Apollo's Warriors

US Air Force Special Operations during the Cold War

Michael E. Haas, Col, USAF, Retired

University Press of the Pacific
Honolulu, Hawaii

Apollo's Warriors:
US Air Force Special Operations During
the Cold War

by
Michael E. Haas

ISBN: 1-4102-0009-4

Reprinted from the 1997 edition

University Press of the Pacific
Honolulu, Hawaii
http://www.universitypressofthepacific.com

Apollo the archer, the lord who strikes from afar,
sends lone warriors clothed in the mist,
or comes on the wind as the night comes down,
beguiles and strikes, unknown but knowing.

—The Odyssey

Contents

Korea

Covert War

The Second Indochina War

Foreword

Since our founding 50 years ago, the US Air Force has been responsible to the nation for controlling and exploiting the air and space environment. We are the nation's Air Force—the only service that provides air and space power across the spectrum, from basic research to combat operations. In *Apollo's Warriors*, Col Michael Haas, USAF, Retired, brings to life the critical, albeit little-known, contributions US Air Force special operations forces have made to the exercise of air and space power.

The author focuses in particular on the period between the Korean War and the Indochina wars of 1950–79. The Korean War marked the first major use of Air Force special operations capabilities during the cold war. Capabilities previously employed during the Second World War were quickly resurrected and used to conduct unconventional warfare missions on the land and sea, as well as in the air. Once these capabilities were available, USAF special operations personnel found themselves constantly engaged in psychological, covert, and search and rescue operations far north of the 38th parallel until the war ended in 1953.

During the period between 1953 and the initial force deployments to Laos and South Vietnam in the early 1960s, the Air Resupply and Communications (ARC) units had the primary responsibility for USAF special operations. Operating in support of US intelligence and US Army Special Forces groups, the four ARC units performed a number of national-level, clandestine, and covert operations behind the Iron Curtain. Backing up this small force, four states activated their own Air National Guard ARC units as a ready reserve force to support special operations.

The role of USAF special operations changed dramatically with the increased involvement of the United States in the Second Indochina War. One of the more interesting changes was the reconstitution of the Air Commando concept of the Second World War. During that war, the Air Commandos conducted effective aerial invasions throughout the China-Burma-India theater. Building on this legacy, the Air Commandos of the Vietnam era initially were the focal point for training Laotian pilots and conducting unconventional warfare operations in Laos. By 1968, they had proved so valuable that their role had been expanded to encompass all USAF special operations in Indochina. As a reflection of this broader mission, the Air Commandos were renamed the Special Operations Forces.

Colonel Haas ends his account noting that this period of prominence for USAF special operations again was short lived. Once the war in Indochina ended, USAF special operations gradually lost their political (and financial) support. And, because of this lack of support, unique capabilities were allowed to atrophy until the failed 1980 Desert One mission demonstrated the need for their restoration.

Although Colonel Haas's work ends at this point, it ably sets the stage for the subsequent USAF special operations successes in Panama, the Persian Gulf, Haiti, and elsewhere. Most importantly, however, he constantly reminds the reader of the professionalism and dedication to service of the men and women of the USAF special operations community. If, by the nature of their service, their exploits must remain largely hidden, their deeds nonetheless earn them the honor and respect accorded to the finest members of the profession of arms.

Ronald R. Fogleman
General, USAF
Chief of Staff

About the Author

Col Michael E. Haas, USAF, Retired, began his military service as a private in the infantry, subsequently moving through eight years of duty in Special Forces, Ranger, airborne, aviation, and psychological operations units. He fought in the Republic of South Vietnam as a flight platoon commander and assault helicopter pilot, completing 968 combat hours.

After entering the Air Force, he served in Special Operations aviation and Special Tactics units, commanded the Pararescue Squadron, and completed tours on the Joint Chiefs of Staff and Headquarters Air Force staffs. He holds USAF command pilot, master parachutist, and free fall qualifications, US Army Special Forces and Ranger tabs, and US Navy diver ratings for open-circuit and closed-circuit scuba operations.

Colonel Haas earned his first master of arts degree in management and a second master's degree in national security affairs from the Naval Postgraduate School. His previous publications include the book *Air Commando! 1950–1975: Twenty-five Years at the Tip of the Spear*, as well as numerous magazine-length articles on special operations theory and practice. He is the advisor on special operations to the Center for the Study of the Vietnam Conflict at Texas Tech University.

Preface

> *The person who has nothing for which he is willing to fight, nothing which is more important than his own personal safety, is a miserable creature and has no chance of being free unless made and kept so by the exertions of better men than himself.*
>
> John Stuart Mill, 1868

The secretive world of military "special operations" is filled with men and women whose dedication, self-sacrifice, and heroism on behalf of their country is seldom acknowledged in public. If John Stuart Mill could come to America a century after his historic judgment to meet such men and women, he would almost certainly understand their modern-day stories without a moment's confusion.

Attempting to capture the history of USAF special operations from the beginning of the cold war to the end of the Second Indochina War is an exercise in humility, the historian's worst nightmare in some respects. The clandestine or covert nature of their worldwide operations, their need (and talent) for deceptive cover stories, and their support to intelligence agencies and special forces of US and foreign countries all combine at different times and places to mislead the unwary researcher.

For reasons which the reader will soon appreciate, I have intentionally avoided the temptation to record every operation, aircraft tail number and type, and technical detail of various weapons and pieces of relevant equipment I encountered in my research. Such a huge collection of dry material would serve no useful purpose with the possible exception of its use as a cure for insomnia. Hopefully of much more interest to the reader is the discovery of many dramatic events that bring new insights into that momentous phase of American history known chiefly by the misnomer "cold war."

The story of USAF special operations during the cold war is not a neutral subject. These unconventional warfare specialists have consistently inspired their supporters and infuriated their detractors. And as the record shows, there have been plenty of both supporters and detractors in places as ideologically diverse as the Pentagon and the Kremlin. Frequently overlooked in the controversy that surrounds our "special purpose forces " is the fact that their employment overseas is invariably directed by the highest civilian authorities, the National Command Authorities (NCA).

Their secret missions to Tibet, Laos, and South Vietnam, to name just a few, underscore their employment in support of national-level foreign policy decisions. That these foreign policy decisions would come to have such a traumatic impact on the American public and the world at large hardly justifies the "cowboy" image with which their detractors have often attempted to slur special operations.

The pattern that emerged from these cold war special operations is one of direct NCA involvement, the temporary issuance to the Air Commandos of a "blank check" for resources, *"must not fail"* command guidance from the check writers, and an aggressive response to such guidance from the airmen in the field. Using unorthodox tactics that often exceed the spirit, if not the letter, of published regulations, the special operations force achieves both success and, of course, the criticism that inevitably follows those who succeed.

How could it be otherwise? What USAF regulation, for example, prescribes the step-by-step procedures and safety standards required to teach illiterate mountain tribesmen to fly T-28 fighter-bombers?

In the end, perhaps the most useful way to look at the Air Force special operations force is from the perspective of an observation made during the Victorian era which I take the liberty to update: "The thing about the Air Commandos is that you don't need them very often. But when you do, you tend to need them very badly."

Michael E. Haas
Col, USAF, Retired

Acknowledgments

Without the unstinting cooperation of Brig Gen Harry C. "Heinie" Aderholt, USAF, Retired, neither I nor any other "Air Commando historian" could possibly have attempted to record the remarkable history of this unique brotherhood. The true story of General Aderholt's remarkable life as leader, fighter, and airman reads like an adventure novel spanning the entire cold war era.

My deep appreciation is extended to both Col Terry R. Silvester, commandant, USAF Special Operations School, and Herbert A. Mason Jr., command historian for the Air Force Special Operations Command. Their active support and guidance were absolutely essential in the team effort necessary to record a candid modern-day history of USAF special operations.

Many of the stories described in *Apollo's Warriors* would never have seen print but for the singular example of security and policy review professionalism exhibited by Mr. Archie DiFante at USAF's Historical Research Agency, Maxwell AFB, Alabama. Also located at Maxwell AFB is the Air University Press and the key staff who for two years have patiently guided me through the myriad of mysteries that eventually lead to the publication of a book: Hugh Richardson, the content editor; Ms. Debbie Banker, the copy editor; Daniel Armstrong and Susan Fair for design, layout, and typeset; and Steve Garst, who provided artwork for the Korea and Covert War sections.

I wish also to thank friend and military historian Meg Jones for suggesting what became our final selection of *Apollo's Warriors* as the title for this book. In the same spirit, my admiration to Kate Thompson and Wayne Thompson, two DynCorp graphic illustrators whose talent and support are found throughout the book.

With apologies in advance for those I may have inadvertently left out, I owe a particular debt to the following: Lester M. Adams Jr., Joseph Barrett, Larry Barrett, Dale R. Bennett, Carl Bernhardt, Bob Brewer, Bob Brice, Richard Brodkin, William Brown, Bert and Karen Cartwright, George Donaldson, Anthony Durizzi, Ed Evanhoe, Frank Fabijan, Jerry Gilbert, John Hagan, Mary Ann Harrison, Lee Hess, "Smokey" Hubbard, Peter M. Hurd, August G. Jannarone, Charles Jones, Edward B. Joseph, Bill Keeler, Jerome Klingaman, Roland Lutz, Bernard Moore II, P. G. Moore, Joe Murphy, Don Nieto, Charlie Norton, Bob Pinard, George Pittman, John L. Plaster, Larry Ropka, Norman H. Runge, Harve Saal, Richard Secord, Dick Shaller, Joe Shannon, Kenneth L. Shook, Connie Siegrist, Bob Sullivan, Ronald Terry, Jacques Tetrick, Janet Ray Weininger, Jack Wheeler, Tom Wickstrom, Joseph Wildinger, Mike Williams, and Jim Yealy.

Prelude

Before the Beginning

In the long course of human history, few individuals or groups can legitimately claim to have achieved a historic "first." There is always someone else, somewhere else, who's done it earlier. And so it is too with the airmen in this book, the United States Air Force's unconventional warriors who flew and fought in the quarter century spanning the Korean and Vietnam wars. Someone else, somewhere else in our Air Force, had indeed flown "special operations" first. But who, and where?

Bernard V. Moore II

The heavily modified B-24 heavy bomber was the mainstay of US Army Air Forces' long-range Carpetbagger flights into German-occupied Europe.

Bernard V. Moore II

Operating deep behind enemy lines was not the kind of work favored by the fainthearted. Judging by the looks of this heavily armed lot on board a Carpetbagger C-47 en route to France in 1944, faint hearts were in the minority.

In Europe, these World War II American airmen flew specially modified aircraft from airfields in England and North Africa. At night, alone, they flew hundreds of miles into German-occupied territory to support national resistance movements and to retrieve downed Allied aircrew members. They were unseen and unheard, and the pain of their subtle sting was not felt by the victim until long after the airmen had returned to the safety of their distant airfields. They proudly called themselves the "Carpetbaggers."

In Asia, a unique, all-American composite aerial force of 348 aircraft supported an all-British ground force. They also flew at night when stealth was required, notably during a spectacular night aerial invasion called Operation Thursday. But these Americans flew mostly in large marauding groups during the day. Like a swarm of killer bees, these unconventional warriors relentlessly hunted their quarry, the Fifteenth Imperial Japanese Army. Their sting was unmistakable; the victim's pain immediate. They became the famous "Air Commandos."

The following brief sketch of these two remarkable groups is presented not as a unit history but rather in recognition that these early airmen truly showed the way in the era when the Air Force's unconventional warfare (UW) heritage began. Carpetbaggers, Air Commandos—to them goes the honor of having truly achieved a first for our country.

Special Operations in Europe*

American aviators had virtually no experience in what was to become known as special operations until mid-1943, when the United States Army Air Forces (AAF) was directed to support the clandestine warfare and secret intelligence activities of the Office of Strategic Services (OSS). The OSS, America's first centralized unconventional warfare and intelligence agency, needed this support to parachute its sabotage and guerrilla warfare teams, resistance organizers, and intelligence agents deep behind enemy lines. The OSS also needed to parachute weapons, ammunition, and other supplies to the various underground resistance groups fighting against their German and Japanese occupiers. For the sake of security, the AAF called these top secret missions "special operations."

Bernard V. Moore II

Combined special operations is evident as this British rigger helps American special forces personnel from the Office of Strategic Services don parachutes for a night infiltration into Europe. The civilian-run OSS coordinated with, but remained independent of, the military services, as would be the case with its successor, the Central Intelligence Agency.

*The author is indebted to Lt Col Bernard V. Moore II for contributing this story.

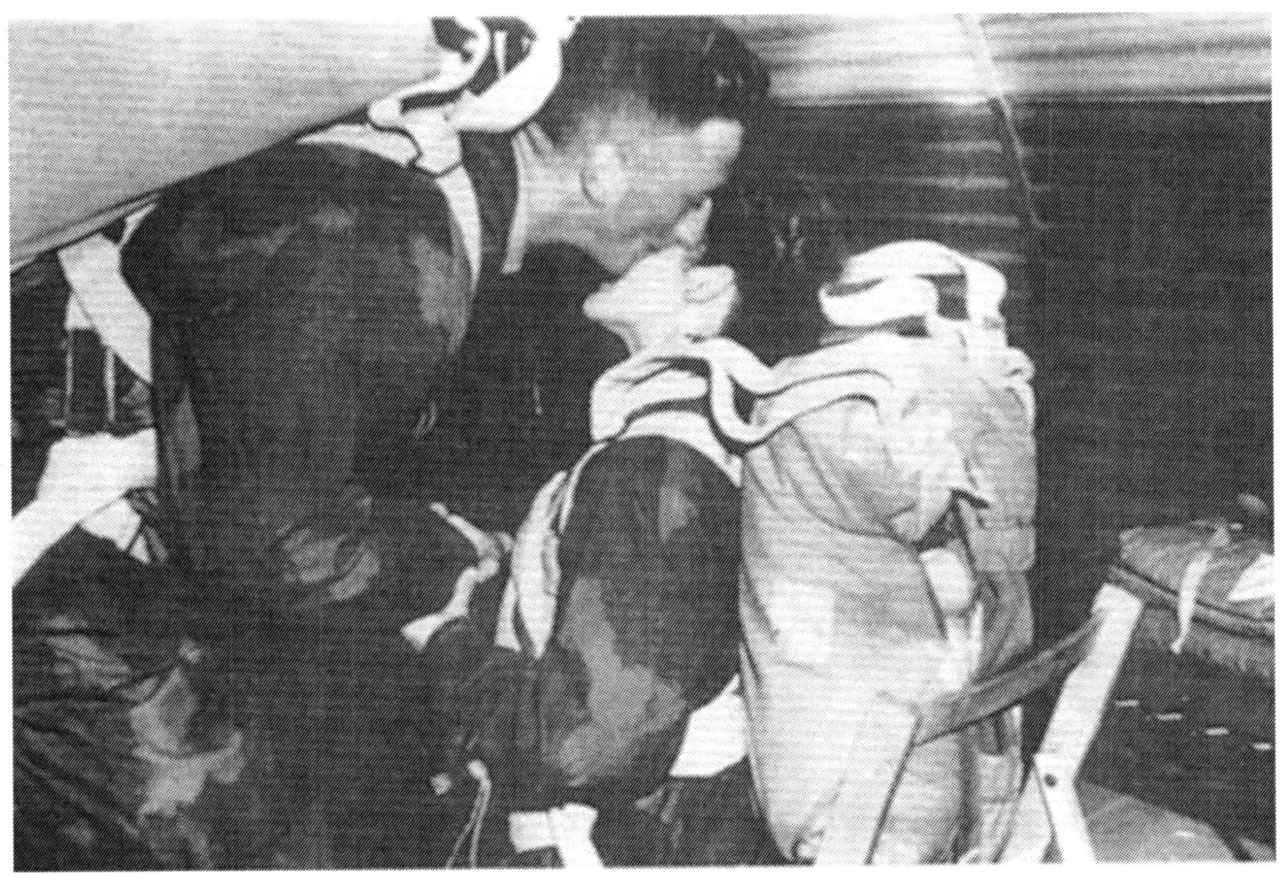

Bernard V. Moore II

A husband gives his wife a "good luck" kiss before boarding a Carpetbagger flight to France. The rare husband-wife team would both be dead within hours, as later reports would show that the drop zone had been compromised and the Germans were already waiting for them when this picture was taken.

In September 1943, the AAF created its first special operations unit in Tunisia. The Special Flight Section was a small outfit that flew specially modified B-17 heavy bombers on clandestine agent infiltration and resupply missions from North Africa to drop zones (DZ) in southern France. Flying its first OSS mission in October 1943, the Special Flight Section developed through experience the specialized tactics and techniques the AAF would employ in flying special operations missions. Experience gained on the early missions over France quickly shaped the distinctive nature of special operations tactics. The missions were almost always flown at night at very low altitude and in extraordinary secrecy.

In November 1943, the Special Flight Section was redesignated the 68th Reconnaissance Group. At the same time, six B-25 Mitchell medium bombers were added to the group to fly short-range resupply missions from southern Italy and the Balkans. In the spring of 1944, C-47 twin-engined transports from regular troop carrier squadrons replaced the B-25s.

In an effort to increase its support to the OSS for the upcoming invasion of France, the AAF added 12 modified B-24 Liberator heavy bombers to the B-17 flight, then based in Tunisia. With the addition of the B-24s, the unit was redesignated the 885th Bomb Squadron (Heavy) (Special). After the liberation of France, the 885th moved to southern Italy, where it flew OSS missions into northern Italy, Yugoslavia, Albania, Greece, Austria, and Germany until the end of the war. But the main focus of the AAF's special operations effort was to take place elsewhere.

In the United Kingdom, the Eighth Air Force set up a much larger special operations force in a top secret project code-named "Carpetbagger." Using two squadrons of highly modified, all-black B-24s, the Carpetbaggers began flying OSS missions over occupied Europe in January 1944. By the summer of 1944, the Carpetbaggers had expanded to four squadrons with 64 B-24s and five C-47s organized under the cover designation 801st Bomb Group (Provisional). The C-47s were used primarily to land at clandestine rough-field landing zones behind German lines in France to insert and recover OSS teams. The Carpetbaggers flew hundreds of successful covert missions to France, Belgium, Holland, and Denmark. In the summer of 1944, the AAF's Air Transport Command also conducted a number of OSS supply drops to Norway under the code name "Project Ball." These missions to Norway were eventually taken over by the Carpetbaggers.

In 1945 the Carpetbaggers, now the 492d Bomb Group, acquired twin-engined Mosquito fighter-bombers and A-26C Invader light bombers for missions over Germany. The A-26Cs were used to parachute and resupply agent teams into high-threat areas deep inside the Third Reich, while the Mosquitos were used to fly high-altitude orbits over these agents while recording their intelligence reports on special radio receivers.

The AAF also flew a small number of clandestine special operations supporting the OSS in the China-Burma-India (CBI) theater. In Asia, the AAF often relied on conventional transport units to fly OSS missions, although a small special operations unit with two ex-Carpetbagger B-24s became operational in China in the last six months of the war.

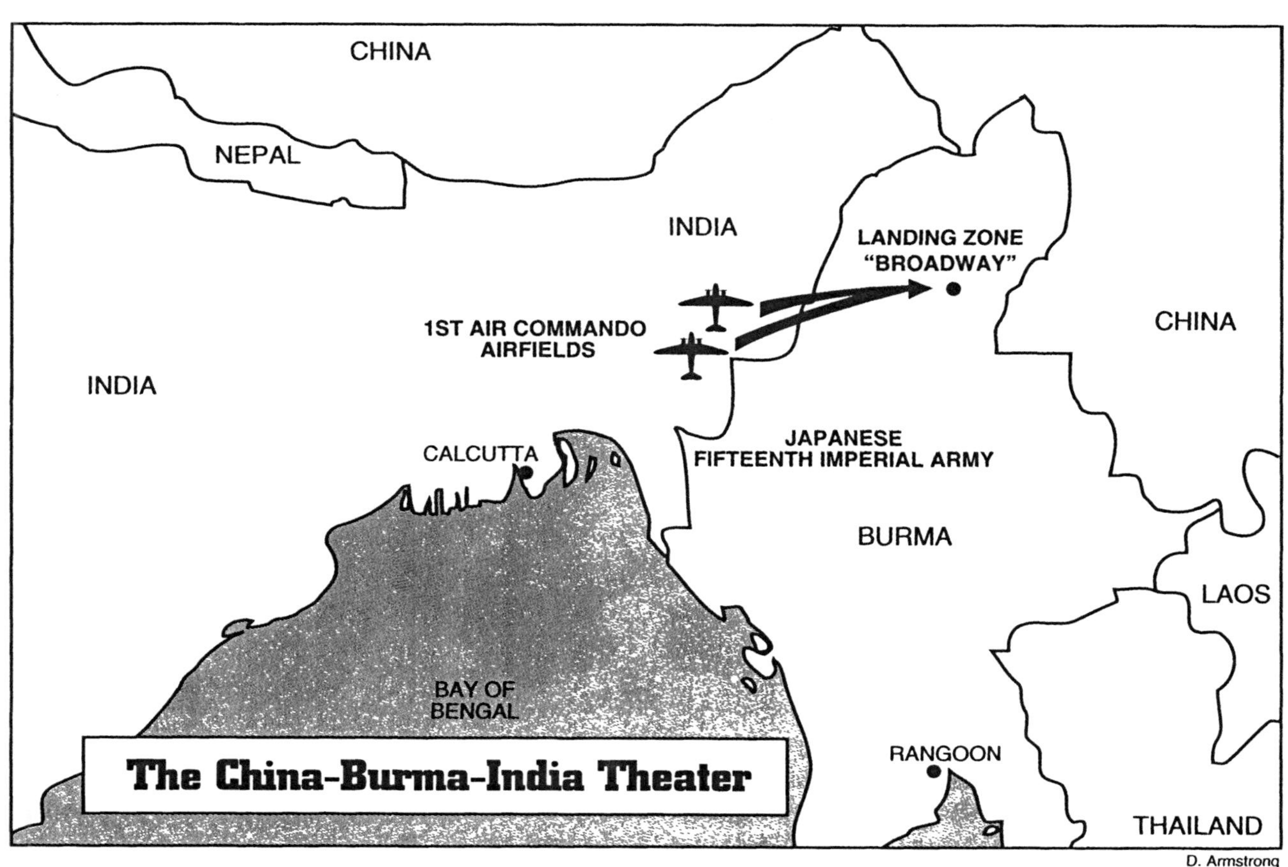

The China-Burma-India Theater

During the course of the war, the AAF's special operations units secretly parachuted and landed several hundred OSS agents and guerrilla warfare teams deep into enemy territory. They also completed thousands of aerial supply drops that enabled thousands of resistance fighters to strike back at their oppressors. The American special operations squadrons waged war from Norway to Manchuria. Succeeding in every theater, they were particularly effective in supporting the Allied campaigns in France, Italy, and Yugoslavia.

Through it all, they maintained a thick cloak of operational stealth to ensure their "invisibility" from both Allied media and enemy defenses. As events were to prove, combat would turn out very differently for the AAF's other unconventional force operating a long way from Europe.

The Air Commandos

Like a brick exploding through a plateglass window, the arrival of the 1st Commando Group in the China-Burma-India theater upset a lot of people. Senior British and American air force officers already in the CBI were openly affronted by the arrival of an independent, provisional force in "their" theater. Worse yet, this force was commanded by a colonel answerable only to the chief of staff of the US Army Air Forces headquartered in Washington, D.C. Ruffled feathers were hardly smoothed with the further news that the newly arrived Americans with their nearly 350 aircraft would become, in effect, the private air force of Brigadier Orde C. Wingate, the most

USAF

The Air Commandos' light-plane force evacuated over 2,000 wounded soldiers from areas so remote that death would have been the only alternative, as indeed it was on previous long-range raids without such air support. The desperate and grateful wounded often kissed the hands of the embarrassed pilots, who daily risked their own lives while abusing the "minimum safe" landing/takeoff standards for remote field operations.

USAF

Air Commando leaders Alison and Cochran, both fighter pilots, weren't inclined to settle for their original guidance from AAF Chief of Staff Gen Henry H. "Hap" Arnold to simply provide air resupply support to British general Wingate's long-range penetration columns. P-51A Mustang fighters and B-25 Mitchell bombers armed with 75 mm cannons were more to everyone's liking—with the notable exception of the Fifteenth Imperial Japanese Army.

controversial and irregular commander in the British army.

The Air Commandos were already in a big hurry when they arrived in India in November 1943. Unconventional, bold, and seemingly reckless to observers unfamiliar with their capabilities, they came to carry out a strategic mission personally directed by the president of the United States. It was a mission intended to change the tide of the two-year-long war in the CBI and, with flying weather restricted to Burma's winter-spring dry season, they had less than six months to get the job done. It was a job so unique that no Army Air Forces manual had ever described it, nor had any squadron ever been formed to accomplish it. Considering the consequences of failure, it was quite a gamble.

Despite the CBI's reputation as a "back-water" theater, the geopolitical stakes involved were enormous. If Japanese forces in Burma could strangle China by isolating it from Allied support flowing through the CBI, thousands of Japanese troops stationed in China could be freed to fight the Allies in the Pacific. And if the remaining Japanese forces could then drive the British from India, the "Jewel of the British Empire," the military, economic, and political blow to the Allies would be incalculable. By mid-1943, the outnumbered British and Indian armies in the CBI were still ill-prepared to counter the threat posed by these two big "ifs."

Too weak in 1943 to counter a planned Japanese offensive with frontal attacks, the British army attempted to disrupt Japanese lines of communication with long-range raiding groups in rear areas. Of the three raiding sorties mounted in Burma during the dry season, two were ambushed quickly and driven back into India; the third eventually returned to friendly lines with only two of every three soldiers surviving the foray. The lack of effective air support, along with the combination of brutal terrain and merciless Japanese attacks, had doomed any future repetition of what was until then the only offensive British initiative in the theater. Only specialized air support could make the difference.

When Gen Henry H. "Hap" Arnold, commander of the US Army Air Forces, selected Lt Col Philip G. Cochran and Lt Col John Alison, both fighter pilots, to implement the Air Commando concept (code-named "Project 9"), he challenged them to be creative. He also gave them a top-priority "blank check" to get it done. They took the check and ran, winning in the process General Arnold's approval for a one-of-a-kind composite force of fighter, bomber, transport, liaison, glider, and helicopter aircraft.

Within 30 days of securing General Arnold's approval, the two officers had assembled a combat force totaling 523 men and 348 aircraft. Thirty days later, the first elements were in India. Tailored exclusively to support Wingate's raiding columns in Burma, this specialist force was to be disbanded at the end of Burma's 1944 dry season. It didn't turn out that way.

By January 1944, the Air Commandos were flying out of two crude airfields 12 miles apart and 100 miles west of the India-Burma border. Intensive training began at once with Wingate's "Chindit" raiders, so named after the mythological Burmese dragons guarding Buddhist temples in Burma. Of particular importance was the ability of C-47 pilots to pull two fully loaded gliders simultaneously at night without aircraft lights. Fighter pilots were cross-trained to fly both P-51A Mustangs and B-25H medium bombers armed with eight .50-caliber machine guns and a 75-millimeter cannon.

The response of the British Chindit officers to their new air force is worth noting. Long frustrated by their inability to develop an effective working relationship with the Royal Air Force (RAF), the Chindit officers were frankly disbelieving the first time Philip Cochran, now a colonel, briefed them on what the Americans had to offer. After Cochran's briefing, one British officer summed up the British response thusly: "Look, even if nine-tenths of what this chap [Cochran] says is b------t, we'll still get twice what the RAF are giving us." The first joint maneuvers made believers out of the Brits, who concluded that "the proportion of taurine dung in Cochran's talk was very small."

Good will and superb tactical coordination developed quickly between the Air Commandos and the Chindits. This in turn proved critical to the outstanding success of what would soon become the most audacious single operation of the entire war in the CBI—Operation Thursday. It was the mission for which the Air Commandos had been formed and sent to the CBI to do, and it took place only weeks after the two organizations were brought together. Operation Thursday was nothing less than the first night aerial invasion of enemy territory. On the night of 5 March 1944, Air Commando C-47s moved Chindit forces in 80 gliders more than 200 miles behind Japanese lines. Obstructions at the landing zone (code-named "Broadway") resulted in the destruction of most of the assault gliders but with remarkably few casualties. Wingate's staff later estimated that 539 soldiers, three mules, and 65,972 pounds of supplies had been air-landed during the night. In the next seven days, additional C-47s from Troop Carrier Command and the Royal Air Force lifted the total to 9,052 men, 175 horses, 1,283 mules, and 509,083 pounds of supplies.

In the space of a few short but harrowing hours, the Air Commandos had accomplished their primary mission, scored a number of AAF firsts, and completely justified the faith put in them by General Arnold. The element of surprise had again proven the dominant factor on the battlefield. For a number of days, the Japanese still had no idea that such a sizable force was operating in their rear.

While Operation Thursday proved the most dramatic feat in the lst Air Commando's short existence, other achievements also proved what a small force of handpicked airmen could achieve with the right leadership. The fighter force flew nearly 1,500 combat missions, losing only five aircraft, while the bombers flew nearly 500 missions with the loss of one B-25. The only C-47 loss came when one of them collided with a water buffalo on a runway at night. The small force of liaison aircraft evacuated 2,200 soldiers without a single combat loss. The success in Burma sparked the creation of the 2d and 3d Air Commando groups that fought elsewhere in the few remaining months of World War II. It was quite a show.

At the conclusion of the war, both Carpetbagger and Air Commando units were deactivated in the overall demobilization program. Only five short years would go by before their skills were needed again. But as history has shown, it was five years too long. With no commitment to maintain its unconventional warfare capability, the United States Air Force would have to reinvent the wheel all over again on the bloody Korean peninsula in 1950.

The Return to War

If the best minds in the world had set out to find us the worst possible location in the world to fight this damnable war, politically and militarily, the unanimous choice would have been Korea!

Dean Acheson
US Secretary of State, 1949-53

Korea 1950

Harsh is perhaps the best single word to describe the landscape of the Korean peninsula. Shaped like Florida but nearly twice the size, the 500-mile-long peninsula is essentially a huge chunk of granite rock. Gouged deeply as if by an invisible jackhammer, the granite forms a peninsula-long washboard of sharp-edged mountains rising steadily from west to east. Alternately baking and soaking in summer's hot monsoon season, the barren rock later freezes in bitter winter storms sweeping down from Manchurian wastelands to the north. The rice paddies that fill the narrow valleys are fertilized by the most commonly available fertilizer—stinking human feces, and this is just the interior.

Korea's 5,400 miles of coastline are equally difficult and dangerous as well for its inhabitants. On the peninsula's western shores, the Yellow Sea rises and falls twice every day with tides that reach the height of a three-story building. On Korea's eastern shores, the Sea of Japan freezes coastal waters to ice every winter, blocking the few safe harbors available. Every year at least one killer typhoon roars across the peninsula.

On top of all this, the Korean peninsula endures one final curse of nature that has brought a never-ending cycle of violence to its proud people: it provides a near-complete land bridge from the Asian mainland to the Japanese islands. Mongol and Chinese armies intent on ending Japan's dominance of the region have used this obvious invasion corridor for centuries. So too have Japanese armies intent on using Korea as a buffer zone to protect the main islands. That was the case in 1945, when the presence of a Japanese occupation army provided the pretext for the

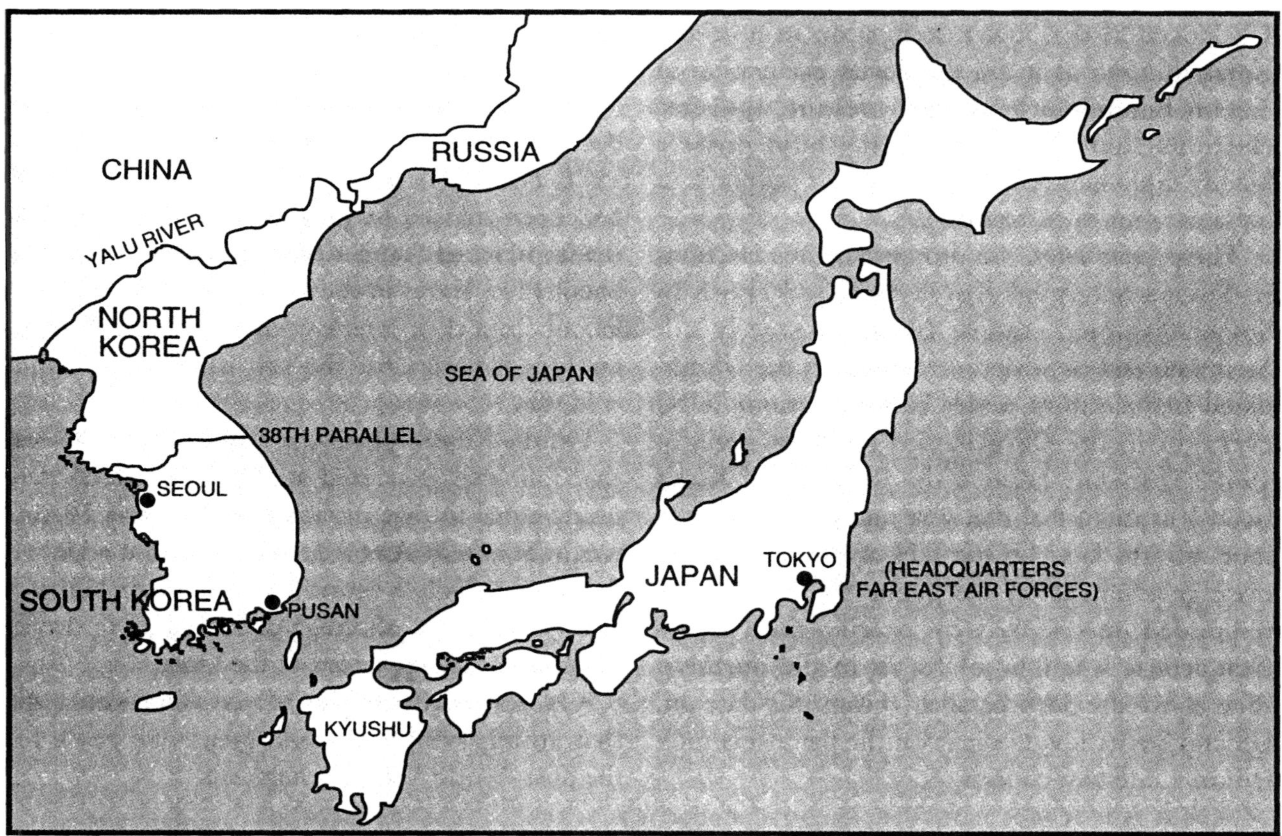

Pointed like a dagger at the region's historical superpower, Japan, Korea's peninsula provided both attack and defense options for adversaries over the centuries, to the bloody despair of its long-suffering indigenous population.

Soviets to use a power ploy that would have consequences not even they could have foreseen.

The Soviet Union declared war on Japan on 8 August 1945, two days before the Japanese formally sued for peace. Although the declaration had no military value, it did allow Soviet premier Joseph Stalin to send his armies into both Manchuria and Korea with no audible complaint from his surprised Western allies. Caught off guard, the US hastily suggested a joint US-Soviet trusteeship of Korea that divided the peninsula roughly in half. The Soviets would accept the surrender of Japanese forces north of the 38th parallel, while the Americans would do the same in the south. The Soviets quickly accepted the US suggestion.

The US proposal to use the 38th parallel as a dividing line totally ignored terrain, lines of communication, indigenous political institutions, and economic resources. These factors were not considered important to Washington at the time. The US looked at the Soviet occupation in northern Korea in 1945 as it did the Soviet occupation of eastern Europe—a temporary measure until free elections could be arranged. It would prove a bloody diplomatic error of monstrous proportions for those sent to correct it.

Three years later, the prospect of free elections in Soviet-occupied Korea matched those in Soviet-occupied eastern Europe—exactly nil. Seeing no end to Soviet intransigence, the US initiated free elections under United Nations (UN) oversight in the US-occupied southern zone in 1948. This zone became the Republic of Korea (ROK) in August of that year and was recognized four months later by the UN as the only legitimate government on the peninsula. The Soviets responded immediately by creating the People's Democratic Republic of Korea in the northern zone above the 38th parallel.* From this date on, US and Soviet involvement on the peninsula took radically different courses.

The Soviets officially completed the withdrawal of their troops from North Korea in 1949, but left behind thousands of Soviet advisors committed to building a fully modern, mobile, and heavily armed army and air force. Within a year, the North Korean People's Army (NKPA) would count 135,000 strong in 10 divisions. This included a large guerrilla force that commenced a violently effective infiltration and disruption of South Korea's embryonic national infrastructure.

Anxious to complete a near-total military withdrawal from South Korea during this same period, the Truman administration's response was minimal. Its Korean Military Advisory Group (KMAG) consisted of less than 500 officers and men. KMAG's goal was to create a South Korean constabulary armed only with light weapons and a few pieces of obsolescent artillery. The gross imbalance of forces could (and would) hardly be seen as anything but a major temptation by North Korean and Soviet leaders eager to test US resolve in the emerging cold war.

The inevitable North Korean hammer slammed down in the early morning darkness of 25 June 1950. Nearly 10 of every 13 soldiers in the NKPA had been massed behind heavy artillery to rout the unprepared South Korean army from the 38th parallel like leaves in the wind. This they did. The fallout from their attack would also change life in faraway America for the rest of a long 40-year cold war.

On the Korean peninsula, the three years of war that followed generated an American death rate nearly equal to that sustained in America's 10-year war in Southeast Asia a decade later. In the United States, the "police action," as President Harry S Truman called it, affected Americans more deeply than they could appreciate at the time:

• It destroyed the short-lived American hope that atomic weapons would guarantee peace for the post–World War II generation.

---

* Because the Republic of Korea and the People's Democratic Republic of Korea are commonly referred to as *South Korea* and *North Korea*, respectively, in most literature, these terms will be used for these two countries hereafter.

Central Intelligence Agency map 504789 3-81

A granite-hard peninsula swept by the worst of nature's winter and summer storms produces a tough population. For centuries Korea would prove even tougher for foreigners who fought and died in its freezing mountains or along the jagged spines of its heat-baked ridges.

• It generated an undreamed of conventional and nuclear military arms buildup by the United States, with a subsequent commitment to use these arms to "bear any burden" in their employment against Communist expansionism in Third World "proxy" wars.

• It generated a mob-like, anti-Communist frenzy of political correctness led by Senator Joseph McCarthy (R-Wisc.) that would ultimately destroy reputations and even the lives of those refusing to be coerced by the fear of mob rule.

In the summer of 1950, however, the serious, long-term implications to American society were not yet a major concern. US foreign policy planners had a far more immediate problem responding to the North Korean attack. In terms of combat effectiveness and global power projection, the US military had virtually ceased to exist following the postwar demobilization fervor that swept the country.

If the Army and Navy's force structure were hurting, the fledgling Air Force was on its knees. From 1945 to 1947, the United States Air Force shrank from 218 to 38 groups, only 11 of which were rated operationally effective.[1]

President Truman distrusted the new Air Force leadership. He made clear his view that the cost of their expensive technology was a threat to his budget-cutting plans for the military.[2]

Secretary of State Dean Acheson's frustrated outburst quoted on the opening page proved as accurate as it was dismal. Worse still for the soldiers, sailors, and airmen sent to Korea, it would also prove as bloody as it was dismal. And lost from memory as if it had never existed was the unconventional warfare expertise learned at such cost in World War II by both the Carpetbaggers and the Air Commandos. It would have to be learned all over again.

Notes

1. Clay Blair, *The Forgotten War: America in Korea, 1950–1953* (New York: *Times* Books, 1987), 9.
2. Ibid.

CCRAK

The Shadow War

During the first several months of the Korean War, both Communist and UN* forces took tremendous military risks in their separate attempts to bring the war to a quick conclusion. At different times both sides nearly succeeded. It was like two boxers abandoning all defense to go for a knockout blow to the head. Neither side could know how long the bout would last . . . or that a third boxer would soon enter the ring.

*The United States provided the overwhelming majority of forces for the UN response to North Korean aggression, suffering in the process a corresponding percentage of the casualties. For the sake of clarity, the author hereafter will use "US" when referring to the allies fighting the Communists in Korea.

The War: Center Stage

In the first round, the North Koreans came within a few short miles of driving US forces completely off the southern tip of the peninsula in the summer of 1950. Facing military disaster, Gen Douglas MacArthur, commander in chief of Far East Command (FECOM), proceeded to break the back of the North Korean onslaught that September with his audacious amphibious assault landing at Inchon Harbor on South Korea's western coast, a move which cut the supply lines of the overextended North Korean forces. But his subsequent decision to send troops north of the 38th parallel to North Korea's border with China prompted a vicious Chinese response beyond what anyone in FECOM or the US had anticipated.

That winter thousands of Chinese "volunteers" drove allied troops southward in retreat through a freezing hell of -30 degrees Fahrenheit temperatures, snow storms, and heartbreaking mountainous terrain. Those who couldn't retreat froze to death where they fell. Only by the narrowest of margins did US airpower avert what could have been the worst military defeat in American history. Round one was over.

The second round consumed the remaining two years of the war. On the ground, it involved trench warfare the likes of which had not been seen since World War I. All the horror, disease, cold-weather injuries, and massive artillery duels that marked the earlier world war were repeated in Korea. Far above the frontal infantry attacks that bled assault regiments white, US Air Force (USAF) and Navy fighters achieved a hard-earned mastery of the air. The first jet aces of the three-year-old USAF became national heroes and the press continued to cover the war closely, at least the war they were allowed to see.

The War behind the Curtain

The "war behind the curtain" that few people would be allowed to see was initially directed by an obscure FECOM staff organization, the "Liaison Group," or FEC/LG. But appearances would prove deceiving, for the bland-sounding Liaison Group was anything but a routine headquarters staff function. It was in fact FECOM's link to a bizarre group of intelligence and partisan organizations controlled by US military and Central Intelligence Agency (CIA) case officers.

FEC/LG infiltrated spies and partisans into enemy territory by air, land, and sea, and its areas of operation ranged from remote mountain ambushes to the private bedrooms of high-ranking Chinese officers. Operationally active but vulnerable to interservice (and military-CIA) bureaucratic rivalries, FEC/LG would see much of its lead role later supplanted by another organization with another intentionally bland acronym—CCRAK (pronounced "see-crack").

In an unusual but not unknown practice in special operations,* FECOM gave the acronym *CCRAK* both classified and unclassified interpretations. The former was known as "*C*overt, *C*landestine, and *R*elated *A*ctivities—*K*orea." The title was accurate but hardly suitable for maintaining the low profile necessary to conduct its mission.[1] The less-inflammatory title "*C*ombined *C*ommand for *R*econnaissance *A*ctivities—*K*orea" was selected for public use.

CCRAK was established in December 1951** and headquartered in the former First Methodist Church compound in downtown Seoul. It was a FECOM initiative intended to centralize control of a peninsula-wide unconventional warfare campaign run by a confusing number of "bandit

*During the Vietnam War, for example, the senior US military headquarters in Vietnam, the Military Assistance Command, Vietnam (MACV), would hide its version of CCRAK under the bland title "Studies and Observations Group."

**The bureaucratic history of UW operations in the Korean War is a story of a continual, often chaotic evolution in organizational titles that had little impact on the mission. In the name of consistency and to avoid unnecessarily confusing the reader, the author has chosen the CCRAK evolution as a reference point. The author readily acknowledges that many early events took place during the tenure of CCRAK's predecessor, the Far East Command Liaison Group.

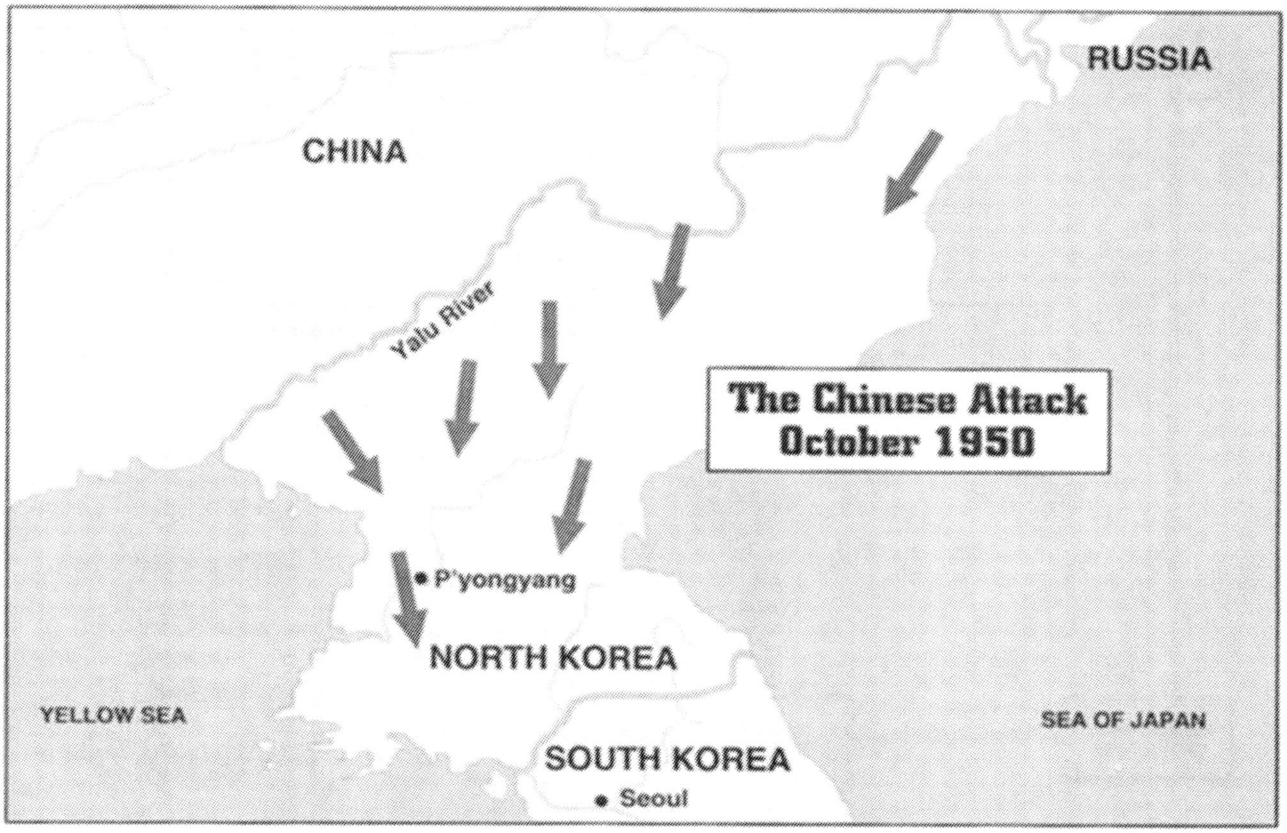

In late 1950, a massive Chinese Communist force unexpectedly struck US and South Korean forces, driving them southward through the frozen landscape of ridges and valleys and threatening to encircle them. Exhausted US marines (below) had to fight their way out.

USMC

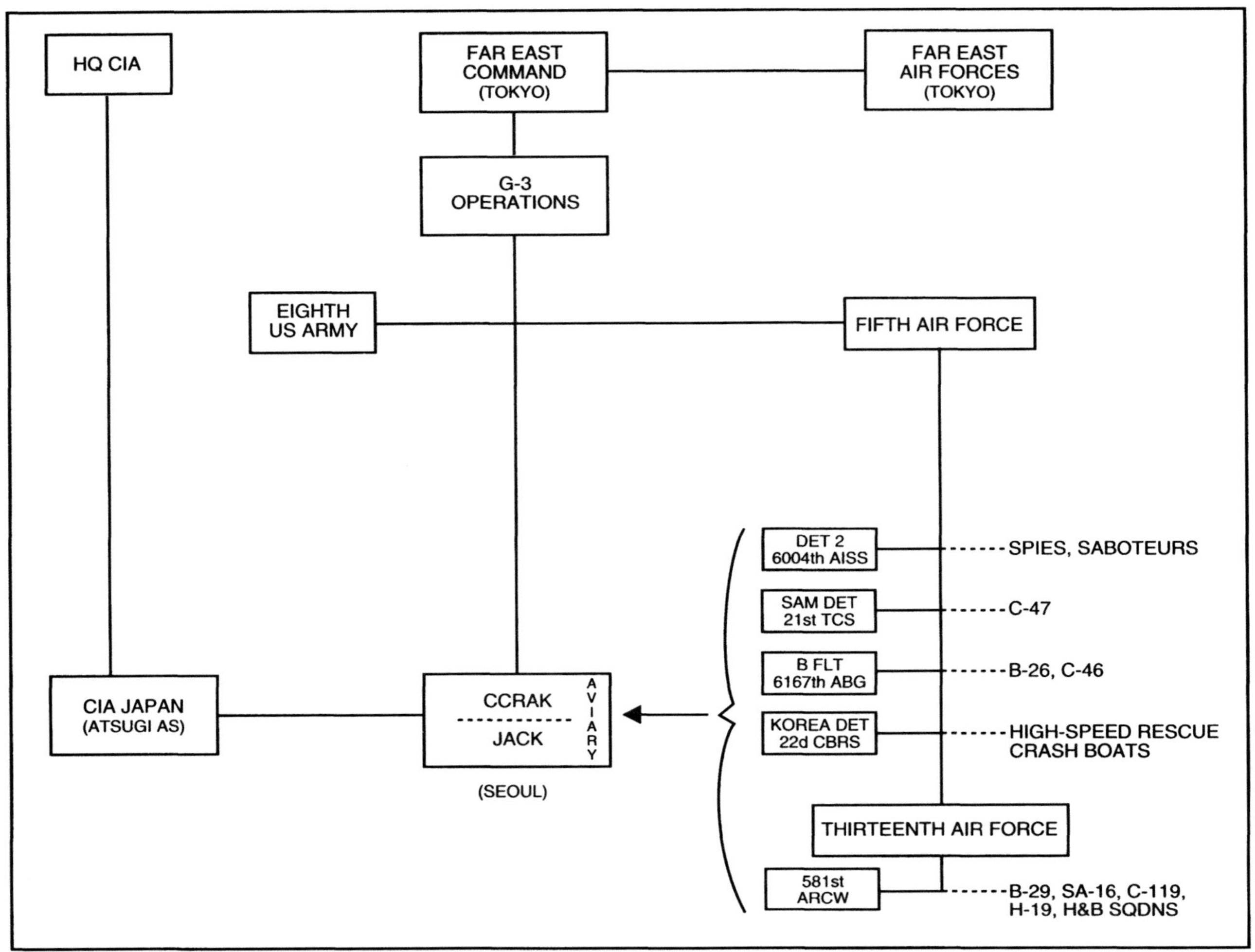

Figure 1. By 1952 USAF special operations air, land, and sea forces were actively supporting FECOM's joint, unconventional warfare component CCRAK. This included JACK, the CIA force within CCRAK.

chiefs" from the military, the CIA, and the South Koreans themselves.[2] In this regard, CCRAK would prove only partially successful as it was not given explicit command authority over its primary partner and bureaucratic rival, the CIA's Joint Activities Commission—Korea (JACK).[3]

While FECOM appointed the CCRAK director, its deputy director could be appointed only by the CIA. Why? In an attempt to secure "rival" JACK's voluntary cooperation, the FECOM plan reserved the deputy director's position for the director of JACK![4] As noted, the FECOM plan was only marginally successful as the new CIA continued to jealously guard its organizational independence (to include JACK) from military control.

The Far East Air Forces (FEAF) headquarters in Tokyo would prove more supportive of CCRAK than the CIA. However, like the CIA, it insisted on maintaining command of FEAF assets cooperating with CCRAK. Despite these internal bureaucratic struggles, CCRAK was still an organization capable of hurting the Communists in a number of ways. In addition to directing a partisan combat force, which by the end of 1952 counted over 16,000 (and growing) armed men, CCRAK infiltrated agents and partisans* by air,

* The terms *partisans* and *guerrillas* are used interchangeably throughout these stories, as the terms are used interchangeably in archival documents from this era.

land, and sea in a number of highly classified operations.

To infiltrate by air, CCRAK continued running the successful air program initially established by FEC/LG. Operation Aviary was the overall code name for parachute operations behind enemy lines,[5] or "north of the bomb line," as the rear area was also called. Agents selected for Operation Aviary were recruited through the Korean Liaison Office (KLO), a subsection of FECOM's still-active Liaison Group. Deep penetration of enemy territory was KLO's mission; the airborne vehicle was Operation Aviary. According to former US Army captain and Aviary case officer Bob Brewer, the survival rate of Aviary agents, at least in the first year of the war, was approximately 70 percent of those parachuted behind enemy lines.[6] Other means of infiltration were also used.

Bob Brewer

Unit 4 (later Special Air Missions [SAM]) commander Capt "Heinie" Aderholt personally tests the SCR-300 radio that finally brought effective communication between Korean agents operating behind enemy lines and SAM C-47s equipped with the same radio modified to include a voice tape-recording machine.

Bob Brewer

An unidentified American advisor conducts a last-minute review of a mission before agents prepare to parachute behind enemy lines. A better-than-average survival rate for the airborne agents early in the war deteriorated to what became virtual suicide missions by late 1952.

To infiltrate overland, CCRAK recruited agents through FEC/LG's Tactical Liaison Office (TLO). These agents were committed to shallow penetration of the front lines for tactical information of immediate use to infantry units on the line. One US officer, one enlisted man, one interpreter, and 20 Korean agents comprised a typical TLO team.[7] As early as September 1950, one TLO team had been dedicated to each US infantry division and to each ROK corps on the front lines. During the initial recruiting program begun in 1950 by FECOM's Liaison Group, American officers

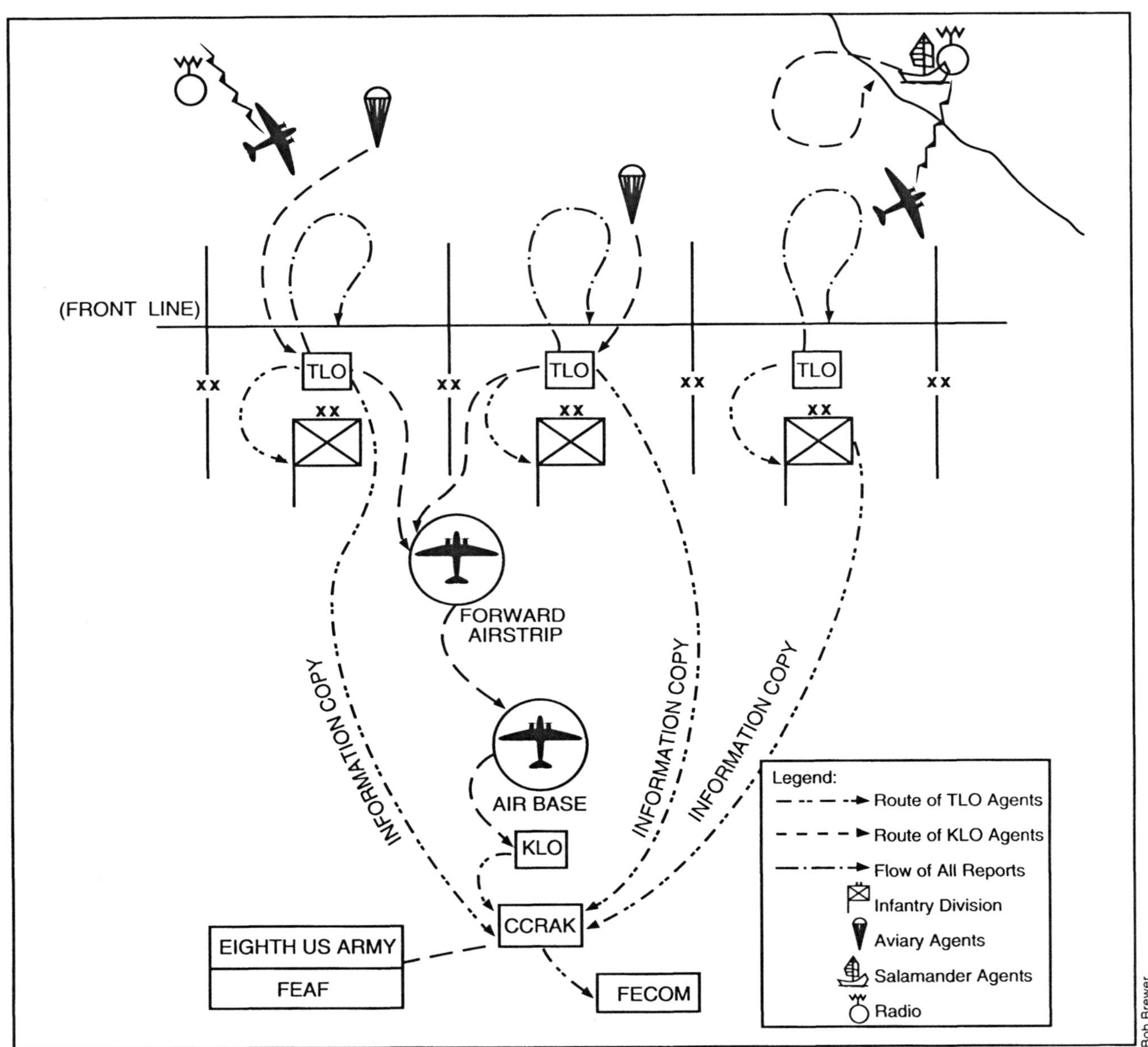

Source: Lt Col Garth Stevens et al., "Intelligence Information by Partisans for Armor" (U) Research Report, vol. 1 (Ft. Knox, Ky.: Armored Officer Advanced Course, 1952), 29. (Confidential) Information extracted is unclassified.

Figure 2. A schematic drawing by a liaison group officer shows air, land, and sea infiltration techniques used during the war. Long-range infiltration by air (Aviary) and sea (Salamander) were conducted by Korean agents from the KLO. Short-range penetration of enemy lines was conducted on foot by agents from the TLO. Both offices belonged to Far East Command's Liaison Group, the predecessor to CCRAK.

Bob Brewer

The exhaustion and strain of extremely high-risk human intelligence (HUMINT) gathering shows on the faces of two returning female agents during a postmission debriefing. For some special missions, female agents parachuted into the target area unarmed and without radios. The success of the mission and personal survival were totally dependent on their individual ability to deceive the senior enemy officers they were sent to approach.

became aware of an obscure religious sect with priceless skills for espionage.

One of the most consistent aspects of foreign domination of Korea throughout the centuries was its religious persecution of Korea's indigenous religions. This created a number of underground "outlaw" religious sects that learned over the years (no doubt at considerable cost in blood) the art of secret communications. Included in these sects was the *Cho'ondagyo,* a group purportedly numbering in the several thousands. After securing the support of this secretive group, Captain Brewer could only marvel at their astounding ability to bring back vital intelligence from situations in which no one else could conceivably have even survived.[8]

To infiltrate by sea, CCRAK again turned to KLO for recruits to execute Operation Salamander. Infiltration by sea was a technique employed on both coasts using a variety of small craft. Operations Salamander and Aviary were both dangerous, but the infiltration risks were obviously different. Partisans infiltrating by sea were frequently required to pick their way through minefields at sea and then through more minefields blockading likely infiltration points on the beaches. Despite these hazards, an estimated 90 percent of the partisans returned from these missions.[9]

Both Aviary and Salamander KLO operations transmitted their field reports back to CCRAK through Air Force special operations aircraft orbiting near their locations. These C-47s were specially equipped with the SCR-300 infantry radio modified to include a voice tape recorder. Meanwhile, the short-range TLO operations continued to rely on word-of-mouth reports from the individual agents upon their return to friendly lines. As crucial as air transportation and communications obviously were to CCRAK, they reflected only two of the many weapons Air Force special operations brought to the fight. Still others would seem so bizarre that it was hard to believe they were Air Force weapons at all.

The USAF special operations force that flew over, walked through, and sailed around Korea's unforgiving granite mountains played a critical role in CCRAK's shadowy war. This colorful cast of airmen fought a very unorthodox war with everything at their disposal, both what they were authorized and what they could lay their hands on. It was a potent mixture of imagination, guts, and opportunity that could (and would) explode in many different directions.

Special operations aircraft flying low-level, night-infiltration missions parachuted spies behind North Korean lines and even further north into Manchuria. A mysterious Air Force intelligence officer commanded a "detachment" of nearly a thousand South Korean spies and saboteurs who infiltrated enemy territory by parachute, on foot, or by his "private" fleet of indigenous junks. Sixty-three-foot-long USAF crash rescue boats armed with quad .50-caliber heavy machine guns and capable of 40-plus-knot speeds landed South Korean partisans and intelligence agents against coastal targets. By air, land, and sea, the Fifth Air Force's special operations teams roamed the peninsula and the surrounding seas at night.

And then there was something the Air Force called an "ARCW" (pronounced "Arc"), which was stashed in the Thirteenth Air Force at faraway Clark Air Base in the Philippine Islands. The innocent-sounding 581st Air Resupply and Communications Wing (ARCW) took the unconventional war to the enemy with heavy bombers, twin-engined amphibians, and the new H-19 helicopters. The Chinese Communists were so incensed by its nighttime activities in Korea (and Indochina) that they threatened the United Nations with an international war-crimes trial for one captured (and badly tortured) ARCW B-29 bomber crew. That crew in fact would become the last group of American military prisoners of war (POW) released by the Chinese after the war. But in the fall of 1950 none of this could have been guessed by the small band of USAF special operators already busy far behind enemy lines.

Aviary and Unit 4 in Action

The concept that became Operation Aviary sprang to life less than two months after the war started, at a time when UN forces were making their last-ditch stand around the southern coastal town of Pusan. Within the embattled enclave, a primitive parachute jump school was fashioned even as South Koreans were recruited by the KLO for intelligence-gathering operations.

Neither the time available nor the facilities on hand would permit training of the agents as fully qualified paratroopers. To the contrary, the parachute infiltration phase of the mission was intentionally de-emphasized for psychological reasons when it was discovered that many of the inexperienced agents viewed the frightening night jump as the most difficult phase of their much more dangerous intelligence mission.[10]

The first Aviary mission followed the offensive breakout of US troops from the Pusan enclave and the daring amphibious invasion of Inchon Harbor. The North Koreans were clearly in northward retreat, but was it a disciplined withdrawal or a rout? What routes was the defeated enemy taking? Where were its armor, artillery, and reserves? Failure to answer these questions had lured more than one seemingly victorious army to their destruction from an apparently defeated foe.

On the night of 26 September 1950, two C-47s from Unit 4, a special detachment of the Fifth Air Force's 21st Troop Carrier Squadron departed Taegu South Airfield (K-37) in southern Korea for northbound flights with a total of nine, jump-trained KLO agents.[11] Five were dropped into one drop zone and four into another, both DZs being located directly in the paths of the retreating North Korean army. All agents were observed landing safely, and eight of the nine successfully reported back to their KLO case officers after returning on foot to friendly lines.

While judged a technical success, this first mission quickly revealed two major problems inherent with early Aviary tactics. The first problem to surface was the inordinate time it took the KLO agents to return on foot through friendly lines. They had infiltrated without radios, and their hard-earned field reports were frequently outdated by the time they were personally debriefed. This would soon be fixed, at least partially, by equipping the agents with AN/GRC-9 radios for communication with Unit 4's C-47s orbiting within line-of-sight range of the radios. Bulky to carry and difficult to operate for the hastily trained

Bob Brewer

Korean agents undergoing parachute training. Parachute jumps were the only practical long-range infiltration tactic for entry into Korea's rugged interior. By late 1952, getting back alive would prove so difficult that one postwar study concluded such missions "were both futile and callous" in their disregard for the lives of those sent on such missions.

agents, the "Angry-9" radio offered only a limited solution. Key examples of both the problem and the potential for success with radio communication would surface that December.

The second problem stemmed in part from the difficulties of the first. To reenter friendly territory, the agents had to first allow themselves to be captured and sent to POW cages for interrogation. Aside from the obvious dangers of being shot by frontline soldiers from either side, the agents could usually count on a hostile reception from US troops even after having identified themselves with a code word. Some were killed attempting to cross the no-man's land separating the front lines, others were co-opted for use by frontline infantry units as laborers, while still others simply disappeared into the vast POW camp populations.

With or without radios, agents in the early Aviary missions were so successful that soon agents were being parachuted into enemy territory as rapidly as they could be recruited and readied. Inevitably, training and mission-preparation time suffered, with predictable losses. The radio communications problem continued to haunt Aviary planners until the SCR-300 infantry radio was introduced. Lightweight and simple to operate, it proved ideal for communications between the agents and the SCR-300-equipped aircraft flying overhead. Communications were enhanced still further by the simple technique of trailing a long coaxial cable behind an in-flight C-47, the cable becoming a giant radio antenna.

Solving technical communications problems was obviously critical. But on at least one important occasion, Unit 4 and Aviary solved an urgent communications problem with ingenuity and a tactic used since biblical times. This notable operation was executed as US and ROK forces retreated southward before the massive Chinese intervention in November 1950. With contact broken between the attacking Chinese and the retreating allies, US military commanders were suddenly in the dark as to where the Chinese were massing for their next attack.

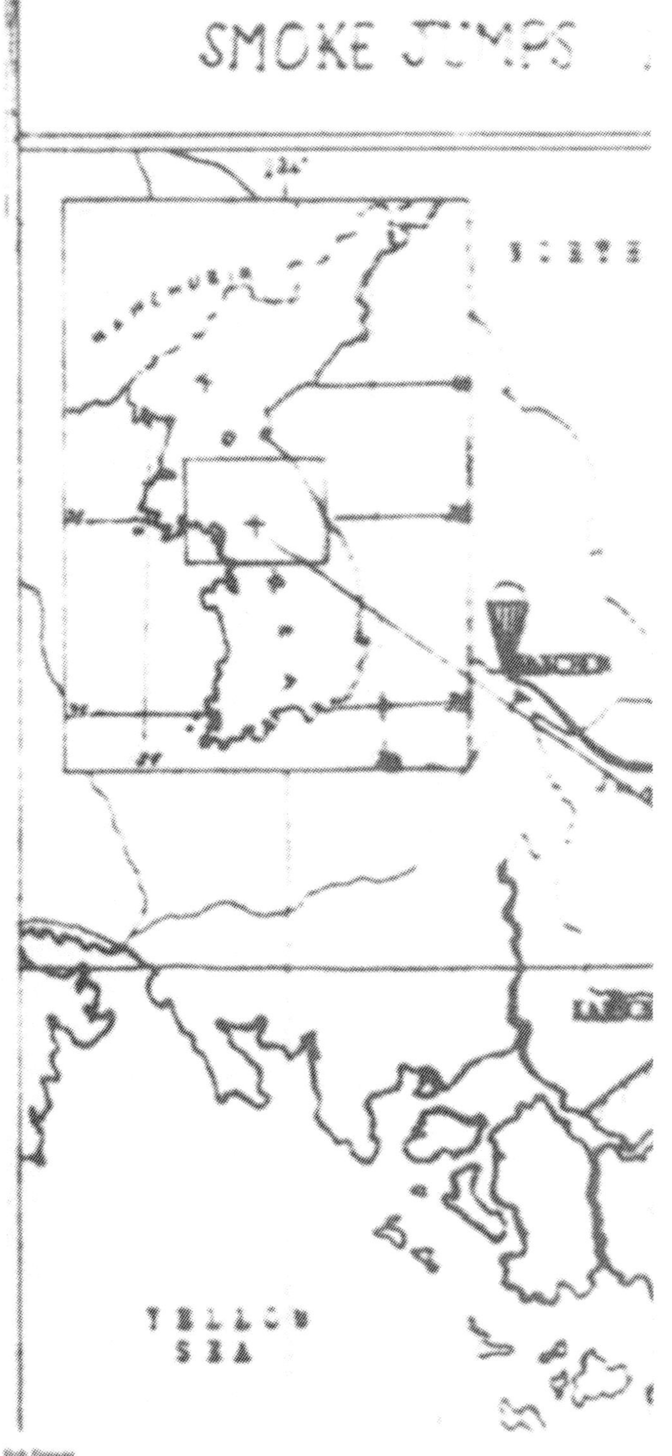

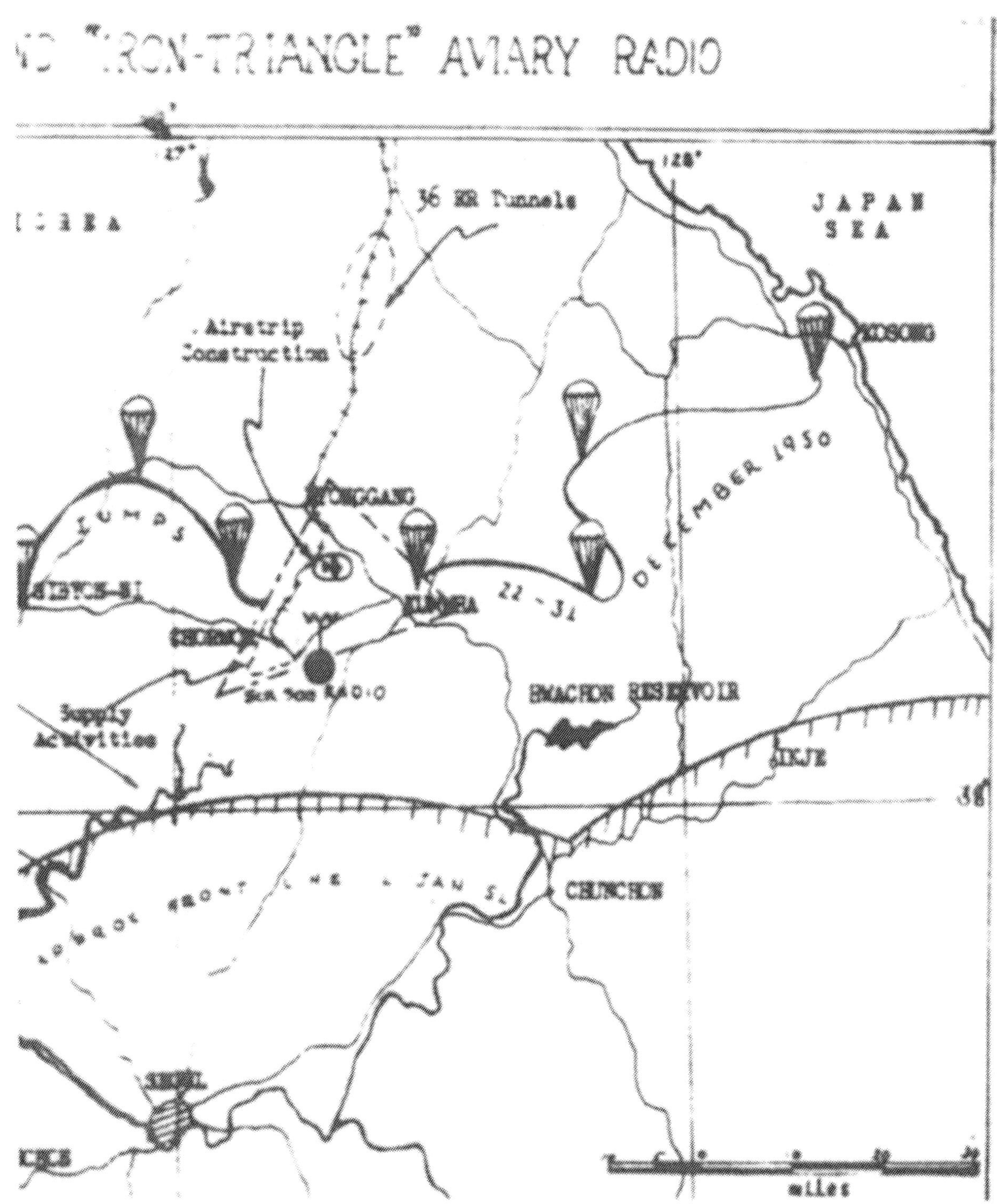

Where will the Chinese strike next? To determine where the next blow would fall, a beaten and retreating Eighth US Army turned to special operations to parachute Korean spotter agents between it and the advancing enemy. A combination of ingenuity and guts soon rushed the answer through a communications system used since biblical times.

Table 1
Unit 4
Unconventional Warfare Missions
January 1951

Date	*Destination*	*Sorties*	*Mission*
1	Wonsan-Chongjin	1	Drop UN Personnel
5	Chinnampo-Tongyang	1	Radio Intercept
8	Chinnampo-Tongyang	1	Radio Intercept
8	Kyongju-Ulchin	1	Supply and Recon
11	Yonan-Hamhung-Chinnampo	3	Personel Drop and Radio Intercept
12	Yonan-Seoul	1	Radio Intercept
14	Hamhung	1	Radio Intercept
15	Sibyonni-Chorwon-Kosong	1	Personnel Drop
16	Ulchin-Seoul	1	Radio Intercept
17	Yonan-Chinnampo-Hamhung	3	Radio Intercept
19	Kumwha-Ch'unch'on	1	Personnel Drop and Radio Intercept
21	Oro-ni	1	Personnel Drop
23	Yonan-Chinnampo	2	Radio Intercept
24	Ulchin-Hamhung	2	Radio Intercept
26	Songu-ri; Kapyong'on; Ch'unch'on; Yanggu; Yangang	5	Personnel Drop
26	Hongwon	1	Radio Intercept
29	Yonan-Chinnampo	1	Radio Intercept
31	Yonan	1	UN Agent Drop

Source: History, 21st TCS, January–April 1951, Historical Data No. 5, Monthly Activity Report, 1 February 1951, Capt Harry C. Aderholt, flight commander, Unit 4.

Not knowing where the next massive blow would come from is an ugly position for any army to find itself in. To find an immediate answer, FECOM turned to CCRAK, which in turn responded with an operation simply referred to as the "smoke jumps." Unit 4 personnel painted the undersides of their C-47s' wings with broad black and white stripes reminiscent of those used to identify Allied aircraft during World War II's famous D-day invasion. They then proceeded to drop two-agent teams across the narrow neck of mid-Korea, 10–20 miles in front of US outposts. Equipped with various colored smoke grenades, the agents went to ground to watch for the enemy and await the presence overhead of the specially marked aircraft. Every day a Unit 4 aircraft flew low level over the path of dropped agents to observe their smoke signals. If the agents had seen Chinese in numbers over battalion strength, they signaled with red smoke; yellow indicated North Koreans; and green signified little or no enemy presence.[12] Despite deteriorating weather that soon led to a solid, low overcast, Unit 4's aircrews observed 25 percent of the total signals possible.[13] It was crude but effective intelligence when nothing else was available to FECOM. Still, it was obvious to all that improved radio communications were a must for most future operations. As usual, the agents were on their own to get back to friendly lines. This time the US was not coming back north.

For all the obvious advantages of radio communications, there still existed a category of mission so dangerous that carrying a radio or even a weapon was not an option. Such special missions were frequently reserved for one small group of KLO agents, or "rabbits" as they became known, recruited from the most unlikely of sources. This group consisted of young women recruited for the KLO by Madam Rhee, wife of South Korea's president Syngman Rhee. A well-known matron of the arts in prewar Seoul, Madam Rhee recruited the women within a small circle of theater actresses. Even to Unit 4's hardened aircrew veterans, the courage of these young women was legendary, especially considering the personal nature of their mission.

One Unit 4 commander in particular who remembers these female agents is Brig Gen Harry C. "Heinie" Aderholt (then a captain), who recalled in a 1986 interview:

> The agents were furnished by the Koreans. We had hundreds of them. Madam Rhee furnished all the women. They had all the movie stars and everybody, the best-looking girls. We put them out over enemy territory during the winter of '50–'51 when the outside air temperature was forty to fifty degrees below zero. They would go out in cotton padded shoes and suits. They wouldn't weigh enough to get to the ground, you would think.[14]

But get to the ground they did. They then followed the mission plan by associating themselves intimately with high-ranking North Korean or Chinese officers in the vicinity. Remaining with these officers long enough to learn units, locations, planned offensives, and so on, they would discreetly drift off in the confusion common to frontline areas to be captured by the closest allied forces. After giving the prearranged code word from a prisoner of war cage, they were released to their KLO case officer for immediate debriefing.

General Aderholt recalls at least one mission in particular. A female agent warned of an impending, unexpected Communist attack in sufficient time to allow US forces to reinforce their weak sector and deal a punishing defeat on the attackers:

> Everyone was frantic. Where have they [the Chinese] gone? We were retreating then . . . the 2nd (US Army) Division had been beaten up and was paper thin. One of them [female agents] came out. She had slept with a lieutenant colonel, Chinese army, and had their whole Order of Battle . . . three or four Chinese divisions had side-slipped about 80 miles and were poised head-on against the 2nd Division. That report saved the day . . . the Marines moved up behind the 2nd Division . . . and kicked the s--- out of them.[15]

The bravery and sacrifices of the Korean agents, many of them refugees or defectors from North Korea, were unquestionable. But there was a dark side to Aviary and other CCRAK partisan and intelligence operations that depended on indigenous personnel intelligence. It was particularly dangerous because it surfaced without warning from the least-expected direction. And it could, and did on at least one tragic occasion, cost the lives of the special operations aircrews that risked their own lives to deliver the agents "above the bomb line." In a word, it was called *treachery.*

The presence of double agents within intelligence or resistance organizations has been a fact of war long before the Korean peninsula was blown apart in 1950. With the never-ending urgency to recruit agents and guerrillas for CCRAK, it was inevitable that some double agents would slip through the screening process to find themselves in a position to hurt their enemy. The inevitable happened in the dead of winter, February 1952, on a night infiltration mission to parachute agents near the Yalu River separating North Korea from Manchuria. Author and CCRAK veteran Ed Evanhoe described the mission for *Behind the Lines* magazine:

> Taking off from Seoul City Airfield (K-16) during the night of 18–19 February, the C-46 Air Commando transport headed east through the night sky under a near-full moon for the first of its multiple drops, saving the most dangerous for last. The first drops were completed successfully, and the plane flew west to a DZ near the Yalu River . . . and into disaster.[16]

Arriving over the unmarked DZ, the C-46 slowed to drop speed and the first of two Chinese

USAF

Returning from an urgent mission, a special operations C-47 from Unit 4 lands at a combat-littered forward airstrip with time-critical information. The special black and white identification stripes painted under its wings identify the aircraft to South Korean agents operating in enemy territory.

agents parachuted out into the night. Hesitating just before he jumped, the second agent lobbed a live grenade into the forward cabin section. The agent was safely out the door under an opening parachute when the grenade exploded, instantly killing or disabling the four remaining Chinese agents and one of the two American jumpmasters. With the aircraft on fire and coming apart in midair, Capt Lawrence E. Burger, the instructor navigator, stayed at the controls to allow the surviving crew members to jump to safety.

The crew members were captured shortly after landing. The next day the Chinese told the navigator, Capt Guy O. King, that four Chinese bodies had been recovered from the wreckage.* The full story of the treachery did not become known

*Was the Chinese interpreter lying or perhaps mistaken? A CCRAK agent working in a nearby military hospital reported shortly after the downing of the C-46 that a wounded American "spy" had been brought to the facility. His description of the American closely resembled that of Sgt George G. Tatarakis, the assistant jumpmaster on the doomed flight. Other agents subsequently reported that an American matching Tatarakis's description was put on a train . . . bound for Siberia.

until the repatriation of the captured crew at the end of the war. Fortunately for the special operations aircrews, this kind of in-flight disaster would prove to be, like shark attacks, as rare as it was horrifying.

Unlike the case of the Burger crew, a lack of evidence or explanation marked most mission failures. Aircrews, agents, or partisans simply disappeared without a trace, and CCRAK officers could only hope they had died instantly before capture and the interrogations could begin.

Despite the personal sacrifice and the heartache of such losses, the war dragged on. The Fifth Air Force continued to send its aircrews north. The partisans continued to fight and die. FECOM's unconventional warfare program was reorganized for a third time in December 1952. CCRAK now reported to a new staff organization, the Special Operations Division, which in turn reported to another staff entity, FECOM's G-2 (Intelligence) function.[17] It would take another war a decade later, again in the Far East, to confront America's military leaders with how much or how little they had learned from their lessons in unconventional warfare in Korea.

Notes

1. Col George Budway, USAF, Retired, former CCRAK officer, letter to Sgt Ray Dawson, USAF, former CCRAK NCO, subject: CCRAK, June 1987; and Ray Dawson, telephone interview(s) with author, 10–14 July 1995.

2. Maj Steve A. Fondacaro, "A Strategic Analysis of U.S. Special Operations during the Korean Conflict, 1950–1953" (thesis, US Army Command and General Staff College, 1988), 71.

3. Ibid., 69.

4. Ibid.

5. Lt Col Garth Stevens et al., "Intelligence Information by Partisans for Armor" (U) Research Report, vol. 1 (Fort Knox, Ky.: Armored Officer Advanced Course, 1952), 29. (Confidential) Information extracted is unclassified.

6. Ibid., 35.

7. Ibid., 19.

8. Maj Robert B. Brewer, US Army, Retired, former FEC/LG officer, to Joseph C. Goulden, author of *Korea: The Untold Story,* letter, 12 December 1984.

9. Ibid., 49.

10. Brewer, "Study Regarding Parachute Agent Problems (U)," Joint Special Operations Center, FEC/LG, 3 September 1950, attached as appendix 2 to Stevens, vol. 2, "Intelligence Information to Partisans for Armor." (Confidential) Information extracted is unclassified.

11. Stevens, 20, 31.

12. Ibid., 43.

13. Ibid.

14. Brig Gen Harry C. Aderholt, USAF Oral History Interview (U) (K239.0512-1716), 12–15 August 1986, 53. (Secret) Information extracted is unclassified.

15. Ibid., 46.

16. Ed Evanhoe, "Reported Alive: Three U. S. Spec Ops Men Still Missing in the Korean War," *Behind the Lines,* November/ December 1993, 42–43.

17. Col Rod Paschall, "Special Operations in Korea," *Conflict* 7, no. 2 (1987): 169.

SPECIAL AIR MISSIONS
USA
20301557

Special Air Missions

CCRAK fought its unconventional war behind enemy lines, much like the legendary Mongol warrior archer with a quiver full of specialized arrows. CCRAK's arrows were intelligence agents, partisans, psychological warfare (psywar) leaflets urging enemy surrender, and even psywar voice broadcasts with the same mission. But like all arrows, CCRAK's weapons were useless without a strong bow to launch them. Seaborne infiltration had its place, but such operations seldom penetrated far inland. Only airborne infiltration could penetrate the curtain of mountains that hid the enemy's positions and maneuvers so well. As events would prove, CCRAK found one of its most effective bows in USAF's Unit 4, introduced briefly in the previous story.

"Special Air Missions" brought US Air Force, Army, CIA, and Korean special operations personnel together for missions "north of the bomb line." The dangerous night missions were flown after the same pilots were used to fly high-ranking State Department and DOD dignitaries throughout Korea during the day. Oddly, no one seemed to question the practice of mixing covert operations and high-visibility VIP flights so closely.

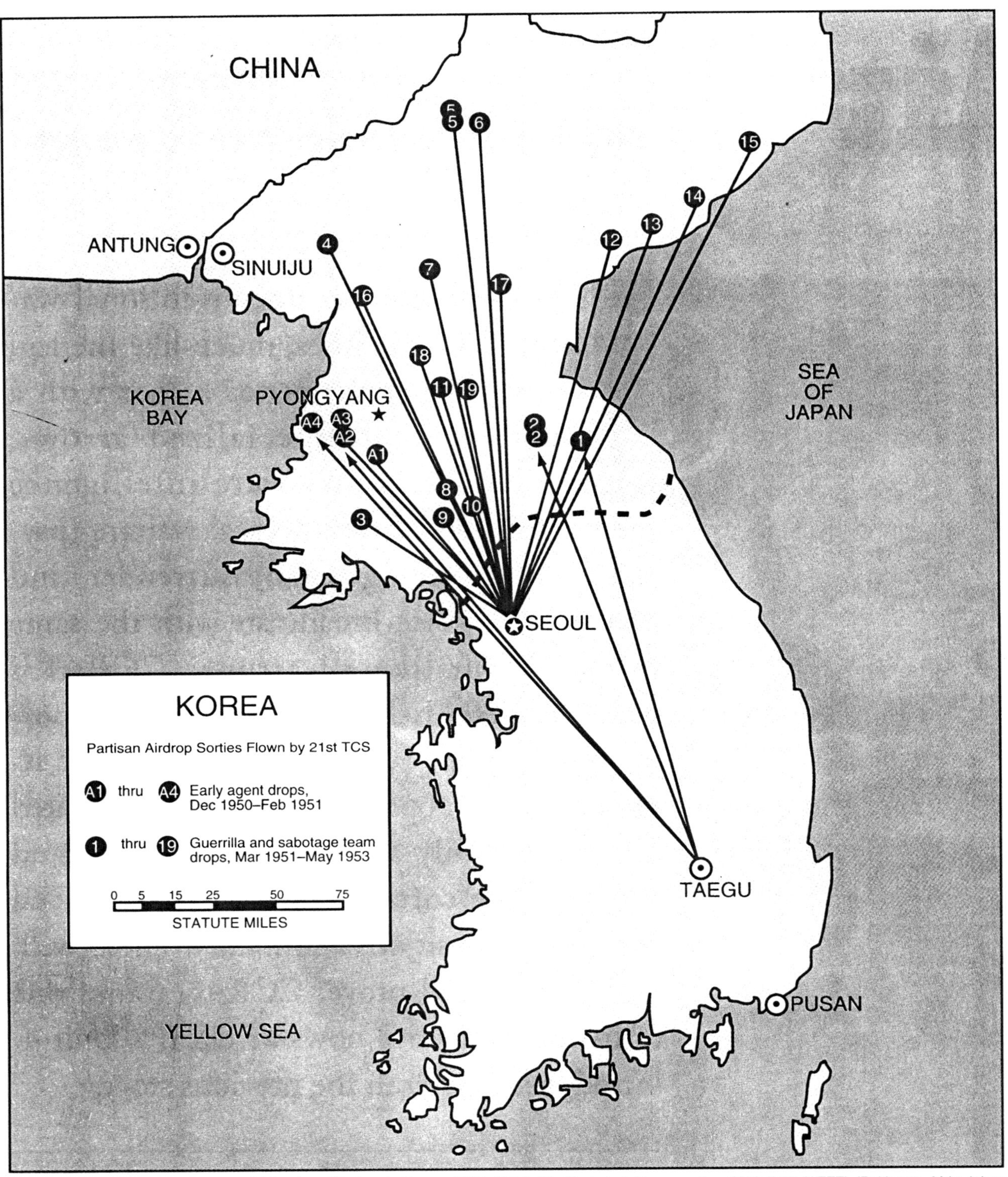

Source: Frederick Cleaver et al., "UN Partisan Warfare in Korea, 1951–1954" (U), Technical Memorandum ORO-T-64 (AFFE) (Baltimore, Md.: Johns Hopkins University, June 1956). (Secret) Information extracted is unclassified.

This unclassified map shows the range and scope of agent drops from both Taegu and Seoul during most of the war, at least those conducted by SAM. Other military and civilian organizations were equally active, but the absence of an effective joint special operations command badly hampered the unconventional war.

Unit 4 belonged to the 21st Troop Carrier Squadron (TCS), officially based on the Japanese island of Kyushu. The wartime reality was that the squadron's overcommitted C-47s were so active everywhere in Korea they seldom made it back to their home base, hence their unofficial nickname, the "Kyushu Gypsies." Activated in July 1950, only eight days after the start of the war, the 21st TCS was under the operational control of the 374th Troop Carrier Wing (Heavy) and received its commitments from the 315th Air Division (Heavy), both headquartered in Japan.

Activated almost immediately following the squadron's start-up, Unit 4 flew its first missions from Taegu Airfield (K-2) in southern Korea following the US breakout from the Pusan perimeter that fall. Unit 4 then relocated to Kimpo Airfield (K-14) just outside the capital city of Seoul, where some of the most important missions described thus far were flown. But there was more to come—much more.

Less than 90 days after Unit 4's arrival at K-14, pressure from the southward attacking Chinese caused the unit to return in February 1951 to the relative safety of Taegu Airfield. Distancing itself from the front lines had obvious advantages, but it also came at the expense of much longer missions for the already extended aircrews. The primary Aviary liaison officer to Unit 4 during this period observed:

> The missions have become much longer since moving our base of operations to K-2. In addition, KLO has stepped up the number of flights per month. It is not fair to expect crews to fly all night on tactical missions and then fly all day on cargo and evacuation runs.[1]

Standard 21st TCS policy was to rotate volunteer crews from Japan to Unit 4 for two-week periods. This policy did not, however, lead to overmanning the unit. It was an exhausting schedule that succeeded beyond what might have been expected, due in part to the fact that many of the aircrew members volunteered to extend beyond their scheduled two-week rotation. A KLO study in early 1951 describing ways to increase the effectiveness of special air-intelligence projects observed:

> Under Captain Harry C. Aderholt, CO of Unit 4, the crews have developed considerable skill in the special techniques required on these special missions. . . . Flying intelligence missions, which often last five or six hours during the hours of darkness, as well as missions during the day, has exacted the utmost in stamina and endurance from pilots and crews.[2]

While the "duty day problem" would remain apparently insurmountable for the foreseeable future, the unit's return to K-2 was followed

Harry Aderholt

Special Air Missions Detachment commander Capt Harry C. "Heinie" Aderholt was already in his second war, but not his last. His unorthodox tactic of arming SAM C-47 transports with napalm bombs to attack truck convoys at night was surprisingly effective but not appreciated much at FEAF headquarters.

USAF

Bad day "at the office" when psychological warfare leaflet bundle breaks open after the main cargo door in a SAM C-47 is already open. Always difficult to assess because of other related factors, psywar in Korea still had many notable successes.

immediately by substantial changes, some of them inexplicable even 45 years later.

Unit 4's return to K-2 that February coincided with a mission letter from higher headquarters, the 374th Troop Carrier Wing. The letter directed the establishment of a Special Air Missions Detachment at Taegu South Airfield on the 20th of the same month. The SAM would

> provide air transportation for US Ambassador Muccio [John J.], Republic of Korea President Rhee, Lieutenant General Ridgway (CINCFECOM), 8th Army Staff, other agencies with legitimate lift requests, and *to operate psychological missions as requested by 8th Army.*[3] (Emphasis added)

And that's what happened next—almost. By day, Unit 4-turned-SAM* aircrews flew "white hat" cargo runs and the highest ranking US officials on VIP flights. At nightfall, the same aircrews switched to their "black hat" work, putting long hours in on dangerous low-level infiltration flights behind enemy lines.

The new SAM was equipped with one B-17 heavy bomber-turned-VIP transport (VB-17), one C-47 transport-turned-VIP transport (VC-47), two "voice" C-47s for aerial psywar broadcasts, and three additional C-47s from the deactivated Unit 4.[4] The VB-17 and VC-47 were piloted by crews from the Fifth Air Force headquarters.[5] The same mission letter changed the existing policy of

*One cryptic sentence in a 374th Troop Carrier Group (TCG) unit history report (March 1951) notes: "The Special Air Mission at K-37 is now responsible for all special missions previously assigned to the K-2 detachment."

assigning crews from the 21st TCS to Unit 4 for two-week rotations by placing all SAM personnel on "indefinite detached service from this [21st TCS] unit."[6]

Noting the threat posed by enemy night fighters to SAM's stepped-up night-infiltration missions, CCRAK suggested modifications to the C-47s to include self-sealing gas tanks, an olive-drab paint scheme (SAM aircraft flew in USAF standard flat-silver metal finish), engine exhaust extensions to reduce visibility of low-flying aircraft to ground observation, and improved radar sets and radios.[7] Of the list, only the last modification was accomplished, with the addition of the SCR-300 radio.

Capt Heinie Aderholt himself saw the hordes of Chinese bearing down on unsuspecting, vulnerable American units like a tidal wave of death. As Aderholt now recalls:

> We saw thousands and thousands of troops, trucks, bumper to bumper! It was a moonlight night, snow on the ground. . . . We flew right down, turned our landing lights on, and they [the Chinese] wouldn't fire. We came back and reported and were told, "Well, the B-26s will get them."[8]

Fortunately for Aderholt, Chinese fire discipline was impeccable. Under strict orders not to betray their positions by firing at low-flying aircraft, they

USAF

Psywar leaflets kept the message simple and used pictures to convey messages to the largely illiterate North Korean People's Army. Psywar leaflets on victorious and advancing NKPA or Chinese "volunteers" early in the war were predictably ineffective and used by the troops for purposes other than that for which they were intended.

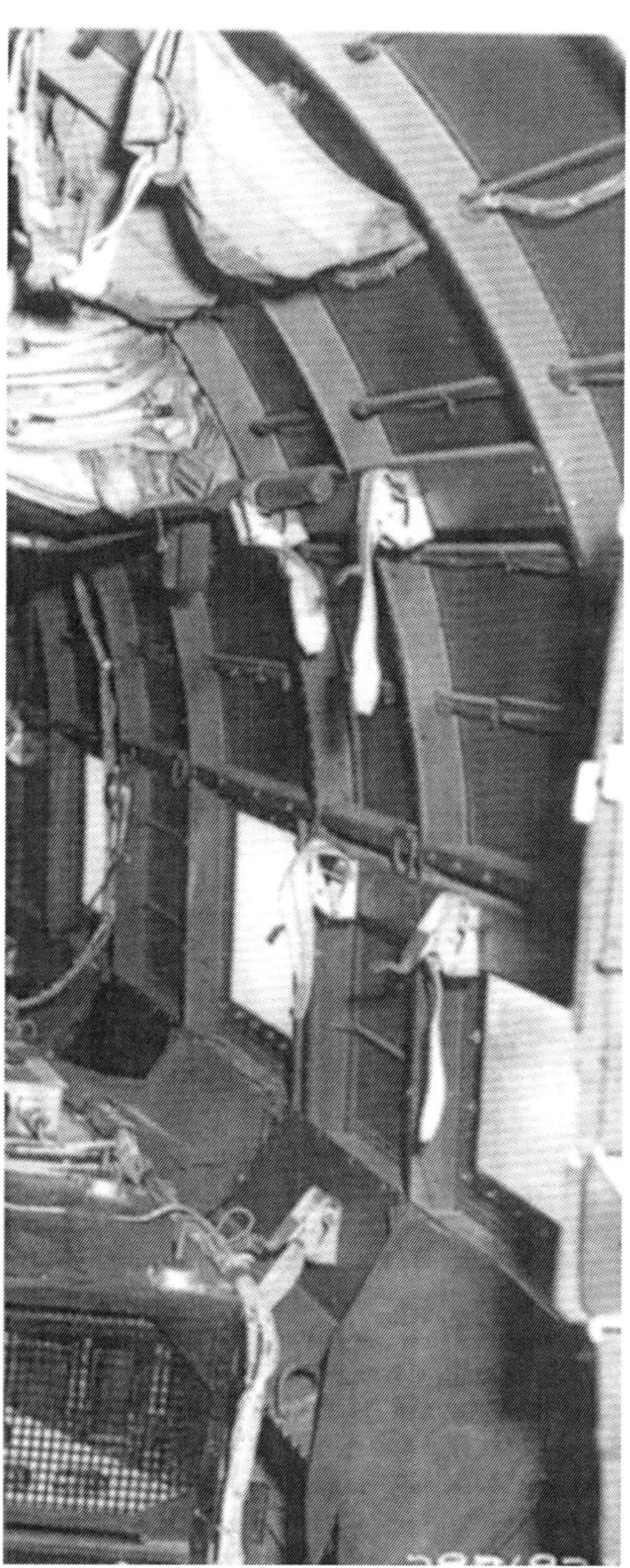

With two C-47s modified with loudspeakers, SAM C-47s experienced notable psywar successes with voice broadcasts to isolated and starving pockets of enemy soldiers. The use of female voices added insult to injury to the North Korean troops, who feared airpower above all other US weapons encountered in combat.

obeyed even when it became obvious they had been spotted. Incredibly, the Chinese still refused to fire even after the young captain attacked the trucks with one of his personal improvisations—napalm "bombs" in fuel drums slung underneath the C-47's fuselage. It was one more way SAM had found to take the war to the enemy. The only stipulation Aderholt placed on his aircrews was that the primary mission had to be completed before they were free to attack targets of opportunity with their unauthorized "C-47 low-level bomber." Although extremely accurate when used, the practice was eventually terminated by a startled FEAF headquarters when it became aware of this particular SAM initiative.[9]

Unit 4/SAM flew virtually all CCRAK-KLO missions early in the war,[10] including the first parachute infiltration of a successful radio-agent team behind enemy lines.[11] This "first" was of critical importance to a demoralized United Nations force in full retreat following the "surprise" intervention of Chinese forces in November 1950. For the second time in less than six months, the US faced the humiliating and bloody prospect of being run off the Korean peninsula. With contact yet again broken between attacking Chinese and retreating allied forces, the urgent question was raised by FECOM: "Where are the Chinese?" The crude "smoke jumps" described previously could be useful, but only if the weather cooperated. However, *cooperative* is not a word often associated with Korean winters.

The answer to FECOM's urgent question was soon forthcoming from the Aviary-SAM team. On the freezing black night of 9 December, a single SAM C-47 inserted a radio-equipped team codenamed "Hotel Victor One" into a desolate track of land in the enemy's path of advance. It was soon

USAF

Unlike the time-consuming psywar leaflets, The Voice could respond immediately to changing battlefield conditions. On occasion, this timing could be exploited to induce the surrender of entire enemy units.

rewarded with a strong signal from the blackness below.[12] How important were the reports transmitted from this single team? One knowledgeable postwar study called it "*the* vital essential element of information" needed by FECOM.[13]

While dropping intelligence agents was a primary mission for SAM, it was only one of many that shared equal priority. Radio intercept missions were highly valued by both FEAF and CCRAK and were a major mission, especially early in the war (see table 1, page 26). Psychological warfare flights, utilizing either loudspeaker-equipped voice C-47s or leaflet drops, also became one of the mainstays of SAM.

Particularly disheartening to Communist soldiers was the sight of a slow-moving C-47 flying pass after pass low over their positions with impunity from the North Korean Air Force. Occasionally, a female voice was used for the loudspeaker messages, adding insult to injury to the enemy below. In fact, field interrogations of defecting soldiers conducted in Korea in early 1951 concluded that voice broadcasts were more effective than surrender leaflets due to the numbers of illiterate soldiers in the Communist ranks.[14] However literate or illiterate, the Communist soldiers could still be counted on to provide a hot welcome to SAM's low-flying psywar missions.

The initial psywar leaflet flights in 1950 were briefed to drop from 2,000 feet altitude,[15] but it soon became evident that this was too high to assure the leaflets landed in the desired area. Flying at 500 feet solved the accuracy problems, and flights continued with standard leaflet loads averaging 3,000 to 4,000 pounds per mission. Predictably, the lower altitude also solved another accuracy problem, this one to the advantage of the enemy below who now had the aircraft within easy range of their machine guns and rifles.

In February 1951, one psywar C-47 from Unit 4 was so badly damaged it was a write-off upon landing.[16] While dropping leaflets near Seoul City, the aircraft had been hit by enemy small arms fire that severed its rudder cables and caused a runaway propeller on the right engine, requiring the engine to be shut down. Barely maintaining aircraft control, the crew made it back to a friendly airstrip, only to find that all remaining hydraulic fluid had to be used to extend the landing gear. With no brakes, the C-47 veered off the runway upon landing, shearing the landing gear, tearing both engines from their mounts, and leaving the aircraft with "the wings bent considerable."

The February crash led to the decision to conduct further low-level leaflet drops at night, but it provided only partial respite from SAM's increasingly violent world. A 21st TCS unit history report for March notes cryptically that "aircraft are receiving battle damage while accomplishing Special Missions in Korea. Three airplanes received major damage and five received minor damage during March 1951."[17] The 21st TCS report for the month of April noted:

> One aircraft from this organization has been missing since the morning of 30 April 1951. This aircraft had four crew members and two psychological warfare men aboard. This aircraft departed from K-37 on a leaflet drop mission in the Kumhwa-Wonsan, Korea, area behind enemy lines. The aircraft commander was heard giving the distress call "May Day" and [an] emergency IFF [identification friend or foe] signal was observed . . . this is the third crew from this organization (SAM) that has been listed as killed or listed as missing since the start of the Korean war.[18]

"To operate psychological missions as requested by 8th Army" would prove to be more than a mission statement for the surviving SAM aircrews. It would also provide a fitting memorial for those whose death came on missions too secret to even be acknowledged at the time by our country.

Notes

1. Lt Col Garth Stevens, "Intelligence Information by Partisans for Armor" (U) Research Report, appendix 4 to vol. 2, KLO letter, subject: Study on Need for Special C-47, 23 January 1951, 213. (Confidential) Information extracted is unclassified.
2. Ibid., 212.
3. History, 374th Troop Carrier Wing (Heavy), 1–28 February 1951, Historical Data No. 1.
4. Ibid.
5. Ibid.
6. Ibid., 3.
7. Ibid., 213.
8. Brig Gen Harry C. Aderholt, USAF, Retired, Oral History Interview (U) (K239.0512-1716), 12–15 August 1986, 32. (Secret) Information extracted is unclassified.
9. Ibid., 39.
10. History, 374th Troop Carrier Wing (Heavy), 1–28 February 1951, Historical Data No. 1, 212.
11. Stevens, 37.
12. Ibid., 11.
13. Ibid.
14. Kilchoon Kim and E. A. Johnson, "Evaluation of Effects of Leaflets on Early North Korean Prisoners of War" (U), Technical Memorandum ORO-T-4 (EUSAK) (Baltimore, Md.: Johns Hopkins University, 20 February 1951), 8. (Secret) Information extracted is unclassified.
15. History, 21st TCS, October 1950, Historical Data No. 5.
16. Ibid., Historical Data No. 14.
17. History, 21st TCS, March 1951, 7.
18. History, 21st TCS, April 1951, 3–4.

B Flygth

Firefly, Leaflet, and Pickup Operations

Twenty-four years after the close of the Korean War, the US government finally declassified the special operations wartime activities of B Flight, 6167th Operations Squadron, Fifth Air Force, United States Air Force. Activated 1 April 1952 in conjunction with a number of Fifth Air Force reorganizations, B Flight was equipped with B-26 medium bombers as well as C-46 and C-47 transports. The flight's black-painted aircraft were a noticeable addition to the growing USAF special operations presence at Seoul City Air Base, a base already referred to by many as "Spook City."

As "welcome mats" go, this bullet-riddled entrance to Seoul City Air Base left something to be desired. Officially designated K-16, the air base was unofficially known as Spook City. Regardless of name, it became the center for unconventional warfare operations during most of the war.

SEOUL CITY
AIR BASE

Even an abbreviated summary of the declassified document describing B Flight's "combat doctrine" in Korea helps explain the long-held secrecy surrounding this unit. The little-known B Flight was created solely for the purpose of conducting:

> CLASSIFIED Missions: Transporting and resupplying personnel and units operating *behind enemy lines* [emphasis added] . . . for the purpose of gathering intelligence information and covert activity . . . or for aiding rescue, escape, or evasion.
>
> PSYWAR Operations: Missions assigned by psychological warfare section of 5th Air Force and/or 8th Army . . . encompassing leaflet drops and speaker missions.
>
> FIREFLY Operations: Flare drops . . . to aid ground units . . . in night combat . . . and bomber A/C in night attack of enemy.
>
> OTHER Missions: As may be assigned by 5th Air Force. This includes *personnel snatch* [emphasis added] with transport A/C.[1]

The combat doctrine document left little doubt in the minds of newly assigned personnel as to the hazardous nature of the duty confronting them. No one was asking for volunteers this time and the three- or four-day period allowed for indoctrination of new members in unit mission and procedures didn't allow for slow learners.

"Classified" missions were initially flown in all three types of aircraft assigned to the flight. Experience soon led the crews to conclude that the glass-nosed (unarmed) B-26, modified with a jump platform in the bomb bay, was the ideal aircraft for these missions.[2]

The platform modification to the bomb bay provided wood benches on the bomb racks on which a maximum of six parachutists could sit en

route to the drop zone. There was still another modification not briefed to the parachutists. As former B Flight navigator Maj P. G. Moore recalls:

> When we gave the green light for the parachutists to jump, they simply slid off the wood benches and dropped. In the event they hesitated, we had a toggle switch in the cockpit that dropped the whole lot . . . bomb racks, benches, and parachutists from the aircraft.[3]

If the spy and partisan parachutists hesitated, perhaps it was because they had noticed the absence of those sent on previous missions, never to be seen again. Things had changed since the early days of the war when individual spies stood a better-than-average chance of coming back.

As noted earlier, the Special Air Missions Detachment of the 21st Troop Carrier Squadron had made the first wartime personnel drops behind enemy lines with mixed results and an agent survival rate approximating 70 percent (see the previous story on "Special Air Missions"). One of the more interesting aspects of these parachute missions is that, contrary to widespread denial both in print and personal accounts that exist to this day, Americans indeed led some of these operations.

The first airborne partisan operation of the FECOM Liaison Group was launched on 15 March 1951 with the code name "Virginia" (table 2). Four US Army Rangers led 19 Koreans on a mission to sabotage railway traffic. The mission failed, with all but five of the partisans killed and one Ranger captured.[4] Three months later, two American, one British, and two Korean guerrillas parachuted behind enemy lines in Operation Spitfire. Two more "UN personnel" led nine Koreans a week later to the same area to reinforce the first party. That mission also failed, although most of the partisans were able to exfiltrate to friendly lines.[5]

Major Moore also recalls taking American parachutists further north—across North Korea's northern border and into Manchuria itself. Moore, who honed his navigator skills in World War II's elite Pathfinder squadrons, used the best maps available for these paradrops into Manchuria—maps published in 1912 and marked "Japanese General Staff."[6]

When going that far north, the B-26s would generally take off from K-16, fly east out over the Sea of Japan and, using a navigation beacon on one of the US Navy's carriers, fly north as far as possible before turning inland to search for the small fires that would mark the drop zone. Sometimes "going up" was the easy part. On the night of 30 March 1953, Moore earned his first

Black-painted B-26s of B Flight on the ramp at K-16 in 1952. The Plexiglas nose indicates use for purposes other than that of the solid-nosed ground-attack version. Six parachutists could be carried in the specially modified bomb bay.

P G Moore

Table 2
Sorties Flown by Fifth Air Force to Drop Partisans behind Enemy Lines 1951–53

Partisan Operation Code Name	*Date*	*Partisan Mission*	*Number Personnel Dropped*
Virginia	15 March 1951	Sabotage	24
Spitfire	18 June 1951	Set-up Base	5
"	25 June 1951	"	11
Mustang	22 January 1952	Sabotage	19
"	16 March 1952	"	16
"	14 May 1952	"	10
"	14 May 1952	"	10
"	31 October 1952	"	5
"	31 October 1952	"	6
Jesse James	28 December 1952	Sabotage	10
"	28 December 1952	"	10
"	30 December 1952	"	10
Green Dragon	25 January 1953	Set-up Base	97
Boxer	7 February 1953	Sabotage	12
"	7 February 1953	"	12
"	9 February 1953	"	12
"	11 February 1953	"	12
Hurricane	31 March 1953	Set-up Base	5
Rabbit	1 April 1953	Sabotage	40
"	6 April 1953	"	6
Green Dragon	19 May 1953	Set-up Base	57
			TOTAL 389

Source: Lt Col Lawrence V. Schuetta, *Guerrilla Warfare and Airpower in Korea, 1950–1953* (Maxwell AFB, Ala · Aerospace Studies Institute, January 1964), 145

Oak Leaf Cluster to a Distinguished Flying Cross (DFC)[7] "just" for bringing his crew home alive.

The language in the DFC citation provides a classic example of a special operations award for valor under circumstances better left unsaid. Selected phrases are useful for those still practicing to read between the lines (comments in brackets are the author's):

Major Moore was a navigator of an unarmed, unescorted B-26 . . . performing a classified night interdiction mission [*interdiction in an unarmed aircraft?*]. . . . This mission penetrated deep into enemy territory in the vicinity of the Yalu River [*no mention of which side of the Yalu River, which separates North Korea from Manchuria*]. . . . The target area [*a drop zone for partisan parachutists*] was near enemy operational airfields . . . guarded by heavy anti-aircraft

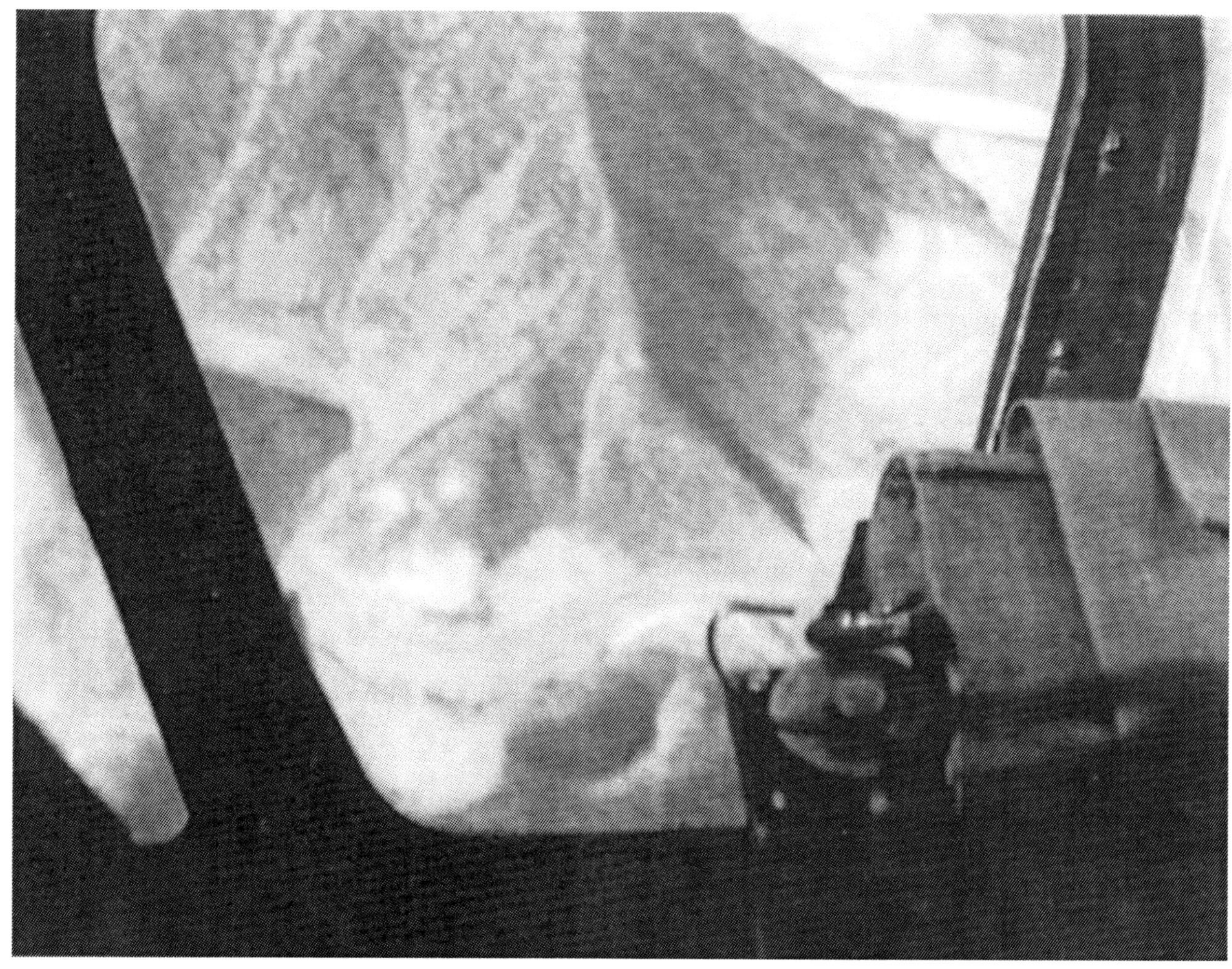

P G Moore

A rare daytime view from the Plexiglas nose of a B Flight B-26 shows Korea's rugged terrain, a geographical reality that made parachute infiltration the only viable long-range entry into the North Korean or Manchurian interior.

> weapons, radar stations, and searchlights. . . . Moore successfully directed the low-flying [*parachute-dropping altitude*] aircraft around and through mountainous terrain [*and the aforementioned searchlights, which had by then caught the intruder in their beams*] . . . to the water [*as in right down on the water!*].[8]

Records of these missions do exist, but they usually avoid mentioning the presence of Americans on the partisan teams.[9] As with all other parachute operations, the partisans were expected to exfiltrate on foot, if they could. And throughout 1952, failed operation after failed operation proved that the chances for mission success matched exactly the chances for individual survival—zero.

The problems were twofold, with the Air Force having its own difficulties to tackle. The USAF personnel rotation policy for Korea created a system in which incoming airmen could rotate home in as little as six months. Good for morale, the policy inevitably placed inexperienced aircrews on special operations missions, demanding much higher levels of expertise and experience. The grossly inadequate three or four days B Flight allowed to "indoctrinate" and train special operations aircrews from nonvolunteer transport pilots highlights the problem.

This situation was further compounded by a later decision to give "two-mission credit" for any single mission lasting more than five hours over enemy territory. Inevitably, partisans and supplies were parachuted into the wrong place. The 6167th Air Base Group (ABG) unit history report for the last six months of 1952 notes, "the primary problem of the Group has been the lack of qualified personnel *due to constant rotations.* Of particular importance is the shortage of *navigators*" (emphasis added).[10] The acknowledged shortage of experienced special operations aircrews had surfaced long before 1952; and in at least one known case, the result was deadly.

The previously mentioned Operation Spitfire had as its objective the setting up of a secret partisan base behind enemy lines. Two jumps, spaced several days apart, got the mission off to a good start. But on 5 July, 10 days after the second jump, an inexperienced crew attempting to resupply the secret camp made a fatal error. Unable to locate the camp at night, the plane returned at daybreak and parachuted the supplies into the camp . . . in front of every enemy eye within sight.[11] Although the team immediately left the area, it was ambushed the following morning with the loss of several lives and the obvious abort of the mission.*

The Air Force had problems, but airborne partisan operations behind enemy lines had reached such grim proportions by late 1952 that they had literally become suicide missions. If the missions were not compromised on the ground by double agents within the partisans, the partisans were killed or captured within days of their infiltration, if not on the DZ itself. The results, if not the particulars, were known to CCRAK planners, leading one well-documented postwar study on the subject to offer the criticism that "these decisions to use partisans against enemy supply routes in airborne operations appears to have been futile and callous."[12]

The psywar leaflet-dropping missions were usually flown with either C-46 or C-47 transports, both types having the main cargo door removed. The more humanitarian leaflets might warn civil-

*Army SFC William T. Miles and a Korean scout held off the attacking Communists long enough to allow the main partisan party to break contact. CIA agents in the enemy rear reported that a wounded American prisoner matching Miles's description was brought to a nearby town shortly after the fight, then shipped to a hospital elsewhere in North Korea. Unconfirmed CIA reports later indicated that Miles was subsequently moved by train to Siberia. He was not among the American prisoners repatriated to the US at the close of the war.

USAF

The C-46 Air Commando was as versatile as it was tough flying "classified" missions, Firefly flare drops, or psywar leaflet missions. It was a C-46 of this type that was downed by a grenade thrown into its interior by a Chinese double agent just before he parachuted out of the aircraft.

ian populations to flee the area before bombers arrived with their lethal cargo. Most messages, however, were aimed at demoralizing the enemy, urging the Communist troops to surrender by using the leaflet itself as a "safe conduct" pass.

B Flight's leaflet drops were made from 7,500 feet, a safer altitude than the much lower levels attempted by the 21st TCS earlier in the war. A 14-inch or 18-inch slow-burning fuse allowed the leaflet "bombs" to drop to a much lower altitude before a small powder charge ignited and broke the bundle open to disperse thousands of leaflets contained in each bomb.[13]

B Flight eventually dropped its early attempts to use its B-26s and C-47s for psywar loudspeaker missions. Flown at 5,000 feet "or lower," these flights took the same enemy ground-fire punishment meted out to all loudspeaker flights. In the

USAF

Million-candlelight-power flares dropped from B Flight C-46s or C-47s could spell the difference between life and death for the infantrymen below. Proudly if curiously dubbed "The Queen of Battle," the infantry suffered every deprivation while awaiting human-wave assaults by Chinese assault regiments attempting to use the night to escape US airpower.

end, B Flight suspended loudspeaker missions with the cryptic note "Due to battle damage and scarcity of speaker parts, this method of psychological warfare has been curtailed."[14]

As in every modern war, attempts to measure the effectiveness of psywar leaflets in Korea proved difficult at best. However, one early war study done in Korea by a research team from Johns Hopkins University concluded that "the (financial) cost of a psywar capture to a conventional kill appears to have a probable ratio of 70:1 in favor of psywar."[15] The same Johns Hopkins study (largely POW interrogations) provided an additional insight that led to yet another special mission for B Flight—this one in direct support of US frontline units. From its field research, the Johns Hopkins team learned that Communist soldiers feared air attack far more than artillery, tanks, or infantry (table 3).[16] The aircraft weapons feared most were machines guns, high-explosive

Table 3
Communist POW Reports of US Weapons Feared Most

Kind of Fighting	*Percent of Total*	*Aircraft Weapons*	*Percent of Total*
Air Attack	82.0	Machine Guns	56.0
Artillery	7.0	High-explosive Bombs	19.3
Tanks	2.6	Rockets	11.0
Infantry	1.6	Napalm	7.4
Not Answered	6.8	Not Answered	6.3

Source: Kilchoon Kim and E. A. Johnson, "Evaluation of Leaflets on Early North Korean Prisoners of War" (U), Technical Memorandum ORO-T-4 (EUSAK) (Baltimore, Md.: Johns Hopkins University, 20 February 1951), 7. (Secret) Information extracted is unclassified.

bombs, rockets, and napalm—in that order.[17] The Communists quickly learned that by moving and attacking at night, they could exploit USAF's near-total lack of night ground-attack capability. USAF countered this tactic in part by turning night into day with B Flight's Firefly missions.

To execute its Firefly missions, B Flight loaded all three types of its aircraft with 1-million-candlepower parachute flares. Entering the target area at night at 10,000 feet altitude, the aircrews were vectored to their specific drop area by airborne or ground controllers. The high-intensity flares were armed in the aircraft and set to ignite at 1,000–1,500 feet below the aircraft. At 2,000 feet above the terrain, each of these flares could illuminate approximately one square mile.[18]

In a war in which the technology for night-vision devices had not yet been perfected, Firefly missions were a tactic that spelled the difference between life and death for the infantry "grunts" below. For example, a maximum effort by B Flight on the night of 29 March 1953 dropped

USAF

Desolate, frozen Manchuria north of the Yalu River, which separates it from North Korea. USAF special operations aircrews were no strangers to this forbidding land.

Table 4
B Flight Operations Statistical Report
1 July–31 December 1952

	JULY	AUGUST	SEPTEMBER	OCTOBER	NOVEMBER	DECEMBER
Classified Missions	69	79	69	88	77	47
Leaflet Missions	142	182	214	202	203	137
Speaker Missions	13	37	29	34	25	10
Flare Missions	79	73	96	116	88	13
Combat Hours	753	879	952	1,127	440	366

Source: B Flight Operations Statistical Report, 1 July–31 December 1952.

1,004 flares to illuminate Communist infantry assaults below in the notorious "Old Baldy" sector of the front lines.[19] Still other special operations tactics were in their infancy during the war, and B Flight would have a chance to test these also.

A Fifth Air Force letter classified secret, dated 29 November 1952, announced a new capability for retrieving downed airmen or agents from enemy-held territory "north of the bomb line."[20] Officially named the "Personnel Pickup Ground Station," it was known more simply by the designated pickup aircrews as "the snatch system." As usual, the simpler name said it all. It literally called for an aircraft in flight (usually a C-47) to snatch an individual from the ground and reel him into the aircraft. The system was similar to the one used by banner-towing aircraft, in which a wire was strung horizontally between two poles, with a second wire leading to the object to be snatched from the ground. An aircraft equipped with a tailhook swooped within a few feet of the ground, snared the horizontal wire, and climbed immediately for altitude, pulling the banner (or downed pilot) up behind it.

In Korea, the horizontal wire was a nylon rope that would stretch when pulled, thereby avoiding the self-defeating prospect of tearing the downed airman in half as he accelerated from zero to a hundred miles an hour almost immediately. The necessary ground equipment would first be dropped to the airman or agent in a 50-pound bundle kicked out of the pickup aircraft. The setup was necessarily simple, as time was obviously of the essence. When the circling aircraft observed the individual ready for pickup, it would begin a low, slow pass to snag the rope with its hook. Successful field trials proved the feasibility of the concept, but all involved noted the extreme vulnerability of the aircraft to ground fire on the low, slow snatch pass.

In the first half of 1953, B Flight attempted two snatch pickups of personnel in enemy territory. The first failed when the airman was captured before the pickup aircraft could reach the scene. The second failed for the reasons feared during the pickup trials. As the pickup plane reached the most vulnerable speed and altitude profile for the pickup, the waiting enemy opened fire, "inflicting extensive damage on the aircraft."[21] A similar ambush in Manchuria, north of the Yalu River, later downed a Civil Air Transport C-47 on its pickup pass.[22] The two surviving

Americans, Richard Fecteau and John Downey, would spend decades in Chinese imprisonment before diplomats could secure their release.

B Flight would fly and fight to the finish in Korea. Its unit history for the last six months of 1953 concludes:

> During the last twenty-six days of the Korean hostilities, seven hundred, eighty-two combat hours were flown with no loss of aircraft . . . two hundred, ninety-one combat missions were flown; one hundred, seventeen were classified; seventy-three were leaflet; and one hundred, one were flare.[23]

It's difficult to maintain an aggressive combat spirit in the waning days of a war. Personal sacrifice becomes meaningless for both victor and loser, and the most basic instinct of all, survival, becomes overwhelming. It's more difficult still when the individual's war is fought behind a cloak of secrecy without even the psychological support of public recognition. Flying single-ship missions into the black void of night becomes the airman's most intimate nightmare when failure means death or capture and torture. One of the least-known special operations units in the Korean War, B Flight did everything that was expected of it until the end.

Notes

1. Memorandum, Combat Doctrine B Flight, 6167th Operations Squadron (U), date obliterated by declassified stamp. (Secret) Information extracted is unclassified.
2. History, 6167th Air Base Group, 1 July–31 December 1952, 9.
3. Lt Col Paul G. Moore, USAF, Retired, former navigator, B Flight, 6167th ABW, Shalimar, Fla., interview with author, 14 March 1995.
4. Lt Col Lawrence V. Schuetta, *Guerrilla Warfare and Airpower in Korea, 1950–1953* (Maxwell AFB, Ala.: Aerospace Studies Institute, January 1964), 146.
5. Ibid.
6. Moore, interview with author, 11 July 1995.
7. Fifth Air Force General Orders 637, Award of the DFC, First Oak Leaf Cluster, to Maj Paul G. Moore, 27 September 1953.
8. Ibid.
9. The author is attempting to have these records declassified as this book is in progress.
10. History, 6167th ABG, 1 July–31 December 1952, page not numbered.
11. Ed Evanhoe, "Reported Alive: Three U. S. Spec Ops Men Still Missing in the Korean War," *Behind the Lines,* November/ December 1993, 42–43.
12. Frederick W. Cleaver et al., "UN Partisan Warfare in Korea, 1951–1954" (U), Technical Memorandum ORO-T-64 (AFFE) (Baltimore, Md.: Johns Hopkins University, June 1956), 94. (Secret) Information extracted is unclassified.
13. Combat Doctrine, 3.
14. History, 6167th ABG, 1 July–31 December 1952, 3.
15. Kilchoon Kim and E. A. Johnson, "Evaluation of Effects of Leaflets on Early North Korean Prisoners of War" (U), Technical Memorandum ORO-T-4 (EUSAK) (Baltimore, Md.: Johns Hopkins University, 20 February 1951), 8. (Secret) Information extracted is unclassified.
16. Ibid., 7.
17. Ibid.
18. Combat Doctrine, 2.
19. History, 6167th ABG, 1 January–30 June 1953, page not numbered.
20. History, 6167th ABG, 1 July–31 December 1952, letter page not numbered.
21. History, 6167th ABG, 1 January–30 June 1953, page not numbered.
22. Brig Gen Harry C. Aderholt, USAF, Retired, USAF Oral History Interview (U) (K239.0512-1716), 12–15 August 1986, 42. (Secret) Information extracted is unclassified.
23. History, 6167th ABG, 1 July–31 December 1953, 5.

The 6004th AISS

Nichols´s "One-Man War"

If I were called upon to name the most amazing and unusual man among all those with whom I was associated during my military service, I would not hesitate for a second in picking out Donald Nichols as that individual. . . . I have often referred to him as a ONE-MAN WAR.

Gen Earle E. Partridge
USAF, Retired

Hundreds of remote, unnamed islands off the west coast of Korea north of the 38th parallel provided ideal launch sites for intelligence and special operations missions behind enemy lines. Untold stories of valor and violence in these islands still remain cloaked in the silence of wartime secrecy.

General Partridge, who commanded the Fifth Air Force during much of the Korean War, had good reason to recall Donald Nichols in such terms. Under Nichols's command, Detachment 2 was arguably the most successful behind-the-lines special operations unit of the war.

Who was this former motor pool sergeant with a sixth-grade education who had 24-hour-a-day access to both General Partridge and South Korean president Syngman Rhee, as well as to a host of shadowy Asian characters whose names will never be seen in print? Who was this master spy who was wounded in close-quarters combat while leading ranger-style night attacks against Communist guerrillas . . . a combat leader who personally conceived, organized, and led a daring heliborne mission deep into enemy-held territory to strip parts off a downed MiG-15 fighter, the most highly sought-after intelligence prize of the war* . . . the innovator of "positive intelligence"?

Nichols himself admits he made up the term *positive intelligence* (PI) in prewar South Korea, where he was already well on the way to establishing a powerful intelligence apparatus both south and north of the 38th parallel separating the two Koreas. In his autobiography *How Many Times Can I Die?* Nichols recalls:

> By this time [1947–48] our unit was really moving in "high, very high" South Korean government circles. All doors were open to us. In those days no one in this area knew or even thought about *Positive Intelligence,*** (Covert Intelligence). We invented it for this area and taught others, as we saw fit, for our own benefit.[1]

"Our unit" was Sub-Detachment K of the 607th Counter Intelligence Corps (CIC) stationed at Kimpo Airfield on the western outskirts of Seoul. Master Sergeant Nichols had joined the subdetachment in 1946 and soon commanded the three-man unit. Extensive use was made of Korean civilian agents, later augmented by South Korean coast guard and air force personnel put, at President Rhee's personal orders, under operational control of "Mr." Nichols. Without realizing it, Nichols's self-styled positive intelligence made him one of the founding fathers of the modern Air Force human intelligence program.[2]

What took Nichols's PI beyond the normal scope of HUMINT was the historical collision of forces beyond any single individual's control—a brutal war fought between populations already toughened by years of deprivation, a young US Air Force still not certain of its limitations, the trust that South Korean president Syngman Rhee (and others) placed in this singular American, and finally, as General Partridge succinctly put it in his foreword to Nichols's autobiography, Nichols's "genius" for intelligence operations. His was the personality that stood in the midst of this violent vortex, a legend to the Korean government and the special operators who knew him but an unknown to this day to the American public.

By 1950 Nichols's CIC subdetachment had become a well-oiled machine with deep penetration and contacts throughout both Koreas. In May 1950, a month before the outbreak of war, his agents pulled off a major coup by persuading a North Korean pilot to defect south with his Soviet-built Il-10 ground attack fighter. It was the first of its kind to fall into US hands, and extensive debriefs of the willing pilot proved extremely valuable to Air Technical Intelligence experts. The plane itself was dismantled for shipment back to the Zone of Interior (ZI), as the continental US was then known in military parlance.

But before this shipment could take place, Nichols's team, as well as the South Korean gov-

*For this mission Nichols received the Distinguished Service Cross, the second highest decoration for valor America can bestow on its military personnel.

**"Negative intelligence" was the practice of denying the enemy from acquiring intelligence on US forces (i.e., the Counter Intelligence Corps's primary mission).

USAF

A rare photo of "Mr." Donald Nichols, a man with good reason to be camera shy. A combination of both "Lawrence of Arabia," and "Dirty Harry," this Office of Special Investigations (OSI) agent was a legend to the Koreans, a confidant of both flag-rank USAF officers and the president of South Korea, the man you turned to when results were too critical to question the methods. He survived assassination attempts in 1948, 1950, and 1953 and endured an attempt by North Korean teams to kidnap his son in Seoul. The teams were quickly identified and "annihilated"—end of kidnapping.

ernment and all Americans in South Korea, had to flee for their lives when 100,000-plus North Koreans poured over the 38th parallel like a huge swarm of killer bees. Leaving "a bloody wake of massacred civilians to mark their rapid advancing line," they forced Nichols's team to abandon their catch.[3] Staying behind on his own volition to destroy abandoned equipment and aircraft at Kimpo Airfield, Nichols himself barely escaped at the last minute by crossing the Han River clinging to the side of a small boat. It was a bitter pill to swallow for the man who had repeatedly warned FECOM that the North Koreans were about to attack.

As it turned out, his warnings had been in vain. As the Fifth Air Force commander later observed, Nichols's reports were "suppressed and disregarded."[4] His last report predicted within 72 hours the "surprise" attack that stunned FECOM and the US government. Not surprisingly, it was a terse report from Nichols in Seoul on the morning of 25 June 1950 that gave FEAF headquarters in Tokyo its first official notification that the war had started.[5]

Promoted to warrant officer the month the war started, Nichols immediately began his own war. Catching up with the retreating Americans in Suwon, he was recognized by the American ambassador to Korea, John J. Muccio, who promptly asked him to maintain personal contact with the heads of the South Korean military services. In July Nichols was relieved of his subdetachment command duties and appointed special representative to the director, Special Investigations (IG), FEAF, a move designed for no other purpose but to free him for "bigger things."

Bigger things came fast as General Partridge was not a commander with much time on his hands. Nichols's first task was to "secure by any means possible" a Russian-built T-34 tank, a weapon Fifth Air Force fighters so far had little luck destroying in their strafing runs. Nichols promptly "borrowed" a tank retriever vehicle from a frontline Army tank unit and secured the desired T-34 under enemy fire. A grateful Partridge awarded Nichols a Silver Star medal for his valor and initiative.

General Partridge then asked Nichols to take care of another urgent problem: Communist guerrillas in the hills overlooking Taegu Airfield were shooting up Fifth Air Force planes flying into that vital air base. Could Nichols help? Nichols led over 20 South Korean soldiers into the hills at night and attacked the guerrillas. His personal leadership on this mission can be judged in part by the grenade fragment wound to his leg incurred during the fight. Nichols's raid permanently stopped the guerrilla harassment of Fifth Air Force planes operating from Taegu.

In that same month, Nichols responded to a third request from General Partridge. Infiltrating 48 South Koreans by parachute behind enemy lines in 13 different missions, he supplied Fifth Air Force with its most complete target list to date. Later that year, he also supplied parachutists for the rescue of a downed B-29 aircrew in North Korea.

The parachutists had "graduated" from a crude jump school Nichols had established to provide for such missions. While observing jump training one day, he observed a plane fully loaded with Korean jump students landing for no apparent reason. Upon learning they had refused to jump, he determined to set the example by strapping on a parachute and warning the students of the consequences if they refused to follow him; after all, he too had never been to jump school. As Nichols relates in his autobiography:

> I really didn't at this time think that it would be necessary for me to jump. However, after we became airborne, I noticed all eyes were on me. When we went over the DZ, old man Nichols jumped. I was quite elated to see the blossoming of every other chute on the plane spread out above me as I dropped.[6]

Positive intelligence had obviously evolved into a special strike force of some kind. Fifth Air Force was not sure what to call it, but they knew they liked it (or at least the Fifth Air Force commander did, and he had the biggest vote). It was time to give it proper support.

A March 1951 letter from the Office of the Deputy for Intelligence, Headquarters, Fifth Air Force provides a rare insight into Fifth Air Force's wide-open approach to intelligence collection. The letter proposes the activation of existing assets (i.e., Nichols's ad hoc activities) into "Special Activities Unit Number One," a unit which would:

> (1) Provide intelligence operations of a *positive nature* designed to meet the objectives of this command.
> (2) Perform operations (sabotage, demolition, and/or guerrilla) necessary to accomplish destruction of specific objectives.
> (3) Assist allied agencies responsible for providing evasion and escape facilities to downed United Nations airmen.
> (4) Coordinate with other allied United Nations intelligence agencies as required by existing directives.[7]

Subsequent interservice/CIA staff meetings deleted "guerrilla warfare" as a task in deference to other agencies conducting such operations. That deletion was, however, apparently offered more in deference to bureaucratic sensitivities than to any real intention to surrender operational prerogatives.

USAF

A most unusual Air Force intelligence-collection vehicle, this indigenous Korean junk acquired by Donald Nichols sits at low-tide awaiting its next mission. The Yak-150 was part of Nichols's "private" fleet that ranged from indigenous fishing vessels to a US Navy landing ship, tank. These vessels plied an active trade to and from seemingly deserted islands that in fact were quite busy.

By this stage of the war, Nichols was providing Fifth Air Force "one-stop service" for requirements ranging from sensitive HUMINT collection to airborne ranger assaults on high-priority targets. Maj George T. Gregory, one of Nichols's executive officers during this period, describes the diverse kind of people Nichols brought to his enterprise:

> His [Nichols's] men included scholars with advanced degrees, and burly athletic types without higher education, but who could walk all night through enemy forests, ride horses, paddle canoes, parachute from low altitudes, kill a man with a single karate blow, and [be] able to speak three or four foreign languages.[8]

Perhaps to reflect its growing stature, Special Activities Unit Number One was redesignated the 6004th Air Intelligence Service Squadron (AISS) later that month. The AISS was activated on the orders of Headquarters FEAF in what appears to have been an effort to ensure top-level control of an extremely sensitive and valuable intelligence/special operations asset. Squadron detachments would continue to be added throughout most of the war, but its overall structure would include the following units and their missions:

> (1) Detachment One: Collect Air Technical Intelligence and conduct prisoner of war interrogations.
> (2) Detachment Two: Collect and disseminate Air Intelligence information. *Due to the unusual nature of this work and other circumstances, both the primary and secondary missions have been classified Top Secret by the Commanding General, Fifth Air Force.* (Emphasis added)
> (3) Detachment Three: Plan, coordinate, and support Evasion and Escape activities for the recovery of UN airmen downed in enemy territory . . . and to assist in the organization and specialized training of personnel necessary to accomplish the basic mission.[9]

Detachment 1 (under the command of Donald Nichols) came first, of course. And before the ink was dry on the new organization's paperwork, Fifth Air Force had a mission for Detachment 1 that would underscore Fifth Air Force's commitment to retain its prerogatives regardless of joint-service sensitivities.

On 1 June 1951, Nichols sent 15 South Korean Air Force saboteurs on a parachute infiltration mission to blow up two railroad bridges. Enemy uniforms, equipment, weapons, and papers were carried by the teams should they need to bluff their way past enemy challenges. The mission failed and all 15 were captured by the Chinese, a rare total loss for Nichols.[10] Detachment 1's mission soon evolved into the more traditional, technical intelligence and POW interrogation roles . . . and Nichols moved over to assume command of Detachment 2, the most aggressive Air Force intelligence unit of the war.

While Detachment 1's mission could usually be accomplished within established intelligence channels, the same could not be said of the other two detachments. In particular, the *"unusual nature . . . and other circumstances"* of Detachment 2's mission led to its description in one postwar study as "the first covert collection agency of a tactical nature in the history of the US Air Force."[11] This quote is a masterpiece of understatement.

Detachment 2 was activated in Seoul on 25 July 1951 with an authorized strength of seven officers (Nichols commanding) and 26 enlisted men.[12] As noted earlier, the latitude of its mission was extremely generous in an operational sense. In a wide-ranging summary, it was authorized to do the following:

> Direct intelligence operations behind enemy lines with special emphasis on . . . positive intelligence . . . coordinate with allied intelligence agencies . . . gather positive intelligence on the effectiveness of (allied) air operations . . . vital points of the enemy's transportation system . . . revetment hide out areas . . . plan and direct such *special operations* as may be required to support . . . Fifth Air Force and Far East Air Forces intelligence missions.[13] (Emphasis added)

Clearly, most of these missions could only be accomplished by "eyes on target," a military euphemism requiring an individual to visually watch the target close up, obviously at great risk to his or her life. What the summary didn't specify was exactly whose "eyes" were to take such great risks, how they were to conduct surveillance in the target area, and, most important to the owner of said eyes, how to stay alive in the process.

The answer to the "who" question could be found in the personnel manning statistics for this United States Air Force detachment. By January 1952, only 5.7 percent of the detachment's 665 personnel were American, with officers representing 1.2 percent of the total.[14] Lack of incoming qualified personnel and the continual rotation out of those who learned their jobs were constant problems (as it was in every other US special operations unit in Korea). In addition, Detachment 2

Ray Dawson

Resupplying partisans by air on Cho-do Island's beaches could be done at low tide in the hands of a skilled C-47 pilot. The trick was to be gone before Korea's notorious tides wiped out the "airfield."

had to deal with one overwhelming operational reality that no number of Americans could remedy. In a nutshell, no "round eye" (American) could go where Detachment 2's agents went. And where did they go? According to a 6004th historical report, "the main difference between its [Detachment 2's] mission and that of *Detachment Number One, is that Detachment Number Two works generally north of the bomb line*"[15] (emphasis added). By July 1952, Detachment 2 had positioned a total of 23 subdetachments north of the bomb line with reports coming into the detachment by radio on a regular basis.[16] By the end of the year, the number would swell to 32.[17] Actual personnel strength would total 11 officers and 47 airmen supervising 900 Koreans, of which 178 came from the South Korean Air Force.[18]

Most of the 700 other Koreans in Detachment 2 had been recruited from the ranks of the UN-supported partisan forces,* where they had proven themselves in combat.[19] Their partisan training and experience as well as their hatred of the Communists posed a peculiar problem for Detachment 2's Korean subdetachment commanders. Most of the former partisans were far more interested in fighting than intelligence gathering, an admirable quality anywhere else but in Detachment 2! Close supervision by their USAF

*Virtually all the UN-supported partisans were North Koreans who had chosen to flee south from the advancing Communists rather than live under their control. For the most sensitive intelligence missions, CCRAK and Detachment 2 found the educated Christian Koreans to be the most reliable agents.

subdetachment advisors (fig. 3) and continual training in intelligence craft were required to keep the discipline problem under control.

One problem definitely *not* under control was the rising death toll of agents in the field. As the Chinese and North Koreans began to comprehend that US forces were not coming back north of the 38th parallel (in 1951), they started reinforcing internal security forces in areas in which Nichols's agents had previously operated successfully. Routine missions became tough, and the tough ones became one-way missions.

The agents weren't the only ones to suffer from this deadly reality. In his haunting memoirs, Nichols talks about the price tag for knowingly sending men to their death, about lonely dark nights in which he confesses, "I hate to call myself a man":

> I had to be the one to give the actual orders when I knew someone was going to be killed. Maybe some of my bosses could have told me how to go about filling some of those requirements; however, I doubt it. They wanted little to do with them. They wanted the

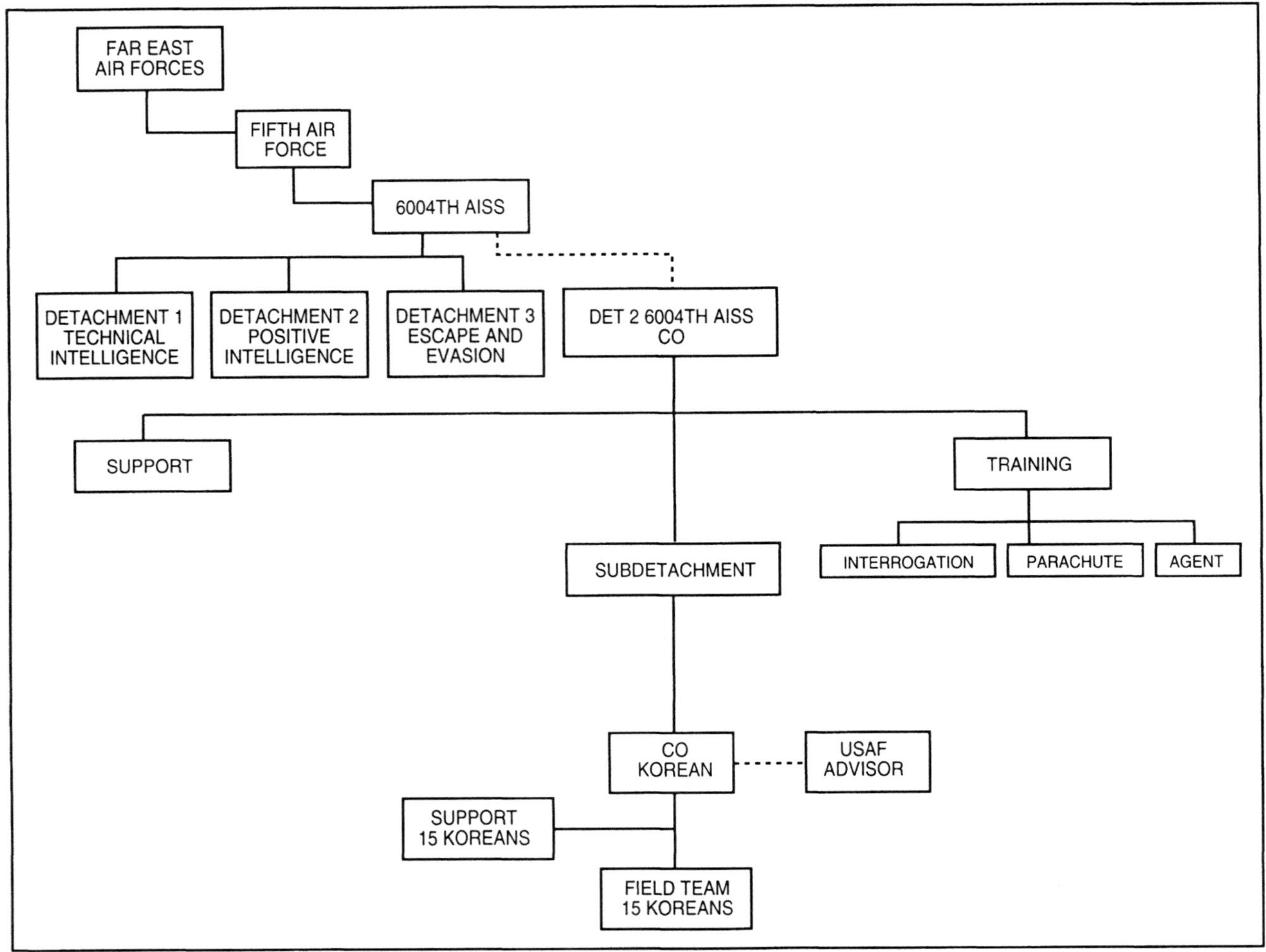

Source: Lt Col Lawrence V. Schuetta, *Guerrilla Warfare and Airpower in Korea, 1950–1953* (Maxwell AFB, Ala Aerospace Studies Institute, January 1964), 100, and History, 6004th AISS.

Figure 3. Detachment 2, 6004th AISS.This chronological "snapshot" of Detachment 2's organization shows the organization by mid-1951. Like virtually all other USAF special operations units involved in the Korean War, Detachment 2 was in a fairly continuous state of organizational evolution throughout the war.

Joe Barrett

An airborne view from a special operations helicopter showing how close some of the islands were to enemy territory on the peninsula. The British navy provided protection for the islands, but on occasion a Communist raiding party could successfully massacre lightly armed island partisans (and their American advisors) and escape before help could arrive.

> answers, and in some cases didn't want to be told how I got them. They knew it meant lives; sometimes many.
>
> It's easy to give an order such as "I want a MiG-15" or "I want some enemy officers, a few enemy tanks to experiment with, some of their 85 mm tank ammo," etc. However, filling these requirements is another problem which requires lives.[20]

With nearly 900 Koreans in the field conducting a form of positive intelligence not found elsewhere in the USAF, it was imperative that Detachment 2 establish its own training program. By the second half of 1952, the detachment had consolidated this training into three schools run by both American and Korean instructors. The curriculums included:

> (1) Interrogation: Agent-trainees were taught the fundamentals and techniques for interrogating both prisoners of war and Koreans they would encounter in the target area while operating behind enemy lines.
> (2) Agent: Trainees learned techniques for accurate intelligence gathering on enemy airfields, aircraft, and radar. Small arms training and guerrilla warfare skills were also included, and physical fitness was emphasized.
> (3) Parachute: As parachute infiltration was the primary means of entering enemy territory, a jump school was organized to teach the basics.[21]

Both in numerical size and bureaucratic power within FECOM's intelligence community, Detachment 2 was clearly growing beyond what anyone could have anticipated at the war's beginning. This growth had not gone unnoticed by others in FECOM who had their own suggestions for Detachment 2's future.

FEAF retained command while Fifth Air Force provided general housekeeping and logistical support to the detachment. Mission coordination was frequently conducted through CCRAK, which also provided mission-specific equipment drawn from CCRAK logistics by special arrangements made through FEAF.[22] This arrangement reflected Detachment 2's secondary mission—support for CCRAK's unconventional warfare campaign.[23]

While Fifth Air Force had no objection to Detachment 2's commonsense cooperation with CCRAK, it did object strongly to an attempt by CCRAK to secure operational control of Detachment 2 following its (CCRAK's) activation in December 1951. Predictably, Headquarters USAF and FEAF supported Fifth Air Force's contention that Detachment 2 should remain under Air Force control throughout the war.[24] Important as these bureaucratic struggles were at the top levels, they were of little interest to the airmen and their Korean agents in the field who remained focused on more important (to them at least) issues.

The basic problem of getting to and from the target area without being detected would continue to grow in the face of the previously mentioned Communist consolidation of their territory. For Nichols and his subdetachment commanders, it was a continual game of trying to outfox the Communists, who, of course, were playing the same game against Detachment 2. Unlike most games, however, the award for second place was death, and not always a quick one at that.

Infiltration by parachute "north of the bomb line" would continue to be the primary, if not the only, practical solution to long-range penetration into Korea's mountainous interior. Early experience in CCRAK proved the effectiveness of radio-parachute teams, and Detachment 2 agents were frequent users of the Special Air Missions Detachment, 21st Troop Carrier Squadron.[25] B Flight also provided transport for Detachment 2 as would the 581st Air Resupply and Communications Wing, a Thirteenth Air Force special operations unit based at Clark Air Base in the Philippines. On occasion, conventional troop carrier squadrons were also used. For all the different units taking Detachment 2 agents north of the bomb line, however, there remained throughout the war virtually only one way back—on foot.

The one viable long-range alternative to air infiltration was seaborne infiltration. The Korean peninsula offers thousands of miles of coastline for infiltrators, and many key road and rail lines run through these relatively flat coastal areas. These geographic and man-made factors made shallow coastal penetrations a realistic tactic for both partisans and agents. Fast, armed gunboats such as those provided by the Air Force's crash rescue boat crews were ideal for partisan raiding parties. But for Detachment 2 agents, stealth and deception—not to mention agent survival—were the keys to mission success. And to that end, the creative Nichols had the clout to acquire local shallow-water craft identical to those used by Korean fishermen.

By August 1952, Detachment 2 had five boats operating throughout the partisan-held islands dotting the Korean coastline.[26] In addition to the infiltration mission, the boats proved invaluable supplying the subdetachments operating from the most remote of these islands. Nichols later added larger ships to his fleet to support his island activities, including a Navy LST (landing ship, tank) for the biggest loads. This support was critical because, as it turned out, there was a lot going on out on these islands.

The islands lying off Korea's western coastline north of the 38th parallel make particularly good launching platforms for partisans raiding and spies infiltrating North Korean coastal areas. Located only a few miles from the shoreline, these islands were far too many in number for the Communists to control at one time. Their obvious proximity to key transportation nodes running along North Korea's coastal routes offered a considerable potential for unconventional warfare operations, a fact not overlooked by Nichols, the CIA, and CCRAK.

The islands offered something else of particular interest to the Fifth Air Force. USAF pilots flying over North Korea knew that a bailout over the peninsula's rugged interior meant almost certain capture and torture. To stand any chance of pickup or even evasion, they had to get at least as far as the offshore islands where US partisan forces (and Nichols's teams) operated. The islands were designated "safe havens," places for the pilots to head if a bailout appeared likely. The safe-haven concept sounded plausible and was certainly good for pilot morale. In practice, however, it rarely justified the pilots' hopes.

As previously described, Detachment 3, 6004th AISS, became Fifth Air Force's designated focal point for its escape and evasion (E&E) program in April 1951. Specific tasking for the detachment included responsibility to plan, coordinate, and support escape and evasion activities for the recovery of UN airmen downed in enemy territory.

Detachment 3's activation was borne of Fifth Air Force's frustration with CIA efforts to date with this program. A Fifth Air Force point paper, "Evasion & Escape Historical Synopsis" summarizing the E&E situation for the first four months of the war makes clear General Partridge's dissatisfaction.[27] Upon asking his staff when an effective underground could be established to assist airmen evading through enemy territory, he was informed:

> All clandestine activities connected with Evasion and Escape are delegated to an agency not under the operational control of the Air Force and that repeated assurances of substantial covert operations within the near future had been received from this agency . . . but as yet no agents had been placed in the field.[28]

By this time, the clandestine E&E mission had already been institutionalized in the CIA, and Fifth Air Force efforts to reclaim the mission met stiff resistance from JACK, the CIA's in-country team. Joint military/CIA meetings held in 1952 added manpower to the E&E program, but the CIA maintained its primacy for covert E&E, at least on paper. In reality, Nichols's agents were too well placed not to be useful, and CCRAK partisans on and near the North Korean coast were obvious players in the "E&E game." It seemed that everyone wanted the mission, but no one gave it a day-to-day priority matching that of more prominent unconventional warfare missions.

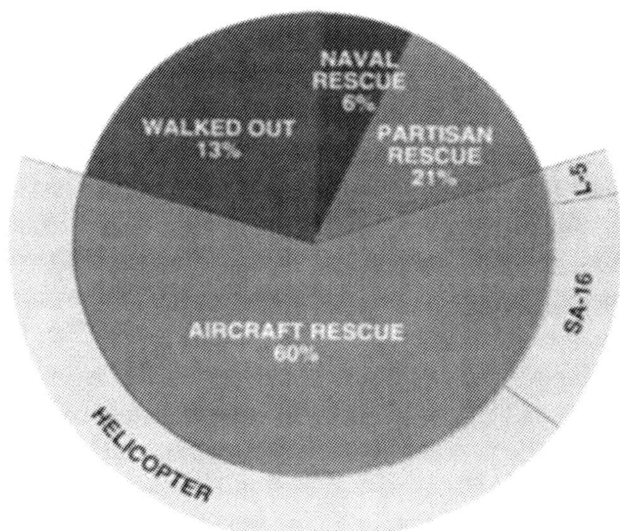

Source: Lt Col Lawrence V Schuetta, *Guerilla Warfare and Airpower in Korea, 1950–1953* (Maxwell AFB, Ala.. Aerospace Studies Institute, January 1964), 100

Figure 4. How Downed Airmen Evaded Capture (Percent) in 77 Cases Reported by Fifth Air Force, July 1950–January 1952.

In a well-researched paper on the subject of airpower and guerrilla warfare in Korea, Lt Col Lawrence V. Schuetta quotes Fifth Air Force E&E reports crediting the partisans or friendly Koreans with helping a respectable 21 percent of 77 pilots who evaded capture after being downed in enemy territory between July 1950 and January 1952 (fig. 4).[29] However, further insight into specific reports makes clear that luck and accident rather than an effective program account for a fair percentage of these "rescues." One well-publicized rescue in particular highlights the problem.

On 1 May 1952, Col Albert W. Schinz, deputy commander of the 51st Fighter Interceptor Wing, parachuted from his battle-damaged F-86 into the sea near a small island off North Korea's western coast. Before bailing out, he contacted RESCAP

(Rescue) with his position and was told to hang on for the night to await pickup the following day.

Making it safely to a nearby island and knowing that his general location was known to Fifth Air Force, he awaited pickup . . . for the next 37 days. In his paper "Special Operations in Korea," Col Rod Paschall, then director, US Army Military Institute, graphically describes what then happened:

> Thirty-seven days later, near starvation and thoroughly disgusted with the US rescue and escape and evasion system, Schinz crawled into his hut for another lonely night of waiting, only to be rudely awakened at two a.m., as he found himself staring into a flashlight and a gun barrel. To his further astonishment, he heard "Whoopee! American colonel!" spoken in broken English by [CCRAK] partisans who were deployed in the area.[30]

Although Schinz was relieved to be picked up at last, his attitude changed when he learned from the US Army lieutenant advising the local CCRAK partisans that CCRAK teams operating in these USAF-designated safe havens were not issued a radio receiver that could pick up distress calls from standard issue USAF survival radios! In fact, Schinz's rescue was purely an accident. The partisans were out looking for another pilot they believed had bailed out in the area.

Schinz was safe, but his rescue would bring tragedy to the partisans who found him. During Schinz's subsequent debrief at the Pentagon, he named the island on which he was rescued by the partisans. Headquarters USAF released the story to *Life* magazine, which published the saga to include the island's name in seven pages of its 28 July 1952 issue.[31] The Chinese apparently read the story because shortly thereafter a large raiding party stormed the island, killing all partisans present.[32] Overall, the behind-the-lines E&E program in Korea was not the high point of CCRAK, CIA, or FEAF unconventional warfare, which continued to grow steadily in other areas. And, like them, the 6004th AISS continued to grow too.

In yet another proposed expansion for the 6004th in the summer of 1953, Fifth Air Force accurately described the 6004th as "the primary collection agency of FEAF."[33] Noting the 6004th's liaison (as an organizational equal) with FECOM's Document Research Office (the CIA liaison with FECOM), the letter assesses the squadron's position relative to other intelligence organizations in FECOM with the following comment:

> While an exact parallel with CIA's operations and Navy's cannot be drawn, it may be noted that in Korea we now have a detachment operation [Detachment 2] on an equal basis with a CIA operation of regimental strength and a Navy operation equivalent of a group.[34]

Considering the rank of senior officers normally commanding regimental or group-sized operations, the presence of Maj Donald Nichols at the helm of Detachment 2 speaks volumes of the special trust and respect Fifth Air Force and FEAF flag-rank officers held for this unique individual.

Anecdotal sources have their obvious human limitations, but from such sources a sketch emerges of the mysterious Donald Nichols. Seldom known to wear military rank and a complete uniform of any type, the Coca-Cola-drinking detachment commander appeared to instill confidence in everyone ranging from field agents to the most senior commanders in FEAF. Ray Dawson, an Air Force NCO serving with CCRAK, recalls the night he went to Nichols's compound in downtown Seoul to discuss operations with him:

> The first thing I noticed was the presence of a large number of Air Force security police outside Nichols's building; usually it was just Korean military police. As I entered Nichols's room it was so dark it took a minute for my eyes to adjust to the light coming from one small oil lamp of some sort. When they did adjust I saw the reason for the Air Force security police outside . . . I was looking at General Partridge [Fifth Air Force commander] and General Doolittle! They were

sitting cross-legged on the floor talking to (a casually dressed) Nichols.[35]

For better or worse, one of the most enduring aspects of special operations is the impact a dominant personality exerts on the organization, its mission, and the desired outcome. Clearly, Donald Nichols saw the possibilities not only for his own intelligence agents but for the synergistic effect that could be brought about by integrating his detachment with CCRAK and other Fifth Air Force special operations units.

Or was it the other away around? In either case, it was, as they say, "a distinction without a difference." Major Nichols distinguished himself and served his country well, at great personal risk, and in doing so made a difference. So did others ranging from the flight crews to flag-rank officers who provided the necessary freedom of action needed to ensure Nichols's success at "the tip of the spear." Special operations and positive intelligence may have been too integrated to separate, but the joint potential was exploited to the fullest. It also engendered still another legend, known only to a few, in the proud legacy of special operations.

Epilogue: Three months after the war ended, a North Korean MiG-15 pilot defected to South Korea, which made good its standing offer of a $100,000 reward for the receipt of a flyable MiG-15. Donald Nichols is credited for a role in the defection although, in the best tradition of the "spook" world, no details of his involvement are available. Two months later, Fifth Air Force activated the 6006th AISS, Donald Nichols commanding.

Donald Nichols retired from the Air Force in 1962, his health failing from a number of diseases to which he was exposed in Korea. He died in June 1992.

Notes

1. Donald Nichols, *How Many Times Can I Die?* (Brooksville, Fla.: Brooksville Printing, 1981), 117.
2. Dr. Diane Putney, "Air Force HUMINT 40th Anniversary," Air Force Special Activities Center (AFSAC) booklet, Fort Belvoir, Va.
3. Nichols, 126.
4. Ibid., 5.
5. Putney, 2.
6. Nichols, 130.
7. Headquarters Fifth Air Force, Office of Deputy for Intelligence, letter, subject: Special Activities Unit Number One (Operating Instructions), 5 March 1951, in "UN Partisan Forces in the Korean Conflict," Project MHD-3, prepared by the 8086th Army Unit (AFFE) Military History Detachment, January 1953, 192.
8. Nichols, 148.
9. History, 6004th AISS, May–June 1952, 31.
10. Putney, 5.
11. Lt Col Lawrence V. Schuetta, *Guerrilla Warfare and Airpower in Korea, 1950–1953* (Maxwell AFB, Ala.: Aerospace Studies Institute, January 1964), 77.
12. Headquarters FEAF, General Orders 336, 20 July 1951.
13. History, 6004th AISS, 1 July–31 December 1952, 37–40.
14. Ibid., 79.
15. History, 6004th AISS, May–June 1952, 28.
16. History, 6004th AISS, 1 July–31 December 1952, 40.
17. Ibid.
18. Schuetta, 99.
19. Ibid., 100.
20. Nichols, 132–33.
21. History, 6004th AISS, 1 July–31 December 1952, 42.
22. Schuetta, 45.
23. Ibid., 89.
24. Ibid., 88.
25. Ibid., 102.
26. Monthly Report for August 1951, 6004th AISS, 8 September 1952, page number blurred.
27. Headquarters Fifth Air Force, report, "Evasion & Escape Historical Synopsis," date obscured on original document.
28. Ibid.
29. Schuetta, 151–53.
30. Col Rod Paschall, "Special Operations in Korea," *Conflict 7*, no. 2 (1987): 167.
31. Schuetta, 186.
32. Col George Budway, USAF, Retired, former CCRAK officer, letter to Sgt Ray Dawson, USAF, former CCRAK NCO, subject: CCRAK, June 1987, 9.
33. Headquarters Fifth Air Force, Director of Intelligence, letter, subject: Reorganization of the 6004th Air Intelligence Service Squadron, 12 September 1953.
34. Ibid.
35. Ray Dawson, telephone interview with author, 3 July 1995.

The 22d CRBS

Special Operations by USAF "Sailors"

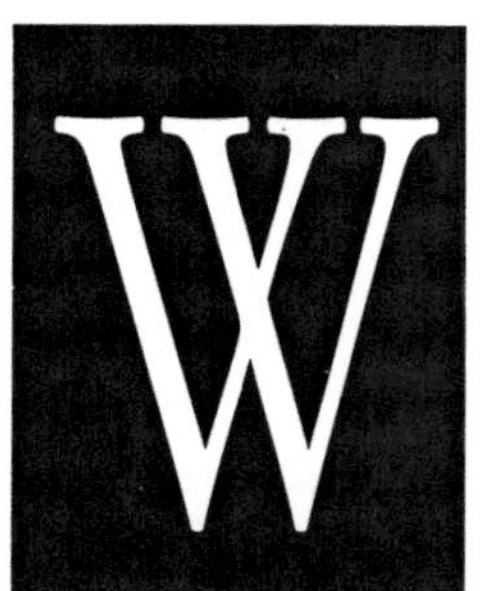

hen the Korean War exploded in mid-1950, the three-year-old United States Air Force was the new kid on the block. And in 1950 the "block" was an all-new national defense structure in which the Air Force was, at least in theory, an equal partner with the more entrenched Army and Navy departments. Ongoing attempts in the Pentagon to define USAF roles and missions (and Army/Navy responses to these changes) were suddenly put on hold as all three uniformed services abruptly turned in their own way to face the bloody emergency in Korea.

The wooden-hulled Air Force crash rescue boats had three, and **only** three, things going for them when the seaweed hit the fan on a night raid along the North Korean coastline: speed, firepower, and the wits of their NCO skippers. With two, high-octane gasoline-powered 1,550-horsepower engines of the same type used to power the F-51 fighter, the boats could push 40-plus-knot speeds in the open sea.

John Hagan

During the Korean War, the 22d Crash Rescue Boat Squadron threw its lot in with a collection of unconventional warfare "pirates" that took the unit a long way from its conventional mission; amazingly, young sergeants like "Boog" Farrish pulled it off.

Few "roles and missions" discussions in the Pentagon were left as wide open as the issue of unconventional warfare. With more zeal than intentional planning, the brash young Air Force proved itself willing to fill this doctrinal void not only in the air and on land, but on the sea itself. The remarkable war record of the Air Force's 22d Crash Rescue Boat Squadron (CRBS) in North Korea's frigid ocean waters would become another legend in the secret world of special operations.

The 22d CRBS had the most humble beginning possible in 1950. Just three months before the war, the last of the USAF boats* had been put in dry storage for shipment back to the US.[1] Airmen and officers with marine-career specialties were scattered to other career fields and one of the first cries to come from Far East Air Forces headquarters when the war broke was "Get our boats and people back together!"[2]

On 7 July 1950, the 6160th Air Base Group activated its boat section at Itazuke Air Base (AB), Japan, with one FP-47 (114-foot boat), one lieutenant, and four airmen.[3] Shortly thereafter it became Detachment 1, 6160th ABG. The detachment commander, 1st Lt Phil Dickey, promptly moved out to reassemble all former boat crewmen still in-theater and whatever boats were still seaworthy.

Dickey found the effort to acquire seaworthy boats easier than getting the crewmen, but Detachment 1 shortly counted seven 63-foot, eight 85-foot, and one 104-foot boats in addition to the original FP-47.[4] His efforts to get the crews back together again, however, brought the lieutenant to the unfavorable attention of several senior officers, themselves frantic to get their own undermanned units ready for war. Phone calls from Fifth Air Force headquarters soon straightened out the senior officers, if not their antipathy toward the young officer. Lieutenant Dickey's word-of-mouth communications among the small crash rescue boat fraternity managed to bring a beginning cadre of 85 airmen back together, and Detachment 1 was soon off to the war.

Detachment 1's small fleet of boats was immediately dispersed by FEAF throughout its entire area of operations. From south to north, the boats were stationed in Guam (Andersen AB), Okinawa (Kadena and Naha ABs), Japan (Haneda, Miho, Ashiya, Itazuke, and Brady ABs), and into the line of fire itself in Korea: Pohang (K-3), Pusan (K-9), Chinhae (K-10), Kunsan (K-8).[5]

*The understandable but erroneous perception persists that USAF "crash rescue" boats belonged to the Air Force Air Rescue Service (ARS), itself activated from the legislation that created an independent Air Force in 1947. With the activation of ARS, the boats reverted to local air base service organizations such as the 6160th Air Base Group described above.

A few boats operating in their designated rescue role in Korean waters went further north of the 38th parallel and the main line of resistance separating the massive Communist and US armies on the peninsula itself. These 85-foot boats, operating near Wonsan Harbor on Korea's eastern coast and especially near Cho-do Island off the west coast, found themselves between hundreds of small, seemingly deserted islands and the coastline itself. And in doing so, they found themselves operating in a war that no one had yet briefed them on, the secret spook war between CCRAK and the Communist forces on the peninsula. Inevitably drawn into this war, they went with the full blessings of the Fifth Air Force.

By stationing themselves so far north to aid allied combat pilots ditching in the sea or even downed airman attempting to evade to the shoreline from further inland, the boats were seen by many as useful transport for another purpose. As the boat crews soon learned, the seemingly deserted islands were anything but empty. Thousands of US-supported partisans were stationed on these islands to conduct unconventional warfare in Communist rear areas directly accessible from the islands. But seaborne transportation was in short supply and fast raiding craft virtually unobtainable, at least until Detachment 1 arrived in the area. Calls were made, meetings were held, and things changed in a big way for the airmen/sailors of Detachment 1.

To assure the needed mission-response time to special operations boat requests (and to control a scarce asset), Fifth Air Force headquarters in Japan

John Hagan

"You don't need guns very often, but when you do . . . you tend to need them rather badly." Borrowed from the Army and mounted on special steel plates built into the hull to absorb the massive recoil, the "quad-fifties" could put 2,000 heavy machine-gun rounds a minute into targets a mile away, rather nice when you need guns rather badly.

directed its own Operations Directorate to assume operational control of Detachment 1, with the 6160th ABG at Itazuke AB retaining administrative and logistical responsibilities. Boats were then placed on 30-day temporary duty status in Korean waters to yet another mysterious spook outfit specializing in warfare behind enemy lines. This, they would soon learn, was the Fifth Air Force's Detachment 2, 6004th Air Intelligence Services Squadron, described earlier as "the first covert collection agency of a tactical nature in the history of the U.S. Air Force."[6]

The boat crews would also learn that attempting to use a unit's title as a means of guessing the unit's mission was a waste of time in special operations. The 6004th's Detachment 2 was a lot more than a "covert collection agency," or at least they sure seemed to need a lot of guns to collect whatever it was they wanted!

They needed fast boats too, and the boat crews soon learned their mission: transport and protect, when necessary, spies and saboteurs from Detachment 2 as well as CCRAK guerrillas on their nighttime forays into enemy-held territory. Their boats had the required size, range, and speed, but something more would be needed for this job if the boats were expected to go within rifle range of the very vigilant and jittery Communist coastal security force.

Different combinations of firepower were experimented with before the boat crews settled on the reliable .50-caliber Browning heavy

John Hagan

The wooden hulls could be penetrated by rifle bullets, and survival in the frozen waters was measured in minutes. The 24-hour-a-day pressure on the young NCOs commanding the special operations boats never relented. Despite numerous instances of battle damage, no 22d CRBS boat conducting special operations missions was ever lost in combat.

John Hagan

The enemy's economic and monetary systems are legitimate targets of war, a fact not lost on Mr. Nichols's imagination or expertise. The wily commander had the boats under his operational control take bundles of forged currency to North Korea for agents to distribute it.

machine gun. Coming out of the barrel at 2,930 feet per second, the heavy slug had a maximum effective range of nearly one mile. Mounted in pairs, they were twice as devastating, but mounted in fours, they became the legendary quad-fifty of the Korean War.

Adapted by the US Army to deal with the human-wave assaults of Communist infantry on the peninsula, they proved equally adaptable to the 85-foot crash rescue boats once steel support plating was added to the deck to absorb the massive recoil. And to those sailing in harm's way, they brought the priceless peace of mind that can only come with protection that puts out a combined rate of fire of over 2,000 rounds per minute. Unwilling to scrimp when it came to their survival, the boat crews also mounted single .50 calibers in gun tubs on both port and starboard sides of their boats. It was a precaution for which they would be grateful on more than one occasion.

Monthly unit histories are terse to the point of frustration for historians trying to shed light on the Detachment 1 airmen/sailors and their Detachment 2 intelligence counterparts, but fortunately it's not difficult to read between the lines of some official reports throughout 1951:

> May: . . . Evacuated 200 UN guerrillas from behind enemy lines to prevent their capture and execution; June: . . . Operating . . . in the Yellow Sea, transported captured Chinese prisoners and friendly guerrillas to rendezvous behind enemy lines; September: Crash boat departed for 5th Air Force (ADV) north of 38th parallel. . . . On two occasions vessel fired upon by shore batteries. . . . Cpl Jim Johnson wounded aboard this vessel.[7]

It was nerve-racking work to attempt to sneak through ice-choked coastal waters at night with a boatload of North Korean partisans, never knowing when or from what direction the darkness might be pierced with a stream of tracer rounds coming straight for the boat. Minus 30-degree Fahrenheit temperatures, ice, enemy artillery and gunfire, and the Yellow Sea's notorious 30-foot tidal flow all added to a lethal environment, one that frequently seemed to be just waiting patiently for a tired boat commander to make a mistake. The Air Base Group's monthly unit histories, written in Japan far from this danger, dutifully record the need for continued emphasis on personal appearance and uniform requirements.

In January 1952, the 6004th AISS Detachment 2's commander, "Mr." Donald Nichols,* acknowledged the contributions made by Sgt (and boat "Master")** James R. Jarvis and his crew on USAF crash boat R-1-667 in North Korean waters with the simple words: "These men have been a great asset to this organization and their departure constitutes a considerable loss." Typical of the special operations world, even this brief, understated recognition for missions unspecified came in a letter labeled "RESTRICTED."[8]

The Communist coastal defense gunners did not appear to share Nichols's appreciation (or maybe they did), as three months later they caught the R-1-667 squarely in their gun sights. The results were noted in a cryptic message found in Detachment 1's unit history report for the month of April 1952:

> Received a message from R-1-667 operating in North Korean waters that they were fired upon and hit . . . holes in and thru the planking on port side, hot water heater jacket punctured, hole in engine room blower, and various holes in galley compartment.[9]

Like the Navy's famous PT boats of World War II, the crash boats' defense was limited to firepower, speed, and the quick thinking of their commanders. Their wooden-hulled boats offered no hope should a serious mistake be made or simple bad luck catch up with its crews.

By the summer of 1952, Detachment 1 had grown significantly from its initial cadre of 85 "sailors." In July of that year, Headquarters USAF reorganized the detachment by activating the 22d Crash Boat Rescue Squadron at Itazuke Air Base.[10]

*One of the most mysterious characters of the spook world in Korea, Nichols's story and that of his positive intelligence detachment is told elsewhere in this book.

**The Air Force authorized the use of naval ratings (e.g., "master," "mate") on the crash boats, while maintaining standard Air Force rank for all other matters.

John Hagan

The "mother" ship resupplied the special operations boats at sea in order to extend their time on-station behind enemy lines.

Squadron strength stood at over 400 officers and airmen as all crash rescue boat detachments in-theater were formed under the new squadron.

On some missions, the boat crews took South Korean marine raiding parties ashore to do what all marines always seem to do best—disturb the peace, wreak havoc on bad guys, and cause sufficient unrest in the neighborhood to necessitate their early departure from the party. Other boat missions were more subtle, such as transporting bundles of forged North Korean currency for delivery to CCRAK agents for further distribution inland.

The enemy's economy has always been a legitimate target in war, and unconventional warfare could exploit opportunities far beyond the obvious use of conventional weapons. For example, in

John Hagan

The "bad guys." North Koreans captured during a coastal raid in 1952 are taken to Cho-do Island for interrogation.

April 1952, FECOM's Liaison Detachment (Korea) published a four-page document titled "Guerrilla Operations Outline, 1952." It candidly notes in paragraph 11:

> North Korean Currency Exchange: Due to the large requirements for North Korean currency and the limited sources available, commanders will encourage bank robberies and other suitable means of procuring this currency.[11]

The 24-hour-a-day pressure from an unforgiving sea and enemy coastal gunners never relented on the young NCOs commanding the boats. And not all the threats came from the coastline. In October of that year, the crew of R-1-664 caught a North Korean junk trying to infiltrate right into the harbor at Cho-do Island, one of the primary offshore US special operations bases. Two prisoners were taken, but the boat then sustained an hour-long attack by North Korean fighter aircraft. The fighters were accurate enough to wound one crewman and inflict minor damage to the boat.[12]

The story of the crash rescue boat crews in North Korean waters is a story of airmen taking the unconventional war to the enemy in a role far beyond the primary coast guard-like duties they signed up for in the beginning. Their courage, seamanship, and willingness to throw in their lot with the "Terry and the Pirates" world of CCRAK made them full-fledged but little-known members of the USAF's special operations heritage.

John Hagan

The "good guys." North Korean partisans, working for the US, returning from a mission on the coast in 1951 are retrieved for return to their island base.

Notes

1. Lt Col Lester M. Adams Jr., former commander, 22d CRBS, to author, letter, subject: History of USAF Crash Rescue Boats, 5 May 1995.
2. Ibid., 4.
3. History, Detachment 1, 6160th Air Base Group, 25 June–31 October 1950, Historical Data Section 5.
4. Adams, 4.
5. Ibid.
6. Lt Col Lawrence V. Schuetta, *Guerrilla Warfare and Airpower in Korea, 1950–1953* (Maxwell AFB, Ala.: Aerospace Studies Institute, January 1964), 77.
7. History, Detachment 1, 6160th ABG, January 1952.
8. Donald Nichols, commander, Detachment 2, 6004th Air Intelligence Service Squadron, to commanding officer, Headquarters Squadron, 6160th ABG, letter, subject: Letter of Appreciation, 11 January 1952, filed in History, Detachment 1, 6160th ABG, January 1952.
9. Nichols, April 1952, 1.
10. Adams, 5.
11. Headquarters FECOM, Liaison Detachment (Korea), to commanders Leopard, Wolfpack, Kirkland, and Baker section, letter, 11 April 1952.
12. Historical data pertaining to Crash Rescue Boats R-1-664 and R-1-676-DPU in the Korean operation, December 1951–August 1953, USAF Historical Division, Maxwell AFB, Ala., December 1954.

LIBERTAS PER VERITATEM

The 581st ARC

USAF's Secret Psywar Weapon

When the first North Korean assault regiments exploded across the 38th parallel in the early Sunday morning darkness of 25 June 1950, the international reverberations rocked the United Nations like an earthquake. Earlier tremors like the Berlin airlift of 1948 and the workers' anti-Soviet rebellions in Eastern Europe had already been felt. It was the first major bloodletting of the cold war, and who knew where it might lead? But despite mounting evidence of the Soviets' global ambitions, these tremors were like danger signals that, strangely, only some in the Western world would or could see.

The 581st Air Resupply and Communications Wing was the only USAF special operations unit organized, trained, and equipped from the start to conduct psywar in the Far East during the early 1950s. The bland-sounding ARCW designation was a cover for a mission more fittingly described with the 581st's motto "Freedom through Truth."

USAF

Home of the 581st, Clark Air Base was strategically located to support psywar special operations in Korea and elsewhere in the Far East. It would be kept busy, much to the chagrin of the North Koreans and Communist Vietnamese.

Fortunately, there were in the Pentagon (as well as in the newly organized Central Intelligence Agency) small pockets of visionaries that did see what others would not or could not acknowledge. What the visionaries saw was Soviet dictator Joseph Stalin's total commitment to the spread of Communism far beyond Soviet borders—and even how he was going to do it. Stalin's primary weapon would be a new kind of war, one that would take the term *psychological warfare* to an extreme never experienced in modern history.

The visionaries in the Air Force understood the potential of psychological warfare, or "psywar" as it came to be called. With Soviet intransigence continuing to manifest itself in Europe (and Korea), Headquarters USAF organized a Psychological Warfare (PW) Division at the Air Staff level in February 1948.[1] Within 24 months, the PW Division was ready to propose specific plans for an Air Force psywar weapon tailored to meet this new kind of war. The plans turned to reality in 1950 when the Air Staff authorized the activation of two "special operations wings" (SOW) in fiscal year (FY) 1952, with three more to be added in FY 1953.[2]

Initial planning called for each SOW to operate under a psywar unit within each overseas theater command.[3] These theater psywar staff units would, in turn, report directly to the PW Division at Headquarters USAF, an odd "stovepipe" arrangement but one that fully reflected the priority attached to the psywar mission at the start of the cold war. On 5 January 1951, the Military Air Transport Service (MATS) was given the mission of organizing, training, and equipping these SOWs, which for security reasons were designated "air resupply and communications wings."[4]

An air resupply and communications service would provide a functional headquarters for the air resupply and communications wings (ARCW, pronounced "Arc"). Never before had the Air Force attempted such an organization on this scale—nor would it ever do so again.

The first air resupply and communications wing, the 580th ARCW, was activated in April 1951 at Mountain Home AFB, Idaho; the 581st ARCW followed three months later at the same base. In the haste to prepare for combat in Korea (and perhaps elsewhere), the first group of personnel rushed to Mountain Home arrived to find the base, working areas, and living quarters in a state of total disrepair. The words *primitive, crude,* and *unsatisfactory* permeate Air Resupply and Communications Service (ARCS) reports of this period. Nonetheless, a sense of urgency drove the first "pioneers" on, apparently with the pragmatic outlook that complaining was acceptable as long as hands and feet kept moving at the same pace as the mouth.

The 581st received orders to report to the Thirteenth Air Force, Clark Air Base, Philippines, by July 1952. The wing arrived on schedule, the aircrews having safely ferried the aircraft across the Pacific while the main body arrived on the US naval ship *General William Weigle*. Not surprisingly, it took the Thirteenth Air Force a little time to figure out just what it was that had flown and sailed into town.

The ARCWs weren't like anything anyone had seen before. Like the World War II Air Commandos in the CBI, the 581st was a "composite" wing with different types of aircraft. But unlike the Air Commandos, the aircraft in the ARCWs were only one part of a multithreat system. And as a "threat system," an ARCW was the only USAF organization built from the ground up for psychological warfare.

Organizations and Missions

By the time the 581st arrived at Clark, it had shed its organic air base and medical groups, units originally included to make an ARCW totally self-sufficient when operating in austere environments. This still left the 581st with six mutually supporting squadrons, all of which had the same numerical designator as the parent wing. The 581st ARCW Operations Plan 3-52 brought it all together.[5]

581st Air Resupply Squadron

The most visible part of the ARCW "spear," this squadron contained all aircraft assigned to the wing. This included 12 specially modified B-29 four-engined heavy bombers, four C-119 (Flying Boxcar) twin-engined heavy transports, four SA-16 twin-engined amphibians, and four H-19A single-engined helicopters. While the World War II B-29s had been pulled from USAF's mothball fleet, all other aircraft came directly from the manufacturer's factories. The 581st would be the only ARCW to actually be equipped with helicopters as called for in the original ARCS concept plans.

Mission: Aerial introduction, evacuation and resupply of guerrilla-type personnel, and aerial delivery of psychological warfare propaganda.

581st Maintenance Squadron

The "maintenance" title is self-explanatory; its meaning obvious. Not so obvious is the operational nightmare that ensues when this critical function collapses. Maintenance is the glue that holds the whole show together.

Mission: Organizational and field maintenance of aircraft supporting psychological warfare and guerrilla operations.

581st Air Materials Assembly Squadron

Originally called the "Airborne Packaging and Supply Squadron," this squadron was expected to be capable of "devising and fabricating slings, containers, and harnesses for the delivery of objects unusual both in size and shape."[6]

Mission: Receive, store, prepare, and distribute for aerial delivery supplies and equipment used by guerrilla-type personnel and psychological warfare propaganda materials.

581st Holding and Briefing Squadron

The most classified of all ARCW units, it provided "facilities for the administration, briefing, and supply of personnel assigned by other agencies for introduction behind enemy lines."[7] Table of Organization 1-1937T, 22 January 1951, called for 260 officers for this one squadron, of which *200 would come from outside the Air Resupply and Communications Service.*

Mission: Secure, house, supply, administer, train, and brief guerrilla-type personnel prior to introduction into enemy-occupied territory.

581st Communications Squadron

This squadron provided the capability to maintain a 24-hour-a-day broadcasting service on four frequencies simultaneously. Unmodified jamming of enemy frequencies was an additional capability. Base station communications functions were augmented by field stations using relay systems if the distances surpassed 1,000 miles.

Mission: Provide secure point-to-point and ground-to-air communications with aircraft and guerrilla-type personnel.

581st Reproduction Squadron

This squadron produced covert propaganda material and overt propaganda leaflets, the latter as a service to USAF units engaged in leaflet attacks in their particular area. The squadron was expected to produce up to 4 million two-color, 5 x 7-inch leaflets per day. According to the Joint Printing Committee of Congress, the 581st Reproduction Squadron in fact had a printing capability equal to that found in all commercial presses (i.e., newspapers, magazines) in the four states of the US Northwest.[8] To make such production quotas possible, the squadron was authorized 16 giant commercial standard offset presses.

Mission: To produce psychological warfare propaganda.

Obviously an ARCW was meant to be extremely flexible, breaking down into whatever size and composition of elements best suited to accomplish a particular mission. To brief FEAF on the capabilities of the ARCW and sort out how the wing would fit into the overall air campaign in Korea (and elsewhere), the 581st commander, Col John K. Arnold Jr., flew to Tokyo to meet with the FEAF staff. From these meetings emerged the following concept of operations (Operations Plan 3-52) for the 581st:

- Four of the 12 B-29s with crews were sent on 60-day rotations to the B-29-equipped 91st Strategic Reconnaissance Squadron, Yokota Air Base, Japan. Each crew was to fly once every four days, completing a total of 15 tactical leaflet-drop missions prior to rotating back to Clark AB.
- The four C-119s and crews were placed on 90-day rotations with the commander of the 315th Air Division designating the particular unit to be supported. Conventional troop carrier missions would be performed during this initial period. Later, the C-119s

Bob Brice

Big, black, and beautiful, the 581st ARCW's 12 B-29 bombers were stripped of all gun turrets, save that in the tail. The navigation/bomb radar dome can be clearly seen, as can the "Joe hole" that replaced the aft-belly turret to allow for parachuting agents to exit the aircraft. This particular bomber is flying over the Philippine Islands on return from psywar duty over Korea.

would find their biggest contribution taking place a long way from Korea—in a place called Indochina.

• Two of the four SA-16s, with crews, were sent on extended temporary duty to Seoul City Airport (K-16) in Korea to support B Flight, the 6167th ABG's unconventional warfare unit. These black-painted amphibians would find their role in coastal infiltration and exfiltration of spies behind enemy lines at night.

• All four of the H-19 helicopters were to be stationed with the 2157th Air Rescue Squadron, also located at K-16. Their mission was identical to that of the SA-16s, with a secondary mission of air rescue of downed pilots.

• All C-118s and C-54s (two each) were reserved for "special" missions, some of which supported an agency beyond the operational purview of the US Air Force—the CIA.[9]

All these deployments represented the activities of just the flying squadrons of the 581st. In addition, large numbers of specialists and mission-tailored teams from elsewhere throughout the wing were sent on continual rotations to other unconventional warfare units in Korea. One set of 581st orders dated 8 January 1953 gives an unusual insight into this overall movement:

4 personnel from 581st Comm Sqdn to Detachment 2, 6004th AISS.

1 person from 581st Resup and Comm Wg attached to "B" Flight.

3 personnel from 581st Resup & Comm Sqdn attached to "B" Flight.

1 person from 581st Hold and Brief Sqdn attached to "B" Flight.

5 personnel from 581st Hold & Brief Sqdn attached to CCRAK.[10]

Tales of the 581st

It was the aircrews of the flying squadrons more than the other personnel that found themselves in harm's way, and their stories tell in graphic detail just how much harm was out there for these psywar specialists.

The Ambush of Colonel Arnold

On 15 January 1953, the 91st Strategic Reconnaissance Squadron notified the 581st ARCW Operations Center at Clark AB that Colonel Arnold, the 581st commander, and the other officers and airmen aboard a 581st B-29 Superfortress were missing in action on a night leaflet drop in the northernmost sector of North Korea near the Chinese border. Nine days later, Peking radio announced the shootdown and capture of the surviving crew members. Colonel Arnold was specifically named as one of the pris-

USAF

Korean laborers load psywar leaflet "bombs" for subsequent long-range B-29 missions over enemy territory. Altitude-sensitive fuses opened the containers at predetermined altitudes depending on the desired dispersal pattern and size of leaflet "footprint."

oners. Peking radio then went dead silent on the fate of the crew.

Already inside China, the ARCW prisoners had only begun their ordeal. Kept handcuffed and chained in solitary confinement for months, the ARCW crewmen underwent grueling mental and physical torture. Eighteen months after their internment and a year after the war was over, the Chinese broke their silence to announce the forthcoming trial of the crew on charges of germ warfare. In October 1954, the crewmen were put through a highly publicized propaganda trial before a Chinese military tribunal and—surprise—found guilty.

The effects of prolonged deprivation and torture showed on the crewmen during the trial, a fact that generated outrage throughout much of the Western world. Efforts by the United States and the United Nations to secure the release of the crew intensified but without apparent impact on China's leaders. Then, following secret negotiations between the US and China in Geneva, Switzerland, in July 1955, the Chinese released the crew on 4 August 1955—the last American POWs released after the Korean War.

Was it coincidence that the massive Chinese effort expended just happened to fall on airmen from an ARCW unit? Unprovable circumstances suggest otherwise.

USAF

Col John K. Arnold Jr., commander, 581st ARCW and mission commander on B-29 radio call sign Stardust 40. The bizarre circumstances of the shootdown and continued torture of surviving Stardust 40 crew members, even **after** the war concluded, raised questions that remain unanswered to this day.

The shootdown of Colonel Arnold's flight, call sign "Stardust 40," was neither the first nor the last of B-29 losses during the Korean War. In fact, only four months prior to the loss of Stardust 40, FEAF had lost five of the giant bombers and suffered damage to another seven on bombing missions in the last 10 days of October alone.[11] That these air-to-air losses to Soviet-built MiG-15 fighters occurred despite USAF fighter escort gives some measure of the threat posed at the time. Reasonably enough, FEAF concluded that until the MiG threat could be neutralized, it had to be avoided.

Limiting the B-29s to night missions was the obvious answer, at least for the time being. The MiG-15 was an effective but fairly crude "day only" fighter with none of the electronics necessary to conduct night-interceptor missions, a fact borne out by their combat record during the war. The temporary measure worked, and losses to night-flying B-29s by MiGs stopped . . . until Stardust 40. Lt Col George Pittman, the 581st Air Resupply Squadron commander at the time, still recalls the secret postshootdown briefing he received at Fifth Air Force headquarters:

> Fifth Air Force radar plots had showed the "day only" fighters rising up to intercept Stardust 40. At approximately the same time, radar-controlled searchlights lit up the B-29, making it an easy target for the cannon-firing MiGs.[12]

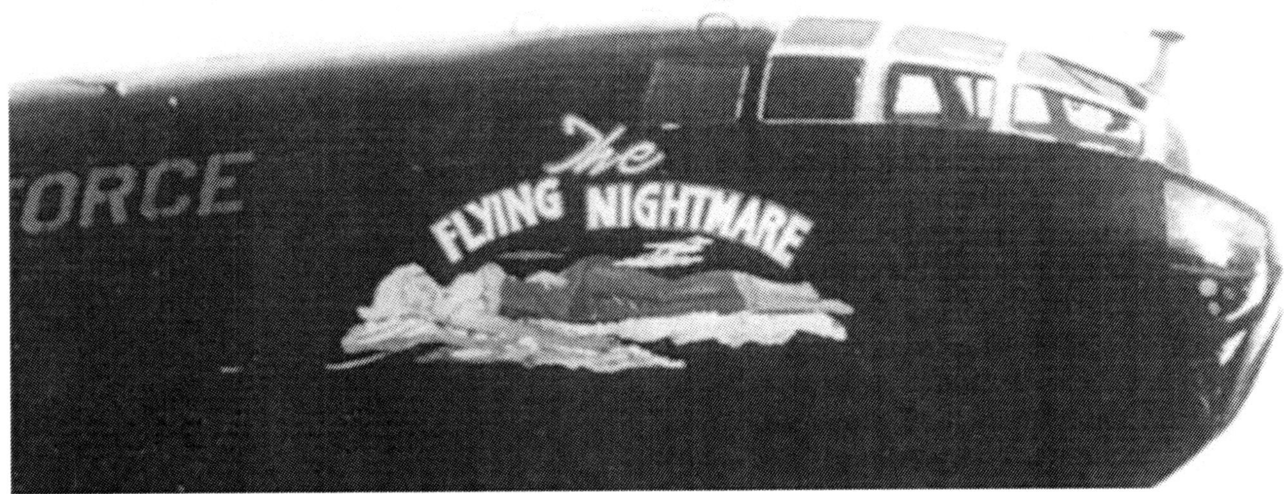

Bob Brice

Night, low-level missions flown **below** 300 feet were simply not one of the requirements considered when the massive B-29 was built in World War II for daylight high-altitude bombing. Such missions proved totally unforgiving to pilot error and took their deadly toll of ARCW aircrews over the years. On 8 September 1955, The Flying Nightmare crashed into the ocean during a night low-level mission. There were no witnesses or survivors. The cause of the cash was never determined.

Stardust 40 was flying approximately 12 miles south of the Yalu River, approaching its final leaflet-drop pass for the night's mission when the MiGs attacked at 2230. Within moments three of the Superfortress's four engines were on fire. Capt Wallace L. Brown, pilot of the bomber, recalls the surviving crew bailing out: "We landed safely in North Korean territory . . . [but] we were scattered all over the countryside."[13] North Korean militia troops rounded up the crew one by one the following day and after a short delay turned them over to the Chinese.

There is no evidence that this combination of radar-controlled searchlights *and* night-attacking MiGs ever occurred before or after the shootdown of Stardust 40. The officers of the 581st believed that the Chinese knew the B-29 was carrying leaflets, not bombs. Leaflet-carrying B-29s had been in the area recently and always flew single-ship missions, as Stardust 40 was doing. More disturbingly, the officers were convinced that somehow the Chinese knew Arnold was on this particular flight. If true, this knowledge would represent the highest possible security breach. The suspicions of the 581st were fueled by what happened within hours of the shootdown and days before Peking radio made its first announcement:

> The early morning edition of the Manila newspapers highlighted the shootdown, quoting Hong Kong newspapers as their source. The newspaper stories were complete with the names and personal details of some of the surviving crew members, including their assignment to the 581st ARCW.[14]

The Communist Chinese links to Hong Kong newspapers did not surprise the Air Force officers. But how could such details of the aircrew have reached Hong Kong within hours of the shootdown? Or were these details already "on file" for use should the Chinese succeed in shooting down the B–29? Did the Chinese know Colonel Arnold was on the crew? Did they know the scheduled flight route? Was Colonel Arnold's presence the only reason for what appeared to be a preplanned aerial ambush? Or was the Communists' extreme sensitivity to the 581st psywar mission a major factor as well? How else could the near-instantaneous reporting of the aircrew's names be accounted for? The answers to these questions remain a mystery to this day.

The Night Shift

The collocation of the 581st B-29s with the 91st Strategic Reconnaissance Squadron provided both the necessary maintenance support and the equally useful operational deception cover for the 581st psywar mission. This successful formula would be used elsewhere in Korea, with the 581st helicopters stationed at Seoul City Airfield. There they would blend in with the 2157th Air Rescue Squadron, another unit flying the same H-19A-type helicopter. There were, however, some "adjustments" made as the "white hat" rescue crowd made room for the "black hat" special operations pilots suddenly thrown into their midst.

Like owls, bats, and other aerial "things" that go bump in the night, the 581st aircrews flying behind the lines during the Korean War did their best work in the dark. This did not sit well with the commander of the 3d Air Rescue Group (ARG)—the unit tasked with providing maintenance support and living arrangements for the 581st helicopters (helos) at K-16. The commander made no bones in giving his views to Lt Col George Pittman, the 581st deputy commander, including his opinion that "helicopter flying at night is too dangerous."[15] In a tense meeting, Pittman reminded the 3d ARG commander that his responsibilities ended with support of the ARCW helicopters, adding, "It's none of your business, don't worry about what they're doing."[16]

The 2157th ARS commander did, however, succeed in having "RESCUE" removed from the sides of the black-hat H-19s. To the 581st helo pilots, it seemed the more conservative rescue squadron didn't want the North Koreans confusing them with the 581st should a helo go down in "Indian country." Considering the fate of the 581st B-29 crewmen in the previous story, the air rescue concerns were not totally without merit.

The first ARCW helo pilots had a few adjustments of their own to make, beginning with the basic fact that they arrived in Korea with no helicopters and no idea of the ARCW mission. When the newly arrived pilots approached Fifth Air Force staff officers for both their aircraft and a mission, the initial response was denial that the 581st even existed! It did, of course, and by October 1952, six pilots, one NCO, and 12 airmen fresh from tech school comprised the Helicopter Flight, 581st ARC Squadron, commanded by Capt Frank Westerman. A long way from their parent wing in the Philippines, they

P G Moore

A black-painted SA-16 amphibian from the 581st ARCW on temporary duty with B Flight at Seoul City Air Base in 1952. Note similarly painted B-26s in the background.

Joe Barrett

Mysterious Cho-do Island was the launch site from which the ARCW helos inserted intelligence agents along Korea's western coastline above the 38th parallel. In addition to the 581st helos, the island was used by numerous other military and CIA units conducting unconventional warfare during the war.

learned early to shift for themselves. With four brand-new H-19A helicopters in their possession, the ARCW helo pilots next learned why Fifth Air Force had been so reluctant to answer their initial questions. Their primary mission was to insert United Nations intelligence agents behind enemy lines by means of infiltration flights at night at the lowest possible altitudes to avoid enemy radar. They would soon learn that this invariably called for them to fly from US-controlled islands off Korea's west coast, skimming the freezing waters of the Yellow Sea as they flew to their blacked-out landing point on the (hopefully) deserted coast.

Without the benefit of today's reliable radar altimeters, night-vision goggles, and sophisticated navigation equipment, these missions demanded superb airmanship at the rawest "stick and rudder" level. Close calls were inevitable. Robert Sullivan, then a second lieutenant, vividly recalls the night he felt the nose of the helicopter tug and dip slightly as he flew the helo's nose wheels into the frigid ocean waters; it would happen again to others.

The Helicopter Flight soon received another lesson on just how far Fifth Air Force was prepared to go to hide the flight's existence from unwanted scrutiny. Though housed with the 2157th Air Rescue Squadron at K-16 and supported by the 3d Air Rescue Group in Japan, it took its missions from B Flight, 6167th Air Base Squadron, another classified unit also based at K-16—except when Fifth Air Force Intelligence (A-2) itself chose to directly assign a mission to the flight. One can hardly fault the Communists (or Fifth Air Force staffers!) if questions regarding the Helicopter Flight generated blank faces and not much else.

The final launching pad for agent-insertion missions was usually Cho-do Island, a bleak rock located only 10 miles from the North Korean coast . . . but 60 miles behind enemy lines. While the British navy protected the coastal islands from retaliatory seaborne attacks, Cho-do's proximity to the coastline provided an ideal platform from which to conduct unconventional warfare missions at night.

Joe Barrett

The four H-19As assigned to the Helicopter Flight, 581st ARCW, were collocated with the 2157th Air Rescue Squadron also flying the same type aircraft at K-16. The attempt to blend black hat special operations and white hat rescue pilots together had its bumps, as when the rescue commander ordered the ARCW pilots to remove RESCUE markings from their helos.

Flying from K-16 during daylight hours, the flight's helicopters would land on Cho-do for fuel and a final mission brief, then settle down for a few hours sleep to await darkness. Flying solo and in complete radio silence, they could only hope that North Korean coastal security forces were not waiting for them at the drop-off point. Not all threats came from the ground, however, and sometimes the threat started long before they crossed the coastline. Lieutenant Sullivan recalls one mission in which they launched with the radio call sign "Treefrog 33":

> Flying an insertion mission north along the coast in total darkness, the crew heard "Kodak" (the radar tracking site on Cho-do) ask, "Treefrog 33, how many treefrogs are out there?" Maintaining radio silence, the special operators refused to respond. Kodak then announced, "Treefrog 33, I am painting five, repeat five, slow moving targets near your vicinity."[17]

Without a word, Treefrog 33 banked out to sea, disappearing silently over the dark horizon en route to Cho-do and safety. On a subsequent

Joe Barrett

This Korean intelligence agent in enemy uniform waits in isolation for a night insertion behind enemy lines from Cho-do. As the Communists tightened their totalitarian grip on North Korea's population, the survival rate of such agents dropped to appalling levels.

Joe Barrett

One of many "souvenirs" found on an ARCW helo following the harrowing daytime rescue of a downed Marine fighter pilot from a frozen reservoir in enemy territory. Another inch nearer the leading edge, the bullet would almost have certainly severed the tail-rotor spar, killing all persons aboard.

night mission, it got trickier still when Kodak asked Lieutenant Sullivan his distance from the drop-off point. This time Kodak's voice came with a faint oriental accent.

As dangerous as the night missions were, the special operators at least had the element of surprise and safety of darkness on their side. But both were lost before the mission ever began when it came to their secondary mission: combat rescue of downed pilots. When called into combat rescue, the ARCW helo pilots attempted to reach the downed pilot before the enemy had a chance to prepare antiaircraft defenses for the inevitable rescue attempt. In contrast, the more conservative air rescue philosophy called for more thorough but time-consuming mission planning. While the former approach was unquestionably riskier to the helo crew, the latter also had a major drawback—the enemy got the same additional time to prepare for the Americans' arrival.

Whatever the choice of tactics, there was simply no way out of a knock-down brawl if the North Koreans were near enough the downed pilot to smell blood. And on 24 February 1953, there was enough blood, enemy soldiers, firepower, and bad weather near a downed Marine Corps pilot to produce three Silver Star medals for two ARCW helo pilots and their Air Rescue Service crewman.

Things were not going particularly well for Marine major Dave Cleeland on this cold February morning. His 100th combat mission had left him wounded, freezing, and lying next to the fuselage of his crashed F4U Corsair in the middle of a frozen reservoir surrounded by North Korean troops about to take him prisoner, if not kill him outright. A lack of local maps and subsequent radio confusion had already deterred two Air Rescue Service helicopters before ARCW helo pilot Joe Barrett* and his crew were scrambled from K-16. Time was running out . . . and the bad news outweighed the good news.

The good news was that the ARCW helo was soon approaching the reservoir and had the crashed F4U in sight. The bad news was that the North Koreans were charging out onto the ice from their positions along the shoreline in a last-ditch attempt to capture or kill Cleeland. Whether what happened next is good news or bad news has a lot to do with whether the reader is American or North Korean.

As the North Koreans rushed toward the pilot, a combination of just-arrived Corsair and USAF F-80 jets orbiting overhead reacted instantaneously, raking the exposed enemy on the ice with their .50-caliber heavy machine gun and 20-millimeter cannon fire. In response, the entire rim of the reser-

*Captain Barrett was no stranger to excitement. A B-17 pilot in World War II, he had returned from his first combat mission over Germany in a bullet-riddled bomber. His second mission was against the Schweinfurt ball-bearing complex on "Black Thursday," the worst day of the war for American bomber pilots. Barrett never made it back from Germany on that mission, spending the rest of the war in a German prison camp.

voir seemed to explode with flashes of gunfire as the North Koreans opened up on the dangerously low-flying fighters. In the midst of this air-ground frenzy, the ARCW H-19 swooped through a hail of ground fire seemingly coming from every direction. Picking up the marine, experiencing a good fright, and taking on several bullet holes (including one to a fuel cell and another through the hand of A2C Thomas Thornton, the 46-year-old crewman), the H-19 crew fled the firefight en route to some well-deserved recognition.*

Sometimes the collocated ARCW and Air Rescue Service crews crossed paths in odd ways. This was never more true than on 12 April 1953 when two F-86 fighter pilots bailed out of their battle-damaged jets over the Yellow Sea. One of the two, Capt Joe McConnell, was already an ace en route to becoming the leading jet ace of the war and a nationally recognized hero. With one ARCW and one Air Rescue helo searching over water for the two pilots, McConnell splashed into the near-freezing waters right in front of Lieutenant Sullivan's helicopter and received a quick pickup courtesy of the 581st. Or at least that's what Sullivan thought until he saw newspaper descriptions of the rescue featuring photographs of an H-19 with RESCUE markings hoisting "McConnell" out of the water. Sullivan later learned that the photograph came from an Air Rescue Service reenactment of the rescue, conducted in a fresh-water lake in Japan.[18] *C'est la guerre!*

During the operational period described here, the six ARCW pilots flew approximately 1,000 hours total on its four helos in the process of flying innumerable ARCW and ARS missions. It remains a matter of considerable (and justifiable) pride to the flight's veterans that these missions were completed without a single accident, combat loss, or fatality. Sullivan, now a retired major, recently offered his assessment of these operational accomplishments with the comment "Not too shabby for a bunch of beginners, huh?"[19]

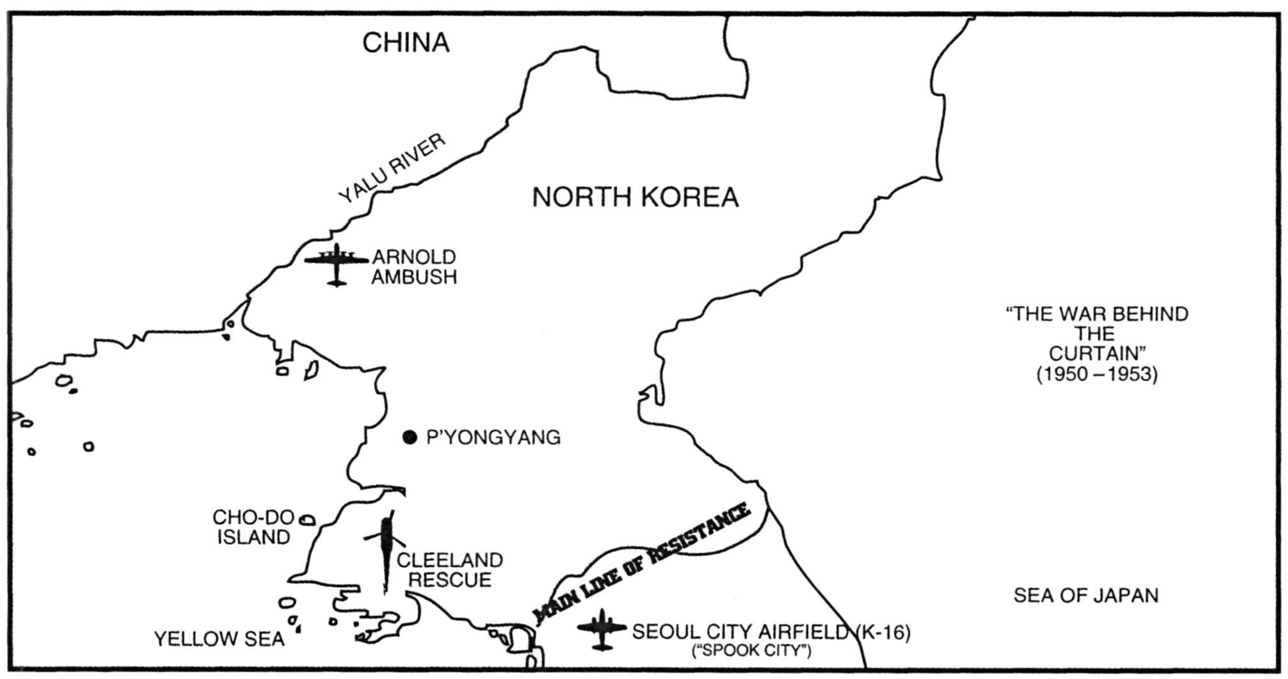

*Grateful naval authorities reportedly proposed to nominate the trio for the Navy Cross. The Navy subsequently demurred after Fifth Air Force responded it would provide its own recognition to the airmen. On 21 May 1953, Capt Joseph Barrett, 1st Lt Frank Fabijan, and A2C Thomas Thornton received Silver Stars for their gallantry.

French C-119 Flying Boxcars sit at Clark Air Base awaiting ARCW and other USAF crews to fly them to and from French enclaves in Vietnam. The subterfuge was minimal, as the vertical stablizers still carry USAF squadron markings, and the twin-tail boom shows a barely erased USAF emblem under the French national insignia.

The 581st "French" Boxcars

While the 581st's B-29 bombers, SA-16 amphibians, and H-19 helicopters roamed the night skies over the Korean peninsula, the wing's C-119 Flying Boxcar transports made their mark fighting Communism farther south . . . a lot farther south.

For the C-119 crews, this fight began in 1953 as the Korean War started winding down. France was by then fighting an increasingly bloody battle to maintain control of its colonies in Southeast Asia. The French needed heavy transports both to ferry supplies, principally into Vietnam, and to support French troops in combat within that region. It was precisely the kind of sensitive, politico-military mission that the ARCW was designed to execute, and the 581st was tapped to participate in it.

Soon the 581st transports were carrying supplies into Haiphong airfield located near the coast in the northern half of Vietnam. Ammunition, vehicles, and barbed wire in particular became high-priority cargo for the C-119s. Other heavy transports from conventional troop carrier units

William E Brown

also joined the intentionally designed, low-profile program. A wary US did stipulate to the French that its air support would not carry French troops into Vietnam, nor would it become involved in combat air support within the country.

As with many special operations, its politico-military implications were handled like a hot potato. The situation was not, however, without occasional humor for the American aircrews. Grover Ensley, a C-119 pilot, recalls his trip to Vietnam in 1954 in which the public controversy and the military reality for the airmen could be summed up in three short phrases: "Congress said we weren't there; the French said we don't want you here; the United States Air Force said stay there!"[20]

As French requests for more air-cargo support escalated beyond what the Eisenhower administration was prepared to support publicly, alternatives to helping the French in less obvious ways were explored. Two mutually supporting plans were devised, both involving 581st personnel. The first aimed at reducing the high-profile presence of increasing numbers of USAF transports in Indochina, the second at providing the French with C-119 qualified aircrews.

To accomplish the first plan, the 581st coordinated a larger USAF effort to fly a small number of active duty C-119s from troop carrier bases in Japan to the 24th Air Depot Wing, collocated with the 581st at Clark Air Base. Towed into the end of one of the huge maintenance facilities as USAF aircraft, the planes would exit the other end of the building with French national markings on the fuselage. *Voilà!* The 581st crews would then fly the "French" C-119s into Vietnam. Worn-out C-119s already in-country would be flown back to Clark for refurbishment at the 24th Depot Wing. As they exited the maintenance depot, the repaired aircraft emerged as USAF C-119s en route back to their bases in Japan.

The 581st training program for qualifying C-119 aircrews had a particular twist of its own. The pilots they were training for combat in Indochina weren't French; they were American civilian employees of the Civil Air Transport (CAT) Company, a CIA-proprietary airline.[21] In addition, the 581st instructors had a rude surprise in store for them the morning they went out to the airfield to meet the first group of eight CAT pilots arriving at Clark for their C-119 conversion training.

Advised in advance that time was short, the 581st trainers had organized an intense three-week course that could, with good maintenance and weather, get the job done. On meeting the CAT pilots, the instructor pilots learned that they had exactly three *days* to complete the conversion training! In a fitting testimony to the professionalism of all, the incredibly high-flying times of the

CAT pilots,* and the sturdiness of Fairchild's C-119, the training was completed on time and without accident. It was by all accounts, however, a program that left both pilots and C-119s panting like winded ponies at the end of the 72 hours.

The CAT pilots did their 581st instructors proud, especially in the last stages of the war when they flew through intense antiaircraft fire to parachute supplies to the paratroopers and Foreign Legion troops in the doomed garrison at Dien Bien Phu. Loss of the garrison in May 1954 signaled the end of France as a colonial power in Southeast Asia. But months before then, the Air Force was already phasing out its air resupply and communications concept.

The Last Act

On 8 September 1953, nine months before the fall of Dien Bien Phu and less than three months after the stalemated conclusion of the Korean War, the Air Force reduced the 581st from wing to group size.[22] Gone were the wing headquarters, the Holding and Briefing, Communications, and Reproduction squadrons. The remaining Air Resupply Group maintained control of the Air Resupply Squadron and its supporting Airborne Materials Assembly Squadron, with the personnel strength of both squadrons declining to approximately half the authorized strength. The group's wartime mission was curt:

1. Supplement theater airlift.
2. Prepare supplies for air delivery.
3. Resupply military units.

The ARC pulse was growing fainter, but it still had its uses for intelligence agencies whose missions were steadily growing in the midst of the cold war. The group was still assigned two C-54 and two C-118 transports, maintained by Philippine Airlines at nearby Nichols Field at Manila. Group crews in civilian clothes flew some classified missions in the C-118s, but for the high-risk missions out of Formosa, only the CIA's CAT crews were used.[23]

So "sterilized" were the C-118s that not only were their exterior markings removed but every serial number on every piece of equipment on the planes themselves. In its semiannual history report for the latter half of the year, the section detailing the hours flown on unit aircraft notes:

> Elaboration on the training and operational missions of the C-54 and C-118 aircraft assigned this organization is withheld due to the high security classification afforded their operations.[24]

The 581st Air Resupply Group left Clark Air Base in October 1954. Its move to Okinawa changed not only its geographical base but transferred control of the group from Thirteenth Air Force to Twentieth Air Force. Four months later, the 581st lost a B-29 on a routine low-level training mission. Flying into a hill on the south end of the island, it was the 581st's first major accident. The following September, a B-29 piloted by Capt Walter A. Prolisce, chief of standboard (i.e., standardization and evaluation), disappeared on an overwater flight resulting in the loss of all 13 crewmen on board. The unit history reports that debris was recovered from the crash area, but not enough to give a clue as to the cause of the accident: "Results of investigation were negative."[25]

In October 1955, FEAF transferred its aircrew survival school from the island of Eta Jima to Okinawa, activating the 6333d Technical Training Squadron (Survival) to the 581st.[26] Its mission was to train all FEAF aircrews in the principles, tactics, and techniques of survival, escape, and evasion techniques. By then, however, the constant rotation of personnel out of the group had so outstripped the numbers of incoming personnel that already serious readiness problems became overwhelming. Inadequate facilities

*Colonel Pittman recalls the *low*-time CAT pilot had *12,000* hours flight time!

and "survival" instructors pulled overnight from unrelated career-field personnel on Okinawa led to predictable results.

The deterioration of operational readiness continued to the point that by December 1955, total aircrews assigned had decreased to three for the B-29s, one for the SA-16s, and two for the C-119s. By then only one crew from each of the three aircraft flights was deemed operationally ready. Without official notification of the group's deactivation, the unit received a series of orders that summer to transfer its aircraft to other locations. In September the 581st was officially deactivated with remaining aircraft transferred to the 322d Troop Carrier Squadron (Medium) (Special).

The end of the trail for USAF special operations in the Pacific ended four busy years after its arrival in the Philippines. Or had it? The "special" designator assigned the 322d TCS was a tip-off that perhaps things were not what they seemed. Indeed they weren't. The operation had gotten smaller and gone deeper underground . . . like a stream that goes underground only to surface much farther away. The wing-level club of the 581st was to be replaced by the more discreet but still deadly stiletto—a weapon more suited to the cold war intelligence activities and covert war that were to become the next proving ground for USAF special operations.

Notes

1. *The 1952 Historical Research Origin and Development of the United States Air Force Psychological Warfare Program, 1946–1952* (Maxwell AFB, Ala.: USAF Historical Division, 1 June 1953), chap. 1, 1.
2. Ibid., 40.
3. Ibid., 41.
4. Ibid.
5. History, 581st Air Resupply and Communications Wing, Operations Plan 3-52, 14 July 1952, Historical Research Agency, Maxwell AFB, Ala., microfiche reel no. K3643.
6. Ibid.
7. Ibid.
8. Col George Pittman, USAF, Retired, letter to author, 13 December 1994.
9. Ibid., 6–7; and idem., interview with author, 10 September 1994.
10. Special Order 5, 581st ARCW, 8 January 1953, as quoted in *Arc Light* 11, no. 1 (January 1955): 9.
11. History, Far East Air Forces, 1 June–31 December 1951, 58.
12. Pittman interview.
13. *Arc Light* 1, no. 4 (October 1985): 3.
14. Pittman interview.
15. Ibid.
16. Ibid.
17. Maj Robert F. Sullivan, USAF, Retired, telephone interviews with the author, April–May 1994. Corroboration provided by Helicopter Flight pilots Capt Joseph Barrett and 1st Lt Frank Fabijan in subsequent interviews.
18. One USAF file photo of the "McConnell" rescue can be found in Larry Davis's *MIG ALLEY: Air to Air Combat over Korea* (Carrollton, Tex.: Squadron/Signal Publications, 1978), 57.
19. *Arc Light* 11, no. 1 (January 1995): 1–3.
20. Col Grover Ensley, USAF, Retired, interview with author, 8 May 1995.
21. Pittman letter.
22. Headquarters Thirteenth Air Force, General Order 63, 1 September 1953, sec. 1, par. 1.
23. Pittman letter.
24. History, 581st Air Resupply Group, 1 July–31 December 1955, vol. 2.
25. Ibid.
26. Bob Koch, telephone interview with author, 20 July 1995.

COVERT WAR

A Cold War Venture

The Air Resupply and Communications Service

By the close of World War II, the American people were more than ready for the good times to roll. Having endured nearly a decade of poverty during the Great Depression and having emerged bloodied but victorious against the totalitarian evils of Japanese and German fascism, Americans felt that the long-awaited promise of good times was just inches from their anxious fingertips. Within three years, however, the promise was already burning those fingers like a hot iron, and the heat was coming from a most unexpected source.

How could our "valiant Russian allies," filmed so favorably for American audiences during the war, suddenly turn against the very country that helped save them from Adolf Hitler? The Soviet threat was not at all subtle, yet Americans could hardly believe what was unfolding before their eyes. They had believed that the threat of global totalitarianism in their times had ended with the destruction of the Japanese and German war machines.

A Chilling Fear

You could smell the *fear.* As if coming from some overlooked egg in the Cave of Evil, Soviet dictator Joseph Stalin was presenting totalitarianism on a scale that threatened to dwarf that of Hideki Tojo and Adolf Hitler combined. Inflammatory rhetoric? Cold war hyperbole? Ask any American old enough to remember the 1950s-era school drills in which children practiced crawling under their desks to protect themselves from Soviet nuclear attack. Frightening times indeed, and one response to that fear came in July 1947 with the passage of the National Security Act. The act created a number of organizations to deal with the Soviet threat, including, significantly, the United States Air Force and the Central Intelligence Agency.

Within 12 months of the creation of these two organizations, small groups of both Air Force and CIA officers were working feverishly in their own spheres to expand a World War II concept that was about to assume a role unparalleled in scope in American politico-military history: psychological warfare. Psychological warfare in the 1950s encompassed much more than merely the dissemination of propaganda. It in fact came to encompass what the 1990s military reader will recognize as "special operations."

Despite the differences in titles and technology over the years, psychological warfare missions, now special operations, remain essentially unchanged. They include unconventional warfare (guerrilla warfare); direct action (commando-type raids); strategic reconnaissance (intelligence gathering); and, of course, psychological warfare (psywar) or psychological operations (psyops). The difference between the latter two is that while psyops can be used on friendly populations and US forces, psywar is reserved exclusively for use against enemy forces and populations. To the handful of military and civilian visionaries who saw how this new cold war would be fought, psywar appeared the most effective way of countering the Soviets in the absence of declared war. Others weren't so sure.

The decision to pursue politically risky psywar weighed heavily on the minds of those who would ultimately be held responsible should specific operations fail, as some inevitably would. The pursuit of psywar, admittedly an extralegal form of warfare, by a democracy founded on the overriding principle of law is an explosive mixture that can burn the handler as well as the target. But most senior officials involved also believed that psywar or something very closely resembling it had to be pursued if the Western world were to survive Stalin's ambitions. The bureaucratic trick was not to be the agency holding the "blame bag" when things went wrong. An excellent study of this era describes the prevailing attitudes in Washington in 1947:

> The task of delineating agency responsibilities for psychological warfare proved difficult. Secretary of State George Marshall opposed taking responsibility for covert actions that might embarrass the Department. ...He favored placing covert activities outside the Department, *but still subject to guidance from the Secretary of State* (emphasis added). . . . Similarly, the military wanted to maintain some control over covert psychological activities without assuming operational responsibility.[1]

This left the CIA, an organization created only months earlier and led by many veterans of its predecessor organization from World War II, the Office of Strategic Services. During the war, OSS veterans had conducted all the psywar/special operations missions described in the previous section of this book, and they had done so while staying beyond the direct control of the military. Despite the large number of military personnel transferred to the OSS, the organization itself had been nothing less than a civilian-run special operations force led by William J. "Wild Bill" Donovan, a charismatic Wall Street lawyer (and World War I Medal of Honor recipient) who answered to only one man, the president of the United States.

By the end of 1948, the young CIA had already developed a limited (and already controversial) covert action capability.[2] But before it could hope to conduct unconventional warfare in Soviet-occupied Europe and Asia, it needed long-range air transport to get its guerrilla warfare agents, weapons, and supplies deep behind the Iron Curtain. Public records of planning sessions between CIA and USAF officers on this subject are predictably scarce, but the records of an unexpected source—the United States Army—shed some light on the subject.

Not until 15 January 1951 did the Army's leading psywar proponent, Brig Gen Robert McClure, succeed in establishing the Office of the Chief of Psychological Warfare (OCPW) as a special staff division at the Department of Army level in the Pentagon.[3] General McClure's vision divided Army psywar into three components: psychological warfare, cover and deception, and unconventional warfare. By then three years behind Air Force and CIA psywar planning, General McClure's attempts to secure USAF long-range aircraft for the Army's proposed guerrilla warfare forces* soon hit a snag. Someone else with the same request had already beaten the Army to the punch.

General McClure's response to this "snag" led to an unusually bitter, three-way fight over roles and missions between the Army, Air Force, and CIA, with the "winner" getting the unconventional warfare mission. The general was clearly suspicious that the Air Force and CIA were already thick as fleas in the "psywar game," and it wasn't hard to see why. Buried in each of the USAF's air resupply and communication wings was a secretive holding and briefing (H&B) squadron, which, as previously described, reserved 200 of its 260 assigned officer billets for personnel "assigned by other agencies." The trail was not hard to follow, and General McClure's suspicions were correct.

Within four months of OCPW's establishment, General McClure was already pressing the Air Force to switch the aircraft in its ARC wings to support the Army psywar mission. Referring to the limitations of Air Force C-47 transports in psywar leaflet drops in the Korean War, he asked the Air Force director of operations in May 1951 to reassign "the special air wings being organized to support CIA activities in Korea . . . for use by [Army] psychological warfare."[4] What General McClure may not have understood at the time was that the Air Force did not view its role in psywar as merely that of air support to the CIA.

By 1951 powerful forces in the Air Force fully intended for the Air Force to become the executive agent within the Department of Defense for national-level psywar. How inclusive would this role be? Coming out of his talks with Headquarters Air Force staff members in the fall of 1951, a clearly dismayed General McClure reported to the Army chief of staff that the Air Force not only disagreed with the Army's view on retardation (slowing the anticipated Soviet assault on Western Europe) but also "felt they [the Air Force] had a major responsibility in the field of unconventional warfare, *which did not exclude the*

*Progressing against opposition through multiple staff offices on the Army Staff, General McClure's plans to establish a Psychological Warfare Center at Fort Bragg, North Carolina, came to fruition with the activation of the center in April 1952. Within the center was the nucleus of his guerrilla forces, today's Army Special Forces, or "Green Berets" as they are more popularly known.

Carl Bernhardt

"Freedom through Truth" was the motto of the Air Resupply and Communications Service (ARCS), a special psychological warfare force activated by the Air Force in 1951. ARCS units worked closely with US intelligence and Army Special Forces to develop an anti-Communist guerrilla capability in Soviet rear areas should the cold war suddenly turn hot.

actual command of guerrillas" (emphasis added).[5] Whatever gave the blue-suiters of the new Air Force the idea that they could actually pull this off? Well, for one thing, *they already were.* And the vehicle that they were using to do it with was the Air Resupply and Communications Service and its tactical air wings.

It was a strange role for the Air Force to assume, but these were even stranger times. With a hot war ongoing in Korea, and Eastern Europe (East Germany and Poland) threatening to explode in anti-Communist rebellion, growing Soviet pressure on Greece and Iran, and lingering memories of the Berlin blockade, the fear of yet another world war could be smelled in the air.

Something ugly was about to go down and it couldn't be stopped. But could it be contained? Could specially trained psywar units, fighting by a different set of rules, make a difference in the fight? The Air Force certainly hoped so, and the air resupply and communications concept was its entry into the fight everyone just knew was coming.

An "Agency outside DOD" Makes a Request

The Air Resupply and Communications Service was activated on a cold February morning on 23 February 1951 at Andrews Air Force Base, just outside Washington, D.C.[6] The high-level impetus for its creation had begun two years earlier when the secretary of defense was requested by "an agency outside the Department of Defense" to "provide support services similar to the type that provided covert airlift operations during World War II."[7] The request clearly had in mind the Army Air Forces' Carpetbagger special operations flown into Nazi-occupied Europe from bases in England and North Africa.

The Carpetbagger comparison was particularly useful in describing the type of "services" expected from the Air Force. While ultimately successful enough to serve as a future model for the ARCS, the Carpetbagger units had initially suffered badly from a low priority within the European theater. The Carpetbagger experience underscored the subsequent convictions of many Air Force planners that unconventional air warfare units "must become part and parcel of the military organization, rather than a crazy quilt of temporary expedients tacked on to the main body during wartime."*

The publicly unidentified agency's request was quickly approved by the powerful National Security Council and sent to the Joint Chiefs of Staff,

*The words are eerily prescient of the same convictions that culminated in the controversial activation of USAF's Special Operations Command (AFSOC) in May 1990. Despite the 39-year separation of the two events, it is also noteworthy that the decisive impetus came from outside the Department of Defense.

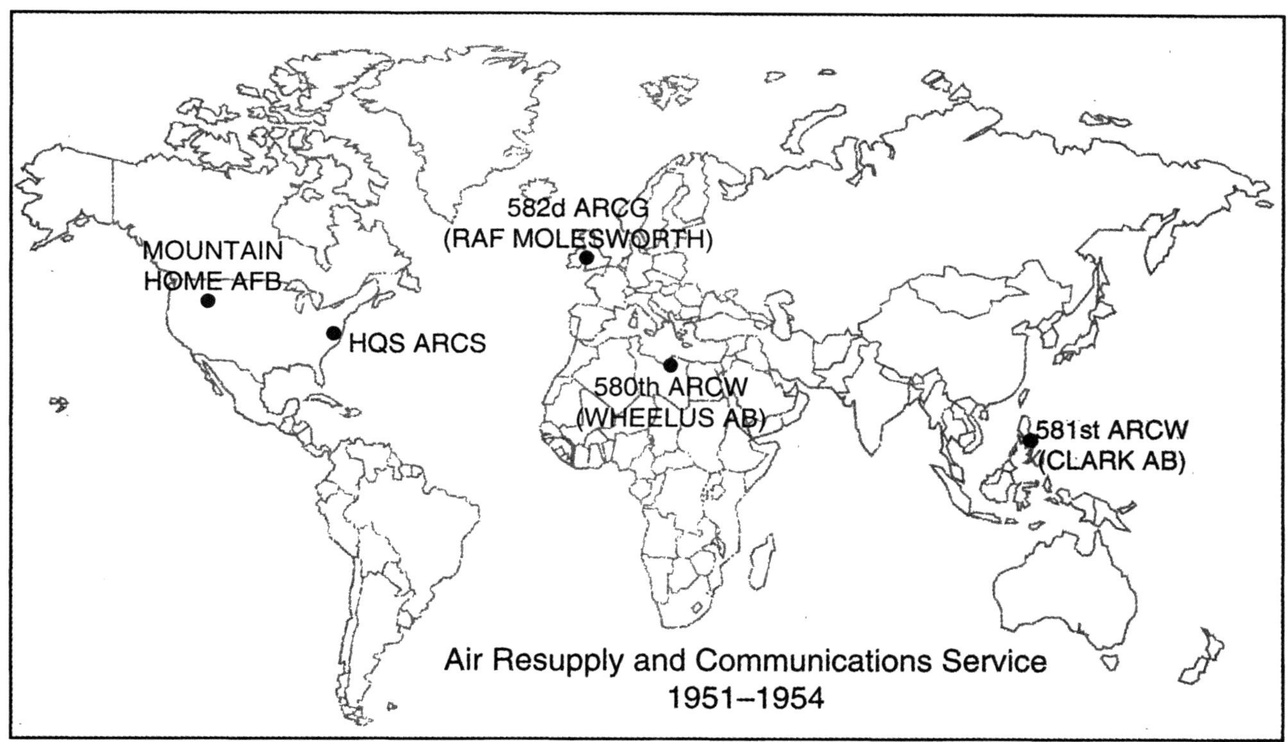

who promptly gave the mission to the Air Force. Headquarters Air Force in turn tasked its Military Air Transport Service to organize, train, and equip the new service and its tactical wings. It was no small task. The plan envisioned nothing less than a service-level command headquarters and seven subordinate psywar wings to be activated in three-month intervals and then be deployed overseas following six months of training.

Incredibly, the first wing was to be activated less than 60 days after the February activation of the service headquarters itself. The frenetic pace of the ARC wing's activation boggles the mind even today. It wasn't just that each ARC wing would require well over 1,000 personnel ranging from heavy bomber mechanics to foreign language specialists; that four distinctly different types of aircraft with very different maintenance requirements were to be used; or even that something called a Holding and Briefing Squadron required selected Air Force officers to undergo Army Special Forces and US intelligence (hereafter USI) tactical training in guerrilla warfare. These would prove the easy problems to solve. The major problem defies understanding even 50 years after the fact. But the bald truth, agonized over repeatedly in official archives, is that even after launching this massive effort, *Headquarters Air Force found itself unable to define the mission of this service and its proposed seven wings!*

Four months after the activation of the service, representatives of the Air Force's major commands met to resolve once and for all the elusive and maddening problem of defining the ARCS mission. Yet even this conference could do no better than conclude with the feeble agreement that "there is an urgent need for a realistic mission letter to each of the major commands."[8] In all fairness to the conference representatives, it must be stated that it was not only the mission itself that defied ready definition but also the unique chain of command proposed for this precedent-breaking service. The official records underscore the problem:

> Compounding the difficulty in clarifying the ARCS mission was the fact that its Wings were actually operational arms of the Psychological Warfare Division, Directorate of Plans, Headquarters, USAF. This division under General [Orrin L.] Grover, was charged with "planning Air Force Psychological Warfare, unconventional warfare and special operations."[9]

Operational air wings being deployed to overseas theaters but commanded personally by staff officers in the Pentagon? It's not difficult to imagine the response of both theater commanders and senior flag-rank officers commanding the fighter, bomber, and transport commands. Despite these fundamental problems, the ARCS program pressed forward at a furious pace with general guidance to prosecute two distinct but related functions:

1. Aerial resupply: Introduce and evacuate ranger-type personnel behind enemy lines and supply them and guerrilla units.
2. Psychological warfare: Prepare psychological warfare material for audio and printed distribution.[10]

A third mission, dubbed "Project Reach High," was later assigned to the service. It required the service to establish . . . *a balloon flying squadron!* This squadron would "employ balloons as an efficient and inexpensive delivery of material to potential enemy target areas."[11] In due course, this squadron was to be activated. For the moment, the service had more pressing problems, chief of which was selecting the type of aircraft required to fulfill the aerial resupply mission. There were some surprising twists in what at first glance seemed to be a simple issue.

Going Too Fast

To "introduce ranger-type personnel and supplies" deep into the Soviet-occupied territories of Eastern Europe and Asia, the service developed demanding operational criteria for its long-range aircraft. These included a 4,000-nautical-mile range; a minimum payload of 4,000 pounds; low-level, long-range navigation capabilities; and, of course, the capability to drop parachutists and resupply bundles. Only one such aircraft in the Air Force inventory was available in the quantity required—the World War II-era B-29 Superfortress heavy bomber. The required number of bombers were soon pulled from the mothball fleet at Robins AFB, Georgia, and restored for duty, some with fuselage markings still showing the number of combat missions flown over Japan.

The Superfortress was not a happy choice for the service, which noted the limitations of using a high-speed, high-altitude bomber for low-speed, low-level, night infiltration missions. The B-29's tendency to stall near parachute-dropping airspeed and its lack of maneuverability at these low airspeeds did not portend well for the mission or the survival of the aircraft itself. Extensive modifications to the giant bomber would be required, but in the end these would still provide only limited operational improvements.

These modifications included removing all guns for self-defense, saving those in the tail turret, and installing a "joe hole" in the former aft-belly gun turret space for parachutists to exit. Resupply bundles would hang like clusters of melons in the bomb bay to be dropped like bombs as the plane passed over the drop zone. Beyond the technical limitations of the B-29 itself, another problem soon surfaced—one that could (and did) prove deadly to inexperienced crews.

The ARCS leadership had acknowledged from the start that the critical key to safely flying a high-altitude bomber for the dangerous low-level ARCS mission depended on the assignment of highly experienced B-29 aircrews. In practice this meant transferring experienced B-29 pilots from other Air Force commands flying the bomber, or at least putting highly experienced pilots of four-engined transports through the B-29 Combat Crew Training Squadron (CCTS) training at Randolph AFB, Texas. The former rarely hap-

Jack F Wheeler

Only the B-29 Superfortress had the range and payload to deliver Ranger-type personnel and their supplies deep behind the Iron Curtain. Unhappily, the giant high-altitude bomber proved difficult to handle for inexperienced crews flying low-level night missions. The bomber depicted, assigned to the 580th ARC Wing in Libya, impacted the terrain at cruise speed on 15 January 1954 while on just such a mission.

pened, as the commander of the 580th ARC Wing's flying squadron noted:

> Without exception all aircraft commanders received by us were recalled officers with low total time and very little experience within the last five years. *The total time within this period, including the B-29 training, ran from 90 to 130 hours.* (Emphasis added)[12]

What took place at Randolph was even less encouraging. Following an inspection of aircrew proficiency at Mountain Home AFB, Idaho, in July 1951, an inspecting officer included in his report to the commander, ARCS, that the director of training at Randolph had said that the ARC wings were receiving the poorest crews completing CCTS in B-29s.[13] Two months later, a flight examiner from MATS's Chief Pilot's Division completed a similar inspection of aircrew performance at Mountain Home, only to recommend that "the C-119 and B-29 schools be investigated to determine whether the least qualified crews are being assigned to ARCS."[14]

By then ARCS had already reported the unsatisfactory aircrew-experience situation to Headquarters MATS along with a request for eight B-29 instructor pilots for Mountain Home. A subsequent ARCS letter to Headquarters USAF further requested an aircrew training squadron be assigned to Mountain Home. As an interim measure, MATS sent one instructor pilot, 1st Lt Robert S. Ross, to Mountain Home while considering the overall problem. Less than 60 days later, Lieutenant Ross and six other crew members of a

580th ARC Wing B-29 died on a night training flight at Mountain Home. The ARCS commander subsequently noted:

> The investigation reveals that a probable cause factor was the practicing of engine failure procedures at low altitudes before the student pilot's operational ability had progressed to the point where he could cope with such practices.[15]

Headquarters Air Force subsequently responded to the ARCS request for instructors with the decision that such a request was "unfeasible" at that time. Additional comments in the response reveal the lack of understanding prevalent among those inexperienced in the dangerous world of low-level night flying:

> It is difficult to believe that any B-29 aircraft commander successfully completing the course at Randolph, and who prior to that course met input criteria for Randolph, could be as deficient as the basic correspondence alleges.[16]

In the 1990s, units of the Air Force Special Operations Command are able to invite key

Jack Tetrick

The air-to-ground extraction of personnel from behind enemy lines was a concept that had been proved to be technically feasible during the Korean War . . . using twin-engined medium transports. The potential use of the 50-plus-ton Superfortress for this mission added an element of excitement not much appreciated by the "volunteer" test pig situated in a cage at the top of the tower seen below and to the left of the B-29's tail. Field tests with this B-29 (no. 44-70113) were conducted at Eglin AFB, Florida, in 1951.

Jack Tetrick

Pentagon officials to visit their bases and "savor" the experience of low-level night flying: the noise and heat, the aircrew tension in the cockpit, and the split-second crew coordination needed to avoid becoming a fireball in the southern pinelands of the Deep South. But in 1951 it was all going too fast. With luck, the inexperienced became experienced and survived. Those without luck . . .

As the Superfortress had never before been used in low-level, psychological warfare missions, the inexperienced crews were further burdened with setting the operational limits of the bomber in this role. Missions lasting up to 20 hours were flown at altitudes below 300 feet to test the limits of human and airframe endurance. Perhaps one of the most bizarre of these tests involved using the giant bomber to execute the air-to-ground "snatch" recovery system developed during the Korean War using much smaller, twin-engined transports.

During the summer of 1951, a B-29 from the 580th ARC Wing conducted trials at Eglin AFB in the Florida panhandle to determine the feasibility of using the bomber to conduct air-to-ground personnel extractions from deep inside enemy territory. Modifications to Superfortress no. 470113 included cutting a 48-inch diameter hole in place of the aft-belly turret and fitting an elongated tailhook—similar to that used by Navy aircraft for carrier landings—to the rear of the B-29. As the bomber swooped down on the "extractee," its tailhook caught a horizontal wire over the individual, who in turn was reeled intact through the 48-inch hole in the aircraft's underbelly . . . maybe.

On the first attempt, a test pig in a small cage atop a tower "fared poorly" after the cable snapped following a successful hook engagement. A subsequent test with a human volunteer was more successful but still resulted in a nasty head gash to the extractee as he was reeled through the too-small opening in the aircraft's belly. While technically feasible, the project was eventually dropped in favor of higher-priority programs. Fortunately for the ARCS, its other aircraft selections proved much easier than the B-29 to employ.

Neither the Fairchild C-119 nor the Grumman SA-16 had the range and payload of the B-29, but both had other advantages over their bigger brother. Both could land on rough-terrain strips, and the amphibian SA-16 could, of course, land on water as well. Reversible propellers on both further reduced the size of landing strips required, greatly expanding the operational potential of the aircraft. Still better, both were coming to the ARCS spanking new from the factory with little need for modification.

To round out its unconventional aerial warfare capabilities, the service proposed the addition of four helicopters to each ARC wing. While only the 581st ARC Wing fighting in Korea would actually receive helicopters, their performance in that war would validate their usefulness for inserting and extracting operatives behind enemy lines. Thus, the final aircraft authorization tables allocated to each wing included 12 B-29s; four C-119s; four SA-16s; and, for the 581st only, four H-19s. The aircraft balance was a versatile mixture and one that would in time prove exceptionally well thought-out.

Psywarriors from Georgetown University to Fort Benning

The understandable predilection of many Air Force officers to concentrate on the "flying side" of the new organization did not, fortunately, tempt the ARCS leadership to minimize the importance of its coequal mission, psychological warfare. To the contrary, from mid-1952 forward, the nonflying aspect of the ARCS mission became the pre-eminent focus of the service headquarters. By that time, the service had developed an outstanding psywar training program unmatched to this day.

The service initiated and managed a three-stage psywar training program that provided carefully selected officers* with the necessary training in international relations, psychology, geography, regional cultures, languages, communications, and propaganda-dissemination techniques. Stage 1 (academic) began with four months of intensive and specially tailored training at Georgetown University's Institute of Languages and Linguistics in Washington, D.C., one of the premier academic institutions in the country. A total of 555 Air Force officers completed this demanding stage of the ARCS psywar course prior to its termination in May 1953.[17]

Stage 2 (psywar training) was conducted at Mountain Home AFB by the 1300th Air Base Wing's** Psychological Warfare and Intelligence School. This second stage supplemented the Georgetown curriculum with practical application and was in turn divided into phases 1 and 2. The first phase transitioned the students from theory to operation with classes in newspaper, magazine, and radio programming techniques.

In stage 2/phase 2, the students were further divided into their future specialties. Some attended the Psychological Warfare Intelligence Officer's Course, while others started in the Psychological Warfare Course for team personnel. The latter course taught advanced propaganda techniques and leaflet operations. Phase 2 training comprised 420 hours of instruction to be completed in 12 weeks, and approximately 95 percent of the Georgetown graduates successfully completed the intensive instruction. From this point on, only volunteers were accepted for specialized stage 3 instruction.

Stage 3 study could involve advanced language study in various government or academic institu-

*One such psywar officer was William Blatty, later known to the American public for his best-selling novel, subsequently turned into a terrifying Hollywood movie, *The Exorcist.*

**The 1300th ABW took the brunt of the unglamorous task of setting up Mountain Home AFB for the ARC program. In addition to basic "housekeeping" chores and the Psywar School, it also helped run the survival school for the ARC aircrews.

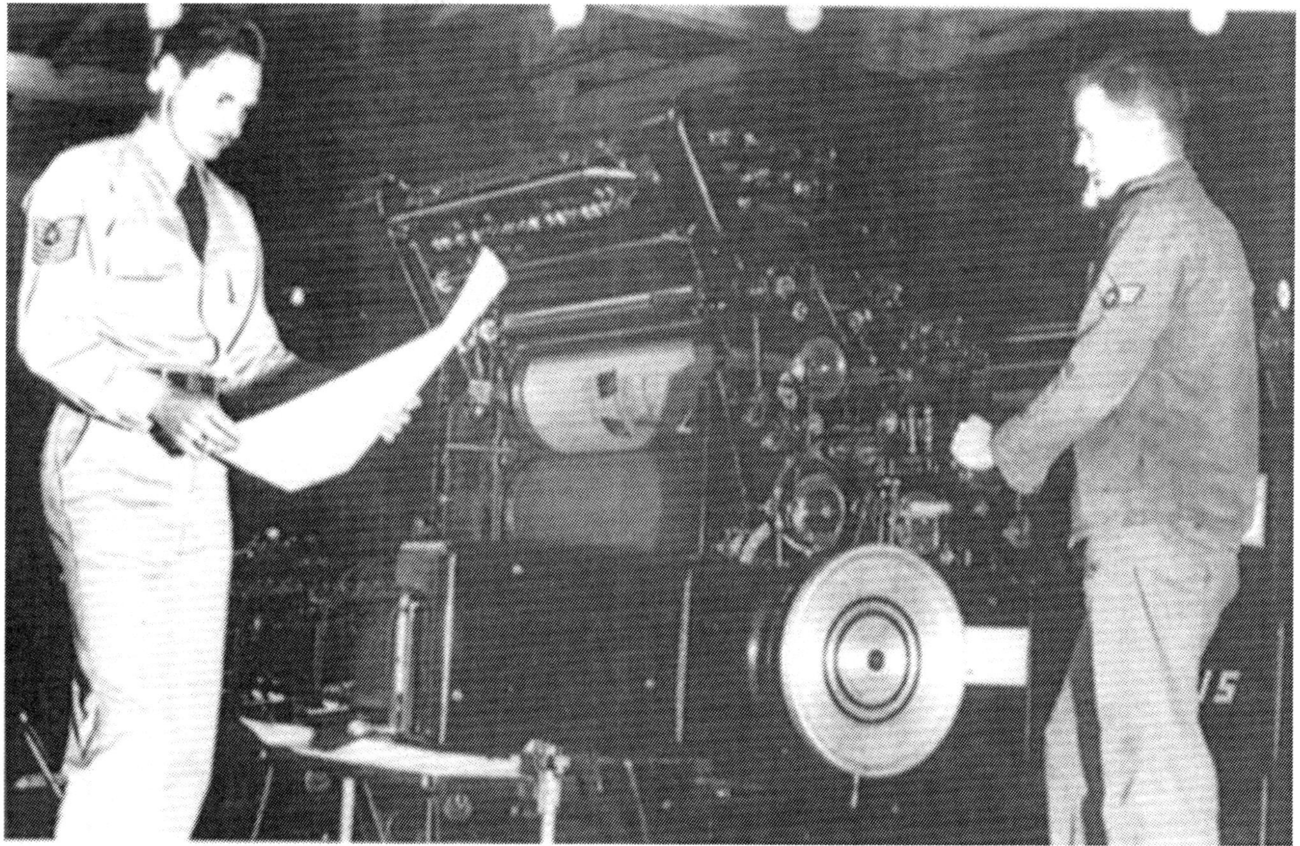

USAF

In each ARC wing, a reproduction squadron equipped with these commercial standard printing presses could produce millions of psychological warfare leaflets within a 24-hour period. The leaflets were conceived and designed by a talented pool of ARCS psywar officers trained at Georgetown University's Institute of Languages and Linguistics in Washington, D.C., at Voice of America broadcasting stations in New York and at other sites in the United States and overseas.

tions, both domestic and foreign, or on-the-job (OJT) training with "government agencies, or advanced intelligence courses in Army or USAF schools."[18] For the select few destined for assignment to the holding and briefing squadrons, it could also include "special" programs to include Special Forces guerrilla training as well as parachute, Ranger, and USI tactical field training at Fort Benning, Georgia.

The concept of Air Force officers undergoing Ranger and Special Forces training was obviously a stretch from the traditional Air Force role. But how much tradition can a three-year-old Air Force have? Besides, if guerrilla warfare was a stretch, what came next was absolutely mind-boggling in an era of nuclear weapons and jet-engined strategic bombers.

The Air Resupply and Communications Service Balloon Program

Records of the ARCS state that "the ARCS balloon program is somewhat difficult to explain." During the summer and fall of 1951, a series of directives, from the Air Force deputy chief of staff, operations, directed MATS to organize a balloon-flying squadron as a cheap alternative for propaganda dissemination into foreign countries.

It was in some respects reminiscent of Japanese attempts during World War II to use fire bombs floated by balloons over America's Pacific Northwest with the intention of igniting fires in the region's huge forests.* MATS in turn passed the mission to the ARCS, which directed the task to its Research and Development (R&D) Division, which was already working feverishly to meet deadlines for aircraft modification and psywar-unique equipment acquisition.

One can almost hear the screeching sound of locked brakes and burning rubber as the R&D staff vehicle slammed into the first roadblock. What could the table of organization and equipment (TO&E) possibly look like for a balloon squadron? And, as with everything else at the time, Headquarters Air Force wanted the balloon squadron *now*—1 January 1952 to be exact. With less than four months of planning time prior to the target balloon squadron's activation date, the R&D staff found itself behind the power curve before it even started. On a more positive note, there could hardly be any existing balloon-flying regulations or established bureaucracies to slow them down!

The January 1952 squadron activation date came and went as Headquarters USAF assessed the proposed TO&E submitted by the service. In the meantime, R&D staffers hungry for technical information descended on Holloman AFB, New Mexico. Holloman was home to USAF's Air Research and Development Command (ARDC), then experimenting with high-altitude meteorological research in Project Moby Dick. Not only did the ARDC have information badly needed by the service R&D team, the unclassified Project Moby Dick provided a very useful cover story for the ARCS's highly classified balloon program, which was dubbed Project Reach High.**

Still pressing forward in March without an approved TO&E, the R&D staffers began to clarify the capabilities that the proposed balloon flying squadron needed to accomplish the following mission:

> The squadron would be able to launch 1,840 balloons monthly, carrying a total of 276 tons of cargo (propaganda leaflets). Mobile tactical ground communication sites would be capable of maintaining communications over a large geographic area. To fill the balloons, it had to be capable of generating 1,152,000 cubic feet of hydrogen gas monthly. Each of its eight Flights was to be mobile and self-sufficient under field conditions.[19]

The use of hydrogen was deemed "dangerous but necessary" by the R&D staffers, who proceeded to build as many practical safeguards into the system as feasible. To predict the necessary favorable high-altitude winds, the Air Force's Air Weather Service would augment the squadron with five officers and three airmen. The Airways and Air Communications Service would further augment it with 31 airmen to track the balloons, which could be launched in maximum winds of 12 knots from a 40-by-17-foot trailer dubbed the "Prairie Schooner."

The balloons themselves were to be manufactured by General Mills of Minneapolis, while the University of Minnesota was contracted to provide a three-month-long course for the personnel who were to launch the balloons.[20] Further, OJT would be provided by the squadron once it was activated.

And activated it was on 1 November 1952 as the 1300th ARC Squadron (Special).[21] It was the first (and last) of the Air Force's special operations balloon squadrons. Never destined for operational

*A small handful of these "balloon fire bombs" actually did accomplish their purpose.

**In its public response to at least one highly publicized "crash of an unidentified flying object" (UFO) in New Mexico during the 1950s, the subsequent Air Force investigation concluded that the observers had mistaken the wreckage of a high-altitude weather balloon for that of a UFO. Noting the speed with which USAF security teams blanketed the crash site and removed the debris, the civilian UFO investigators openly challenged the Air Force findings. Could this debris have come from a Project Reach High balloon?

deployment, the squadron nonetheless deserves its hard-earned niche in the history of USAF special operations. If the World War II Air Commando motto "Any place, Any time!" had been remembered during this period, it could perhaps have been expanded to claim "Any place, Any time, Any which way we can!"

Operation Think

By late 1952, it was beginning to look like the Air Force really was going to take the lead Department of Defense role in unconventional warfare. From high-altitude psywar balloons to low-altitude aerial resupply to "blue-suit special forces," the ARCS's hot enthusiasm and three years of experience supporting the CIA appeared to give the Air Force the lead role in DOD psywar/special operations. If such a wide-ranging, wide-open program confirmed the worst fears of General McClure, it seemed that little could be done about it for the moment. And when the Air Force chose another canny Scotsman, Brig Gen Monro MacCloskey, to assume command of the service in September 1952, it must have seemed to the Army that the die had been cast.

USAF

A veteran of special operations flights over Europe during World War II, Brig Gen Monro MacCloskey assumed command of the Air Resupply and Communications Service in September 1952. As its second commander, he inherited a command so controversial that Headquarters USAF could not reach a consensus on how to define its mission, even after the multiwing service had been activated!

General MacCloskey proved to be an inspired choice to command the ARCS. His command of a Carpetbagger squadron in World War II made him one of the few officers in ARCS with previous experience in special operations. And as his performance in the Pentagon would soon demonstrate, he was an articulate and powerful spokesman for the Air Force's most controversial command. All of his formidable skills would be tested immediately upon his assumption of command, as his arrival had been preceded only two months earlier by a Headquarters Air Force decision to drastically cut back on its plans for a psywar force.

Quoting manpower restrictions, the Air Staff announced in the summer of 1952 its intention to cut the planned number of ARC wings from seven to four (three proved to be the final number actually activated). During the same period, Headquarters MATS declared its intent to deactivate the ARC Service, as its primary function of managing the training of subordinate ARC wings could no longer be justified with the deployment of these wings overseas. Such training and facilities still required were to be transferred to the Tactical Air Command (TAC).[22]

General MacCloskey dissented from MATS's view that the training of personnel for deployed ARC wings did not appear to warrant any special arrangement, and he was dubious of the support TAC's "fighter Mafia" would provide ARCS's psywar and aerial resupply missions. He began his own psychological operations campaign in the Pentagon.

Though convinced that the service had a unique contribution to offer the Air Force, he was also enough of a realist to understand that it had to justify its continued existence by first demonstrating that such a unique contribution could come from nowhere else in the Air Force but from ARCS. The air resupply mission could not be quoted as such a contribution, as both MATS and the Air Staff had already cited their position that this mission did not warrant special training or assignment considerations. ARCS's psywar mission, on the other hand, was unique and, better yet, a strong case could be made that it was very much needed to counter Soviet propaganda.

Less than 30 days after taking command of ARCS, the quick-moving general successfully presented his case to the Air Force's deputy chief of staff, operations, with members of the Air Staff's Psychological Warfare Division in attendance. With this renewed support, MacCloskey initiated Operation Think, a program that challenged the imagination of the greatest single psywar resource in the United States government: ARCS's 500-plus thoroughly trained psywar officers. The challenge took form in the development of psywar programs designed to counter the Soviets' own massive and disturbingly successful psywar efforts. During the following five months, two Operation Think programs in particular drew praise for their effectiveness.

The first was "Atom's Evening," a classic cold war propaganda counterstroke to Soviet propaganda. Still not caught up with the US in the development of its own nuclear stockpile, the Soviets attempted to neutralize America's will to use its nuclear advantage by demonizing the Strategic Air Command and its "horror weapons." The ARCS program parried the Soviet move with its own program, stressing that the US would do what it had to do if the Soviets went from cold war to hot war with a frontal assault on Western Europe. Atom's Evening went a long way toward neutralizing the Soviet campaign.

The second program, coined "Troop Indoctrination," recommended that language and regional-area specialists be placed on the staffs of overseas installation commanders to maintain favorable relations between US troops and the foreign populations in which they were living. The psyops program correctly gauged that no amount of US propaganda or public relations would overcome poor behavior by American military personnel in the local communities.

As successful as these Operation Think initiatives proved, Headquarters Air Force could not help but observe that the Air Force was picking up the financial and manpower costs for what were essentially national-level propaganda programs. Gone were the days when the Air Force's psywar proponents held sway for the lead role in DOD's special operations commitment. In April 1953, the Air Staff indicated that "ARCS should confine itself to projects requiring implementation only by the Air Force."[23] The Air Staff guidance effectively signaled the end of its interest in a special operations force at the service command level.

The ARCS experiment had lasted just over three years, coming to a final end with Department of Air Force Letter 322 and General Order 174, issued by the Military Air Transport Service, deactivating the service effective 1 January 1954.[24] But like ripples spreading outward from a stone cast into a pond, the activities of the ARCS's overseas wings had gathered too much momentum to be turned off like a light switch. Three still-active ARC groups were deployed overseas. Not only was the "agency outside the Department of Defense" that had initiated the birth of ARCS still in business, but its need for the Air Force to "provide support services similar to the type that provided covert and overt operations during World War II" had not diminished.

Notes

1. Alfred H. Paddock Jr., *US Army Special Warfare: Its Origins* (Washington, D.C.: National Defense University, 1982), 52.

2. Ibid., 40.

3. Ibid., 89.

4. Ibid., 97.

5. Ibid., 135.

6. History, Air Resupply and Communications Service, 1 July–31 December 1953, pt. 1, "The ARCS Mission and Program," 1.

7. Ibid., 2.

8. Ibid., 4.

9. Ibid., 5.

10. Ibid., 2.

11. Ibid., "Balloon Launching Squadron," 79.

12. Ibid., 117.

13. History, Air Resupply and Communications Service, 1 July–31 December 1951, 115.

14. Ibid.

15. Ibid.

16. Ibid., 116.

17. Ibid., 57.

18. Ibid., 58.

19. Ibid., "Balloon Launching Squadron," 87.

20. Ibid.

21. Ibid., 130.

22. History, Air Resupply and Communications Service, 1 July–31 December 1953, 10–11.

23. Ibid., 20.

24. Ibid., pt. 1, "The ARCS Mission and Program," 1.

The "Cold ARCs" and the Iron Curtain

Libertas per Veritatem! ("Freedom through Truth!") The spirited motto of the 580th Air Resupply and Communications Wing rang out like the challenge to Communist propaganda it was meant to be. Even its emblem seized the spirit: brilliant red, yellow, and blue colors cover a shield mounted with proud horse heads and that universal symbol of peace, a wreath of olive branches. But then there is an odd shadow in this bright picture.

A night pickup in the Caspian Sea, March 1956. Within minutes this 580th SA-16 Albatross crew would learn whether mission security had been maintained . . . or whether they were flying into an ambush.

Steven C. Garst

What are two sinister-looking, all-black airplanes doing in the midst of these gay colors? And why the large sword piercing the very heart of the peace symbol as if to warn that all who abuse the bearers of the olive wreath could suffer "substantial penalties"?

To the 580th ARC Wing went the honor of being the first ARC wing. Activated on 15 March 1951, less than 60 days after the activation of the Air Resupply and Communications Service itself, it was a unit hustling to catch up before the race ever started. And as all pioneers in every new endeavor learn, breaking a new trail is tough on the good days and downright dangerous on the bad ones. The tough part started early as the advance group of the 580th arrived at Mountain Home AFB, Idaho, only to discover that the base had been essentially abandoned since the close of World War II. Tumbleweeds were stacked to the top of many maintenance buildings and barracks . . . inside the buildings!

Another major problem afflicting the 580th in the early days was that the sudden influx of personnel into Mountain Home outpaced the arrival of the equipment necessary for them to perform their jobs. A lack of tools for aircraft maintenance, printing machines for leaflet reproduction, and even radios for the communications squadron plagued all efforts to get the wing up and running. Perhaps remembering the cliché "Idle hands are the devil's workshop," the 580th's first commander, Col William O. Eareckson, came up with a creative and useful, if decidedly unpleasant, idea to keep the troops busy: a rugged survival school complete with escape and evasion (E&E) and interrogation phases.

The 580th even managed to secure the loan of Maj John Fillingham from the British army as a "survival adviser" for its school. Although archival references to the major are unfailingly polite, they do describe Fillingham as "an authority on the subject." Any reader familiar with the British army's enthusiasm for realistic field training will know that Fillingham's survival course earned its name the hard way.

In November 1951, the 580th got both an overseas deployment notice (to Wheelus Air Base, Libya) and a new wing commander to take them there. Col John R. Kane had won the Medal of Honor in one of World War II's legendary brawls, the low-level bombing AAF by heavy bombers of the Ploesti oil refineries in Nazi-occupied Romania. The 580th airmen were probably less thrilled to learn what else their new commander won at Ploesti—the nickname "Killer."

Hustling as usual to make another short-notice deadline, the 580th had by early December moved the bulk of its squadrons to Camp Kilmer, New Jersey, and its aircraft echelon to Westover AFB, Massachusetts. Tearful good-byes had already been made to families now far away, mountains of gear had been stored in containers at the ports, and flight plans had been drawn up. The big adventure was about to start!

Then, without warning, the balloon burst. The deployment orders were canceled, citing "political unrest in North Africa" as the reason. The truth was more sinister,* but it was not for public release even to the 580th as new orders were issued: return to Mountain Home and continue training. Staff officers could hardly believe their eyes as they read the orders. The morale of the officers and airmen anxiously waiting in the drab

*The former commander of the 580th's Holding and Briefing Squadron recounted to the author another explanation given to him at the time by friends in the CIA. Six months prior to the 580th's scheduled deployment, two British intelligence officers, Donald MacLean and Guy Burgess, stunned England with their defection to the Soviet Union. MacLean had been receiving classified reports of American intelligence plans from his friend Kim Philby, then England's senior intelligence liaison officer to the CIA. The subsequent CIA damage assessment estimate reportedly concluded that the 580th's links to the CIA (of which Philby had been informed) had almost certainly been exposed. The deployment was put on indefinite hold pending further investigation. Years later, Philby himself was found to be a Soviet spy.

embarkation barracks turned as dark as the New Jersey winter nights. Keeping a stiff upper lip, the 580th historian wrote that

> the morale of the troops took a sharp drop at the word of the return, because—in the minds of most of the personnel—Mountain Home in the winter was not the most desirable place in the world to be.[1]

Using its own aircraft to return its personnel to Mountain Home, the 580th directed all flyable aircraft to proceed through blinding snowstorms and icy runways afflicting the East Coast to complete the airlift back to Idaho. Remarkably, no accidents occurred. While most of the wing resumed training in "not the most desirable place in the world to be," those with language specialties went elsewhere.

In January 1952, the 580th sent nine officers to New York City for 75 days of on-the-job training in propaganda dissemination at the US government's Voice of America (VOA) radio station.[2] This original group was later augmented by 13 other graduates of the Georgetown University program, who likewise delivered VOA's foreign-language broadcasts into Communist-controlled Eastern Europe. A list of the tongues spoken by the 580th's foreign-language specialists clearly indicates the wing's wartime area of operations. They included Armenian, French, German, Greek, Italian, Lithuanian, Spanish, Tatar, and Turkish.[3] Seven months more would pass before the foreign-language specialists would get the chance to practice their proficiency closer to their target areas.

January 1952 was also of note for a bizarre event happening a long way from the bright lights of New York City's VOA offices. During a night training mission over southern California's Death Valley, one of the 580th's twin-engined Albatrosses encountered a combination of bad weather and even worse luck. With the Albatross steadily and involuntarily descending due to severe icing conditions and the subsequent loss of one engine, the crew made the prudent decision to bail out before the aircraft collided with something much harder than ice.

Alas, as if pouting from the departure of its "fair-weather friends," the now-pilotless SA-16 continued its flight in a descending but still-controlled manner. It eventually crash-landed on its own accord in a manner that would have likely resulted in light injuries at worst had its crew stayed on board with their hands off the controls. *C'est la vie!*

Blue Suits, Green Berets, Hidden Faces

As the first of the air resupply and communications wings to be established, the 580th frequently found its activities the center of debate in the acrimonious Army-Air Force-CIA bureaucratic struggle for "ownership" of the nation's unconventional warfare mission. This proved especially true for the Holding and Briefing Squadron, which, despite its bland name, put Air Force officers in roles nearly identical to those claimed by the Army's Special Forces and the USI's guerrilla warfare specialists.

Air support for unconventional warfare was one thing, but the 580th's Specialized Warfare Course for its H&B officers was breathtaking in its brashness. Not only was the Air Force seemingly going for a piece of the "ground action" of the unconventional-warfare mission, it was actually going to its bureaucratic antagonists in this competition (the Army and USI) for the training necessary to accomplish this goal!

This was the bureaucratic turf battle ongoing in Washington when Maj Edward Joseph reported to Mountain Home AFB in the summer of 1951 for his yet-to-be-determined assignment in the 580th. With two heavy-bomber combat tours in the Pacific in World War II under his belt, he had every

Edward B Joseph

The USI compound at Fort Benning, Georgia, was known simply as Training Center One. Air Force and Army unconventional warfare specialists as well as intelligence personnel were housed here in the early 1950s while undergoing various phases of parachute, weapons, demolitions, and tactics training.

reason to believe another flying tour lay ahead or perhaps a staff position following his completion of the demanding psywar course at Georgetown University. It didn't exactly work out that way.

The 6'5" former captain of his Columbia University wrestling team got his first clue regarding the 580th's plans for him when he discovered one of his in-processing interviewers was from USI. Shortly thereafter, he received the news that he had been selected for command of the H&B Squadron and, in the process, was designated as one of the small handful of Georgetown graduates selected for the Specialized Warfare Course at Fort Benning, Georgia. Stage 3 training was to be quite an eye-opener.

The USI compound at Fort Benning, designated "Training Center One" (TC-One), had buildings that were used as hospitals in earlier days. In addition to intelligence personnel, TC-One housed Air Force H&B officers who were also undergoing unconventional-warfare training by a cadre of Green Beret instructors housed elsewhere on the post. During the morning, both USI and H&B officers attended parachute training at Benning's well-known jump school. In the afternoon and evening, they returned to TC-One for Special Forces and USI training in weapons, demolitions, communications, and guerrilla warfare tactics.

The training was intensive because H&B officers were expected to provide similar training to the guerrillas they were "holding and briefing." For example, ARCS Individual Training Standard 50-2-2, dated 15 January 1952, demanded that H&B officers be proficient in:

(1) the instruction of light machine guns, heavy machine guns, rifles, carbines, pistols, mortars, bazookas, recoilless weapons, and grenades;

(2) the instruction of demolition procedures and field expedients used in demolition activities;

(3) performing the duties of an aerial delivery technician (jumpmaster); and

(4) performing duties as members of a reception committee and as parachutist members of a reception committee when qualified.[4]

Edward B Joseph

Guard duty at the "front gate" to the 580th's section at Wheelus Air Base, Libya. The view didn't get much better farther down the road.

It was a tough selection process, especially when one remembers that only 5 percent of the graduates of both the Georgetown University (stage 1) and Mountain Home (stage 2) psywar training were selected for the Specialized Warfare Course (stage 3).

Six months later, the 580th finally started its long-awaited trip to North Africa. Surface echelons sailed in July and September aboard the US Navy Ship (USNS) *General R.E. Callen* and USNS *General Hodges*, respectively. The B-29s departed Westover with a refueling stop in the mid-Atlantic Azores Islands before proceeding on to Wheelus AB, Libya. The shorter-range C-119s and SA-16s departed Westover with flight plans that took them to Iceland, England, and Italy before the final leg into Wheelus. With the movement also came a change in the wing's reporting channels as the 580th ARC Wing left the jurisdiction of the ARCS for that of an overseas theater command.

This photo, never destined for an Air Force recruiting poster, shows the 580th's early living quarters at Wheelus Air Base. "Garden City," as it was dubbed, drew mixed reviews from a group that had earlier cleared out stacks of tumbleweeds a story high from inside their wooden barracks at Mountain Home AFB, Idaho.

Setting up their operation from scratch at the far end of Wheelus, members of the 580th once again found themselves in "rustic" surroundings that must have made some of them regret bad-mouthing their experiences in Idaho. It was "tent city" for the first group, and it would stay that way for months. By this time, however, the Mountain Home-toughened veterans were indeed living proof of the old pioneer adage "The cowards never started and the weak died along the way." It was just as well they landed ready because Killer Kane was anxious to move forward with some very definite ideas on the direction the 580th should take.

And the first direction the wing commander took his B-29 bombers was *down*. During the 1943 Ploesti mission, Kane and the other bomber commanders had taken their B-24 heavy bombers to the target in formation at *500 feet*. On flights out over the Mediterranean Sea, Kane now determined to show his B-29 pilots they could do as well or better. Veterans of these hair-raising flights

Edward B. Joseph

report that the huge bombers were flying so low over the sea that their propeller blasts were leaving "rooster tails" in the water behind them!

Flying low-level missions in the pitch-black nights over North Africa's deserts put the B-29s at a more practical, but still dangerous, altitude of 500 feet. The bomber was equipped with the HTR-13 obstruction-warning radar developed expressly for such missions. However, the operative word here is *warning*. Unlike the more advanced systems of the future, this system did not take control of the aircraft to raise it above terrain obstacles in its flight path. In the desolate Libyan deserts during the mid-1950s, the HTR-13 could only warn the pilot to pull up or to mark the spot where the aircraft would collide with the ground. Indeed, it happened in January 1954 when a B-29 impacted the ground at cruise speed on just such a low-level mission.

Regardless of such tragedies, the 580th had little option but to continue training with its Army "cousins" in Europe—usually the Army's 10th

Green Berets from the 10th Special Forces Group parachute from the bomb bay of a 580th B-29 onto the Libyan desert. Special Forces and other unconventional warfare specialists frequently trained with the 580th.

This excellent photo of the busy 580th ramp at Wheelus Air Base, Libya, shows three types of aircraft flown by the ARC wings.

Carl Bernhard

Special Forces Group (Airborne), based in Germany's magnificent Bavarian Alps, although the 10th routinely came to Libya for parachute and desert survival training with the 580th's squadrons. To accurately mark the drop zone for the Green Berets, the B-29 navigator sitting in the bomber's Plexiglas nose would use the famous Norden bombsight developed during World War II. Fortunately for the paratroopers, the sight proved equally effective for bodies as well as bombs, even at 1,000-foot jump altitudes.

As useful as this training was, the 580th would not be allowed to forget it was only a means to an end. And the "end" for this mission would inevitably take place behind the Iron Curtain.

The SA-16s' "Silent Successes"

Like most of nature's amphibians, the SA-16 Albatross was a creature that excelled in neither land nor water environments. Its real value lay in its ability to function in both environments. And for a special operations unit that could hardly expect access to established airfields in Soviet-controlled territory, the rugged SA-16 made every lake, river, and inland sea a possible landing site. And there was always the possibility that the 580th would be called upon to exploit that capability.

The sturdy Albatross cruised at 140 knots and could stay aloft for up to 16 hours with maximum allowable fuel. In this configuration, even its wing-mounted floats held fuel (200 gallons in each float). Unquestionably the most versatile aircraft in the ARC wings, the SA-16 could carry Special Forces teams to every conceivable location on land and water, day or night.

Shortly after its arrival in Libya, the 580th got another bonus with the arrival of four spanking-new SA-16s from the Grumman factory in Long Island, New York. "Someone" had obviously put the highest priority on the order, as all four SA-16s had sequential tail numbers (17252, -3, -4, and -5) right off the production line. Perhaps not wanting to look a gift horse in the mouth, the happy SA-16 pilots didn't stop to question why they had suddenly become so important.

With new aircraft, the SA-16 flight began flying classified courier missions involving both material and personnel throughout the Mediterranean, southwest Asia, and southern Europe. The flight's versatility was becoming more apparent every month, and the crews went where the action was. The action came in many different guises and so did the official explanation for these seemingly routine flights. For some special flights, however, there would be no explanation of any sort. There couldn't be, because as far as the US government was concerned, these flights never happened.

In late 1955, an SA-16 pilot from the 580th reported to the US Embassy in Athens, Greece, for a most unusual mission briefing. The stranger in civilian clothes didn't bother to identify himself, and the pilot wasn't foolish enough to press the point. This mission called for a night, low-level infiltration behind Stalin's Iron Curtain into the area of the Balkans where the borders of Yugoslavia, Bulgaria, and Greece meet. Once there, the aircraft would make a clandestine landing in the darkness on a lake from which three individuals would be extracted and returned to Greece.

This type of mission would be recognized as a success only if it was followed by total public silence. Failure, on the other hand, would lead to an embarrassed American president attempting to explain to the world media what one of our aircraft—not just any aircraft, but a special operations amphibian—was doing on the wrong side of the Iron Curtain. That night no words were exchanged between the aircrew and the trio when the men were pulled into the aircraft or again when they were delivered to Greece. The SA-16 and its crew returned to Wheelus at dawn, and the dark curtain of secrecy silently closed behind them.

Kenneth L. Shook

The rugged and versatile SA-16 Albatross amphibian could land on crude dirt strips as well as on rivers and lakes, day or night . . . on either side of Stalin's Iron Curtain.

The curtain wouldn't stay closed for long. When it opened again, the "show" started with distress signals from an operation so sensitive at the time that officially it didn't even exist. Unlike the carefully planned, discreetly executed Balkans extraction, this mission urgently demanded an immediate, open-sea rescue mission of a national asset in broad daylight. Despite these differences, this mission did have one critical factor in common with the Balkans job: it had to be pulled off without anyone even knowing it had happened. It wasn't the rescue of a pilot in distress that caused the problem. Rather it was what he was flying and, more important, where he was coming from.

The high-altitude, all-black U-2 "weather reconnaissance" jet was in trouble as it glided down from the ink-blue stratosphere without a sound. With its usually reliable (and only) engine flamed out, the U-2 could continue its silent westbound glide beyond the Albanian coastline and the Iron Curtain . . . but not far enough to cross the Adriatic Sea to reach a friendly airfield in Italy. Time was growing shorter by the minute, and a very wet destination awaited the U-2. The Adriatic Sea would therefore provide the stage for a drama in which the twin curtains of secrecy protecting special operations and strategic reconnaissance would either open and close silently . . . or open to a Soviet-orchestrated media frenzy condemning the "US aggression against the peace-loving Socialist countries of the world."

As the U-2 ditched in the sea, the 580th was there with its trusty Albatross, exactly where and when it was needed. Mission accomplished, the special operations crew returned the pilot to safety and themselves to the most flattering compliment they could (and would) receive—total silence.

If "Freedom through Truth" was the 580th's official motto, its growing reputation for discreet performance in the Mediterranean might better have been described with another motto: "Silent Success." Whatever the motto, the demand for silent success continued, as the 580th discovered in March 1956 when another of its SA-16 pilots sat before another civilian-clothed individual in another US Embassy a long way from Libya. This embassy was in Tehran, Iran, and it was in this mile-high city in Persia that he learned for the first time what he and his crew had been training for during the previous month. It was a mission that would take the Albatross north into still higher latitudes . . . right through the Iron Curtain for a night rendezvous in the Caspian Sea.

This was to be another extraction mission: this time that of a man, a woman, and two children. Prior to their departure from Tehran's Mehrabad Airport, the SA-16 crew followed standard procedures by filing a night flight plan that had several legs. Of course, all legs would be reported in stages at the expected times to the local flight-tracking facilities. First flying a deceptive outbound heading from Tehran at a radar-observable altitude, the crew then descended below radar detection and turned north for a night rendezvous at sea they could only hope was not a trap. Such things had happened before.

Crossing the northern Iranian border into Soviet airspace, the crew continued north, proceeding far over the Caspian before sighting a trawler near the designated position. Exchanging silent, coded light signals with the boat, the SA-16 began its descent to the black waters below.

Blacked-out night water landings in the SA-16 were essentially an instrument approach to impact with the surface. They were also a superb infiltration tactic when combined with the highly trained US Special Forces teams.

Kenneth L Shook

USAF

The Airborne Materials Assembly (AMA) Squadron stored thousands of Communist-bloc and US weapons for aerial delivery behind the Iron Curtain. Rations were also stored after first having their English language labels removed and replaced with the language spoken in the country for which the rations were destined.

When the radar navigator called "50 feet," the pilot raised the nose of the aircraft to impact angle, and the Albatross touched down in the sea for a perfect landing. That's the way it was for night, "lights-out" water landings, which in essence were nothing more than an instrument approach to impact.

Having made it thus far, the Albatross taxied close to the darkened boat. Was this rendezvous a double-cross such as that set for the ill-fated CIA airmen who had attempted a night extraction mission in Manchuria during the Korean War? The only two survivors of that crew were still in Chinese prisons.

This time it went according to plan. The family loaded silently aboard the SA-16, and the amphibian became airborne without further delay. With the radio operator faithfully reporting timely and sometimes bogus positions, the 580th aircrew flew back to the Mediterranean Sea for yet another night rendezvous with a boat at sea. Again the coded signals and a subsequent water landing to transfer the family to another dark boat on another dark sea.[5]

The following duty day at Wheelus was pretty much like the one before it. And why not? It was just as hot, just as boring, and besides, nothing had happened.

From H&B to AMA

The H&B Squadron had deployed to Libya with the rest of the wing in the summer and fall of 1952 and soon began working closely with the Green Berets stationed in Germany. The Army

Special Forces troopers would frequently come to Wheelus for joint weapons and demolition training, as well as for the previously mentioned desert survival training in the barren wastelands south of the airfield. Other anonymous individuals from USI would also attend these training sessions before moving on to places and missions of no concern to the H&B trainers or Major Joseph. The major was, however, destined to be privy to the secrets of another unit within the 580th, one that warranted barbed wire fences and 24-hour-a-day security to provide the needed privacy.

When Major Joseph assumed command of the 580th Airborne Materials Assembly Squadron in 1954, he discovered the true logistical power inherent in an ARC wing. Like his old H&B Squadron, the AMA Squadron was far more active than its innocuous title would suggest. Rigging parachutes and preparing nonstandard-sized bundles for parachute drop were routine activities, but it was what went into the bundles that told the true story of the AMA.

Stored in the AMA warehouses were thousands of Communist-bloc small arms weapons, waiting for the day they would be packed and "para-dropped" behind the Iron Curtain to anti-Communist partisans. Purchased on the international arms market, there was no way they could be traced even should anyone bother to try. All had been stripped down, cleaned, and test fired by AMA armorers before being stacked for future shipment.

In addition to the weapons, field rations had been purchased for delivery to resistance movements present or anticipated in Communist-controlled territories. Unlike the Communist-made weapons whose source was self-evident, the rations had to be "sterilized" to hide their origin. Each individual item had its English-language label removed and replaced by a description of the same item in the language of the country for

USAF

These 580th AMA riggers are customizing packages for airdrop. Packing nonstandard-sized bundles for parachute drop was just one of the AMA's specialties.

which it was intended. Both weapons and rations packaging did have one thing in common, however, and that was the unique manner in which they were packed for long-term storage.

"Seal and peel" was a technique developed specifically to protect AMA's weapons and rations from every conceivable combination of weather. The process was as simple as it was effective. For example, a Soviet-built assault rifle and extra magazines of 7.62 mm ammunition were tightly wrapped in cloth, then briefly dunked into a liquid solution, and retrieved. Within minutes the cloth bundle would harden to a tough, quarter-inch thick, brown-colored plastic shell that would protect the contents even if submerged in salt water. Shipments of both weapons and rations were exported in this configuration to various "customers" on a number of occasions.

In addition to AMA personnel, USI maintained a liaison office within the protected compound to ensure a prompt response to its own needs in the region. The integration of its people into the 580th's airlift and logistical system gave the US the capability to support a range of both military and USI special operations across vast distances while still maintaining the low profile that was mandatory for success in a high-stakes competition neither Washington nor Moscow were anxious to publicize.

In September 1953, Headquarters Air Force reduced its three ARC wings from wing to group size, losing in the process their capability to produce psywar materials (the Reproduction Squadron), direct support (the Holding and Briefing Squadron), and long-range communications (the Communications Squadron) to Army and USI guerrilla forces in the field. Other than a small group headquarters, only the flying squadron and, significantly, the multipurpose AMA Squadron remained in the groups. Despite this reduction in capability, the 580th Air Resupply Group remained active for the remaining 36 months of its existence primarily through its support of the Army Special Forces in Germany.

General Order 37, Headquarters Seventeenth Air Force, dated 12 October 1956, ordered the deactivation of the 580th Air Resupply Group at its home base in Libya. With minimal fanfare, its personnel and remaining aircraft were transferred to other duties and bases. Appropriately, the 580th left town in much the same manner it had flown its silent-success missions behind the Iron Curtain.

The Last of the Breed

To the 582d ARC Wing goes the honor of being the last of the breed. Activated on 24 September 1952 at Mountain Home AFB, the 582d carried the scarlet and gold colors of the ARC "stable." The wing was fortunate in that its first commander, Col Robert W. Fish, was a Carpetbagger veteran of special operations flights into occupied Europe during World War II. Before it could deploy overseas, however, it, along with the other two ARC wings already deployed, was downsized to group status in September 1953.* The reduction took authorized strength levels down from 1,200 overall to 137 officers and 463 airmen.

As with the 580th ARC Wing, the reduction in size from wing to group took place despite a substantial increase in ARC support to the Army's Special Forces units. In fact, the downsizing took place during the same period in which the 582d was providing around-the-clock support to stateside-based elements of the 10th Special Forces Group during Exercise Cleo, a massive, joint-service unconventional warfare exercise conducted in

* Concurrent with this downsizing was the deactivation in Washington, D.C., of the Air Resupply and Communications Service headquarters itself.

Georgia's Chattahoochee National Forest. During Cleo, the 582d's B-29s, SA-16s, and C-119s parachuted over 600 personnel and nearly 300 containers for a combined total of over 1,000 tons of airdrop support.

Like the other ARC wings, the 582d was initially assigned 12 B-29s, four C-119s, and four SA-16s. With the reduction to group status, its initial requirement for four helicopters was dropped for good. In February 1954, the 582d Air Resupply Group deployed these aircraft along with its Air Materials Assembly Squadron and support staff to RAF Molesworth, their operational base in England.[6] With this deployment, control of the group was transferred from the Military Air Transport Service* to Third Air Force, itself based in England.

From RAF Molesworth, the 582d provided the bulk of air support given to the 10th Special Forces Group following the latter's complete transfer from Fort Bragg, North Carolina, to Bad Tolz, Germany. Night flying was emphasized as usual to include amphibious training with the reliable SA-16. But the ARC "experiment" was clearly winding down in the face of tighter defense budgets, the costly expansion of the Strategic Air Command within USAF, and the eventual Defense Department decision to give the Army the bulk of the unconventional warfare mission.

Third Air Force General Order 86, dated 18 October 1956, deactivated the 582d Air Resupply Group effective 25 October of the same year.[7] With its deactivation (and that of the other two ARC groups), USAF further distanced itself from peacetime involvement in unconventional warfare. From the seven ARC wings envisioned in 1951, only three had been activated and, as has been seen, all three were subsequently reduced to airlift support-only groups in less than 36 months. The end of an era had come . . . or had it?

The "last of the breed," the 582d Air Resupply Group also provided unconventional air warfare support to the 10th Special Forces Group based in Germany's Bavarian Alps.

The month before the 582d was deactivated, another unit was activated at RAF Molesworth with little fanfare. Oddly enough, it had two of the same aircraft types flown by the 582d, with two flights of C-119s and one of SA-16s; long-range C-54 four-engined transports later replaced the C-119s. The new unit was designated the 42d Troop Carrier Squadron (Medium) (Special). Personnel attached to the 580th's AMA Squadron at Wheelus when both groups (580th and 582d) were deactivated soon began arriving at Molesworth to continue doing what they did best with the 42d. Even so, a small detachment of AMA specialists remained active at Wheelus.

*MATS had taken over the headquarters supervision of the 582d, the only ARC unit remaining in the continental US following deactivation of the Air Resupply and Communications Service.

Jack Wheeler

These 10th Special Forces troopers sit in the bomb bay of a special operations B-29 en route to a drop zone in the mid-1950s. Note the original Special Forces patch on the officer's left sleeve.

On the other side of the world, much of the same was going on at the 581st's final base on Okinawa, where the Air Force activated the 317th Troop Carrier Squadron (Medium) (Special). Oddly enough again, the operational activities of these two squadrons are almost totally ignored in official USAF archives.

But could two troop carrier squadrons adequately take up the special operations load formerly carried by three group-sized ARC units? Apparently some thought not. And the unknown "they" had taken the precaution to look elsewhere once the US Air Force made known its intentions to deactivate the active duty ARC groups. That

USAF

Activated at RAF Molesworth just before the deactivation of the 582d Air Resupply Group in 1956, the mysterious 42d Troop Carrier Squadron (Medium)(Special) continued to make good use of the C-119 (and the SA-16) to support the Army's Special Forces. A similar squadron was activated on Okinawa just before the 581st ARG was deactivated.

"elsewhere" turned out to be right back at the Pentagon, in the offices of the Air National Guard. And by late 1955, the tangible results of that precaution could be found on the runways of Air Guard bases in California, West Virginia, Maryland, and Rhode Island.

Notes

1. History, 580th ARC Wing and 580th ARC Group, 1 November–31 December 1951, 1.

2. History, 580th Holding and Briefing Squadron, 1 January–29 February 1952, 13–14.

3. Ibid., 29.

4. Document in author's possession from interview with Col Edward B. Joseph, 18 September 1995, Arlington, Va.

5. Maj Ken Shook, USAF, Retired, interview with author, 8 August 1995, Tempe, Ariz.

6. History, 582d ARC Wing, 1 January–30 June 1953.

7. History, 582d Air Resupply Group, 1 July–25 October 1956, 1.

"En Garde!"

The Guard Gets the Nod

By 1954, Air Force plans to phase out the remaining three active duty air resupply groups by 1956 brought Headquarters USAF face-to-face with the same thorny question it had attempted to answer in 1950: who will provide air support for military and CIA unconventional warfare forces in the event of war? While Air Force enthusiasm for special operations had clearly waned, the potential for the cold war to suddenly turn hot clearly had *not*. At a minimum, a low-cost cadre of aircrews and aircraft had to be maintained somewhere by someone. But where, and by whom?

A year later, the answers to these questions became evident following a complex series of interdepartmental meetings in Washington, D.C., and several state capitals. In the end, the Air National Guard in California, West Virginia, Maryland, and Rhode Island agreed to activate air resupply groups to train for the Air Force's wartime unconventional warfare mission. Despite this state-federal agreement, however, the sensitive nature of the ARG mission was deliberately downplayed within the states themselves for quite some time.

In the absence of an active duty force, the decision to go to the Air Guard had one great advantage in its favor. Unlike the never-ending personnel rotations that characterize the active forces, Air Guard personnel frequently spend their entire careers flying and maintaining the same aircraft. The overwhelming advantage of such continuity has been frequently demonstrated in tactical competitions in which air guardsmen outperform their active duty contemporaries. This experience proved doubly fortunate as no concerted effort seems to have been made to channel ARG personnel leaving active duty into these new Air Guard units.

From 1955 to 1970, the Air National Guard's unconventional warfare units in California, West Virginia, Maryland, and Rhode Island were designated Air Resupply, Troop Carrier, Air Commando, and finally, Special Operations Groups. Regardless of the titles, the air guardsmen were for many years the primary special operations asset of the US Air Force.

In California, the 129th Air Resupply Group was formed in April 1955, and the 130th ARG was activated in West Virginia that October. Maryland activated its 135th ARG two months earlier, and Rhode Island activated its 143d ARG in November of the same year. Concurrent with the establishment of the four ARGs came the obvious issue of what aircraft would be selected for them.

Initially all four state ARGs were equipped with both the C-46 Commando and the SA-16 Albatross. While the C-46s were phased out within the first years, the versatile Albatross amphibian continued to become the standard workhorse for the Air Force's unconventional air warfare missions. The standardization of one type of aircraft within the ARGs further simplified operational and maintenance programs, which in turn expedited the pace at which the guardsmen could hone the necessary skills for their new mission.

While the pace at which the ARGs grew tactically proficient varied slightly from state to state, the substantial personnel experience levels alluded to earlier kept the overall program to a fairly uniform and high operational standard. The experiences of Rhode Island's 143d Air Resupply Group are typical of what all four states went through. They provide an interesting insight into the events that occurred the first time the Air National Guard became involved in the unique world of special operations.

When the Rhode Island Air National Guard (RIANG) activated the 143d ARG, it truly took a step into the unknown. Prior to the activation, the state's flying experience had been limited to its 152d Fighter Squadron, which, as events were shortly to prove, provided the bulk of the man-

143d RIANG

This black SA-16 of the 143d Rhode Island Air National Guard is seen at Marana Air Park, Arizona, in 1964 during Operation Sidewinder, a rare opportunity for the Air Guard special operators from four states to train together . . . under the watchful eyes of the intelligence community, which maintained a strong interest in their proficiency.

power for the new ARG.* The new group consisted of a group headquarters, as well as the airborne materials assembly and air resupply squadrons. Within the first year, another reorganization would occur that would streamline the group functions into a single air resupply squadron.**

A change of this nature in the nation's smallest state could hardly go unnoticed, and indeed local newspaper articles of the day provided considerable coverage of the new unit. Feeder stories from the RIANG Public Affairs Office describe the air resupply mission simply as considerable but not totally accurate in terms of "providing air transportation for airborne forces" and "long-range movement of personnel." In contrast to the public posture, an undated 143d ARG briefing of this early period, given to Rhode Island's adjutant general, tersely notes, "The mission of this unit is classified and will be explained in detail at a later time."

The mission was, of course, identical to that of the active duty ARGs the guardsmen were replacing—unconventional and psychological warfare. With the organization established and the aircraft coming in, the most pressing question quickly turned to the subject of training. Single-ship, low-level flying in and out of remote airstrips both day and night, not to mention water operations, were a long stretch for a group of fighter pilots used to high-altitude, daytime formation flying. There was, however, an agency that could provide the necessary training for unconventional air warfare training at a place called simply "The Farm."

Shortly after the 143d came together, an operations officer from the group staff, as well as the flying squadron's commander, operations officer, and intelligence officer, received orders to report to a USI training facility in Virginia, about an hour's flying time south of Washington, D.C. For

* Similar transitions were taking place in other states.

** This reorganization distinguished the RIANG from the other three states, which maintained their air resupply units at group strength.

143d RIANG

The Air Guard pioneered the use of floats on the U-10 Helio Courier, a versatile and rugged liaison aircraft found in all four Air Guard special operations groups. In a pinch, the use of fire-retarding foam on dirt airstrips could provide expedient but safe takeoff and landing strips for the float-mounted U-10s.

the next two weeks they underwent an intensive training course in the skills necessary to fly and survive behind enemy lines.* Having completed the training, this cadre returned to Rhode Island to pass on their knowledge to their aircrews.

In the ensuing years, the guardsmen would learn that while their mission would remain essentially unchanged, little else would remain static in their organizations. The C-46s were largely phased out by 1958, the same year in which units from the four states underwent name changes that converted the air resupply units to troop carrier groups.** In 1963, all units were designated Air Commando Groups, following the revival of the active duty

* Records from West Virginia's 130th ARG indicate USAF active duty special operators based in Okinawa and England were also brought back to train some Air Guard ARGs.

** Initially designated the 143d Troop Carrier Squadron (Medium), the 143d grew to group status by 1962. The following year, it was redesignated yet again as the 143d Air Commando Squadron/Group.

Air Commando force at Hurlburt Field, Florida. Five years later, in still another name change, both active and Guard units became special operations squadrons/groups/wings.

If organizational titles were fluid, the arrival of additional types of aircraft also added versatility to the Air Guard's special operations capabilities. All units began picking up the new U-10 Helio Courier, a single-engined, short takeoff and landing (STOL) liaison-type aircraft ideally suited for remote area operations. Both the California and West Virginia units received the big C-119 Flying Boxcars to replace their C-46s. In the absence of active duty special operations forces in the late 1950s, all USAF expertise in this field clearly belonged to the Guard. It was a reality that provided the West Virginia's 130th an unusual opportunity throughout 1960–61.

During these two years, the West Virginians were tasked through Tactical Air Command to assist in the training of USAF's highly classified Jungle Jim program, the active duty precursor to the 1st Air Commando Wing and Special Air Warfare Center (SAWC) at Eglin AFB, Florida. It was quite a turnaround for the Guard, which normally found itself downstream of Air Force

Bizarre looking but ultimately proven effective, this "second generation" air-to-ground recovery system was developed by Robert Fulton Jr. for the US Navy, Air Force, and Intermountain Air, a CIA-proprietary airline operating at Marana Air Park, Arizona, during the 1960s.

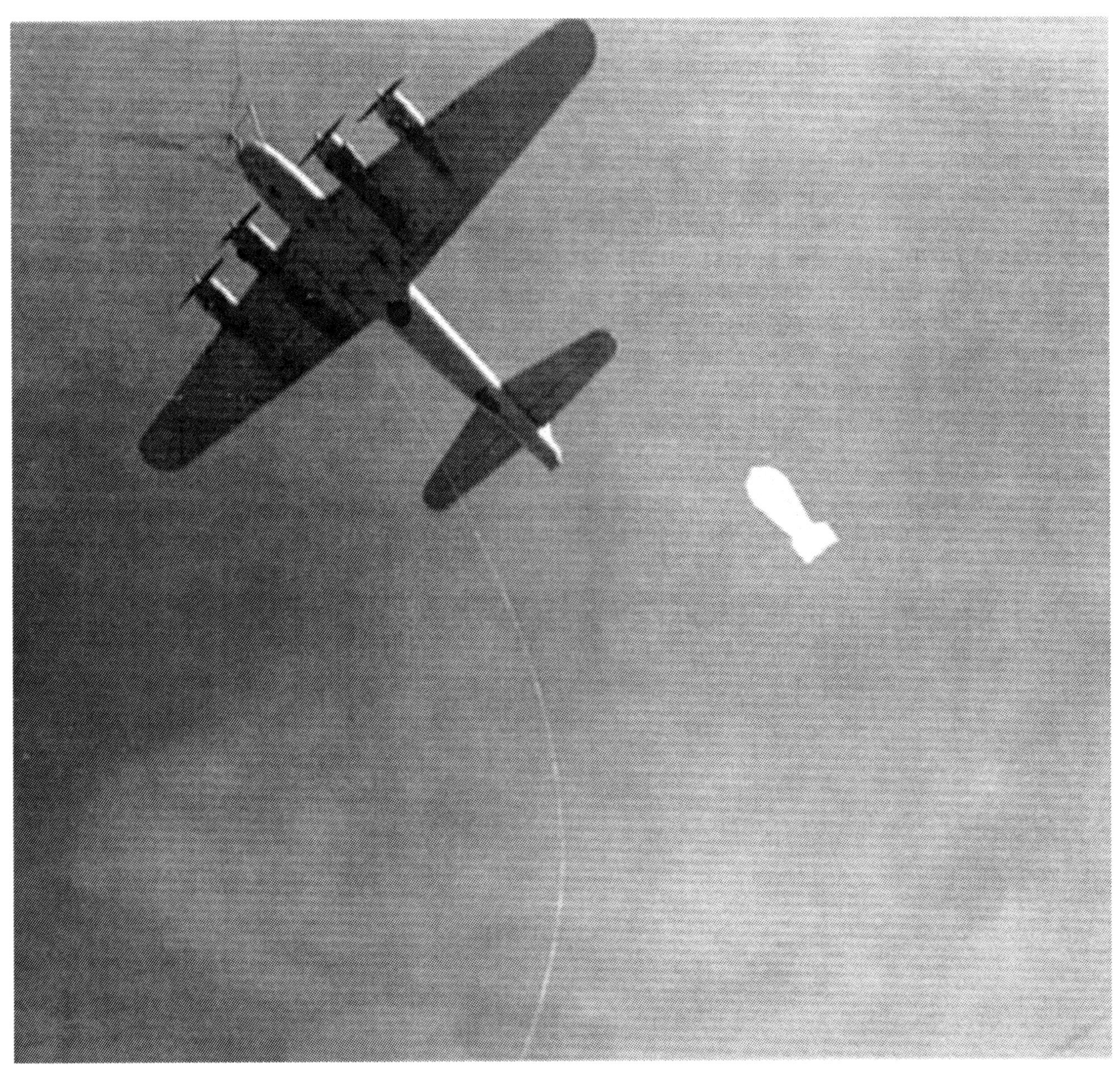

143d RIANG

A moment after the B-17's nose-mounted "fork" engages the cable, the balloon is cut free, permitting the individual tethered to the cable (while sitting on the ground) to be winched into the aircraft. Early efforts didn't always work out that way. In one spectacular, "confidence building" demonstration to a group of pilots, the mannequin hit the ground twice after liftoff before being dragged into nearby high-tension wires, setting off a huge display of sparks and cutting power to parts of the base!

priorities for equipment and training. It was also a nice payback for the faith invested in the Guard during the lean years when all USAF's "special operations eggs" were placed in the Guard "basket."

In the spring of 1964, all four Air Commando Groups came together for a rare opportunity to train during Operation Sidewinder. The training site itself was appropriate in that Marana Air Park, located 20 miles northwest of Tucson,

Arizona, was home to a number of USI proprietary airlines, as well as other unrelated federal departments. While little was said directly to the guardsmen, the presence of civilian strangers observing their mission briefings and flight performance made it clear their proficiency was being monitored. It was also at Marana that the Guard was introduced to the latest evolution in air-to-ground recovery systems, a weird-looking setup patriotically called the "All-American System."

Unlike the Korean War "snatch system" that used a tailhook at the rear of the aircraft to grab a wire attached to the "extractee" on the ground, the All-American System used a Y-shaped fork arrangement mounted on the nose of the aircraft to snare a cable leading from the individual on the ground to a balloon floating a couple of hundred feet above. When the nose-mounted fork engaged the balloon cable, the balloon broke away, and the extracted individual sailed away safely from the ground to be reeled into the aircraft by winch a few minutes later.

At least that was the plan. Like the early Korean War efforts, this second-generation pickup system generated its share of hair-raising moments for aircrews who found their plane entangled in cables and bits of balloon when things went wrong. In one spectacular demonstration to a crowd of spectators, the mannequin extractee rose into the air following cable engagement, only to be smashed back into the ground twice before being hauled through nearby high-tension electrical wires in a shower of sparks, knocking out power to parts of the base!

If Operation Sidewinder proved a useful opportunity for the four units to demonstrate their special operations skills together, other opportunities to train overseas came to the Guard units individually. In the 1960s, South and Central America beckoned, and Panama in particular provided an excellent training site. Unconventional warfare training, psychological warfare leaflet drops, and even jungle-survival school were on the curriculum for the guardsmen operating in the Canal Zone. In addition, numerous humanitarian missions were conducted by the guardsmen using their amphibian and STOL aircraft to reach remote villages and coastal towns. The Rhode Island special operators even took two SA-16s and a support aircraft to the Democratic Republic of the Congo in 1970 to conduct underwater seismic testing for the US Navy in Lake Tanganyika.

In June 1971, Maryland's 135th Special Operations Group (SOG) was redesignated a tactical air support group, with the Tactical Air Command becoming the gaining command. Its HU-16s and U-10s were phased out to be replaced by the 0-2A Skymaster. Four years later, California's 129th SOG became the 129th Aerospace Rescue and Recovery Group, part of the Military Airlift Command. During that same year, both Rhode Island and West Virginia SOGs were equipped with the C-130 transport and were redesignated tactical airlift groups. The special operations era for the Air National Guard passed into history . . . or did it?

If the enthusiasm for special operations forces seems to fluctuate within the military community, the enduring reality is that the need for these skills in a seemingly still-dangerous world never diminished entirely. West Virginia's C-130s were seen years later at Hurlburt Field, Florida, home of the Air Force Special Operations Command. And the Pennsylvania Air Guard's 193d Special Operations Wing, the only Air Guard unit assigned to AFSOC, still makes a unique, low-profile contribution to AFSOC with its six specially equipped EC-130E Commando Solo aircraft. The 193d is the only USAF unit capable of providing airborne radio and television broadcasts. When not supporting AFSOC missions, the 193d provides specialized support to the Air Force Intelligence Agency as its secondary mission. Clearly the sensitive files for Air Guard special operations duties must still be marked "Ongoing."

"The Most Frightening Desert in the World"

"Bandits" on the Roof of the World World

While the signing of the Korean War armistice in 1953 did little to ease global cold war tensions, the loss of an estimated 2.4 million casualties[1] on both sides does appear to have influenced a turn away from large-scale bloodletting during the following decade. Almost as if by mutual agreement, both Western and Communist-bloc powers turned to a more discreet, if still vicious, form of warfare. Intelligence agencies developed formidable paramilitary capabilities, which in turn were bolstered where and when required by supporting military special operations, or *spetsialnoye nazhacheniye** forces. It was from these secret "wars in the shadows" that some of the most effective future Air Commando leaders of the 1960s would learn their craft.

---

*A Russian term for "special purpose" military units.

Throughout the 1950s, successive US administrations tasked the Air Force to support such paramilitary operations by providing clandestine aid to a number of anti-Communist rebellions, including one taking place in the remotest and darkest of these shadow wars. The barren and freezing mountain kingdom of Tibet, located on Communist China's southwestern flank, was by anyone's reckoning a long way from anywhere else. One nineteenth-century traveler recorded his impression of the unforgiving terrain as "the most frightening desert in the world." Populating these desolate areas were the proud Khamba and Amdo tribes, a predictably tough people with a long and proud warrior tradition in irregular warfare.

When Chairman Mao Tse-tung ordered his People's Liberation Army (PLA) into Tibet in 1950, the army entered through the forbidding Chamdo region, home of these fiercely independent tribesmen. Within a few short years, the

heavy-handed Chinese occupation provoked a rebellion among the Khamba and Amdo, who became vilified as "bandits" in the Chinese propaganda machine. Much to the dismay of the Chinese, these tribesmen rebelled with such ferocity that by 1957 the vastly superior Chinese invasion forces found themselves fighting an 80,000-strong, horseback-riding guerrilla army that seemed to come out of a nineteenth-century Rudyard Kipling poem.[2] But the Chinese contin-

Michel Peissel

Tough face, tough land. One nineteenth-century traveler described the desolate homeland of the Khamba and Amdo tribesmen as "the most frightening desert in the world." Ultimately the rebellion would be suppressed only by the massive numbers and ruthless tactics employed by the Chinese.

USAF

There is a reason why Tibet is often called "The Roof of the World." With the "lowlands" at 13,000 feet, the loss in 1958 of even one of the C-118's engines at these altitudes would have led to almost certain disaster for both crew . . . and the US government's plan to maintain "plausible denial" during the clandestine operation.

ued to have one advantage that was even more indispensable than their superior numbers: the brutal geography of Tibet itself made outside Western support to the guerrillas almost impossible.

In responding to the Eisenhower administration's decision in 1957 to provide clandestine support to the Tibetan resistance, the intelligence community quickly encountered its first major obstacle. Without the expertise and equipment to conduct long-range clandestine air missions it needed just to get to Tibet, the program appeared doomed before it had even started. But where could it get the help it needed?

The last of the active duty air resupply and communications groups had been deactivated the previous year. One of the only two remaining USAF troop carrier squadrons (medium) (special) still dedicated to special operations was based on Okinawa, but its aircraft did not have the required performance. And neither for that matter did the special operations Air National Guard units based in the United States.

The needed expertise turned out to be right within the intelligence community itself in the form of a select group of both young and experienced USAF officers seconded to intelligence duties from the Air Force. A few of these seconded officers were assigned to Detachment 2, 1045th Observation, Evaluation, and Training Group (OE&TG)* on Okinawa.[3] Most of this small team, like Capt (later Col) Ed Smith and Lt (later Deputy Assistant Secretary of Defense) Lawrence Ropka, were new to the unconventional warfare business. But the commander who set the pace for these special operators had already established himself as a formidable unconventional warfare fighter and leader in Korea.

Heinie Aderholt's Korean War combat experience in "special air missions," introduced in earlier stories, proved especially useful to the young group assembled on Okinawa. Now a major commanding Detachment 2, 1045th OE&TG, he was soon to become one of the most influential (and controversial) Air Commandos in Southeast Asia. But that was to come later. For the moment, the high-altitude, high-risk flights to Tibet demanded his most imaginative effort.

The reality of supporting the intelligence operation in Tibet proved a daunting task for the Detachment 2 planners. There *is* a reason why Tibet is often referred to as "The Roof of the World." It is a country whose lowlands are located at an elevation of 13,000 feet! Fundamental to the entire problem was simply that of finding transport aircraft with adequate range and payload performance to operate under these extreme conditions.

Prior to 1959, Detachment 2's largest aircraft, a four-engined C-118 transport, had been frequently used for flights conducted by Civil Air Transport, a CIA proprietary airline operating throughout Asia. And CAT had indeed been busy during the earlier stages of the cold war. According to the highest ranking USAF special operations officer at the time, Brig Gen Edward Lansdale, CAT had by 1959 completed numerous overflights of mainland China and Tibet.[4]

For the Tibetan operation, the C-118 was loaded on Okinawa with Communist-bloc weapons and supplies already rigged for parachute drop over guerrilla strongholds in Tibet. Proceeding to Clark Air Base in the Philippines to pick up fuel and long-range communication specialists, the plane then overflew Indochina en route to its final destination at Kermatola, an abandoned World War II airfield located 20 miles north of Dacca, in East Pakistan. From Kermatola, the Air America** crews would take the C-118 on the final run north into Tibet.

Unfortunately, Detachment 2 had only one C-118. And by 1958, the Tibetan resistance movement was growing dramatically, outstripping in the process Detachment 2's inadequate air support.

*The 1045th reported to the 1007th Air Intelligence Group, collocated with and reporting in turn to Headquarters USAF, Plans and Policy Directorate, in the Pentagon.

**CAT was renamed Air America during this period.

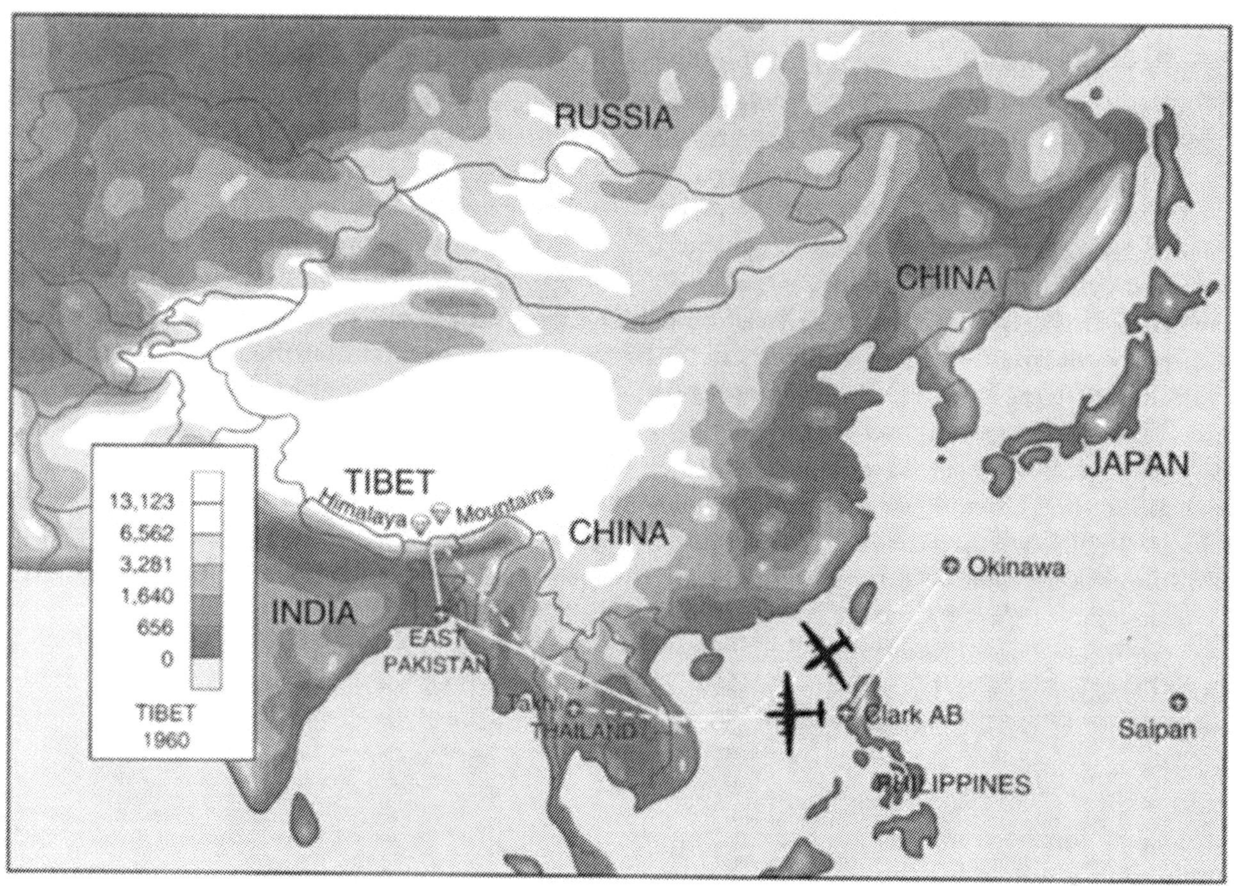

D Armstrong

The extreme range and altitude demands of the Tibet Operation required the highest standards from both aircraft and crew performance.

Worse still, the C-118's power limitations at Tibetan altitudes limited its payload to an unsatisfactory 9,000 pounds per flight. Even with the C-118's limited payload, the loss of even one of its four engines over Tibet's jagged mountains would make the loss of the aircraft and its American crew virtually inevitable, taking with them in the process any hope of maintaining "plausible denial" of US support. By early 1959, the inadequacy of the C-118 had become so obvious to all that top priority was placed on finding a replacement aircraft.

The new Lockheed C-130 just coming off the production lines was the obvious choice for this operation. With four powerful turbine-powered propellers, a range of over 5,000 miles, and a 20,000-pound payload, it was (and arguably still is) the best long-range tactical transport in the world. Best of all for this operation, it could carry this payload at Tibetan altitudes and could be made available, *if* the right strings were pulled, in the required numbers. Already in hot demand throughout the Air Force, the only C-130s then available in the Pacific were assigned to the Air Force's 315th Air Division based in Japan.

To tap clandestine Air Force C-130 support for Tibet, US intelligence approached the Office of Special Operations (OSO),* the division within the Office of Secretary of Defense charged with providing military support to the intelligence

* General Lansdale's office was in the OSO at this time.

community.[5] Pressing the national priority of their operation, the intelligence spokesmen soon obtained the needed Air Force response. And as the operations tempo increased, so did the reputation of the Detachment 2 planners.

With its short runway, the old airfield in East Pakistan was abandoned as a launch point in favor of much better facilities located at Takhli Royal Thai Air Base in northern Thailand. Under the direction of Aderholt's Detachment 2, USAF C-130s began flying into Takhli for removal of all visible USAF fuselage markings and for replacing their crews with Air America aircrews, who flew the final leg over Tibet.[6] First one, then as many as three C-130s, would arrive at Takhli prior to the all-important monthly "full-moon windows."

The arriving USAF crews would return immediately to home base in another aircraft, leaving behind Detachment 2, USI, and Air America personnel along with the Tibetan guerrillas to conduct the missions. With the passage of time, Detachment 2's self-confidence, common sense, and imagination overcame every obstacle to provide the publicly invisible but all-critical air support. And it did so without the loss of a single aircraft or crew during the entire campaign.[7]

To reduce the chance of Chinese detection, the Air America aircrews flew their "sterilized" C-130s northwest from northern Thailand, flying across inadequately chartered mountainous terrain with no reliable navigation aids save the navigator's celestial-plotting skills.[8] To further mask the flights from possible Chinese intercept, all missions were flown at night, during the 10-day "moon windows" that allowed at least some visual reference with the dark terrain below. Monsoon weather restricted the program still further, to dry-season-only flights.

While night and remote terrain factors helped in the avoidance of detection, they obviously complicated the mission planners' efforts to find the easiest routes in and out of Tibet. One planner recalls assembling old French maps in which the same river, running across different map sections, was disjointed by miles when the map sections were brought together. To execute these high-risk missions, the contract aircrews were paid the remarkably low sum of $350 for a "routine high-risk[!]" mission; $500 "if unusual hazards" were involved.[9]

A typical mission might carry a number of weapons and supply pallets rigged for airdrop, along with a small team of a half-dozen Tibetan parachutists who had finished their guerrilla training.[10] It was a measure of the difficulty of these missions that on occasion they exceeded even the extreme long-range capability of the C-130. If shifting winds or mechanical problems caused mission deviations, discreet diplomatic arrangements allowed continued use of the Kermatola airfield in East Pakistan.[11]

Not all of Detachment 2's special operations were performed in southern Asia. As early as 1957, USAF transports began flying Tibetan guerrilla recruits, many who had never even seen an airplane before, from East Pakistan to a special training facility on Saipan, one of the US-administered islands in the Marianas.[12] To maintain the required security of the Saipan facility, flight plans into the island were filed with flight-following facilities as over-water navigation training, with the aircraft dipping down below radar-observation level to make the run into Saipan. Low-level routes were used on takeoff, climbing to radar-effective levels once safely away from the island. On Saipan, the Tibetans were put through map reading and radio communications training, capped with parachute training, before their airborne insertion back into Tibet.[13]

By 1959, Detachment 2 was also organizing flights that took carefully screened guerrilla recruits all the way to Peterson AFB, Colorado, located some 70 miles south of Denver. The airfield was of course only a transfer point for the Tibetans, who were immediately bussed higher into the Rocky Mountains to Camp Hale, a former World War II Army training site near the mining town of Leadville.[14] There they were put

USAF

With all USAF markings removed, Air America contract crews flew the long-range C-130 Hercules on the dangerous final flights into Tibet in the late 1950s. Tibetan guerrillas, some trained in Colorado, returned to their homeland by parachute from these "skyboats," as the Khamba and Amdo tribesmen called the big planes.

through a demanding training curriculum including weapons, demolitions, communications, and guerrilla tactics. At an elevation of over 10,000 feet, the camp was as close to "home" as their US advisors could hope to find for the mountain tribesmen. During field exercises at Hale, the Tibetans astounded their trainers with their physical endurance, the agility with which they traversed the most difficult terrain . . . and their passion for their US-issued weapons. One Tibetan source estimated that about 170 Tibetans passed through Camp Hale between 1959 and 1962.[15]

Following their training, they were quickly flown back to Asia. Shortly thereafter, they were parachuted from the "skyboats," as the guerrillas called aircraft, onto Tibet's high-desert plateaus. When Tibet's most important religious leader, the Dalai Lama, fled his country in March 1959, Colorado-trained Tibetans played a key role in his escape. When the ranking Chinese general in Tibet ordered his 50,000-man army to close all mountain passes to India, Khamba guerrillas guided the group across the 17,000-foot Che Pass and set up the clandestine air resupply drops that were crucial to the success of his safe arrival in India.[16]

By early 1960, the guerrilla movement was flourishing with a string of tactical successes in the countryside. But in the face of these successes, the Chinese responded with increasingly ruthless counterinsurgency tactics. Women and children, by now the only inhabitants left in many villages,

Michel Peissel

The Tibetan guerrillas boasted a long and successful tradition of irregular warfare over the centuries. Proud, fierce, and possessing phenomenal physical endurance at extreme altitudes, the mountain and desert tribesmen proved to be quick learners at US guerrilla training camps.

were reportedly used as human shields in front of Chinese troops assaulting guerrilla strongholds and monasteries. In the face of such tactics and the overwhelming Chinese superiority in numbers, the rebellion inevitably began to falter.

Another blow came in 1960 when the Chinese moved an entire air division into western China to attempt intercept of the essential night resupply airdrops.[17] During this same period, growing Indian and Burmese political pressures further restricted overflight routes, making the missions all but impossible. The downing of Gary Powers's U-2 reconnaissance jet over Russia later that year and President Dwight Eisenhower's subsequent decision to cease all overflights of Communist countries eventually brought an end to USAF special operations support to the Tibetan operation.[18]

While Tibetan resistance continued,* America's attention was being drawn toward a growing conflict in Southeast Asia. In the decade that followed, Air Force special operations would flourish to an extent never seen before or since.

---

*In yet another cold war twist, Soviet airdrops to the guerrillas became common by 1966, following the Sino-Soviet rift. Unlike earlier US "plausible-denial" operations, the Russian diplomats were quite open in admitting their support. See Michel Peissel, *The Secret War in Tibet* (Boston: Little, Brown and Company, 1973), 234.

Notes

1. Clay Blair, *The Forgotten War: America in Korea, 1950–1953* (New York: *Times* Books, 1987), 975.
2. Michel Peissel, *The Secret War in Tibet* (Boston: Little, Brown and Company, 1973), 105.
3. USAF Oral History Interview, Brig Gen Harry C. Aderholt, 12–15 August 1986 (U) (K239.0512-1716), 53. (Secret) Information extracted is unclassified. Also see General Aderholt's interview with the author, December 1993, Fort Walton Beach, Fla.
4. Christopher Robbins, *Air America: The Story of the CIA's Secret Airlines* (New York: G.P. Putnam's Sons, 1979), 84.
5. L. Fletcher Prouty, *JFK: The CIA, Vietnam and the Plot to Assassinate John F. Kennedy* (New York: Carol Publishing Group, 1992), 95–96. See also John Prados, *Presidents' Secret Wars: CIA and Pentagon Covert Operations since World War II* (New York: William Morrow and Company, 1986), 148, 158, for description of OSO.
6. Detachment 2 mission planner, interview with author, 20 January 1994, Fort Walton Beach, Fla. See also Keven M. Generous, *Vietnam: The Secret War* (New York: Gallery Books, 1985), 108.
7. Ibid.
8. Ibid. See also Prados, 158.
9. Detachment 2 mission planner interview.
10. Prados, 158.
11. Detachment 2 mission planner interview.
12. Chris Mullin, "Tibetan Conspiracy," *Far Eastern Economic Review*, 5 September 1975, 32.
13. Ibid.
14. Prados, 163.
15. Mullin, 33.
16. Ibid., 162. See also "Tibet: A God Escapes," *Newsweek*, 13 April 1959.
17. Brig Gen Harry C. Aderholt, interview with author, 6 November 1994, Fort Walton Beach, Fla.
18. Ibid., 166.

The Bay of Pigs

"They Had No Air Support"

Fidel Castro, 1961

By their very nature, "special operations" fire the imagination with visions of elite military forces courageously fighting against great odds to accomplish what others seemingly cannot. No better example of this phenomenon can be found than that of the media glamorization of the American military's Air Commandos, Green Berets, and sea-air-land (SEAL) teams during the Vietnam War. Not nearly so glamorous, however, is the tension, fear, and paranoia that characterize the reality of a special operations mission in progress.

Castro inspects the wreckage of the B-26 piloted by Alabama Air National Guard's Pete Ray, one of 80 Alabama and Arkansas guardsmen contracted to support the invasion. Four of the 16 ANG aircrew members died in aerial combat over the Bay of Pigs.

Such a mission typically combines these elite military units with the US intelligence community, perhaps foreign nationals from the country in which the mission will take place, and even third-country nationals deemed useful to the effort. This inherently explosive combination of strong-willed bureaucracies and different nationalities is then placed in a pressure cooker, the mission itself, before a final touch of heat is added. This hot political torch can turn, and has more than once turned, this already volatile combination into a witch's brew that explodes over the fire in all directions.

In America's cold war history, this heat has frequently taken form in the personal involvement of the White House during either the planning or execution phases of the operation, if not during both. It remains one of the most enduring hallmarks of American special operations after World War II. Examples are those conducted during the administrations of presidents John F. Kennedy (Bay of Pigs, Cuba), Richard Nixon (Son Tay, North Vietnam), Gerald Ford (the *Mayaguez*, Cambodia), Jimmy Carter (Desert One, Iran), and Ronald Reagan (Nicaragua). On one level, such involvement may simply reflect a president's legitimate interest in a high-risk mission, driven in part by the personal and political embarrassment he will suffer should the mission fail. President Nixon's involvement in the 1970 attempt to rescue American POWs from Son Tay prison provides such an example.

At the other extreme, White House involvement may actually involve operational command from the president and his advisers to the special operations force in the field. And no better example of this level can be found than that which occurred during five days in April 1961 in a special operation just 90 miles south of Miami. All early hopes for success as well as the subsequent failure of the operation evolved around the effective use of airpower. Also very pertinent was the domestic political landscape in the US in the months leading up to the operation.

As was usually the case every four years during the cold war, the American presidential campaign had a Republican candidate questioning whether his Democratic rival was "soft on Communism." In this regard, the Nixon-Kennedy campaign in 1960 certainly proved no exception. When the Democratic candidate, President John F. Kennedy, won by the narrowest of margins and took office in January 1961, the new presence of a Communist Cuba on America's doorstep was a political challenge his administration could ignore only at considerable domestic political risk.

Operation Pluto

By the time of his inauguration, however, President Kennedy already knew that the outgoing Eisenhower administration had sanctioned a CIA proposal to begin preparing a paramilitary operation (Operation Pluto) against the Castro regime. Allen Dulles, director of Central Intelligence,* had placed the project under Richard Bissell, his deputy assistant for plans and one of the CIA's rising stars. A Yale graduate, the exceptionally eloquent Bissell was sometimes referred to as the "brightest man in Washington."

The preparations for Operation Pluto had been under way for some months, and the time was rapidly approaching for the new president to make a "go-no-go" decision on the operation that was scheduled a short three months away.** Even in the cynical atmosphere of Washington, few could guess that before it was over this witch's brew would explode from the fire, burning almost everyone but the intended target itself.

The tactical concept for Pluto was not complex. In a nutshell, 1,500 Cuban exiles who had been trained, equipped, and organized by the CIA

*The CIA chief is dual-hatted as the director of Central Intelligence because the position is also the titular head of all federal intelligence agencies.

** At President Eisenhower's direction, the CIA director briefed candidate Kennedy the previous July on the general outlines of a proposed paramilitary operation to oust Castro. After assuming office, Kennedy was again briefed on the operation, learning in the process that it had grown significantly in scope over the preceding months.

Janet Ray Weininger

Fifteen World War II-era bombers were purchased by the CIA from the Air Force "boneyard" near Tucson, Arizona, and refurbished for the operation. Note the vertical stabilizer covered in cloth to hide aircraft markings. To bolster the deception that the invasion was the plan of defecting Cuban military officers, the exile B-26s were painted with the national insignia of the Cuban air force.

would conduct an airborne and amphibious invasion of Cuba at a remote beach adjoining the Bahia de Cochinos (Bay of Pigs), approximately 120 miles southeast of Havana. Critical to the success of the operation was control of the air by the exiles. This would be provided by an air force equipped with 15 World War II-era B-26 bombers and supporting C-46 and C-54 transports, all flown by Cuban exiles. All exile forces would be launched by air and sea from a secret base in Nicaragua.

The hoped-for end result of the operation was that a successfully established beachhead would spark a general uprising of the Cuban public against Castro, who was believed to have already alienated large segments of the Cuban population.* US involvement in the operation was to be masked with the cover story that the revolt was initiated by military defectors within Cuba. The CIA had never attempted a "covert" operation of this size before, but then again never had the American public experienced a Communist country only 90 miles from its shores. The political pressure on the White House to do something was immense.

In fact, the CIA had been busy "doing something" for months. The recruiting of the Cuban ground force had gone well even if the need for tight-lipped secrecy failed to impress the passionate Cuban exiles. Even Castro had drawn public attention to the exiles then training in Guatemala. It was the air component of the invasion force that demanded the most careful analysis, not only because it was indispensable to success but

* A growing volume of evidence over the following years pointed to a much lower level of anti-Castro resentment than that reported at the time. Wishful thinking on the part of the US and a ruthless suppression campaign by Castro against internal dissent appear to account in large part for the misleading intelligence reports.

because two of the most obvious questions involved the source of aircraft and flying crews to man them. And the man who had to answer those questions was one of Bissell's deputies, Stan Beerli, an Air Force colonel seconded to duty with the CIA as chief, Development Projects Division (DPD), a special projects division dedicated to programs not specific to a particular regional division.[1]

After discussions with his deputy for air operations, Col George Gaines, and others, Beerli committed DPD to purchasing 15 B-26 medium bombers from the Air Force's "boneyard" at Davis-Monthan Air Force Base near Tucson, Arizona. Factors favoring the choice included the fact that the Cuban air force flew the same type, if not the same model,* of the bomber; its capability to fly the long distance from Nicaragua to Cuba and back; and its powerful armament of eight .50-caliber heavy machine guns in the nose, wing-mounted pylons for air-to-ground rockets, and an internal bomb bay that could carry 500-pound bombs.

The major drawback of the B-26 was that it had no air-to-air fighting capability should Castro's T-33 jet fighters attack with their cannon. This limitation was not deemed critical, however, because the air plan itself placed the highest priority on destroying all of Castro's limited fighter force on the ground with a surprise attack two days before the actual invasion. Additional strikes were scheduled to follow immediately should any of the fighters survive the first attack.

The bombers were pulled from the boneyard, refurbished, and flown by Air Force and agency pilots to a remote training base in Guatemala. To support this strike force, additional twin-engined C-46 and four-engined C-54 transports were procured to haul cargo and drop the exile paratroopers on invasion day. Eventually a total of 22 aircraft were procured. During the same period, a simultaneous effort was under way to identify and recruit suitable pilots from within the Cuban exile population in Miami. With difficulty, some 40 former commercial and military pilots were selected for additional training by American instructors. But where to find instructors for a dangerous mission, especially those with current B-26 expertise?

As it had so often done in the past, the CIA turned to the Air National Guard, with whom it had developed a close relationship over the years. As CIA officers soon learned, the Alabama Air National Guard (AANG) had only recently retired the B-26s of its 117th Tactical Reconnaissance Wing (TRW) in Birmingham. To make

* The Cuban air force models featured Plexiglas noses, as opposed to the solid-nose models retrieved from the boneyard. It was a seemingly small difference, but one that would backfire badly and publicly on the American plan on the opening day of hostilities.

Alabama ANG archives

Brig Gen George "Poppa" Doster, (left) commander of the Alabama Air National Guard, sits atop the cockpit of an Alabama ANG B-26. The charismatic leader recruited 80 Alabama and Arkansas guardsmen to train exile pilots for the operation.

The 117th Tactical Reconnaissance Wing of the Alabama Air National Guard had only recently retired its B-26s, the same bomber chosen by CIA officers for the exile air force. (below)

Alabama ANG archives

discreet contact with Maj Gen George "Poppa" Doster, commander of the AANG, the agency used another Air Force pilot already seconded to the agency and, better yet, one known personally by the general.

Maj Heinie Aderholt, Alabama born and raised, had never left the agency after the Korean War nor had he lost his contacts in his home state. The fact that his brother had served in the AANG didn't hurt either, and the presence of a familiar face and experienced special operations officer like Aderholt was reassuring to Doster.

Doster responded enthusiastically to the agency request for aircrews and support personnel, and the charismatic "Poppa" soon pulled together a group of 80 current and former air guardsmen from both Alabama and Arkansas, 16 of them pilots. Briefed in the headquarters building of the 117th TRW, the guardsmen were told to prepare cover stories for their absences, complete with a personal history they could relate plausibly to an interrogator.[2] The training team was completed with the addition of another half-dozen agency-contracted pilots who, like their Guard counterparts, were designated for instructor-only duties. Combat missions were not envisioned for an operation the State Department insisted had to "look Cuban."

To run the training program in Guatemala, Colonel Gaines put General Doster's group to work running the B-26 tactics program, while agency personnel trained the transport pilots and provided armament, logistical, and security functions. Most of the Cuban pilots had little or no previous experience in either bombers or large

The four C-46s seen here at the CIA training base in Guatemala would soon drop the exile paratroop force into Cuba hours before the main amphibious landing. A number of C-54s such as the one seen at the far right were used primarily as preinvasion cargo haulers.

Janet Ray Weininger

transports, a fact bringing considerable pressure to bear on both the exiles and their American instructors during the short training time available. To expedite training and a team spirit, the Cubans were housed in three separate barracks, each holding either B-26, C-46, or C-54 aircrews. Despite all efforts, however, the training tempo was such that by the time training was completed in Guatemala, two C-54s and two C-46s were lost due to a variety of causes.[3]

From the standpoint of secrecy, training, organization, and equipment, the operation by this time had become a classic special operations mission in all but name. And as the invasion date approached in the spring of 1961, the exiles' flying skills had improved markedly, so much so that their senior flight instructor expressed absolute confidence that they could successfully pass any US Air Force flight checks.[4] Still, there remained one nagging problem that could not be postponed any longer: another base closer to Cuba had to be found, and soon.

Rafael Garcia

Symbol of the Cuban exiles' "Phoenix" air force.

Again Major Aderholt entered the picture—this time as the point man in the effort to find a launch point isolated enough to minimize public

exposure, yet still close enough to Cuba to place the invasion beach within the combat radius of a fully loaded B-26. This search ultimately led the major to a prophetic meeting with one of the most interesting and durable dictators in Central America. Securing the use of the remote airstrip at Puerto Cabezas on Nicaragua's eastern coast would provide the CIA with the closest launch point it could reasonably expect to find while still maintaining the needed secrecy. This, of course, was dependent on Nicaragua's president, Anastasio Somoza, being willing to take the political risk of supporting the US against a fellow Latino leader.

Flying into Nicaragua at night in civilian clothes as representatives of a large US corporation operating in Central America, Major Aderholt and an agency official met with Somoza at two A.M. to ask for use of Puerto Cabezas. The wily Somoza agreed in a manner that left no doubt he knew exactly what was going on: *"I know who you are. I'm willing to support you, but be sure you get rid of that [SOB], or you are going to have to live with him for the rest of your life."*[5] The next day the major flew to Puerto Cabezas with Somoza's son (like his father, a West Point graduate) to sketch the area to be developed as the invasion launch point.

In February, the Pentagon sent three colonels to Guatemala to review the exile force and invasion plans. The Air Force colonels' report carried the ominous warning that, given the B-26s' lack of air-to-air combat capability, their failure to destroy all of Castro's offensive aircraft in the first attacks could jeopardize the entire operation.[6] Fortunately, "all of Castro's offensive aircraft"

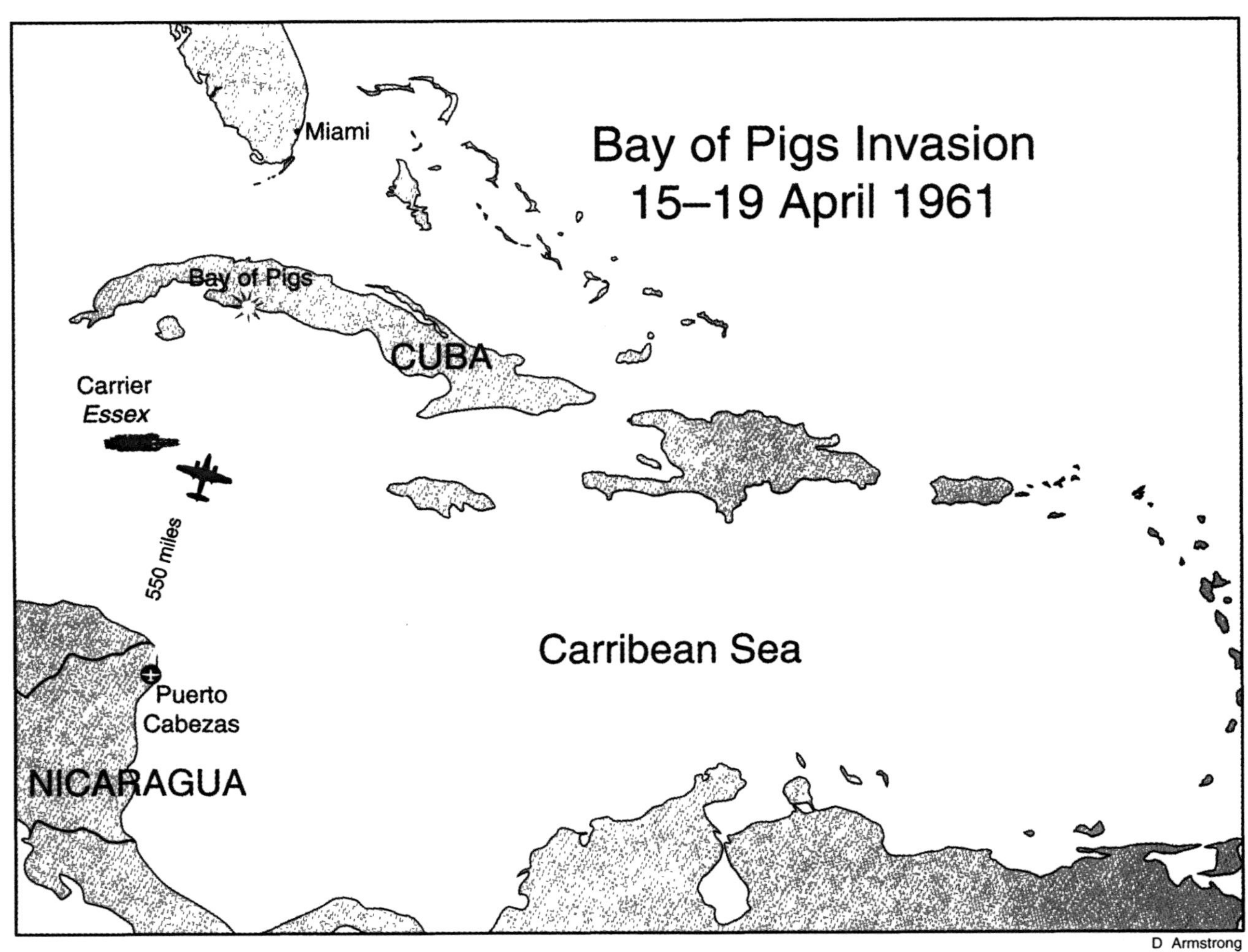

amounted to two B-26s, two World War II-era Sea Fury propeller-driven fighters, and two T-33 jet fighters armed with four cannon. And what could possibly stop 15 heavily armed B-26s from destroying this small force on the ground in a single surprise attack?

In comparison to the tension and excitement in the exiles' camp a month before the scheduled invasion, the situation in the White House can only be described as political agony. Just five weeks before the invasion, President Kennedy rejected the agency's proposed operation as "too spectacular" (i.e., too American-looking) and asked for additional options. During the following weeks, an increasingly skeptical Kennedy continued to withhold formal approval while still allowing final preparations to go forward.

Bissell had his own internal problems and was just barely able to talk two of his top Pluto aides from resigning in despair over the continuing last-minute changes to the plan by the White House and State Department. The exiles moved from Guatemala to Puerto Cabezas. At this point, the invasion was growing a life of its own, and, as history records, 15 April marked the point of no return for the invasion.

On Saturday* the 15th, two days before the airborne/amphibious invasion, the exiles launched their dawn air attacks on the three airfields housing the six aircraft that could potentially doom the invasion. To ensure the maximum possible effect from the element of surprise, the agency plan called for launching all 15 B-26s, with follow-on missions later that day and the 16th if required. As it turned out, Castro was only one of many to experience a nasty surprise. Others included the agency planners and the exile air force. On the afternoon of the 14th, President Kennedy telephoned Bissell to discuss the operation and in particular the all-important first air strikes. Upon learning that the plan called for a maximum 15-plane effort, Kennedy overrode the plan over the phone by insisting on a "minimal" effort to mask US support.[7] Bissell decided that six B-26s, plus two spares, would meet the president's intentions. In Puerto Cabezas, surprised and dismayed case officers launched all eight. But it was a ninth B-26 that would create more public havoc than all the other eight combined could inflict on Cuban airfields.

To meet White House demands that the operation must appear to be the work of disaffected Cuban military officers, a deception plan had been developed calling for a "defecting" Cuban B-26 to land in Miami on the 15th with news of an anti-Castro revolt. The landing was carried out as planned, the Cuban ambassador to the United Nations protested loudly, the US ambassador responded with righteous indignation against the "false" charges . . . and then the roof caved in on the United States. Through a gross oversight, the "defecting" B-26 was of the hard-nosed model, while all Cuban air force B-26s featured the Plexiglas model. Worse yet, the president had decided not to make his UN ambassador privy to the invasion plans. Publicly and personally embarrassed, the ambassador vented his private angst on the White House.

Back in the White House, skepticism gave way first to alarm and then to near panic. Even after learning that the much-reduced initial air strikes had left at least two Sea Fury fighters and two T-33 jet fighters untouched, the president personally vetoed the planned "insurance" air strikes scheduled for the next two days. At Puerto Cabezas, surprise gave way to anger as American and Cuban pilots watched success slipping through their fingers. Remaining hopes turned on the possibility that the Cuban T-33s weren't serviceable after all.

It wasn't until the afternoon of Sunday the 16th, less than 24 hours before D day, that the president authorized a second B-26 attack against Cuban airfields to take place at dawn the

* A Saturday was deliberately chosen as the attack day, with the expectation that weekend media coverage would as usual be less intense than that during the regular work week.

following morning. Every Cuban and American at Puerto Cabezas knew this strike would be their last chance to get the remaining T-33s and Sea Fury fighters on the ground. High-altitude U-2 photographs had shown them where every surviving fighter was located, and Colonel Beerli's staff had already sent the target lists to the field officers.

That Sunday night, the airfield was a scene of frenetic activity as the bombers were fueled, loaded with bombs, and double-checked by maintenance personnel. But far to the north, in Washington, D.C., another drama was being played out, one that doomed the operation even as the B-26s were being prepared for the mission.

Late that same Sunday afternoon, Lt Gen Charles P. Caball, USAF, the number two man at CIA and the ranking officer for the day while Dulles was away on a speaking engagement, stopped by Colonel Beerli's office for an update. Unaware that the president had authorized a second air strike, Caball apparently decided to cover himself by double-checking Beerli's assurances with Secretary of State Dean Rusk, although the secretary had no position in the chain of command. In light of the secretary's known opposition to the operation, Caball's decision proved to be the generator of yet another critical "no" decision.

In his subsequent call to the president (with Bissell and Caball in the room), Secretary Rusk voiced his opposition to the D day air strike, after which President Kennedy reversed his decision made earlier in the day to Bissell. At that point, Rusk asked General Caball whether he wished to speak to the president personally. "There's no point in my talking to the president," the general responded with a shrug.[8] Despite his cancellation orders on the air mission, however, the president allowed the exile invasion to proceed.

Cuban exiles in paratroop training make their first jumps over the airfield in Guatemala. Numbering just under 200, the paratroops secured the beachead for the 1,500-strong main force arriving by ship later the same day.

Joe Shannon

Joe Shannon

Following his B-26 training in Guatemala, former Cubana Airlines pilot Gustavo Ponzoa flew in the critical preinvasion air strike intended to knock out Castro's small fighter force. White House orders to reduce the strike force by half, and its refusal of follow-on strikes against the air bases, permitted two T-33s to escape destruction. It would prove to be two too many.

Hours later, nearly 200 Cuban exile paratroopers floated down onto Cuban soil from five C-46s and a C-54, landing just beyond the Playa Giron airfield that would support their postinvasion forces. Back at Puerto Cabezas, the furious but disciplined Americans had already informed the Cubans of the air strike's cancellation order from Washington. An agency pilot recalls the Cuban pilots' reaction to the stand-down, "They came to me . . . actually crying . . . expecting me to explain this. . . . I could not . . . it was an impossible situation for me. I have never felt worse or more hopeless."[9]

Later that morning, a second set of missions for D day were authorized by the White House, with the strict proviso they be limited to close air support only for the ground force at the beachhead. Taking off at staggered intervals after daylight to ensure near-continuous cover over the beachhead, 10 B-26s flew on the 17th . . . right into everyone's worst nightmare. Circling over the Bay of Pigs like birds of prey, the cannon-firing T-33s

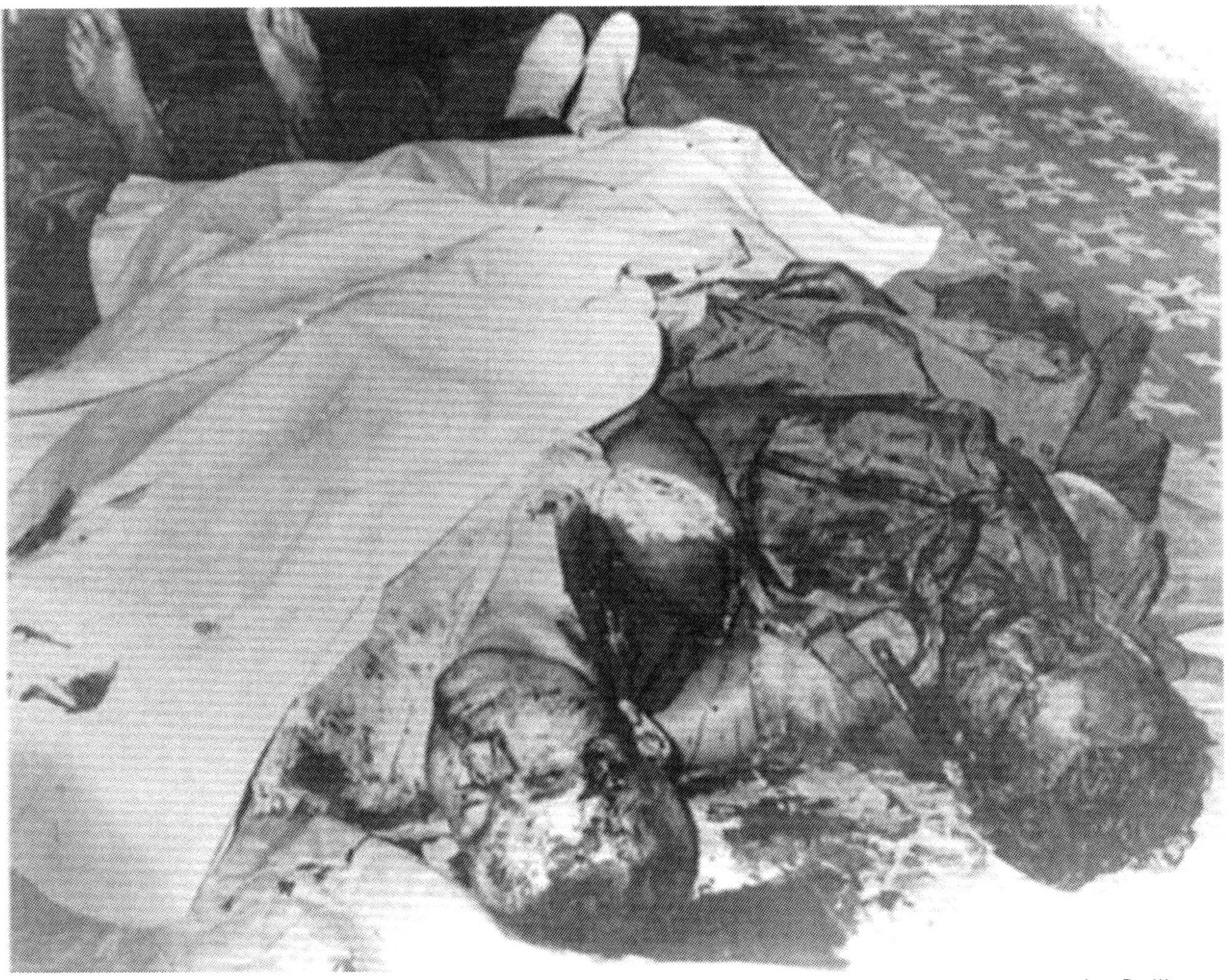

Janet Ray Weininger

The price of defeat. Americans Pete Ray and Wade Gray survived the crash of their B-26 on the battlefield but were killed moments later resisting capture. Half the exile B-26s were lost in combat, virtually all of them shot down by T-33 jet fighters.

and the Sea Fury fighters were waiting for the B-26s. Fully half of the 10 bombers that made it to the beachhead never returned. The T-33s were known to have accounted for at least four of the five losses. So helpless to air attack were the bombers that one was shot down by a T-33 pilot who had not flown at all during the three months leading up to D day; another for five months. The Cuban pilot who sank one of the exiles' small ships off the beachhead had never fired the guns on his aircraft prior to that date. As a postinvasion CIA internal report notes:

> Castro's order that the first target which should be taken under attack was the shipping that was bringing the forces into Cuba—this was exactly what had been predicted in the 22 January 1961 briefing for Secretary Rusk and repeated during the Bissell and Caball meeting with Rusk on the night of 16 April.[10]

The aerial disaster of the 17th led to two predictable phenomena back at Puerto Cabezas. The first was the collapse of the morale of Cuban exiles. Fatigue from the long missions and the shock of losing so many friends in a single day took their toll, but worse was the realization that assurances of American air support were hollow. By Tuesday the 18th, only a handful of them were prepared to go back to the beachhead and into the teeth of the T-33s.

The second phenomena also manifested itself on the 18th, and this one came from the American pilots at Puerto Cabezas. Most of the American instructors had become close friends with the Cubans over the preceding months of hard training and shared the Cuban exiles' view that Castro's Communist government was an "insult" to both Cuba and the United States. On the 18th, two flights of three bombers each headed toward the invasion beach. Four of the six planes were flown by Cubans, the remaining two by Americans as flight leaders of the two groups. This first commitment of American pilots to fly combat strike missions in Operation Pluto was directed by an agency pilot with the operational authority granted his position as the senior air commander at Puerto Cabezas.[11]

The flights on the 18th proved both productive and lucky for the exiles. Productive because the Americans found one of Castro's tank/infantry convoys of 60 to 70 trucks approaching the beachhead and attacked with bombs, rockets, cannon fire, and napalm. Several hundred casualties were reported in a two-mile stretch of highway that was left in fire and smoke.[12] Lucky because T-33s were reported over the beachhead one minute after the bombers left the scene.[13]

The good fortune of the 18th proved to be a deadly exception, for reality returned with a vengeance on the 19th. On the night of the 18th, a handful of Alabama Air Guard B-26 instructors at Puerto Cabezas stepped forward when an agency pilot asked for volunteers for the next day's combat. Bolstering their spirits was the word from Washington that for the first time US Navy fighters* would be over the beachhead from 0630 to 0730 (the attack window) to fend off the T-33s.

The next morning, the ensuing slaughter in the air was a repeat of that of the 17th. Of the five bombers that actually made it to the beachhead, only three returned. Navy "cover" arrived too late, a mistake in timing after which the Navy claimed that the B-26s came over the beachhead an hour earlier than planned and before the Navy fighters could take off from the carrier *Essex*. Adm Arleigh Burke of the Joint Chiefs of Staff (JCS) later claimed that Colonel Beerli confused the difference in time zones between Cuba and Washington, a charge he hotly denied. Lost were both bombers flown by guardsmen. Crew members included Riley Shamburger, Wade C. Gray, Pete W. Ray, and Leo F. Baker. Ray and Baker were killed in a shootout after surviving the crash of their bomber near the beachhead. The Cubans on the beachhead surrendered later the same day, out of ammunition and under unceasing attack from Castro's army and air force.

Aftermath

Immediately after the collapse of the operation, the captain of the *Essex* was ordered to personally burn all orders and ship's logs (navigation, communication, combat information center, etc.) covering the period of the invasion,[14] an action permissible only by direct order of the president.[15] Later that month, the *Essex* returned to home port, bringing with it, in the words of the *Essex*'s air officer, "a load of anger, frustration, humiliation, and remorse."[16]

Left unanswered because they have never been officially asked were other questions about the "mistake in timing" for the air cover. Even if the time zones were confused, how could the *Essex*'s radar (or the radar of its outlying escort ships)

*From the US Navy aircraft *Essex*.

Janet Ray Weininger

At a White House awards ceremony after the aborted invasion, Richard Bissell, with award certificate in hand, is flanked on his right by Allen Dulles, the CIA director, and on his left by President Kennedy. The president had already sacked both Dulles and Bissell for their role in the failed operation, which may account for the unhappy expressions on their faces.

have failed to pick up the incoming B-26s? And what of the continuous message traffic from Puerto Cabezas to the CIA representative on board the *Essex* regarding the B-26s' flight?[17]

The Alabama and Arkansas guardsmen returned home with strict orders to keep their mouths shut. The families of the four dead guardsmen were informed that the men died in an aircraft accident when the C-46 in which they were flying crashed into the sea.[18] It would be years before they learned the truth. Of the four, only Pete Ray's body was ever returned (in 1979) to the United States. The location of the remains of the other three are unknown.

On 22 April, President Kennedy invited retired Army general Maxwell D. Taylor, a distinguished World War II hero, to head a committee investigating what went wrong with Operation Pluto. Representing the JCS and CIA, respectively, were Admiral Burke and Allen Dulles. The president's younger brother, Robert F. Kennedy, represented the White House's interests. With the possible exception of General Taylor, the objectivity of the committee members remains a subject of some debate. In *Bay of Pigs: The Untold Story*, author Peter Wyden writes that even before the first Taylor Committee meeting, "RFK had warned the presidential circle harshly in the Cabinet Room that they were to make no statements that did not back up the president's judgments all the way."[19]

Two months and 358 pages later, the Taylor Committee report was submitted to President

Kennedy. Fidel Castro's answer to the same questions posed by President Kennedy to the committee was uncharacteristically shorter. When asked after the invasion why the exiles had failed, he replied simply, "They had no air support."[20]

While publicly assuming responsibility for the Bay of Pigs disaster, President Kennedy had other views on actual accountability for the loss. In a meeting with Bissell shortly after receiving the Taylor Committee report, the president informed him,"If this were a British government, I would resign, and you, being a senior civil servant, would remain. But it isn't. In our government, you and Dulles have to go, and I have to remain."[21]

It was an oddly warm way of telling the CIA's director and deputy director for plans that they were out. In fact, Bissell was later requested to accept a position on a White House advisory group, a request he declined. In December 1962, the captured exiles were released from Cuban prisons and returned to the United States. In return, Castro received a $53-million ransom in food and medical supplies for his cash-strapped regime.

Notes

1. Transcript of oral interview of Col Stanley Beerli by Jack B. Pfeiffer, 2 February 1976, on the Bay of Pigs Operation, tape no. 1, side A, Janet Ray Weininger collection, Miami, Fla.

2. Albert C. Persons, *Bay of Pigs: A Firsthand Account of the Mission by a U.S. Pilot in Support of the Cuban Invasion Force in 1961* (Jefferson, N.C.: McFarland & Company, Inc., 1990), 13.

3. Edward B. Ferrer, *Operation PUMA: The Air Battle of the Bay of Pigs* (Miami, Fla.: Open Road Press, 1975), 66.

4. Transcript of oral interview of CIA employee by Jack B. Pfeiffer, 6 February 1976, on the Bay of Pigs Operation, tape no. 1, side A, Janet Ray Weininger collection, Miami, Fla.

5. Brig Gen Harry C. Aderholt, USAF, Retired, Oral History Interview (U) (K239.0512-1716), 12–15 August 1986, 84. (Secret) Information extracted is unclassified.

6. Peter Wyden, *Bay of Pigs: The Untold Story* (New York: Simon and Schuster, 1979), 99.

7. Ibid., 170.

8. Ibid., 200.

9. CIA employee to Jack B. Pfeiffer, letter, subject: Bay of Pigs, 20 May 1976, Janet Ray Weininger collection, Miami, Fla.

10. Jack B. Pfeiffer, "The Taylor Committee Investigation of the Bay of Pigs," 9 November 1984, approved for release by CIA, 18 March 1968, 49. Janet Ray Weininger collection, Miami, Fla.

11. CIA employee to Jack B. Pfeiffer letter.

12. Persons, 85.

13. Ibid., 8.

14. Wyden, 299.

15. Capt William C. Chapman, US Navy, Retired, "The Bay of Pigs: The View from PRIFLY (Paper presented at the Ninth Naval History Symposium, US Naval Academy, 20 October 1989), 3. Janet Ray Weininger collection, Miami, Fla.

16. Ibid., 37.

17. CIA employee interview, tape 2, side A.

18. Janet Ray Weininger, interview with author, 30 November 1995, Miami, Fla.

19. Wyden, 289.

20. David Atlee Phillips, *The Night Watch: 25 Years of Peculiar Service* (New York: Atheneum, 1977), 110.

21. Wyden, 311.

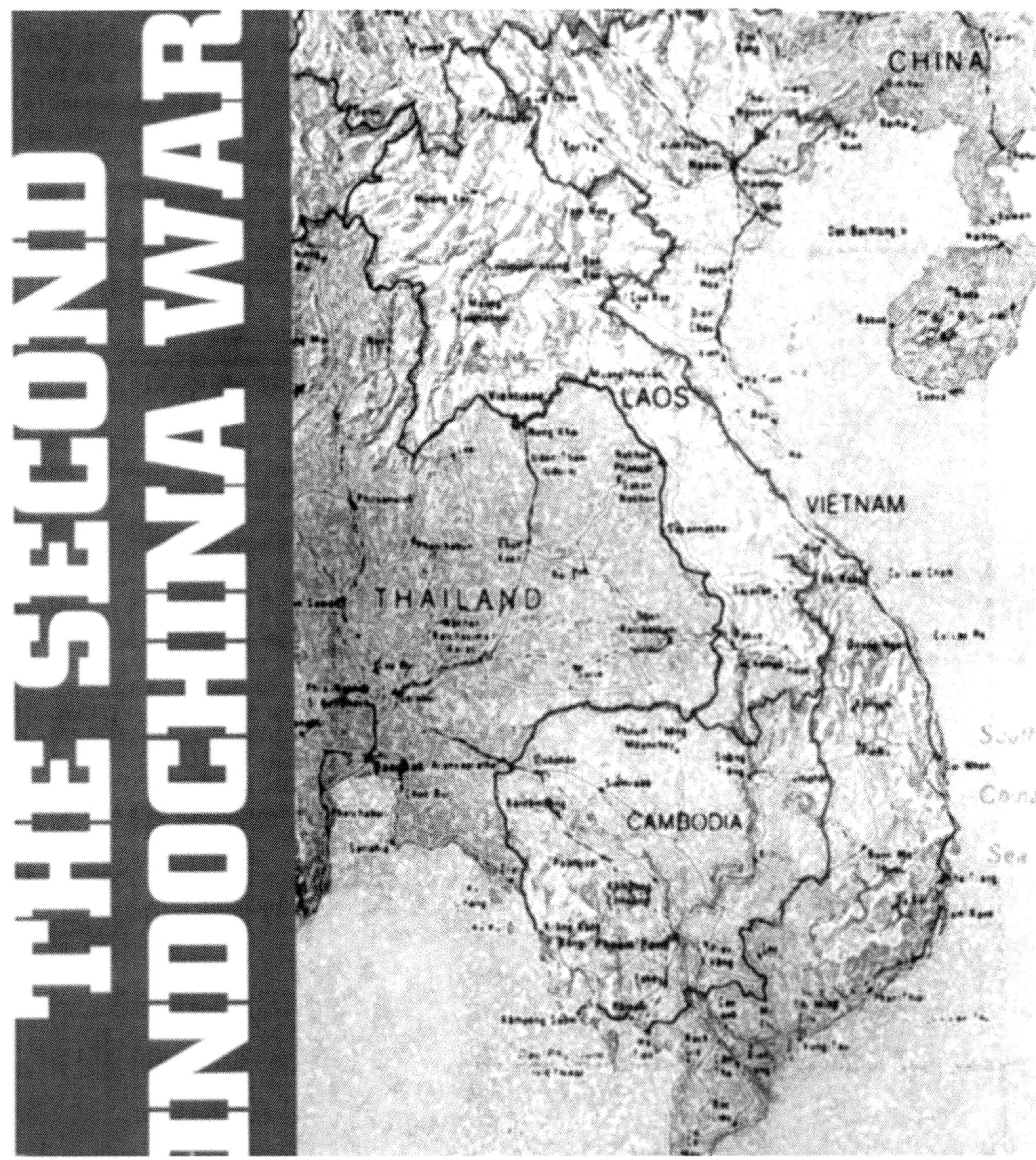
THE SECOND
INDOCHINA WAR
CHINA
LAOS
VIETNAM
THAILAND
CAMBODIA

Laos 1961

The Key Domino

Laos is far from America, but the world is small . . . the security of all Southeast Asia will be endangered if Laos loses its neutral independence.

President John F. Kennedy
23 March 1961

Air Commando Association

Two poorly clad and armed Hmong irregulars reflect the state of affairs before the advent of Operation Momentum, the USI program that turned the fierce mountain people into the most effective anti-Communist fighting force in Laos. It was a proud claim for which they paid dearly.

In the remote, jungle-covered mountains of Southeast Asia, there exists a small kingdom little bigger than the state of Utah with the mystical name "The Land of One Million Elephants and a White Parasol." The population is gentle and courteous to a fault with strangers, despite centuries of colonial dominance by foreigners, or *farangs* as they are called in the native language.

And when the French *farangs* reluctantly relinquished control of their colonies in Southeast Asia in 1954, the people of the newly independent kingdom hoped to avoid the continued regional violence by pursuing an ideologically "neutralist" policy that reflected their inoffensive culture . . . and political naiveté. Six short years later, their country would begin a decade-long trial by fire that ended with their hopes smashed in a hail of violence that eclipsed their worst nightmares.

The kingdom that could not escape its destiny—that was ultimately swept up in this violent confrontation—is more widely recognized by its official name, Laos. Its misfortune is found in its geography. Bordered by Communist China and North Vietnam to the north and east, and pro-

Western South Vietnam, Cambodia, and Thailand to the south and west, Laos was, in cold war terms, simply in the wrong place at the wrong time.

While the US did not sign the Geneva Agreements of 1954 that ushered France out of the colonial business in Indochina, it did agree to respect the terms of the agreements . . . *as long as the signatory countries did likewise.* As for Laos, a number of provisions in the agreements made clear the international intent to keep the kingdom politically neutral in the East-West cold war. Most significantly, the agreements called for the permanent removal of all foreign troops (with the exception of a small French training mission) from Laotian soil.

The agreements were signed in an atmosphere of distrust and mutual suspicion held by all signatories, as well as by the US observers present. Dubious from the start of Russian, Chinese, and North Vietnamese sincerity to respect Laotian neutrality, the Eisenhower administration decided to bolster American influence in Laos with a substantial influx of foreign aid. By the end of 1957, the US was spending more on foreign aid per capita to Laos than to any other nation in the world.[1]

But money wasn't enough. Substituting Communist guns for Yankee dollars, both Russia and China airlifted war materiel directly into Laos to support the Pathet Lao, their Communist surrogates in Laos. Better armed and politically motivated than the government's *Armées du Laos* (Lao Armed Forces, or FAL), the determined Pathet Lao brought the East-West ideological competition down to the most basic choice for the simple Laotian: fight the Americans and face hardship, or fight the Communists and face death.

For most of the Lao population and their leaders, it proved a relatively easy decision. As the resolve of the pro-Western leaders in the Laotian government melted before dramatic Pathet Lao advances, alarm spread throughout the Eisenhower administration. With the bloody precedent established by Joseph Stalin in post–World War II Eastern Europe, the US had come to believe in the "domino theory," in which the fall of one country to Communist subversion inevitably meant its neighbor was next on the list of Communist targets.

Within a year of the Geneva Agreements, the Royal Lao Government (RLG) was discreetly but actively lobbying the US government for military aid to combat the growing Pathet Lao advances and fill the financial gap left by the French decision to cease funding the FAL. In January 1955, the US responded to the lobbying by establishing the Program Evaluation Office (PEO) within the US Embassy in Vientiane.[2] Initially staffed with only a handful of civilians whose primary purpose was the funneling of US money to the FAL, the PEO languished as an effective anti-Communist instrument until the pivotal year of 1959.

That year would prove to be the point of no return for both the US commitment to fight communism in Laos and the tactics it would use there. It began with the first major expansion of the PEO, during which US intelligence sources "loaned" two officers to the program.[3] Working under PEO cover and designated "Controlled American Sources" (CAS),[4] the two officers worked with both the FAL and a group that would soon prove the only effective anti-Communist fighting force in Laos, an ethnic tribe called the Hmong (Free People).[5]

Fierce hill tribesmen proud of their independence, the Hmong (pronounced "mong," the "H" being silent) were led by their premier chieftain, Vang Pao, a major in the FAL. Living in scattered villages throughout northern Laos, the Hmong were perfectly situated to detect and delay the Pathet Lao attempting to infiltrate the *Plaine des Jarres* (Plain of Jars), commonly called PDJ.* The

*The *Plaine des Jarres* receives its unusual name from the hundreds of large jars that litter the plateau. Cut out of stone by unknown inhabitants of the area, their background remains an unsolved mystery.

Jerome Klingaman

Air Commando Jerome Klingaman and an unidentified USAF officer on the Plaine des Jarres, the plateau named for the hundreds of large jars cut from stone by a still unknown civilization lost in time. The bitterly disputed area was a major battleground during America's "secret war" in Laos.

flat plateau lies astride the major invasion path from North Vietnam to the Laotian capital city of Vientiane, located a hundred miles farther south.

But even an expanded PEO wasn't enough. In July 1959, the civilian-clad US Army brigadier general running the PEO received approval to secretly bring in 107 US Army Special Forces soldiers to train regular FAL units in unconventional warfare.[6] The Special Forces worked low-profile in civilian clothes under PEO cover to avoid conspicuous violation of the 1954 Geneva Agreements forbidding foreign military forces in Laos.[7] But if anyone was fooled, it wasn't the North Vietnamese. For soon after the arrival of the American soldiers, Radio Hanoi broadcast the "US Invasion of Laos."[8]

But as with everything else to date, the Special Forces teams weren't enough. Training soldiers to fight doesn't mean they will fight, and the FAL drifted through the following two years of training with no marked improvement. If the FAL continued to disappoint US expectations, more encouraging events were taking place with the Hmong. By December 1960, the Hmong under Vang Pao were proving receptive to efforts by a very unusual CAS* officer to organize them into an effective guerrilla force. The USI-Hmong program was to be called Operation Momentum.[9]

Bill Lair was not only a USI paramilitary officer living in Thailand and married to a prominent Thai national, he was also a legitimate captain in the Thai National Police.[10] More significantly, he was the founder of the Thai Police Aerial Resupply Unit (PARU), an elite Special Forces-type unit made available to the RLG in 1961 to train and fight alongside the Hmong.[11] But as valuable as the Hmong guerrillas were proving to be for the US ground combat strategy in Laos, the remoteness of their mountain villages created critical organizational, training, and resupply problems. With neither roads nor airfields near most villages, air delivery was the primary means of providing food, weapons, and equipment to the guerrillas.

As recruiting of the Hmong brought in thousands of potential fighters, their very success created urgent demands for an improved resupply system. Responding to these demands from field officers, USI headquarters responded on Christmas Day 1960 with a support directive to its secret aerial detachment on Okinawa. Previously introduced to the reader with its cover name, USAF Detachment 2, 1045th Observation, Evaluation, and Training Group, this USI-USAF unit located on Kadena Air Base would play a major role in America's "secret war" in Laos (and elsewhere) over the next several years.[12]

A Blue Major in the Black World

The Air Force special operations officer commanding the detachment read the headquarters directive with enthusiasm. It called for the immediate airdrop of 2,000 weapons to the Hmong.[13] And he knew exactly how to do this, having gained considerable experience during the Korean War under similar circumstances. In fact, he was still participating in an ongoing USAF/USI/Air America** operation then resupplying pro-Western guerrillas in Tibet.[14] Already familiar to the readers, the commander was none other than Maj Heinie Aderholt.

While the subsequent parachute resupply drops were successfully completed by the USI-contract aircrews, it was already obvious by early 1961 that the escalating war in Laos demanded some means of landing at least small liaison aircraft near the Hmong villages. But even if the villagers were willing to hack out crude dirt airstrips on the steep hillsides, neither the USI community nor the Air Force had a short-takeoff/landing aircraft capable of operating in the extreme altitude and temperature conditions found in northern Laos.

If the problem was tough, it was at least simple to understand: no STOL airplane meant no effective anti-Communist guerrilla force. And no effective anti-Communist guerrilla force meant the Pathet Lao and their North Vietnamese patrons could walk into Vientiane at their leisure. Clearly, something had to be done, and fast.

The solution was found in just two words: *Helio Courier*. This commercially built, rugged little airplane was made for backcountry flying from the most rugged airstrips. With flaps extending from the rear of the wing and slats extending forward from the wing's leading edge at slow airspeeds, the plane could almost hover in a

---

**Controlled American Source* was the term that identified US intelligence officers.

**In September 1959, the name of this proprietary airline in Asia was changed from Civil Air Transport to Air America.

Air Commando Association

The arrival in Laos of the short-takeoff/landing Helio Courier brought a badly needed solution to the seemingly insoluble problem of reaching mountainous Hmong villages by some means other than parachute. In the hands of a skilled pilot, the Helio Courier could almost hover in a strong wind.

30-knot wind. Aderholt had been a USI project officer for evaluation and procurement of the Helio Courier prior to his assignment to Okinawa and had persuaded the agency to purchase two of them for testing.[15]

The purchases were not made without internal resistance, however, and then not until the senior USI director personally supported the project. To this end, Aderholt himself flew the director on a cross-country night flight at an altitude never exceeding 500 feet, landing three times in dark, deserted farm fields to demonstrate the plane's capabilities.[16] What the director's staff thought of Aderholt's potentially risky demonstration, if they knew of it, is not a matter of record. But a USI proprietary airline began purchasing Helio Couriers* soon after Aderholt's involvement in Laos, eventually buying a dozen or more of the highly successful aircraft.[17]

But without at least a flat patch of dirt, even the vaunted Helio Courier was still useless. To solve the second half of this tandem problem, Aderholt, Bill Lair, and a small handful of USI pilots developed and extended a system of dirt airstrips throughout Laos that became known as Lima Sites (LS). Many of the Lima Sites were literally scraped off mountain tops by nearby Hmong using only hand tools, providing a severe challenge even for the Helio Courier. Aderholt recalls one Lima Site in particular:

> We had one named *Agony*. It was a b----h. It was 5,200 feet above sea level. In one place, it was 20 feet wide, and it was along two ridges. They had dug off one side of two hills and put it in the middle, and it was 600 feet long. You couldn't get in there after the sun started heating; you would get convection.[18]

The tactical implications of the seemingly simple Helio Courier/Lima Site combination went far beyond the modest concept of getting small liaison planes into backcountry villages. For one thing, it demonstrated again that unorthodox thinking for "low intensity conflicts" could still produce relatively cheap, effective answers to low-technology problems. For another, this timely combination provided the critical support necessary for the US to pursue for a decade its only viable ground war option—use of the Hmong guerrillas to slow North Vietnamese expansionism in northern Laos.

From the start there were always two wars in Laos. The "little" but more devastating war to Laotians was the US-led Hmong war against the Pathet Lao and North Vietnamese. The larger one was the multibillion dollar effort by the US to

Aderholt Collection

A typical airstrip located next to a typically remote Hmong village in the northern mountains of Laos. Such crude airstrips, complete with curves and major dips, were cut out by the Hmong wielding nothing more than handheld tools. The "Lima Sites," as they were dubbed by the Americans, were also the lifeline to keeping the Hmong in the fight against ever-increasing numbers of North Vietnamese troops.

*The Air Force also purchased a number of Helio Couriers, designating the aircraft the U-10 ("U" for utility).

A J Durizzi

The Air America transport pilots trained by Water Pump to fly AT-28 combat sorties were dubbed the "A Team." Capt A.J. Durizzi, one such fighter/transport pilot, also flew the C-7 Caribou, seen here being pushed backward by villagers to the very edge of a Lima Site airstrip. With every foot of "runway" counting for takeoff, the pilots used every trick to stay out of harm's way. Sometimes it wasn't enough.

close down North Vietnam's primary supply route to South Vietnam, a network of roads later made world famous as the Ho Chi Minh Trail. And with support to the Hmong up and running, Aderholt turned his attention to yet another tasking in 1961—this one for "the big war."

No Faces, No Serial Numbers

By 1961 Washington was already receiving unmistakable evidence confirming the growing North Vietnamese use of the Ho Chi Minh Trail as its primary logistics pipeline supporting the "liberation" of their South Vietnamese brethren. Even more blatant and threatening to Laotian stability were the Communist advances across the Hmong homelands on the *Plaine des Jarres.* The belated confirmation that the North Vietnamese had never really left Laos after 1954 further convinced both the US intelligence community and the Joint Chiefs of Staff that something more than low-level support to the Hmong was needed to oust the North Vietnamese from Laos.

These politico-military convictions drove the White House decision to place a covert* aerial unit capable of "armed reconnaissance" within striking range of the *Plaine des Jarres* and the Ho Chi Minh Trail. As at least a nod to the Geneva Agreements of 1954 was still deemed in order by the State Department, an overtly American military presence was out of the question. Again messages flowed

*A "covert" operation differs from a "clandestine" operation in that the former seeks to hide the identity of the operation's sponsor, while the latter seeks to hide the operation itself. See Joint Pub 1-02, *Department of Defense Dictionary of Military and Associated Terms,* 1 December 1989.

from USI headquarters to Okinawa asking for proposals. Aderholt's staff responded again with an idea that was approved on 21 March 1961 and given the code name "Project Mill Pond."[19]

The strike aircraft selected for Project Mill Pond was one USI had considerable and successful experience in previous cold war operations: the World War II-era B-26 Invader.* To bring together the 16 or so B-26s required for Mill Pond, USI combined the handful of operational bombers in its possession with a nearly equal number of B-26s pulled from its supply base and aircraft boneyard at Camp Chenen on Okinawa.**

Some of the Mill Pond aircraft were painted all black while others remained flat-metal silver. But all the bombers were totally devoid of any national insignia, or even the standard serial numbers painted on all vertical stabilizers.[20] Flown from Kadena AB to Thailand were 12 B-26s and two RB-26 reconnaissance variants.[21] The long flight was made nonstop in total radio silence to avoid unwelcomed attention.[22]

Just as the B-26s were "sanitized" with their removal from the Air Force inventory, the Air Force pilots selected to fly them were similarly sanitized.[23] For the individual this meant going through all the official and formal steps of resigning from active military duty. Having completed these steps, his real military records were sent to a special intelligence unit, while substitute, authentic-looking records continued through the military's "out-processing" system.[24] The individual might be required to provide a cover story for friends and family explaining his decision to leave active duty, and all relevant personal records (credit cards, bank checks, etc.) were changed to reflect the individual's new civilian identity.

The process of being sanitized, or "sheep-dipped" as it is widely called in the special operations community, is not a program taken lightly by the potential volunteer. For while he continues to be promoted along with his military peers (noted in his secret files) and returned to official military duty following completion of the operation, he can hardly miss the whole point of sheep-dipping. It allows the US government to deny any involvement or knowledge of his activities should he be killed or captured by the Communists. "Faceless" and a long way from home, he is totally on his own if things turn sour.

Eighteen Air Force pilots with previous B-26 experience were thus sheep-dipped and given first-class tickets to Bangkok, Thailand.[25] Upon arrival, they were placed in the employment of a cover company, Bangkok Contract Air Services, and flown 120 miles up-country to the Royal Thai Air Force Base (RTAFB) at Takhli.[26] They were soon joined at what they dubbed "The Ranch"[27] by a number of USI and Air America pilots also experienced in the B-26. All this activity took place against a background of escalating tensions in Laos caused primarily by the growing success of the Pathet Lao on the *Plaine des Jarres.*

As the tensions reached a crisis point, President Kennedy approved on 9 March 1961 a plan to launch the B-26s against advancing Pathet Lao positions on the *Plaine des Jarres.*[28] On 16 April with the bombers fueled and loaded with munitions and final aircrew briefings completed, the crews were given commissions in the Royal Laotian Air Force (RLAF).[29] But upon reporting to the flight line the next morning, the crews learned their first combat mission had been canceled.

As the reader will recall, something else of momentous political proportions was already taking place on the other side of the world on the day of the scheduled Mill Pond strike. On that day, the

---

*Originally designated the A-26 ("A" for attack) for its introduction into World War II, the Invader was later redesignated the B-26 ("B" for bomber) following the Air Force retirement of the original B-26, the Martin-built Marauder.

**Records as to the exact number of B-26s used for Mill Pond are not available—a result of the deception plan that called for the "sanitizing" of the aircraft to intentionally obscure their original ownership.

full political impact of the disastrous Bay of Pigs invasion of Cuba came crashing down on the White House. Personally and politically stunned by events taking place 90 miles south of Miami, President Kennedy ordered the Mill Pond air strike canceled. Major Aderholt passed the word to the Mill Pond crews that events in Cuba lay behind the White House decision to halt the mission.

The Mill Pond B-26s stayed in Thailand throughout the summer of 1961, flying training missions and remaining combat ready should the need arise. In addition, a handful of tightly controlled photoreconnaissance combat missions were flown over Laos with the two RB-26s included in the Mill Pond detachment, all without mishap. The pilots' flight logs were completed as usual, but not for B-26 flights and not in Asia. For the official record, these flights were flown with the Air Force Reserve's 1001st Operations Group at Andrews AFB, Washington, D.C.[30] Ultimately, the bombers were flown to the Republic of South Vietnam later that year to join the Air Commandos and the growing struggle in that country.

To some in Washington the departure of the Mill Pond B-26s for Vietnam seemed akin to firemen going to a new blaze before the first had been put out. They would soon be proved right. For in the kingdom of One Million Elephants and a White Parasol, the flames never died and the heartache had just begun.

A Primer in "Cold War 101"

Less than a decade after the end of the cold war, many covert operations conceived and frequently carried out by the United States seem, in retrospect, to be acts of near folly, if not worse. But these operations were carried out by intelligent, well-trained men whose dedication and patriotism were beyond reproach. The Mill Pond operation is a case in point. If President Kennedy had ordered the air strike into Laos, he would have had every reason to expect newspaper headlines the following day similar to this:

Bangkok Contract Air Services Attacks Laos!
Thai Commercial Company Launches 16 Bombers;
US Denies Involvement

The point here is, who could have believed this cover story would survive media scrutiny for even a single day? Why, then, even bother with a cover story so bizarre as to be useless if actually used? Well, for one thing, it had worked before for the US and would do so again in the future.

When the Chinese Communists shot down a transport from USI's proprietary airline (Civil Air Transport) flying inside Chinese territory during the Korean War,* the normally hyperactive Chinese propaganda machine failed to even mention the plane's shootdown for an entire year. And in the mid-1960s, years after Project Mill Pond, Cuban exile pilots from the Bay of Pigs operation were noted flying against Communist-supported rebels in the Belgian Congo. Their employer? A USI cover company called "Anstalt Wigmo."[31]

Again Communist propagandists chose not to push to a United Nations showdown the presence of USI combat pilots in Africa. Part of the reason, of course, was that the Soviets were playing the same game in the field with their proxies.**But perhaps the major reason is found not in the field, but in the cutthroat atmosphere of international politics played for keeps.

The continued success of obviously false cover stories used by both the US and the Communist bloc was dependent on both sides choosing to

*See "Firefly, Leaflet, and Pickup Operations," 40.

**Fidel Castro's high-profile subordinate, Che Guevara, also fought briefly in the Congo with a Cuban contingent. One Cuban B-26 pilot recalled to the author a particular day in which the two Cuban groups met in combat, exchanging heated insults over the radio.

accept even the most shallow of cover stories. And the rationale for this seeming absurdity was found in a mutual determination not to launch nuclear war unless either side perceived its homeland as being directly threatened. To avoid this mutual disaster (the appropriate acronym was MAD, or Mutually Assured Destruction), both sides worked from a twisted but relatively safe political logic. If Superpower A acknowledges an attack by Superpower B against one of A's surrogate forces, then Superpower A must either retaliate and risk unacceptable escalation or lose highly valuable political "face" with its worldwide surrogates. For example, a US Air Force attack against the Pathet Lao would likely have forced just such a response from the Communists. But if Superpower A chooses to accept Superpower B's cover story, no matter how ridiculous (e.g., Bangkok Contract Air Service bombers), Superpower A avoids being pushed into an undesirable escalation in a place and time not of its choosing.

Ridiculous? Perhaps. But for 40-plus years it kept either superpower from launching a nuclear war that would have incinerated a fair segment of the human race, including almost certainly this reader and his family. In an unsatisfactory world, perhaps the "near folly" alluded to earlier in this short primer had more going for it than many people realize.

Notes

1. Roger Warner, *Backfire: The CIA's Secret War in Laos and Its Link to the War in Vietnam* (New York: Simon and Schuster, 1995), 23.
2. Kenneth Conboy, *Shadow War: The CIA's Secret War in Laos* (Boulder, Colo.: Paladin Press, 1995), 17.
3. Ibid., 21, 28.
4. Philip D. Chinnery, *Any Time, Any Place: Fifty Years of the USAF Air Commando and Special Operations Forces, 1944–1994* (Annapolis, Md.: Naval Institute Press, 1994), 170.
5. Warner, 41.
6. Keven M. Generous, *Vietnam: The Secret War* (New York: Gallery Books, 1985), 70.
7. Ibid., 104.
8. Ibid., 71.
9. Warner, 47.
10. Conboy, 57–58.
11. Ibid. See also Warner, 31–32.
12. Conboy, 25.
13. Brig Gen Harry C. Aderholt, USAF Oral History Interview (U) (No. K239.0512-1716), 12–15 August 1986, 96. (Secret) Information extracted is unclassified.
14. Ibid., 66, 77. See also Conboy, 29.
15. Brig Gen Harry C. Aderholt, USAF, Retired, "Setting the Record Straight," *Arc Light* 11, no. 4 (October 1995): 1.
16. Brig Gen Harry C. Aderholt, USAF, Retired, interview with author, 9 January 1996, Fort Walton Beach, Fla.
17. Aderholt, "Setting the Record Straight," 1.
18. Aderholt, US Oral History Interview, 78.
19. Dan Hagedorn and Leif Hellstrom, *Foreign Invaders: The Douglas Invader in Foreign Military and US Clandestine Service* (Leicester, UK: Midland Publishing Limited, 1994), 133.
20. Ibid., 134.
21. Conboy, 52.
22. Hagedorn and Hellstrom, 134.
23. Ibid., 133.
24. Col L. Fletcher Prouty, USAF, Retired, *The Secret Team: The CIA and Its Allies in Control of the United States and the World* (Englewood Cliffs, N.J.: Prentice-Hall, Inc., 1973), 172–73.
25. Hagedorn and Hellstrom, 133.
26. Ibid.
27. Timothy N. Castle, *At War in the Shadow of Vietnam: U.S. Military Aid to the Royal Lao Government, 1955–1975* (New York: Columbia University Press, 1992), 34.
28. Conboy, 51.
29. Castle, 35.
30. Ibid., 135.
31. Hagedorn and Hellstrom, 150.

Off the Record

Laos 1964
THE BRUISED DOMINO

North Vietnam broke the 1962 agreements before the ink was dry.

Averell Harriman
Assistant Secretary of State
for Far Eastern Affairs

Water Pump's primary mission from the outset was to train the "C Team," RLAF pilots designated for checkout in their US-supplied AT-28s. Despite initial difficulties in training that forced the US to turn to the A Team and B Team for quick results, the C Team had grown sufficiently by 1970 to take over all AT-28 missions in Laos. Standing with these C-Team pilots, dressed in the required civilian clothes, is US Air Force combat controller "Mr." Roger Klair, call sign "Smokey Control."

Even as the joint CIA-USAF project in Laos, Project Mill Pond, was winding down in late 1961, Communist infiltration and attacks within Laos continued to escalate. In fact, on the same day President John F. Kennedy canceled the Mill Pond air strike into Laos, he ordered US Navy and Marine Corps elements of Joint Task Force 116 (JTF 116), the US contingency force for Southeast Asia, into the China Sea as a demonstration of US resolve.[1]

For President Kennedy, the little kingdom of Laos was becoming much like the proverbial "tar baby"— a sticky problem in which the harder one struggles to escape, the more firmly one becomes stuck to the problem. But for a brief moment at least it seemed that the high-profile JTF 116 deployment had worked, as the Communists promptly responded with an agreement to participate in negotiations on the future of Laos that were to take place in Geneva later that year.

The 1962 Geneva Agreements, essentially a repeat of the 1954 agreements, called for the expulsion of all foreign troops already in Laos by 7 October of that year. The week before the deadline, the United States publicly removed its 666 military personnel through checkpoints manned by the United Nations International Control Commission (ICC) observers; the North Vietnamese evacuated exactly 40,[2] leaving behind an estimated 10,000 more.[3]

Despite appearances, the initial North Vietnamese goal was not the military conquest of Laos, but rather control of the remote eastern regions of the country through which ran its all-important logistics pipeline southward into South Vietnam. Whoever controlled the pipeline controlled the ultimate outcome of the Vietnamese war, a fact not yet predominant in American national-security thinking in 1962.

From the start, the political makeup of the ICC doomed any chance that it could fulfill its mission to ensure the political neutrality of Laos as specified in the Geneva Agreements. Comprised of members sent from pro-Western Canada, "neutral" India, and Communist Poland, the ICC included a proviso in its rules that all members agree on when and where alleged violations of the neutrality rules would be inspected. And a simple "no" from the Polish (or Indian) delegation could prevent any inspection from taking place. And on the rare occasions all sides agreed to inspect a site in Communist-held areas in Laos, the Pathet Lao simply refused them permission. It was a tense situation that could turn bloody without warning.

When on one occasion in 1963 the ICC attempted to enforce its mandate to inspect a site under Pathet Lao control, the two helicopters carrying the inspection team were shot down by Communist gunfire.[4] As for North Vietnam's bald-faced denials of its presence in Laos, they became accepted as diplomatic lies about which nothing could be done, nothing *official* anyway.

For the record, the United States still supported the 1962 Geneva Agreements calling for the removal of all foreign troops from Laotian territory. Off the record, sentiment ran deep in the US State and Defense Departments that the North Vietnamese had been making a mockery of the agreements from the start. It was under these circumstances that a national security rationale based on *realpolitik* evolved in Washington that public support for the agreements could not be allowed to block a military response to North Vietnam's aggression. But how to have both a political and military response?

As Communist expansion in northern and eastern Laos spread unchecked through 1963, the Royal Laotian Government solved the problem for the Kennedy administration by discreetly lobbying the US government for military support. High on the RLG's priority list was the replacement of its World War II-vintage, propeller-driven training aircraft, modified with wing-mounted machine guns for ground attack missions. But what to replace them with, and how to provide the flight training without drawing public attention?

Air Commando Association
A Water Pump T-28 trainer, devoid of all national insignia, departing Udorn Royal Thai Air Force Base in the early 1960s. Rugged and simple to fly, it proved an excellent choice for the American, Thai, and Laotian strike pilots trained by the Air Commandos for war in Laos.

While modern jet aircraft were clearly beyond the flying and maintenance capabilities of the Royal Laotian Air Force, the two-seater T-28 trainer still used by the United States for military pilot training was selected as an effective replacement. And it could be made available from stocks given earlier to South Vietnam. First question resolved.

Also favoring the T-28 selection was the recent US Air Force activation of its newly formed Air Commandos, counterinsurgency specialists organized for just this type of Third World "problem." The Air Commandos had developed considerable expertise in exploiting the combat capability of the rugged and simple T-28, which—when modified for the ground attack role—was redesignated the AT-28D. Second question resolved.

Like a shy young couple made for each other, all the Royal Laotian Air Force and the Air Commandos needed by late 1963 was an introduction. And within months, the Pathet Lao would unwittingly ensure that the introduction was made as a result of their alarmingly successful offensive in the spring of 1964.

In March 1964, Secretary of Defense Robert S. McNamara approved the deployment of a Special Air Warfare Center detachment from the Air Commando base at Hurlburt Field, Florida, to Udorn Royal Thai Air Force Base, Thailand.[5] Within a few short weeks of the secretary's memo, Detachment 6, 1st Air Commando Wing, was hanging its "Open for Business" shingle out in the hot Thai sun. The original deployment was designated Project Water Pump, the name that stuck to the program throughout the following decade. Ostensibly just one of many Air Commando training teams fanning out throughout the Third World in the early 1960s, Water Pump was in fact a one-of-a-kind mission. And that mission was nothing less than providing the senior US official (SUSO) in Laos a secret air force with which to fight a secret war.

Project Water Pump's mission would be executed with several mutually supportive programs. To accomplish its primary mission of training RLAF aircrews and mechanics without technically violating the 1962 Geneva Agreements, the Laotians would be brought outside politically neutral Laos to Udorn RTAFB. If the US was fudging on the agreements—and it certainly was—Washington's policy planners could still point to the wholesale cheating in progress by their North Vietnamese adversaries.

The Air Commandos would also maintain the initial four AT-28s they brought to Udorn, supplement RLAF combat sorties in Laos if directed by the SUSO in that country, and provide a nucleus of combat air expertise should the US activate a major contingency plan in the area.[6] Yet another program would send Water Pump's civic-action teams into Laos and northern Thailand's rural border areas, the latter a payback to the Thai government for its support and a move deemed necessary to protect the growing number of USAF squadrons in Thailand from guerrilla attack.

Remarkably, all this activity was set in motion by a total initial cadre of only 41 Air Commando volunteers sent to Udorn for six-month-long tours, with replacements to arrive as the initial cadre rotated back to the US. Led by colorful and aggressive Maj Drexel B. "Barney" Cochran, the superbly trained and motivated Water Pump team would have its ambitious mission expanded still further within weeks of its arrival at Udorn. In fact, training began almost immediately for both civilian Air America pilots and Royal Thai Air

USAF

The T-28 trainer could be turned into a ground attack fighter (redesignated AT-28, "A" for attack) with the addition of .50-caliber heavy machine-gun pods and external bomb racks slung under each wing. This pristine Air Commando example operated from the Air Commando base at Hurlburt Field, Florida.

Force volunteers seconded to combat duty in Laos to bolster the still small RLAF AT-28 force.

With the threat (North Vietnamese aggression in Laos) identified and a covert response (Project Water Pump) in place, there remained only the requirement for a deception plan to shield the effort from public scrutiny. But what a deception plan! The RLG couldn't admit that it requested US support and still maintain its public and political "neutrality." The Thai government couldn't admit its support to the US and Royal Lao governments, which by definition also violated the 1962 agreements. The Kennedy administration had the same problem as the Thai government, with one bizarre complication: to avoid generating an unwanted escalation of tensions with the Soviet, Chinese, and North Vietnamese Communists, it had to help its enemies "save face" by keeping Water Pump's activities from public view.

Air Commando Association

Like the Water Pump operation itself, Detachment 6's Air Commandos did not waste a lot of time on appearances, as their detachment sign shows. Initially deployed to instruct only Royal Laotian Air Force pilots, the detachment was directed almost immediately to include American and Thai mercenary pilots for AT-28 training.

A Wilderness of Mirrors

Inside Washington, an elaborate process evolved in which the United States publicly denied having a combat role in Laos. Once committed to this stance, however, it had little choice but to make its political SUSO in Laos an unofficial "field marshal" for the secret war. It was a charade that would grow to incredible complexity in the following years.

Inside Laos, the SUSO decided if and when US military planes could overfly Laotian territory. And if granted permission to overfly, what targets could be struck and even what specific types of munitions could be used against those targets. The power granted the civilian SUSO was a bitter pill for theater military commanders to swallow, but there it was.

Inside Thailand, this "smoke and mirrors" deception continued with nothing, including Water Pump, being what it appeared to public eyes. Stripped of all its cover, Water Pump's primary mission was to provide an American ambassador with a private air force to fight a secret war.

Inside Udorn RTAFB, Water Pump's priorities were shifting as fast as the changing politico-military situation around it. The handful of RLAF pilots sent to Udorn were too few and too technically inept to offer any hope of near-term success over the battlefield. And their Buddhist inclination not to hurt (or get hurt by) their fellow human beings, an admirable trait anywhere but on a battlefield, showed itself early to the dismayed Air Commandos. And much to the dismay of the American SUSO in Laos, the North Vietnamese were demonstrating on the battlefield their success in finding a work-around to this Buddhist "drawback."

The SUSO wasn't made any happier to discover that the aggressive Air Commandos on their own had also figured out a work-around to the RLAF's lack of zeal. While the option of using the Air Commando instructors themselves for selected combat missions had been present from the start, it risked exposing the all-important political charade that American military personnel weren't fighting in Laos. And the aggressiveness of the Air Commandos actually worked against them by further fueling the SUSO's fear of their being shot down. The Air Force attaché to Vientiane recalled the SUSO's response to the Air Commando enthusiasm:

> We had to get kind of hard-nosed because the SAWC people . . . were really gung-ho—all of them were. Under a leader like Barney, everybody was just ready to do anything they could. They would sometimes come across the river [into Laos] and one got caught. The Ambassador brought it to my attention . . . and said we would really have to clamp down.[7]

The problem with "clamping down" on the Air Commandos was that it didn't solve the problem of finding an effective air-strike deterrent against the Pathet Lao. Clearly the long-term solution lay with Water Pump's original mission to train Asian AT-28 pilots. The SUSO's torment lay in the reality that there would be no need for a long-term solution if a short-term solution were not found immediately.

Teaching the "ABCs" of the Secret War

In desperation, the SUSO in Laos cabled Washington on 18 May with an extraordinary and politically expedient alternative to direct US military support.[8] The cable left a remarkable trail of heartburn across Washington that reached from the Riverside entrance of the Pentagon clear over the Potomac River to the flag-bedecked C Street diplomatic entrance to the State Department. It was bold, imaginative, and, most important, pragmatic. In a nutshell, it called for Water Pump's Air Commandos to begin training American civilian fighter pilots for combat missions in Laos.[9] Washington agonized for two days before cabling an affirmative response.

Air America, the CIA proprietary airline operating in Laos, immediately sent five pilots (one ex-USAF; four ex-USMC) to Water Pump for quick AT-28 checkouts.[10] Speed was essential with the first group, dubbed the A Team, as their first combat mission came only a week later. On 25 May, five Air America-piloted AT-28s armed with 500-pound bombs, machine guns, and rockets attacked a one hundred-foot-long bridge in Pathet Lao territory.[11] The mission was a mixed success, however, in that two of the fighters had been riddled with bullet holes. If the potential for success had been demonstrated, so too had the potential for the still too hot political disaster that would follow the capture of a shot-down American.

To minimize the political risk, the SUSO restricted use of his civilian fighter pilots to armed escort missions involving rescue attempts for downed military and civilian (e.g., Air America) aircrew. In addition, the two-seater AT-28 would be flown by a single pilot on combat missions.[12] To maximize the operational potential, Water Pump immediately set to work to lengthen the AT-28 conversion training.

Anthony J. Durizzi, former Navy pilot and Air America captain, recalls the Air Commando training he entered in August 1964 in the third Water Pump AT-28 course for American civilians:

> I was in a class of eight, the usual size class for this training. The course had been expanded to three-weeks duration to include ground school, a flight checkout, formation flying, and a week on the gunnery range. After completion of training, we were allowed to maintain proficiency on the AT-28s any-

time we were in Udorn and found the time to fly them. This proficiency flying was done on our "off time," and we weren't paid for it. The AT-28s were armed with two .50-caliber machine guns mounted in pods under the wings, with two more pods mounted outboard of the guns, each of which carried 14 2.75-inch air-to-ground rockets. Our two Air Commando instructors were particularly aggressive and determined to give us their best effort.[13]

The Air America AT-28 pilots went on to fly a number of carefully selected combat sorties, in particular flying armed escort for often dramatic rescue missions of downed American pilots. For risking their lives they were paid $200 a day, whether they remained on the airfield on rescue alert or flew multiple combat missions.[14] Durizzi further recalls the mission profiles:

> When called for armed escort missions, we were always brought together in groups of four, the number of aircraft that were sent aloft for each AT-28 mission. If four were called, an additional four were immediately put on alert, as the AT-28's fuel endurance limited us to an hour-and-a-half flight time. I would estimate 20–25 guys were checked out by the Air Commandos during the length of the program.[15]

But while the civilian fighter pilots proved an aggressive and effective solution in the field, they also brought undesirable political baggage. A captured American pilot would still provide a rich propaganda coup for the Communists, whether military or civilian. And American "mercenary" combat pilots hadn't been sanctioned since the glory days of Gen Claire Chennault's "Flying Tigers" in World War II's China-Burma-India theater. The "civilian fighter pilot" program was finally phased out in 1967, when the A Team was replaced by the B Team—another successful group of Water Pump-trained fighter pilots that had in fact been flying and fighting alongside the A Team from the very start.[16]

Alarmed at the prospect of North Vietnamese expansionism along their border, the Thai by 1964 were offering a combination of overt and covert support to the Americans. Overtly, they offered the use of RTAF bases in Thailand and Thai troops to South Vietnam. Covertly, they provided the B Team, just when the SUSO needed them most. In his authoritative book *Shadow War: The CIA's Secret War in Laos*, author Kenneth Conboy reveals:

> Four days before the first A-Team mission . . . a decision had been made to form a B Team of Thai volunteer pilots—named Firefly—who would conduct some of the most sensitive strike missions originally intended for the Air America contingent. Also, in contrast to the RLAF, the Thai would remain completely responsive to the U.S. Embassy [in Laos].[17]

Like their US counterparts operating in Laos, the Thai volunteers were sheep-dipped from the RTAF. They flew AT-28s with RLAF markings and wore civilian flight suits with no rank. Although skilled pilots, their reluctance to fly in bad weather or at night limited their overall contribution to the SUSO. On the other hand, their previous experience in T-28s and the similarity between Thai and Lao languages made them much easier to train than the then-still minuscule number of RLAF pilots going through Water Pump's flight school. On 27 May 1964, scarcely a week after the first Air America pilots arrived in Udorn for Water Pump training, five Thai volunteers reported for their AT-28 checkout.[18] A year later, Water Pump had graduated 23 Thai Fireflys, each of them expected to complete 100 combat missions during his six-month tour in Laos.[19]

To coordinate targets and flight control for the Firefly program, two Water Pump Air Commandos were discreetly moved to Wattay Airport outside Vientiane to establish an air operations center (AOC).[20] The successful B Team program continued until 1970, when the size of the RLAF pilot

Air Commando Association

The Thai mercenaries trained by the Air Commandos at Udorn were known as the "B Team." After being "sheep-dipped" from the Royal Thai Air Force, they were hired for six-month-long combat tours in Laos. The Thai pilots proved both resourceful and brave in combat at a time when US military pilots were not yet allowed into Laos. Note AT-28s with Royal Lao roundels on their fuselages in the background.

force finally permitted all-Lao manning of its assigned AT-28s.[21]

If the RLAF pilots lacked the aggressiveness necessary to be effective over the battlefield, there still remained one other Laotian possibility. The Hmong, as noted earlier, were taking the brunt of ground fighting (and therefore casualties) throughout the country. During a visit to the US in 1963, their leader, Vang Pao, toured the Air Commando base at Hurlburt Field, Florida, raising the possibility of including selected Hmong in the Water Pump flight school. The presence of Hmong pilots flying over their brethren fighting below would be a matter of considerable pride to Vang Pao and his people. Somewhat reluctantly, the US agreed to support this request from its most effective ally in Laos and tasked the Air Commandos to make it happen.

USAF's Air Training Command (ATC) would not likely have been impressed with Water Pump's flight school facilities or unorthodox training methods. On the other hand, the Air Commandos had problems beyond ATC's worst nightmare. Only the first two Hmong reporting to Water Pump had received any previous flight instruction—a few hours of local civilian instruction in little Piper Cubs. It wasn't until the succeeding Hmong pilot candidates presented themselves at Udorn that the Americans learned their new students had never so much as driven an automobile. Nor could they read or write in English, and their spoken English vocabulary was . . . ah . . . small.

In his official USAF memoirs, Brig Gen Harry C. Aderholt, originator of the Water Pump concept, recalls how these Hmong were trained to fly fighter-bombers in combat: "How do you teach . . . an illiterate Hmong . . . the theory of flight? You don't. You tell him, 'When you push the stick this way, Buddha makes that wing go down, and that turns the aircraft.'"[22]

Another problem with the Hmong was their small physical size, which prevented them from seeing out the T-28's cockpit while keeping their feet on the aircraft's rudder pedals. Air Commando solution: wire small 2 x 4 blocks of wood to the rudder pedals and give thick pillows to the student pilots for their seats. Each morning the proud Hmong students went to the flight line with helmets in one hand and pillows in the other.[23]

Short they might have been, but no one who ever watched them fight faulted the Hmong for courage. Incredibly, 19 Hmong graduated from Water Pump to become ground attack fighter pilots.[24] And like all AT-28 pilots flying in Laos, they took the radio call sign *Chaophakao* ("Lord White Buddha").[25] The best of them, Lee Lue, went on to become one of the most famous strike pilots in all Indochina, a legend known to US Air Force and Navy pilots throughout the region.

Air Commando Association

To the deeply religious Thai and Laotian AT-28 pilots, a blessing for their attack aircraft from a Buddhist monk was a significant ritual.

The Hmong pilots were the pride of their people, but they were not invincible. Whereas their American counterparts finished their six-month or one-year tours with a boisterous party and medals on their chests, the Hmong simply flew until they were killed. And the maelstrom that swept through the Hmong population on the ground showed no more mercy for those in the air. By the end of the war, 16 of the 19 Hmong pilots were dead.[26] Among the fallen was Lee Lue.

Air Commando Association

Hmong pilot Lee Lue reported to the Air Commandos at Udorn RTAFB for attack pilot training with little more than a few hours of local flight instruction in Piper Cubs. A gifted pilot, he graduated as an AT-28 attack pilot in January 1968. As he flew up to a dozen combat sorties a day, he became a legend throughout Southeast Asia for his courage and skill.

Committed solely to Laos, Project Water Pump was designed much as a sniper rifle is designed for one and only one use. Used only rarely against the growing defenses of the Ho Chi Minh Trail, Water Pump's real target was the North Vietnamese Army (NVA) and Pathet Lao forces attacking the Hmong guerrilla forces in northern Laos. From 1964 forward, brutal combat between the lightly armed Hmong guerrillas and their Communist foes became continuous as both sides seesawed back and forth across northeastern Laos and the strategically located *Plaine des Jarres*, north of the Laotian capital of Vientiane.

Obvious to all involved, and the reason for Water Pump's activation, was the military fact that without air support of some kind, Vang Pao's guerrillas were no match against the Communists. But even as Barney Cochran's trainers were moving into high gear for their primary mission of training Asian pilots, an even higher priority interrupted the schedule. This interruption involved search and rescue (SAR) missions for American pilots shot down in an area in which the US government denied even their presence. Like Project Water Pump itself, the cause of this interruption also had a code name.

In the Vietnamese language, its classified title was "*Doan 559*." The secret wasn't so much the identity of the organization itself—the 559th Transportation Division, Rear Services Directorate, of Hanoi's Ministry of Defense—but rather its mission. Simply maintaining and protecting an obscure road network in a remote region would hardly seem to justify the extraordinary measures the Democratic Republic of Vietnam (DRV) expended to hide the 559th's mission. Unless, of course, this obscure road network was the same highway about to become famous around the world in its English translation nickname, "The Ho Chi Minh Trail." For an investment of this importance, lying to the world about the presence of thousands of North Vietnamese troops in "neutral" Laos, was all part of the propaganda war.

In 1964 the Ho Chi Minh Trail had not yet become the massive death trap for the thousands who would die on and above its road network in the years to come. But the North Vietnamese Army was already busy sending critical war supplies and troop reinforcements south through the Laotian panhandle by this time. And like honey drawing bees, the NVA activity brought US reconnaissance jets overhead to monitor the traffic. But these "bees" weren't legally supposed to be there, and the political repercussions of an American military pilot shot down and captured in Laos continued to be a recurring nightmare in Washington.

The inevitable shootdown happened nearly three months to the day after Water Pump's activation. Lt Charles F. Klusman, US Navy, was shot down while flying an RF-8A single-seat jet over the Ho Chi Minh Trail on 6 June 1964. Fortunately, an Air America transport flying in the vicinity heard Klusman's "*Mayday!*" call and organized an immediate search and rescue effort. In Vientiane, Col Robert Tyrrell, the Air Force attaché, requested permission from the SUSO to use American-flown AT-28s as armed escort for the Air America helicopters en route to Klusman's location.[27]

With the prospect of Americans being shot down looming over his head, the SUSO declined, sending instead his Thai Fireflys.[28] The Thai, however, were unable to communicate with Klusman, and with one helicopter crewman wounded from ground fire, the initial rescue team left the area. Pressing the issue again with the SUSO, Colonel Tyrrell secured permission to

Air Commando Association

As Water Pump's ad hoc civic action program spread out from Udorn RTAFB to reach more rural areas, the sight of its red ambulance brought hope and relief to many. The old vehicle was pulled from salvage at Udorn, put into running shape by off-duty mechanics, and manned by volunteers trained by the Air Commando medics.

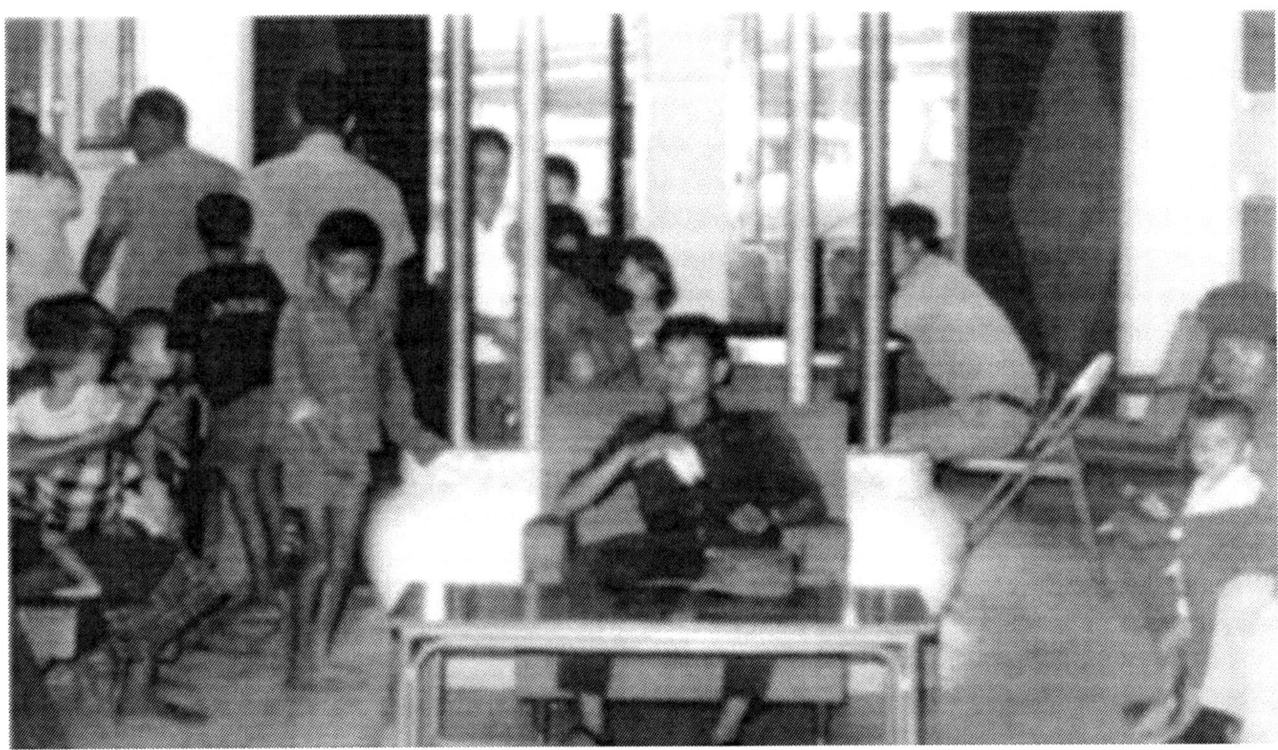

Roland Lutz

When Air Commando medic "Doc" Roland "Hap" Lutz started an after-hours sick call for the local Laotians in the main room of the US enlisted quarters at Savannakhet, Laos, the response quickly overwhelmed the building. With the help of off-duty military and civilian volunteers, he later supervised the building of the one (and only) Royal Laotian Air Force hospital in the country.

use Water Pump pilots in AT-28s, followed by a pair of Air America-piloted AT-28s to support the next rescue effort later that day. This time the SUSO agreed, but unknown to the Americans, Klusman had already been captured.[29] While Klusman was eventually rescued,* future shootdowns over the Ho Chi Minh Trail were clearly inevitable.

As effective as Water Pump was proving, the scale of war in Laos would soon come to dwarf the small output of the Air Commando school at Udorn. With this expansion would come an increase in the number of US air strikes unimaginable in 1964, as well as the military air rescue assets needed to retrieve the corresponding increase in downed pilots. But even as this "big war" grew, Water Pump continued to fight in a number of ways, one of which brought relief to untold numbers of Thai and Laotian civilians caught between the warring armies.

Water Pump's medical team arrived with the first Air Commando deployment in early 1964. Initially intended to support only Water Pump personnel, it began holding off-duty sick call for the local populace. Local Thai officials soon noticed the initiative and encouraged expansion of the unofficial program. This pioneer civic-action program later became the model for a much larger-scale program spread throughout the rest of Thailand and beyond.

*Though captured, he managed to escape four months later and was rescued by an Air America helicopter. In the years and hundreds of shootdowns over Laos that followed, only one other pilot managed to escape from Communist captivity in Laos and reach freedom.

To work under such primitive conditions with the threat of sudden violence always present required a physical and mental stamina beyond what one might be expected to find in a stateside hospital ward. And as former CMSgt Roland "Hap" Lutz recalls, the Air Commandos had some unusual ideas for weeding out unsuitable volunteers:

> Having responded to a notice asking for volunteers for the new Air Commandos, I was interviewed by a full colonel, who asked me a number of questions: Would I volunteer to work overseas in civilian clothes? Work in rural and possibly hostile areas? Volunteer for parachute training? I later learned had I answered "no" to a single question, the interview would have been terminated immediately.[30]

Having answered in the affirmative to all interview questions, Lutz was given the "opportunity" to demonstrate his determination in the next phase of selection conducted by a group of psychologists at Lackland AFB, Texas:

> I was made to stand in a tub filled ankle deep with ice water, with arms outstretched while a "shrink" grilled me with innumerable questions about why I had volunteered for this assignment. The object was to see how long I could hold out, and the minimum time, if there was one, was never revealed to me.[31]

Chief Lutz survived the Lackland "interview" and, after substantial Air Commando "tradecraft" training in the US, was subsequently deployed to Udorn RTAFB with the second Water Pump

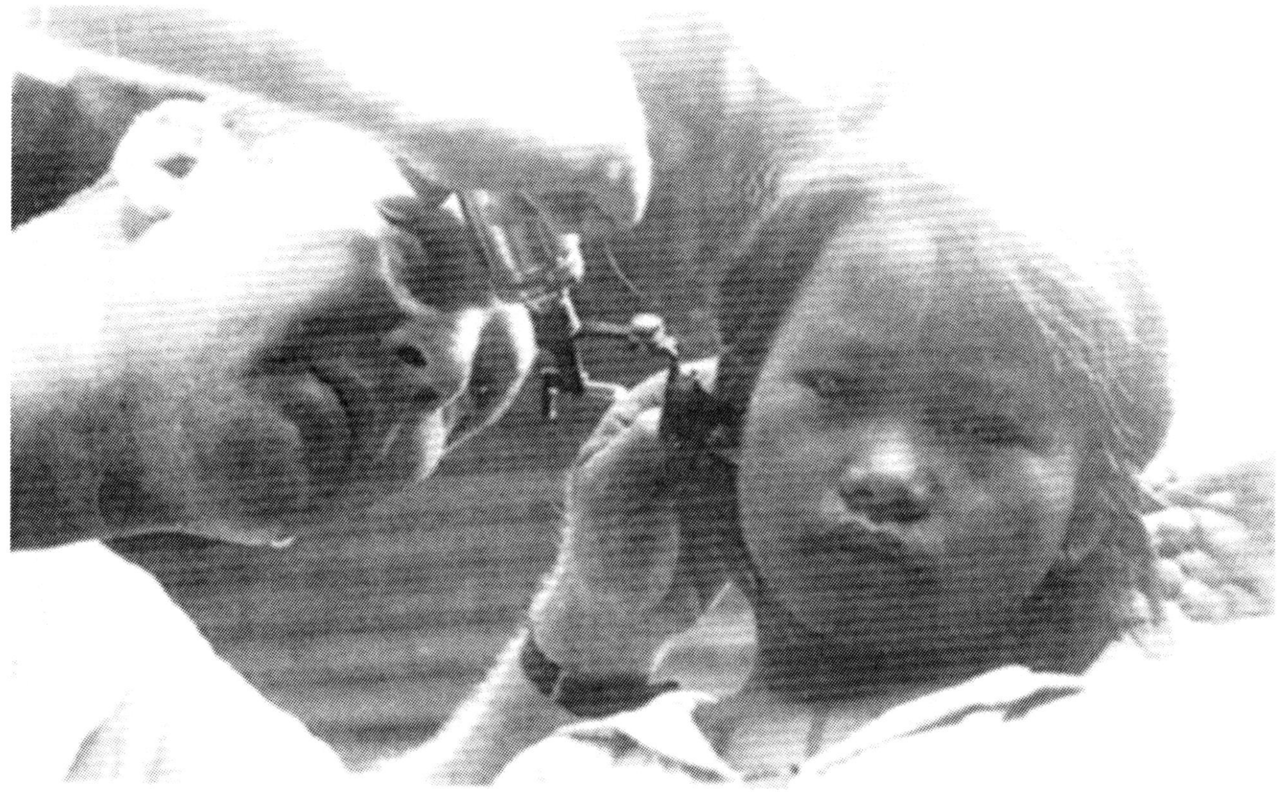

Air Commando Association

Water Pump Air Commando Ted Dake takes a look during a civic action medical tour to a local village. A fully qualified flight surgeon, pilot, and parachutist, Dr. Dake was typical only in the way unusual people were drawn to the challenges and dangers of Air Commando duty in the Third World.

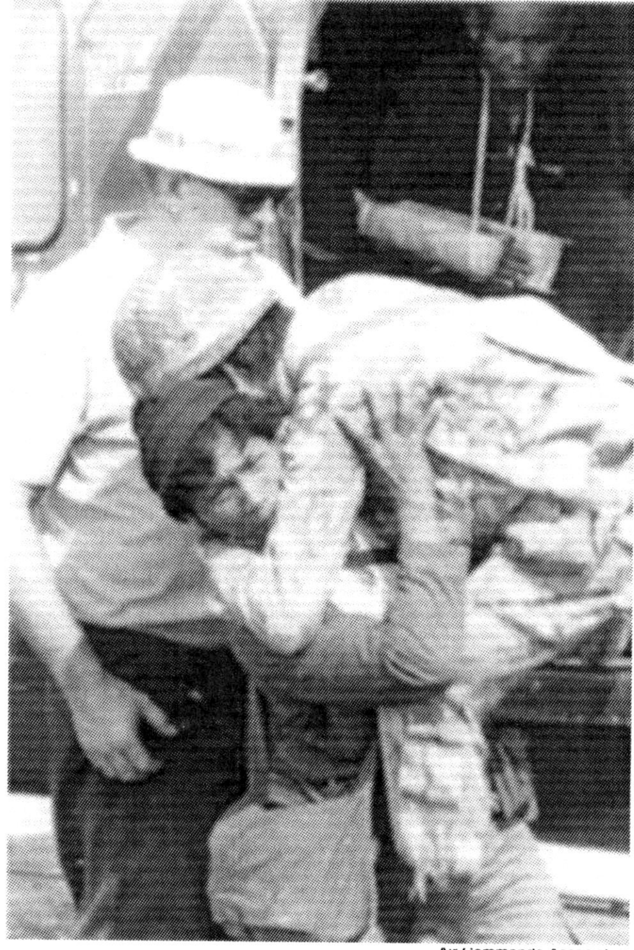

Air Commando Association

Air Commando medic Frank Dean supervises the unloading of wounded from a helicopter after an unknown battle. Air Force noncommissioned officers such as Dean were frequently the senior and perhaps only medical personnel working out of the low-profile air operations centers run by the Air Commandos in Laos.

deployment. He went on to complete five additional Water Pump deployments, surviving, as the Air Commandos say, "with two more stripes and 20 more years than he had a right to expect." His first three deployments to Water Pump returned him to Udorn, while his next three deployments sent him straight to Laos. His tours in Laos, beginning in 1970, brought with them some very unusual duty for a medic.

Duty in Laos was a dream come true for independent-minded Air Commandos. There was simply no end to the opportunities to put their cross-training to use. For Hap, this included loading .50-caliber ammunition belts into RLAF AT-28s, inserting detonation fuses into bombs slung underneath the aircraft, and helping out wherever and whenever needed, all in addition to tending to the medical needs of other American personnel at the base.

During the day, official duties were completed, while at night Laotian military and civilian patients queued up outside the outer room of the enlisted quarters "villa" for nighttime sick call. Enthusiastic volunteers from both the US military and civilian force in the community provided the needed manpower to assist the Air Commando medics. In Laos, in particular, the Air Commando doctors and senior medics brought the civic-action concept close to its full potential. With the help of a number of military and Air America employees volunteering labor during their off-duty time, Lutz oversaw the building of the first (and only) Royal Laotian Air Force hospital, located in the southern town of Savannakhet.

Despite these humanitarian efforts, the cold reality of combat in Laos demanded even the Air Commando medics occasionally become involved in more lethal operations. For Chief Lutz, this took form in directing air strikes against Communist forces attacking the southern town of Dônghèn in 1966.

Water Pump continued in operation for the duration of the war in Laos, continuing to support the secret American effort in that country. Detachment 6, as it was still formally known, later became part of the 606th Air Commando Squadron in 1966, which in turn became the 56th Air Commando Wing the following year.

Much later in the 1970s, the detachment would train its sights on another priority target. This time it would be a classic foreign internal defense mission against the genocidal Khmer Rouge in the land of Angkor Wat.

Charlie Norton

Towering trees amidst the wild landscape of eastern Laos dwarf a vulnerable Air America helicopter on final approach. AT-28s flying combat escort for helicopter rescue missions were hard pressed to protect the helicopters from enemy ground fire at this stage of the pickup.

Notes

1. Kenneth Conboy, *Shadow War: The CIA's Secret War in Laos* (Boulder, Colo.: Paladin Press, 1995), 54.

2. Roger Warner, *Backfire: The CIA's Secret War in Laos and Its Link to the War in Vietnam* (New York: Simon and Schuster, 1995), 84.

3. Keven M. Generous, *Vietnam: The Secret War* (New York: Gallery Books, 1985), 106.

4. Conboy, 99.

5. Ibid., 108.

6. Philip D. Chinnery, *Anytime, Anyplace: A History of USAF Air Commando and Special Operations Forces, 1944–1994* (Annapolis, Md.: Naval Institute Press, 1994), 94.

7. Col Robert L. F. Tyrrell, USAF Oral History Interview (U) (K239.0512-895), 12 May 1975, 25. (Secret) Information extracted is unclassified.

8. Message from US Embassy (Vientiane), dated 18 May 1964, DDRS 1990, as cited in Conboy, 114.

9. Ibid., 109.

10. Ibid.

11. Ibid.

12. Anthony J. Durizzi, former Air America captain, interview with author, Kirkland, Wash., 23 February 1996.

13. Ibid.

14. Ibid.

15. Ibid.

16. Conboy, 160.

17. Ibid., 109–10.

18. Ibid., 110.

19. Ibid., 154

20. Ibid.

21. Ibid., 264.

22. Brig Gen Harry C. Aderholt, USAF, Retired, USAF Oral History Interview (U) (K239.0512-1716), 12–15 August 1986, 98. (Secret) Information extracted is unclassified.

23. Jane Hamilton-Merritt, *Tragic Mountains: The Hmong, the Americans, and the Secret Wars in Laos, 1942–1992* (Bloomington: Indiana University Press, 1993), 153.

24. Aderholt, 98.

25. Hamilton-Merritt, 153.

26. Aderholt, 98.

27. Tyrrell, 45.

28. Ibid.

29. Ibid.

30. CMSgt Roland "Hap" Lutz, USAF, interview with author, 2 February 1996, Fort Walton Beach, Fla.

31. Ibid.

A-26
Working the Trail
THOMPSON

The Propeller versus
Jet Controversy

Laos 1966

THE BLOODY DOMINO

I was briefing General Sweeney one time . . . and he said, "I want to tell you one thing, you are no different from anybody else in the Air Force, that silly [Air Commando] hat and all." I told him, "General Sweeney, we are a hell of a lot better than the average guy I've seen in the Air Force." Boy, that didn't set very well at all!

Col Harry C. Aderholt

The exchange between Gen Walter C. Sweeney Jr., commander of Tactical Air Command, and Colonel Aderholt went far deeper than a sarcastic comment about the distinctive Air Commando bush hat (the USAF's version of the Green Beret) or a personal boast about the relative performance of Air Commando personnel. Both officers were looking at the growing conflict in Southeast Asia (SEA) and the Air Commando mission within USAF from distinctly incompatible viewpoints.

By command, General Sweeney was a major force in the development of the Air Force doctrine designed to counter the major cold war threat to the US: the Soviet air force. Without hope of matching the Soviets' numerical superiority, the Air Force was committed to meeting that threat with an ultramodern, all-jet force using the latest technology. Given the finite funding available, it was not a commitment that looked kindly on the diversion of vital resources to other purposes, such as the military "aberration" steadily growing in SEA.

By precedent, the Air Commandos were by 1966 the most experienced USAF combat outfit in SEA. They had arrived in South Vietnam five years earlier in an "advisory only" role, only to be committed to direct combat within the year. From the start, the Air Commandos were trained, equipped, and organized to adapt to the people, the land, the weapons, and the culture of the war they found wherever they were sent. In the absence of an Air Force doctrine applicable to their unconventional activities, the Air Commandos developed a pragmatic approach to combat: if USAF doctrine brought victory, use it; if it didn't, junk it and find a doctrine that would.

By experience, Colonel Aderholt had long since established his formidable unconventional warfare credentials. During the Korean War, he had flown night, low-level infiltration missions deep behind Communist lines while commanding Fifth Air Force's Special Air Missions Detachment. Seconded to the intelligence community during the postwar years, he provided unconventional warfare planning and oversight expertise to a series of paramilitary operations by US intelligence ranging from Cuba to Tibet to Laos.

It was Aderholt who flew down from Laos to meet the first Air Commando leaders upon their arrival in Thailand in early 1962, providing them with briefings on special operations in SEA.[1] Upon his return to the US, Aderholt was transferred to the Air Commando base at Hurlburt Field, Florida, with the specific task of spreading his unconventional warfare expertise gained in Indochina. In the following years, Colonel Aderholt, later a brigadier general, would go on to serve more combat tours in Southeast Asia than any other Air Force officer.

Four years later, as the opening quote suggests, a number of things weren't setting very well with General Sweeney or within the Air Force overall. And the outburst between USAF's senior fighter pilot general and its most experienced unconventional warfare officer was only one of the visible cracks that were beginning to show the internal rancor. Fueling that rancor was a faceless enemy moving silently southward under the jungle-covered mountains of eastern Laos, gliding slowly but irresistibly like a giant snake.

This deadly, well-camouflaged snake was nearly invisible to Air Force eyes, but it struck back viciously when it sensed danger. Worse yet, like a mythical serpent cut into pieces again and again, it kept bringing itself back together . . . steadily carrying its venom southward towards the South Vietnamese and American forces defending the Republic of Vietnam. The "snake" was the North Vietnamese Army, the likes of which the United States Air Force had never before encountered.

As a matter of perspective, it's useful to bear in mind that the USAF unconventional warfare effort in Thailand and Laos from 1961 to early 1965 was dedicated primarily to supporting Vang Pao's anti-Communist Hmong forces in the northern sectors of Laos. The Helio Courier/Lima

Site combination, Mill Pond, and particularly Water Pump were not aimed so much at the snake gliding down the Ho Chi Minh Trail as at the North Vietnamese and Pathet Lao forces gathering near the *Plaine de Jarres.*

It was just as well that Water Pump's visionaries did not have ambitions for using its graduates against the Ho Chi Minh Trail. In supporting Vang Pao's operation alone, the death rate among the Laotian and Hmong AT-28 pilots was abominable. After five years of steadily turning out RLAF AT-28 pilots from Water Pump, the net increase in Laos was minimal. And the reason was as simple as it was grim. The attack pilot graduation rate had barely exceeded the death rate of the graduates, who simply flew until they died.[2]

A bigger stick was needed if this snake was going to have its head pinned in the dirt. And the still-confident Americans were sure they had just such a stick with which to do it.

Snake Country

The "stick" would be American-flown fighter-bombers, authorized for the first time to conduct armed-reconnaissance missions against North Vietnamese targets found in Laotian territory. Begun in December 1964, the highly classified program, code-named Barrel Roll, marked a substantial escalation of America's "secret war" in Laos. Despite (or perhaps because of) the attendant political risks, however, Barrel Roll was at best a hesitating application of airpower. Intended more to warn Hanoi of US resolve than to accomplish any significant stoppage of North Vietnamese use of the Ho Chi Minh Trail, its failure to accomplish either goal was soon apparent.

Stung by the manner in which Hanoi dismissed his Barrel Roll "warning," President Lyndon Johnson responded in April 1965 by directing an Air Force/Navy "maximum effort" against the Ho Chi Minh Trail.[3] Barrel Roll was retained in northeastern Laos while a new area, dubbed "Steel Tiger," covered the trail as it traversed through the Laotian panhandle. Increased tactical air strikes were ordered, and for the first time the USAF's giant, eight-engined B-52 strategic bombers joined the stick thrashing the Ho Chi Minh Trail. Results: intelligence figures showed the 1965 NVA infiltration numbers more than doubled over those of 1964.[4]

In addition to their legendary endurance, members of the NVA had accomplished this feat through expert use of camouflage, underwater bridges not visible to aerial view, and tactics such as throwing gasoline-soaked rags along roads to seduce strike pilots into believing they had struck meaningful targets.[5] There was more bad news for the Air Force:

> In the first quarter of 1966, PACAF intelligence believed the DRV [North Vietnam] had added about 110 miles of new or improved roads to sustain truck traffic. The Defense Intelligence Agency credited the DRV with having about 600 statute miles of truck-sustaining roads in the infiltration corridor . . . at least 200 of which were capable of . . . year-around operations.[6]

The individual NVA soldier slogged on foot down the 600-mile-long Ho Chi Minh Trail for two to three months before exiting somewhere in South Vietnam. But supplies were carried in vehicles. As early as 1965, an estimated 51 percent of these supplies went south in trucks on the steadily growing road network. The percentages would grow.[7]

The low-tech NVA was proving the worst of all possible targets for a high-tech air force better suited for an opponent in its own league. To incredulous intelligence officers, the snake actually seemed to be growing stronger on the diet of American bombs. In April 1966, Pacific Air Forces (PACAF) intelligence estimated 32 antiaircraft gun batteries and 54 automatic weapon sites

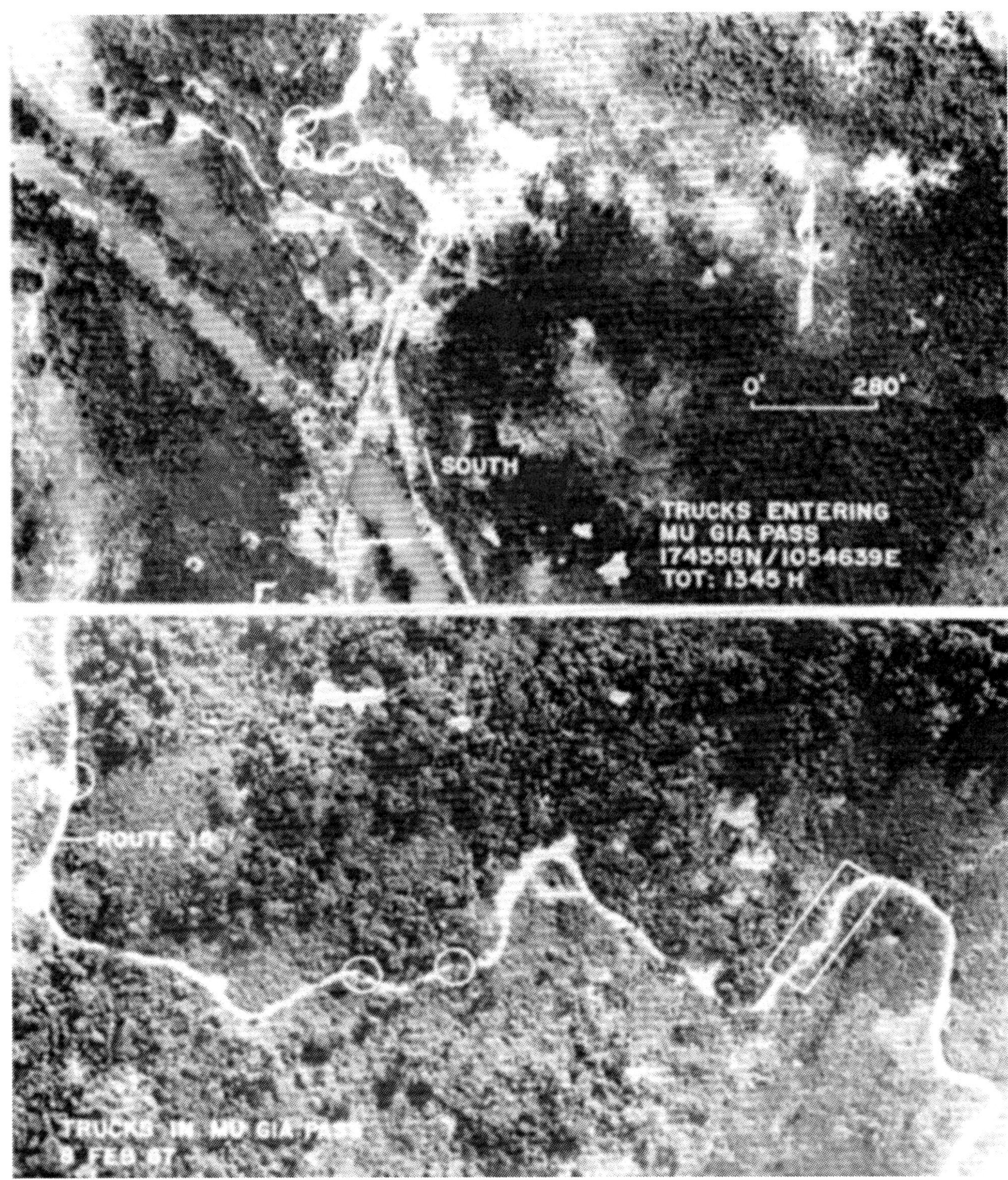

USAF

In early 1967, North Vietnamese truck convoys were still moving down the Ho Chi Minh Trail through Laos in broad daylight. The North Vietnamese government blandly denied even the existence of the trail, while the US kept secret its multibillion-dollar effort to stop the flow of deadly cargo gliding steadily toward South Vietnam.

near Mu Gia Pass, one of the key transportation entry points from North Vietnam into Laos.[8] Only three months later, PACAF upped their estimate to 302 antiaircraft artillery (AAA) sites around Mu Gia.

Thousands of laborers worked around the clock to expand the Ho Chi Minh Trail and repair damage caused by US air strikes. Some were North Vietnamese volunteers, many of whom were young women given room and board, clothing, and the equivalent of $1.50 per month; others were prisoners and local Laotians who had been conscripted.[9] Like the pragmatic Air Commandos, the only doctrine the NVA seemed to care about was what worked in their neighborhood.

Tigers and Eagles Go Snake Hunting

With the consent of its Thai allies, the United States Air Force decided to do a little "neighborhood renovation" of its own in the spring and summer of 1966. This action took form in two initially separate Air Commando deployments from the United States to Nakhon Phanom (commonly shortened by Americans to "NKP") Royal Thai Air Force Base, smack on the Thai border with Laos . . . and less than 60 air miles from the nearest section of the Ho Chi Minh Trail.

NKP was a perfect base for the independent-minded Air Commandos. As Air Commando veteran Tom Wickstrom recalls:

> [NKP] was far enough in the jungle to make it an undesirable point for visiting brass . . . a short enough PSP [pierced-steel planking] runway to discourage anything that consumed kerosene [i.e.,jets] from landing except in extreme emergencies . . . uncomfortable enough that the crews were happy to fly combat missions in return for an occasional "motivational" trip to Bangkok . . . and, finally, big enough to hide all the men and equipment purloined from other unsuspecting organizations throughout the world.[10]

The first deployment, code-named "Lucky Tiger," activated the 606th Air Commando Squadron (Composite) at NKP on 8 March 1966.[11] Formed initially to consolidate ongoing USAF support to the counterinsurgency capabilities of the Royal Laotian Air Force and the Royal Thai Air Force, the 606th was unlike anything the Air Force had put together since the formation of the original World War II Air Commandos.

Lucky Tiger brought together a wild mix of aircraft, including (A)T-28 trainer/fighter aircraft, C-123 twin-engined short takeoff and landing transports, UH-1 single-engined helicopters, and the previously described U-10 Helio Courier liaison aircraft. "Composite" was an understatement for such a gaggle, and the Air Force would soon extend the mix even further.

The U-10s in particular would never receive the attention later given the violent nightly forays flown over the Ho Chi Minh Trail by the Air Commando strike squadrons. But they certainly took their share of the risks and carried their share of the load. Tasked to conduct airborne psychological warfare missions in unarmed aircraft over enemy territory, they flew with their own style. Flying both loudspeaker and leaflet-dropping missions, they proudly used the radio call signs "Loudmouth" or "Litterbug," depending on whether the specific psywar mission called for voice or paper delivery to the enemy below. Sometimes special intelligence gave the U-10 pilot a rare opportunity to spook the enemy in a very timely way.

One such opportunity came in 1968. Joe Murphy, then an Air Force captain serving as an intelligence officer at NKP, recalls a unique experience while working on Operation Igloo White, a special program to detect NVA movement on the Ho Chi Minh Trail through the use of acoustic listening devices. He and others monitoring the listening devices at NKP were flabbergasted to hear two apparently low-ranking North Vietnamese Army soldiers talking about their personal hardships. Incredibly, the two soldiers did not realize they were talking within "earshot" of one of the listening devices, which was transmitting their conversation back to Thailand with excellent clarity. While the first soldier worried about the fidelity of his wife back home, the second complained of an illness which he feared might be terminal and for which no medical aid was available.

Realizing the psywar potential of this unexpected "gift," an all-night effort commenced at NKP between intelligence, psywar, and the U-10 squadron to launch a special loudspeaker flight. The following morning, NVA soldiers on the Ho Chi Minh Trail heard Loudmouth overhead, confirming the worst fears of the two soldiers and identifying both by name and unit. The first was assured that the soldiers in a home-defense unit located near his village would indeed be tending to his wife's needs, while the second was mournfully told his disease would indeed soon prove fatal.

Was the U-10 mission simply a small bit of cruelty inflicted on two unfortunate soldiers? Not at all. For one thing, the cargo of misery and death the two were helping transport to their neighbors in South Vietnam did not permit the Air Commandos the luxury of personal empathy for the two. But far more important from the psywar perspective was the common nature of the fears expressed by two soldiers a long way from home.

From this perspective, the two soldiers themselves were not so much the target of the psywar message as they were simply the messengers. The real target of the loudspeaker broadcast was the morale of all NVA soldiers within earshot. If unseen Americans were close enough to overhear their most intimate conversations, then no matter how thick the jungle, how dark the night, how good their camouflage, enemy soldiers were conscious that Americans could always be out there, somewhere, watching, listening . . . waiting to strike.

The second deployment, code-named "Big Eagle," moved Detachment 1, 603d Air Commando Squadron (ACS), to NKP from England AFB, Louisiana, in May 1966.[12] The detachment consisted of eight B-26K propeller-driven bombers sent to undergo combat tests in Laos. An early glitch arose prior to their arrival when the Thai government expressed its concern at having foreign "bombers" on its soil. But the problem was finessed smoothly when Secretary of the Air Force Harold Brown simply redesignated the Big Eagle B-26Ks as "attack" aircraft, hence their new designator "A-26A."[13]

These K model 26s were a big improvement over the B models first issued to the Air Commandos in Florida in the early 1960s. At a cost of 13 million dollars, the On Mark Engineering Company in Van Nuys, California, converted 40 of the bombers to the upgraded K configuration.[14] Rebuilt fuselage and wing components, more powerful engines, wingtip fuel tanks, additional wing pylons to carry more munitions, and improved avionics all combined to produce one of the most deadly fighting machines of the war in Laos.

Although collocated with and supported by their 606th brethren at NKP, Detachment 1 kept its affiliation with the 603d ACS until December of that year before it too became amalgamated into the Lucky Tigers. Armed with machine guns, rockets, and bombs, the heavily armed aircraft added a considerable punch to a "composite" squadron that was by now looking very much like a modern-day version of "Richthofen's Flying Circus." And the ringmaster for this "circus" was none other than the ubiquitous Heinie Aderholt, who arrived in December to assume command of the Lucky Tigers.

Never at a loss for ideas and with years of experience in Laos, the colonel knew exactly where to

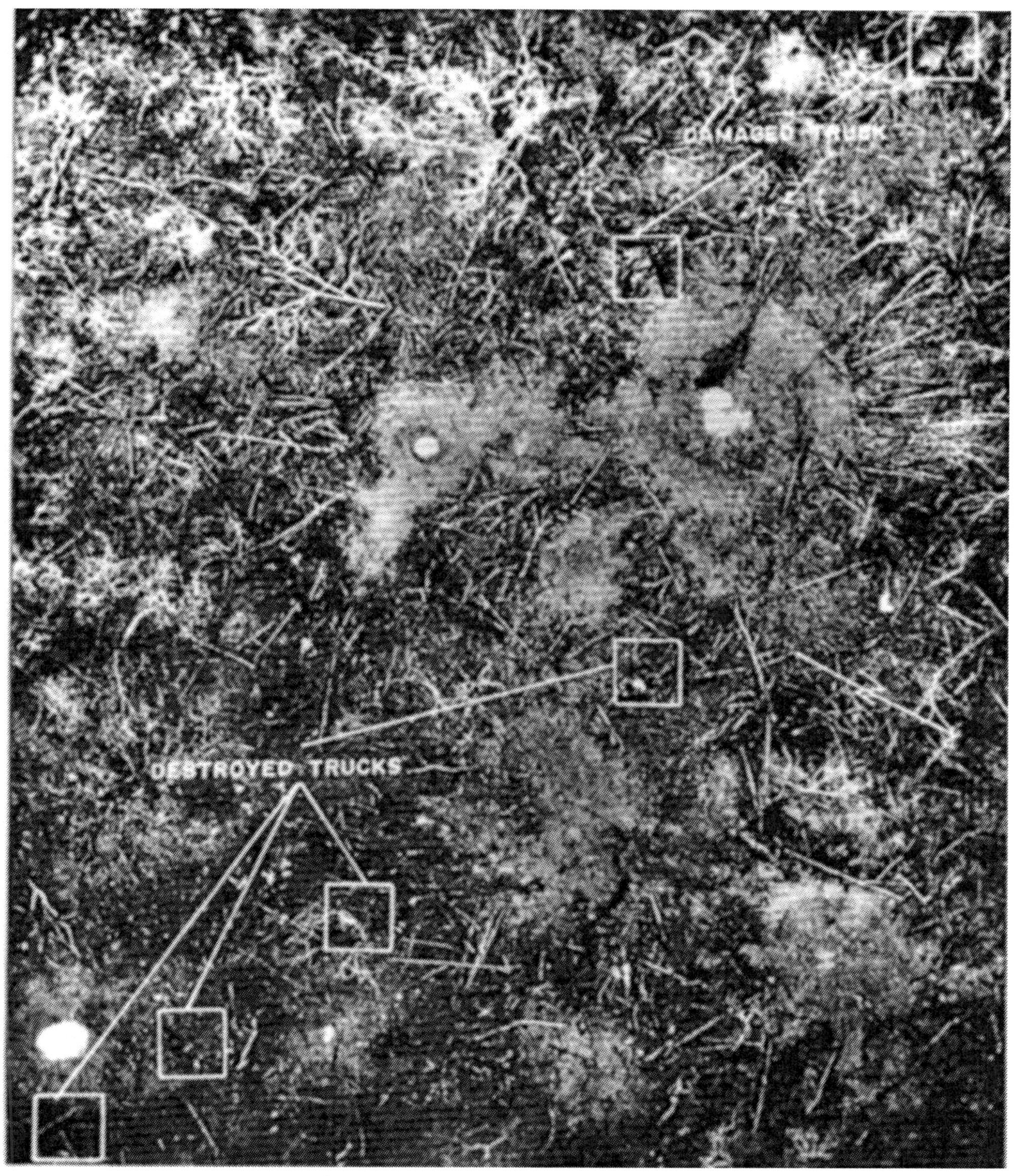

USAF

Silence and desolate destruction are all that mark the grave site of a violent night encounter with fury and fear on both sides. Success or mere survival by either side the previous night counted for nothing in tomorrow night's brawl . . . and there would be one.

find the snake. The 606th headed straight for the Ho Chi Minh Trail . . . and into the two toughest opponents it would face in Southeast Asia: North Vietnamese antiaircraft defenses and senior USAF officers committed to a totally modernized, all-jet Air Force. Of the two, both the colonel and the squadron would survive only one.

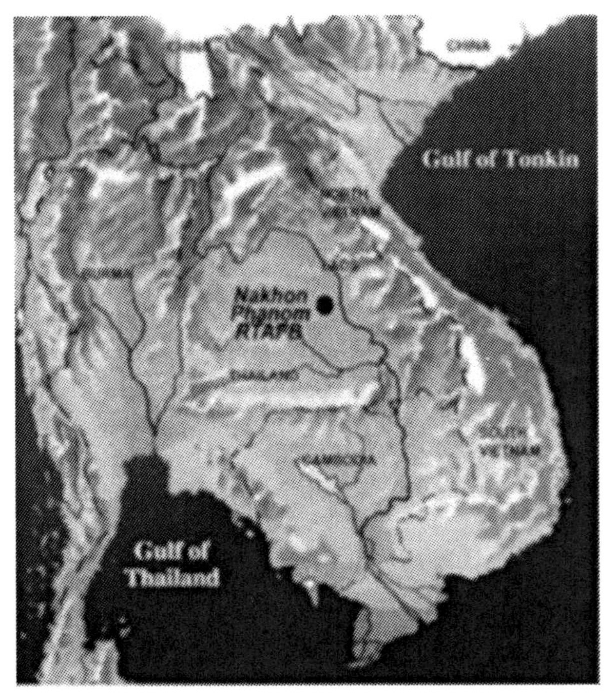

The Nimrods

What had started out in May 1966 as a six-months-only combat trial for the A-26s turned into a dangerous, three-year-long snake hunt. On some nights, the A-26 "stick" hurt the snake badly. On other nights, the snake's venom left only flames, molten aluminum, and broken Air Commandos in its trail. From the darkness below, its fangs would find a fatal spot deep in the belly of 11 Nimrods before their hunt was over. But in early 1966 that was all yet to come.

56th ACW Aircraft Nakhon Phanom RTAFB

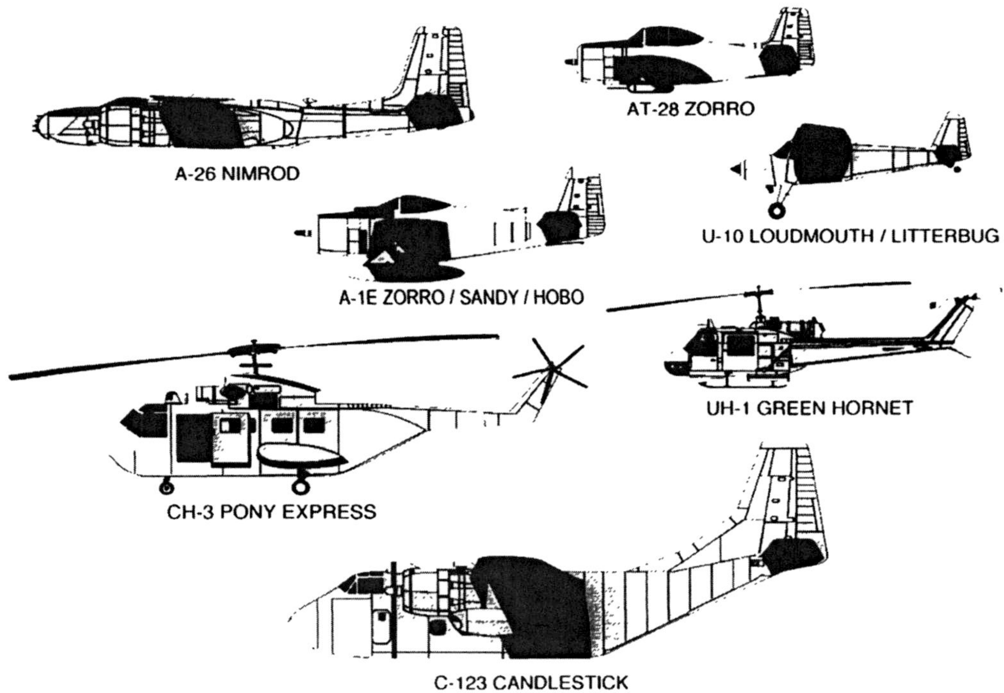

As Detachment 1 began its first orientation flights over the Ho Chi Minh Trail, its aircraft took with them the radio call sign "Nimrod." The call sign soon became synonymous with the aircraft themselves during what became their prolonged "trial through fire" in Southeast Asia. And as an early wartime report observes, the trial standards were designed from the start to push the aircraft and crews to the limit of their capabilities:

> The aircraft were directed to operate at night in a single ship concept, completely blacked out. . . . The full weapons spectrum of the A-26A would be employed: eight .50-caliber nose guns; eight wing stations and 12 bomb bay stations; 10,000 pounds of conventional aerial munitions in all feasible configurations.[15]

The Big Eagle trial got off to a slow start as the Laotian monsoon season began drenching the country soon after the arrival of the bombers. But by the fall of 1966, improving weather began to make possible the full nighttime truck-killing potential of the Nimrods. Like sharks drawn to blood, the Air Commandos sought out the North Vietnamese truck convoys that became their nightly prey. That December the A-26s were credited with 80 percent of all USAF truck kills for the month in the Steel Tiger area despite having flown only 7 percent of all USAF sorties![16]

The A-26's firepower, communications capability, and loiter time over the target made the aircraft very popular with everyone (with the probable exception of North Vietnamese truck drivers). Innovative tactics helped, too, as the following account by a Nimrod pilot reveals:

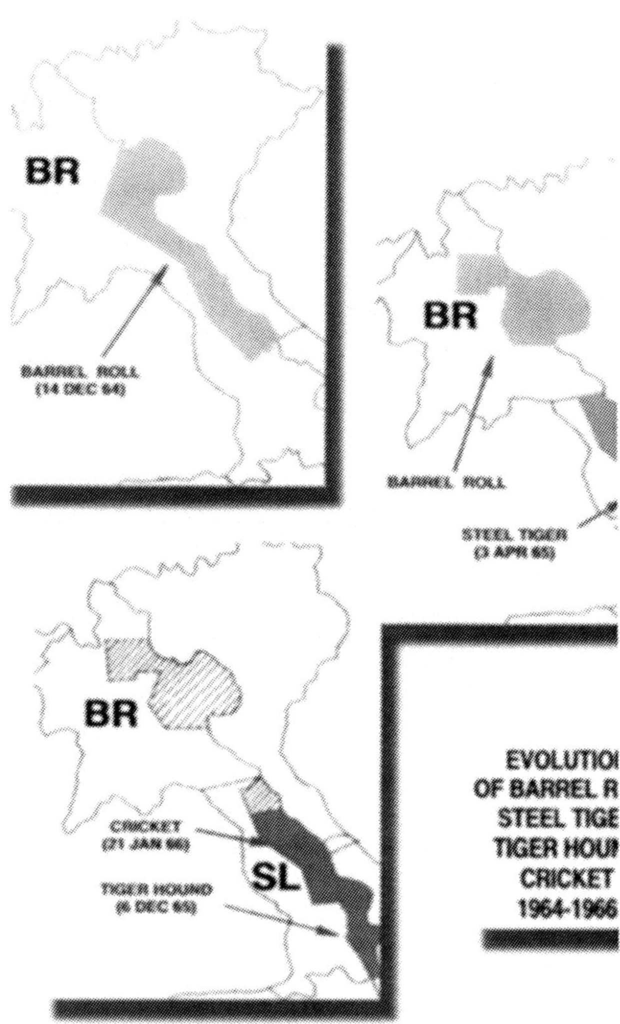

> At dusk, one good road cut [one requiring immediate repairs] is made at a selected interdiction point . . . the A-26 then retires from the scene and loiters nearby [4,000–6,000 feet altitude] while the supporting flareship then drops marker flares [commonly referred to as "bricks" that burn for approximately 45 minutes after hitting the ground]. The [C-123 Candlestick] flareship then departs the scene and as a ruse, dispenses six million candlepower MK-24 parachute flares as though accompanied by an attack aircraft. Prior to burnout [of the original two bricks] the A-26 rolls in, blacked out. . . . Backed-up trucks and road repair crews have been repeatedly surprised by this tactic.[17]

Official reports were enthusiastic in their results-achieved versus sorties-flown descriptions of the A-26's night interdiction tests. What it took in terms

Tom Wickstrom

An A-26 pilot from the 609th Air Commando Squadron poses inside the bomb bay with two Mark-34 Funny Bombs. The World War II-era incendiary bombs each contained several white phosphorous bomblets, which burst from the barrel as they fell in flight.

of human effort to generate these numbers, however, was something that would never find its way into an official report. Through their laughter and their tears, the Nimrod crews recorded some of their thoughts in an unofficial squadron log called "The Funny Book." Some excerpts give quite an insight into this human drama:

> (Nimrod 30): Off 1+45 late. Aborted -645 because #1 gen wouldn't come on-line. Didn't know when I was well off. Was given -644 and after one aborted T/O for low torque we went off into murk. After crossing the river [into Laos], we lost both generators and battery went flat. Jettisoned in NKP area and made no flap landing (Thunderstorms, 22-knot crosswind).
>
> (Nimrod 37): Absolutely the worst display of ordnance delivery I have seen in quite some time! And I did it!
>
> (Nimrod 31): Got four trucks, destroyed POL [petroleum, oil, and lubricants] storage areas, 13 secondary fires and three explosions in two areas. Had usual amount of ground fire, but refused to kill any of the gunners. They were so bad, we feared they might be replaced.
>
> (Nimrod 29): Worked in close proximity to numerous red-orange tracers, jutting karst, and thunderstorms. Snapped out of our complacency when two jets invaded our area, at our altitude, and made a couple of 360-degree turns with their lights on. Four 37 mm gunners extremely accurate. Fun and games.[18]

Considerably less "fun" to record, however, was the inordinately high number of dud munitions noted by the Nimrod crews in their log. Exposing their lives in flying low-level attacks through bad weather, at night, below surrounding mountain tops, and through increasingly accurate ground fire was scary enough. But to do all this and still see the exposed trucks below continue to drive right through a shower of unexploded bombs is to know the real meaning of "helpless rage." Fortunately, help was on its way and, like the A-26 itself, came from a World War II-era idea.

The Air Commandos called it the "Funny Bomb" because of its odd shape. There were still hundreds of them left over from World War II, during which they had been dropped by the thousands on Japan from low-flying B-29s. Who discovered the remaining supply and how they found their way to NKP is still the subject of some dark mystery. But their effectiveness was anything but "funny" to those who saw the incredible results of a well-placed bomb run. Nimrod veteran Tom Wickstrom describes the bomb:

Tom Wickstrom

The most dangerous predator on the Ho Chi Minh Trail in 1967 takes off at sunset for the night's hunt. The World War II-era bombers were rated "nine times more effective but four times more vulnerable" than jet aircraft against truck traffic and antiaircraft defenses on the trail. The "prop versus jet" controversy would become a bitterly divisive issue within the Air Force during the war.

> With its content of jellied fuel, CBU [Cluster Bomb Units], and Willie Pete [White Phosphorous], it had a little bit of something for everyone. It split its casing and ignited its contents while still falling, giving the appearance of a burning water fall. When it hit the ground, the CBU bomblets blew it around so it covered approximately a football field. Anyone or anything in that area was . . . gone.[19]

The Funny Bomb proved the most reliable bomb available to the Air Commandos before the limited stock was used up. As much an improvement as the Funny Bombs were, the Nimrods were about to get still more help as another propeller-driven airplane was about to join the lineup for the nightly battles.

Zorro!

The Nimrods unquestionably had the biggest stick in the Lucky Tigers, but not the only one. The dozen or so Lucky Tiger AT-28Ds also had some clout of their own, and to a fighter like Aderholt anything with wings could and should be thrown into the fight. And so it happened, with the AT-28s beginning their first combat missions on 9 January 1967 with the call sign "Zorro."[20]

The AT-28s were fitted with two .50-caliber machine-gun pods, one under each wing, as well as six external pylons with a combined total capacity to carry 3,500 pounds of bombs and

USAF

What a difference a war makes. The folded wings of this beat-up Air Commando A-1 clearly show the aircraft's Navy heritage, as well as the rigors of combat.

external fuel tanks.[21] An unusual variety of radios and navigation equipment also allowed the Zorros to communicate with other strike aircraft, airborne and ground forward air controllers (FAC), and even the USI guerrilla teams surveilling the Ho Chi Minh Trail at various points.

Like the Nimrods, the Zorros started off with relatively simple daytime missions designed more for pilot orientation than for inflicting damage on the enemy.* But given the growing AAA threat along the trail, the emphasis from the start was to move into the night interdiction role as soon as possible. And with the addition of a second crew member in the back seat, single-ship night interdiction missions began five weeks after the first daylight mission.[22]

By early March 1967, the 606th ACS was conducting nightly interdiction operations with 10 A-26s and an equal number of AT-28s.[23] The

*And like the Nimrod experience, the Zorros lost their first plane and crew to enemy gunners on one of these "simple" orientation flights over the trail.

USAF

This picture perfect A-1H sitting at Hurlburt Field, the Air Commando base in Florida, provides a dazzling display of the armament carried by the legendary Skyraider. Nothing else in the Air Force inventory could match the beast's combination of combat payload, accuracy of munitions delivered, ability to absorb punishment, and loiter time over the target.

following month, the 606th was deactivated, with its forces immediately activated at NKP as the 56th Air Commando Wing (ACW), a more appropriate reflection of the size of the unit. In the ensuing months, the 56th grew more, especially in terms of firepower.

The Skyraiders

In conjunction with its activation, the 56th assumed command of the propeller-driven A-1 Skyraider attack aircraft of the 602d Air Commando Squadron, then based at Udorn RTAFB, another major field west of NKP. The Korean War-vintage A-1s were incredibly rugged and capable of carrying more munitions than World War II's famous four-engined B-17 Flying Fortress. Designed and built for Navy use, approximately 80 E/H/G variants of the Skyraider were transferred to the Air Force for the Air Commandos.

The 602d pilots flew from Udorn with the call sign "Sandy" and specialized in escorting USAF rescue helicopters deep into Laos and even North Vietnam to retrieve downed airmen. It wasn't until March 1968 that the 602d moved to NKP to join another specialized A-1 squadron already at the "propeller base." The 1st ACS "Hobos," whose squadron flag already carried battle streamers from years of combat in South Vietnam, had been transferred to NKP from its previous base at Pleiku, in South Vietnam's central highlands.

The Hobos specialized in "seeding" the Ho Chi Minh Trail with "gravel"—thousands of small firecracker-like explosives that detonated when

Sitting just aft the bomb bay in an A-26 at Nakhon Phanom Royal Thai Air Force Base, Maj Tom Wickstrom innovated the use of the Starlight scope to observe NVA truck traffic moving below a fully blacked-out and undetectable A-26 flying overhead. The harness was a thoughtful touch, as the observer was required to extend his upper torso out over open bomb bay doors to get a good view of the Ho Chi Minh Trail.

Tom Wickstrom

stepped on or driven over by vehicles. When detonated, the gravel was designed not to kill or destroy but rather to activate the thousands of camouflaged acoustic sensors previously airdropped along the trail for the previously described Igloo White program. Upon detecting a detonation, the Igloo White sensors automatically relayed the activity back to monitoring stations in Thailand, thereby alerting the Americans as to the location of North Vietnamese movement.

The high-tech electronic system was totally automatic—almost. The "manual labor" part fell to the Hobos, who had to fly over the trail in broad daylight, at treetop level to seed accurately. It was not only manual, it was downright dangerous once the North Vietnamese gunners figured out what the funny-looking stuff coming off the A-1's wings really meant to them.

The last A-1 squadron to join the 56th at NKP was the Zorros of the 22d Special

Air Commando Association

C-123K Provider transports belonging to the 606th Air Commando Squadron had a special night mission over the Ho Chi Minh Trail. After observers first detected truck traffic below with a handheld Starlight scope, the C-123 "Candlestick" missions exposed the trucks with six-million candlepower aerial flares. And like sharks following a blood trail, the strike aircraft followed the reddish-tinted flares to the hapless trucks.

Operations Squadron (SOS).* Activated in late 1968, the 22d picked up the night interdiction mission from the smaller AT-28s they replaced, along with, of course, all the NVA gunners that came, literally, with the job. The Zorros also picked up the burden of the A-26s as they left SEA in 1969.

As the A-1s moved into their innovative roles over Laos in 1967, a number of other innovations were also taking place, especially in the night interdiction mission. It was during 1967 that the 56th first began testing the effectiveness of the handheld Starlight scope** for spotting trucks traveling through the darkened terrain below the aircraft, primarily in the Barrel Roll sector at this stage of the war.

While the narrow confines of the AT-28 canopy soon revealed the limitations of the scope with that aircraft, the A-26 showed more promise. Better yet, the impatient Aderholt had another card up his sleeve that promised to expedite still faster the experiments in his wing. The "card" turned out to be a navigator so eager to fly in the A-26 he accepted a bizarre proposal from the 56th commander. Aderholt confesses:

> I told Tom Wickstrom that if he wanted to fly and fight from the front of the A-26, he had first to figure

*In 1968 USAF redesignated all Air Commando units "Special Operations."

**The US Army's Starlight scope was initially intended for use by an individual infantryman, who looked through it like a standard telescope. The scope's technology magnified any source of light (e.g., stars or the moon), several thousand times, resulting in a surprisingly clear (if green-tinted) image of objects within its range.

Air Commando Association

As commander of the 56th Air Commando Wing, Col Heinie Aderholt sent his Air Commandos in Thailand against the toughest opponents they would ever face: the North Vietnamese Army and powerful Air Force generals committed to an all-jet Air Force. The controversial colonel and Air Commandos would survive one, but not both.

> out a system for making the Starlight scope effective from the plane. I needed a third set of eyeballs in the -26s for the scope, and I also had some enlisted Combat Controllers who weren't getting any combat pay or tax breaks. They were available if Wickstrom could figure something out.[24]

What Major Wickstrom figured out was that by lying head forward and face down on the belly of the aircraft, with the top half of his body extended out over the open bomb bay, he could get a great view of the ground below. With a harness that kept the bottom half of his body secured to the aircraft, and using the Starlight scope hanging from a bungee cord just in front of his face, he could get the same great view at night.

And the great view Wickstrom got on the third night test mission resulted in the North Vietnamese Army losing seven trucks, along with their drivers and supplies—an impressive debut. A man of his word, the wily Aderholt subsequently rewarded Wickstrom by allowing him to risk his life on future missions from the front of the A-26! While the limited number of enlisted combat controllers restrained the program, such innovations continued to rack up an ever-growing tally of truck kills by propeller-driven aircraft fighting over the Ho Chi Minh Trail at night.

Wickstrom's success with the A-26/Starlight combination followed his earlier successes combining the Starlight scope's capabilities with those of the C-123 Provider transports assigned to the 56th ACW. In the C-123, a crewman looking through the scope from an open hatch in the belly of the transport's cargo bay from an altitude of 4,000 to 6,000 feet over the Ho Chi Minh Trail got an excellent view of any activity taking place under the C-123's flight path. By adding an aerial flare capability to the Provider, the "Candlestick" concept was born.

When a totally blacked-out Candlestick detected truck traffic, strike aircraft (also blacked-out) were called over the convoy, which was still oblivious to what was going on above it. With the strike aircraft ready, the C-123 dropped its six-million-candlepower flares and "marker bricks" over the trucks and flew out of the immediate vicinity. The results were dramatic, both at the moment and in the rise in USAF's end-of-month truck-kill tallies.

USAF records show that during their first eight months of combat, the 10 A-26s were credited with 275 trucks destroyed and 246 more damaged; also hit were 1,223 truck parks, resulting in 1,033 secondary explosions. In addition, the fledgling AT-28 effort added an additional 42 trucks destroyed and 68 damaged, as well as numerous secondary explosions on unidentified targets.[25]

The 56th's price tag for these statistics included battle damage to 25 A-26s, three of which never returned from the fight over the Ho Chi Minh Trail.[26] Three AT-28s had also suffered battle damage, one of which was lost.[27] However, there was another price tag for the Air Commando successes, and it was coming a long way from the deadly Ho Chi Minh Trail.

William H. Sullivan, the US ambassador in Laos, had been watching with growing dismay the increasing number of jet aircraft sent over the Ho Chi Minh Trail throughout 1967 by the Saigon-based Seventh Air Force headquarters.[28] At issue was the undeniably superior accuracy of propeller-driven aircraft against ground targets versus the equally undeniable superior survivability of high-speed jets in the face of the trail's growing AAA network.

For "his" war in Laos, the ambassador was an unabashed advocate of the 56th's propeller planes. He ensured his views were known to Seventh Air Force commanders in South Vietnam, going so far as to press the Air Force in 1967 to put the 56th ACW under his control for use exclusively in Laos. When that initiative failed, Ambassador Sullivan, along with the deputy ambassador to South Vietnam, solicited an analysis from the Office of the Secretary of Defense (OSD) regarding the effectiveness of propeller-driven aircraft versus jets against surface transport targets in Laos.[29]

The OSD response sparked a trail of Air Force protest that spread halfway around the world, from the Pentagon to PACAF commanders in Hawaii to Seventh Air Force headquarters in Saigon. The analysts appeared to support the ambassador's advocacy of propeller aircraft with calculations (based on the first eight months of 1967) showing that

> prop aircraft destroyed 12.8 transport targets (trucks/watercraft) per 100 sorties at a cost of $55,000 per target. Jets (F-4s and F-105s) destroyed 1.5 [transport targets per one hundred sorties, at a cost of $700,000 per transport target.] By replacing two F-4 squadrons with two A1-E squadrons (no additional A-26 or AT-28 aircraft were then available), 1,200 more trucks and watercraft could be destroyed or damaged in the next 12 months at a savings of $28 million.[30]

The report proceeded to add that because propeller-driven aircraft were four times more vulnerable than jets compared to AAA, the price tag for replacing the F-4 squadrons would likely be the loss of 18 more (prop aircraft) and eight pilots.[31] Projected losses for the F-4 squadrons, should they be left in-theater, were apparently not calculated.

Even with a healthy margin for error factored in, the nearly 14:1 cost ratio in favor of propeller versus jet strike aircraft was impressive. A second report, issued in May 1968, showed an even more dramatic gap favoring the props in the truck-killing role. While the cost per vehicle destroyed/damaged by F-105s came to $118,000 for each truck, the cost for achieving the same results with the A-26 amounted to $5,900 per truck, a nearly 20:1 ratio.[32]

Curiously, no one seems to have challenged Seventh Air Force's use of the F-105, a supersonic fighter designed to carry nuclear bombs, for the truck-killing role in the Laotian bush. While the OSD report was correct in describing the lack of additional A-26/AT-28 aircraft available for the ground attack role in Laos, it neglected to mention that the Navy had approximately 150 more A-1s available for transfer to the Air Force, if requested. As the record shows, the request never came.

The propeller versus jet debate finally boiled over in a very personal way for the Lucky Tigers' commander when Ambassador Sullivan chose to press a very reluctant Seventh Air Force commander, Lt Gen William W. "Spike" Momyer, on the subject of reinforcing the battlefield successes achieved by Colonel Aderholt's A-26s. As the 56th ACW commander, Colonel Aderholt had recently experienced General Momyer's wrath for pointing out the superior battle-damage assessments achieved by the A-26 over the F-4 when both types of aircraft were committed to the ground attack role in Laos. Unfortunately for Aderholt, the politician receiving this brief was Senator Stuart Symington (D-Mo.), who represented the district in which the F-4 was manufactured!

The colonel's "good integrity/bad judgment" faux pas had been neither forgiven nor forgotten by General Momyer, one of USAF's staunchest proponents for an all-jet Air Force. Aderholt's luck hadn't been much better with General Momyer's deputy, Maj Gen Charles R. Bond Jr. When seasonal winds at NKP generated cross-winds too strong for light O-1 observation planes to take off on the base's only runway, the mission abort rate soared for the O-1s.

Aderholt's pragmatic solution had been to have bulldozers level a dirt runway heading directly into the prevailing winds for use by the O-1s. That solved the mission-cancellation problem, at least until General Bond paid a visit to NKP to congratulate the colonel for the much-improved O-1 operational rate. Aderholt recalls:

> [General Bond] said, "Hey, you really solved this [O-1 mission-cancellation rate]. What did you do to stop these aborts in the O-1s?" I took him down and showed him [the dirt runway]. He said, "Did you get permission for this . . . from headquarters Seventh Air Force?" I said, "No sir." He said, "Close it right now!" Next day we started aborting again; high winds.[33]

With the failure of the colonel's "better to beg for forgiveness than ask for permission" policy, he had few illusions about his personal stock with Seventh Air Force headquarters. And as he sat in the briefing room in Udorn, Thailand, in November 1967, listening to Ambassador Sullivan press General Momyer for more A-26s in Laos, he knew he was on the endangered species list.

> After hearing the Ambassador out, General Momyer looked at me, then turned back to Sullivan and said, "The colonel is not familiar with all the Air Force requirements. The -26s he has requested are deployed to SOUTHCOM [Panama]." Old Sullivan looked at him (Momyer) and said, "Well, Spike, I didn't know they had a war in Panama."[34]

Things moved quickly after the Sullivan-Momyer meeting. Citing a need for more "integrated" operations at NKP, Seventh Air Force headquarters established a Steel Tiger Tactical Unit Operations Center (TUOC) at the base "to more or less direct Seventh Air Force operational control over all Nakhon Phanom based units."[35] This move effectively removed the 56th Wing commander from operational control of his aircraft, in the process relegating him to administrative-only support for the wing. The rationale for the Steel Tiger TUOC was explained by General Momyer in the following terms: "The organization of this force [TUOC] will permit unit commanders at Nakhon Phanom to concentrate on their assigned mission, rather than get their energies diluted trying to cope with operational problems beyond their assigned missions."[36]

The Panama-based A-26s stayed in Panama. In 1969 the last of the A-26s were withdrawn from combat for lack of spare parts and combat attrition. Most of the flyable aircraft were flown straight to the Air Force's aircraft boneyard in Tucson, Arizona. Five were sent to South Vietnam in a variety of noncombat roles. Another era had passed, but not the bloodletting.

Not until the Nimrods left SEA were all A-1s brought to one location. The 6th "Spads" SOS was disbanded at Pleiku, South Vietnam, with its assets joining the 1st, 22d, and 602d SOSs at NKP under the 56th SOW. New weapons brought to the Ho Chi Minh Trail by one side brought new countermeasures by the other. It was much like two exhausted boxers being handed baseball bats to decide the match once and for all. But between 1969 and "once and for all" lay hundreds of attack missions and hundreds of thousands of antiaircraft shells. . . . Though bleeding badly, the snake was winning.

Notes

1. Brig Gen Harry C. Aderholt, USAF, Retired, Oral History Interview (U) (K239.0512-1716), 12–15 August 1986, 115. (Secret) Information extracted is unclassified.

2. Kenneth Conboy, *Shadow War: The CIA's Secret War in Laos* (Boulder, Colo.: Paladin Press, 1995), 365.

3. Ibid., 56.

4. Jacob Van Staaveren, *Interdiction in Southern Laos, 1960–1968: The United States Air Force in Southeast Asia* (Washington, D.C.: Center for Air Force History, 1993), 104.

5. Ibid., 146.

6. Ibid., 144.

7. Keven M. Generous, *Vietnam: The Secret War* (New York: Gallery Books, 1985), 128.

8. Van Staaveren, 144.

9. Generous, 126.

10. Lt Col Tom Wickstrom, USAF, Retired, "Nimrods, Truck Killers on the Trail," *Air Commando Association Newsletter*, July 1968, 1, 8–13.

11. Van Staaveren, 209.

12. Warren A. Trest, "Lucky Tiger Combat Operations," Project CHECO (Contemporary Historical Evaluation of Counterinsurgency Operations) report, (U) Headquarters PACAF, Directorate of Tactical Evaluation, CHECO Division, 1. (Secret) Information extracted is unclassified.

13. Van Staaveren, 160.

14. Dan Hagedorn and Leif Hellstrom, *Foreign Invaders: The Douglas Invader in Foreign Military and US Clandestine Service* (Leicester, England: Midland Publishing Limited, 1994), 156.

15. Trest, 6–7.

16. Hagedorn and Hellstrom, 159.

17. Trest, 21.

18. Excerpts from the log received from Lt Col Tom Wickstrom, USAF, Retired, former Nimrod, Orange County, California.

19. Wickstrom, 13.

20. Trest, 30.

21. Ibid., 26.

22. Ibid., 33.

23. Ibid., 42.

24. Brig Gen Harry C. Aderholt, USAF, Retired, interview with author, 1994, Fort Walton Beach, Florida.

25. Trest, 42–43.

26. Ibid., 42.

27. Ibid., 43.

28. Van Staaveren, 242.

29. Ibid.

30. Ibid.

31. Ibid.

32. Jack S. Ballard, *Development and Employment of Fixed-Wing Gunships, 1962–1972* (Washington, D.C.: Office of Air Force History, 1982), 99.

33. Aderholt US Oral History Interview, 181.

34. Ibid., 189.

35. Trest, 45–46.

36. Ibid.

Laos
INSIDE THE DOMINO

Wars are to be fought and won, not to justify contemporary doctrine.

Butterfly 44

One of the most striking differences between mainstream Air Force and Air Commando combat operations during the war in Southeast Asia was the relative usefulness of contemporary doctrine and high-technology systems to their respective efforts. Nowhere was this more evident than in the "secret" war in Laos, where Air Commandos flew, lived, and sometimes died far removed from mainstream Air Force doctrine; at airstrips and camps so remote and crude that only the simplest tactics and weapons (e.g., World War II-vintage aircraft) would prove effective.

At the bottom of this doctrinal and technological "food chain" in Laos were the Air Commando combat controllers. Beginning in 1961, these all-volunteer, parachute-qualified sergeants had been

Charlie Jones

A captured Pathet Lao officer (in dark jacket) is interrogated personally by Hmong General Vang Pao (wearing an Air Commando bush hat). Persuaded to cooperate, the Communist was placed aboard a small aircraft to point out the location of his former unit, which was promptly bombed.

Lewis Dayton Jr

The Ho Chi Minh Trail in Laos could be an all-weather paved road, or a well-worn trail capable of hiding dangerous numbers of North Vietnamese soldiers under the thick foliage. Without forward air controllers like the "Butterfly" sergeants, the "Mach 2 monsters," as one American ambassador called jet aircraft, had no hope of hitting well-camouflaged targets like this path.

handpicked from conventional Combat Control Team (CCT) squadrons throughout the Air Force for intensive training in unconventional warfare with the just-activated Air Commando force. Armed only with rifles and radios, wearing no armor protection thicker than their cotton fatigues, the CCTs were (and still are) trained to parachute into austere or enemy-controlled territory to establish aircraft- or parachute-landing zones for follow-on, main-force units. In Laos, they evolved into something else unforeseen even by the Air Commandos. Working closely with Gen Vang Pao's irregulars, they fought a "no quarter given or asked" kind of war against the North

Vietnamese and Pathet Lao Communists. Hard work in peacetime and dangerous in war, it wasn't the kind of work favored by the fainthearted, which accounts for the all-volunteer requirement for combat control duty.

Not surprisingly, Air Force Chief of Staff Curtis LeMay's start-up of the "Jungle Jim" program in April 1961 attracted independent-minded ("stubborn as a mule" also comes to mind) individuals looking for difficult challenges. Jungle Jim was the proving ground for USAF's activation of the Air Commandos, the Air Force's response to President John F. Kennedy's challenge to the military to develop a force capable of fighting the "Communist revolutionary warfare" then sweeping much of the Third World. One of the first to respond to the call for combat control volunteers was Capt Lemuel Egleston, nicknamed the "Gray Eagle" for his hair color.

Egleston soon proved a key figure in establishing the all-critical trust between the Air Commando aircrews flying their aircraft into blacked-out airstrips at night and the Air Commando CCT, often only an unknown voice guiding the pilot over his radio. One measure of this trust can be judged by the fact the controllers on these airstrips were using only flashlights with cut-out, Styrofoam coffee cups taped to the lens as directional beacons to guide the incoming aircraft.[1]

Captain Egleston's imagination and initiative led to another idea, one that proved visionary, timely, and definitely unauthorized. By "bootlegging" instructors from USAF's Air Ground

Charlie Jones

Unmarked civilian aircraft, such as this Continental Air Services Pilatus Porter, proved an ideal forward air control platform for the Butterfly sergeants.

Charlie Jones

Two Air Commando Skyraiders loaded for bear await target identification from Butterfly 44. Photographed from a civilian-piloted Continental Air Services aircraft, the "propeller show" over Laos consistently provided the highest tallies for enemy targets destroyed per sortie.

Operations School, then at nearby Keesler AFB, Mississippi, Egleston began teaching a select number of CCT sergeants the USAF techniques for controlling fighter air strikes against ground targets—techniques taught mainly to officer-pilots at the time.[2]

Included in this select group was then-Technical Sergeant (TSgt) Charles L. Jones, a master parachutist with over 250 jumps, a 12-year career that included combat missions in the Korean War, and—unknown to him at the time—a few gray hairs of his own in the months ahead. Several months later in 1966, Sergeant Jones was tapped for his first tour to Laos to assess what role Air Commando CCT might play in a war that didn't officially exist.

As American military personnel other than the embassy attachés were not officially allowed in Laos, Jones, like all other American and Thai combatants entering Laos, was promptly sheep-dipped to civilian status. For Sergeant Jones, this meant surrendering all military identification and uniforms and substituting instead civilian clothes and papers identifying him as an employee of a commercial firm operating in Laos. "Mister" Jones had arrived. And waiting for him was a major problem tailor-made for his skills.

Strike pilots attacking the Ho Chi Minh Trail and other targets in Laos had a particularly difficult time in pinpointing their targets in the rugged, forested terrain. Jagged mountains and low-hanging clouds all combined to weaken the effectiveness of the aerial interdiction program, even when targets could be found. Target identification in particular was proving near impossible for pilots flying high-speed jet aircraft, who at best had only seconds to acquire the target and release their bombs.

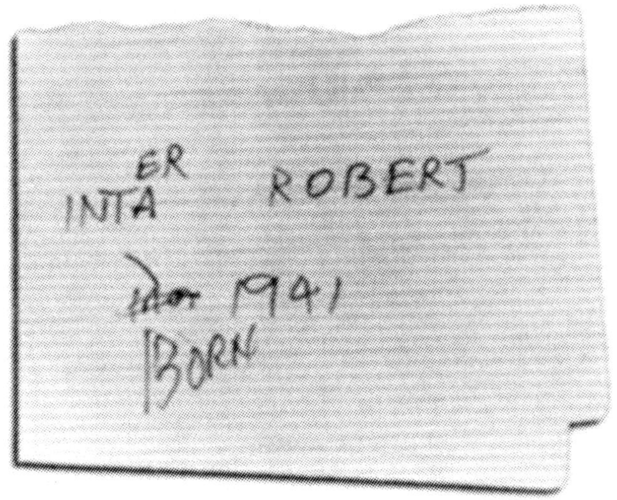

Charlie Jones

This note shows the attempted Hmong spelling of a dead airman's identification as copied from his dog tags by the patrol discovering his body in the jungle. Unable to extract the airman due to nearby enemy troops, the Hmong patrol leader gave the note to Thai mercenaries who forwarded it to Air Commando Charlie Jones. The airman's body was later recovered at Jones's request and buried with full military honors in the US.

What was missing was a coordination link between the fighters and their targets—someone intimately familiar with the terrain, flying in something slow enough to pick out targets all but invisible to fast-moving tactical jet aircraft. Unfortunately, the United States Air Force had no such pilots or aircraft in Laos, or anywhere else. It had long since disbanded the Mosquito airborne forward air controllers that had operated so effectively during the Korean War. It did, however, have Jones and his peers, a group that would soon prove highly innovative even by Air Commando standards.

What Jones and company had going for them was imagination, initiative, excellent (even if it was unauthorized) training to control air strikes, and a lack of USAF regulations spelling out the limitations of young sergeants in Laos. What they needed was an "airborne link" from which to control the attacking jets. Enter Air America and Continental Air Services, two US civilian firms operating small, propeller-driven aircraft and helicopters under contract to the Laotian government—aircraft now available to carry out Jones's plan.

Thus began the "Butterfly" concept, so named for the radio call sign of the first airborne CCT in Laos. As the first Butterfly, Jones became "Butterfly 44." The small handful of other controllers subsequently began using "Butterfly" with different numerical designators. Flying in civilian clothes, operating from civilian aircraft, the Butterflies soon became adept at controlling both propeller-driven Air Commando aircraft operating over Laos, as well as US Air Force and Navy jet fighters coming from bases in South Vietnam, Thailand, and aircraft carriers of the Seventh Fleet.

Even foreign pilots were controlled through the Butterfly net. Laotian, Hmong, and Thai Firefly mercenary pilots were vectored to targets, with Butterfly talking continuously to strike pilots, the civilian American pilot sitting next to him, perhaps friendly troops on the ground, and the Laotian or Thai interpreter sitting behind him. It was definitely a Rube Goldberg setup by any standard, but also a big improvement over the old standard.

May 1966 found Jones discussing a particularly difficult operation with the Thai mercenary running field operations at Site 2, a mountain-top camp 45 miles northeast of Gen Vang Pao's headquarters at Long Tieng. Jones learned that a Hmong patrol had just come in with a report that it had found the body of a dead American airman some miles away but was unable to recover the body due to the presence of enemy in the immediate area.

The Thai commander could only give Butterfly 44 the Hmong patrol's note with an attempted spelling of what had apparently been the dead man's name, copied from his dog tag. At Jones's request, the Hmong subsequently reentered the dangerous territory, this time returning with the airman's body. With this recovery, confirmed identification was later made and next of kin notified for a burial with full military honors in the United States. It was a small touch of humanity in a war known for its atrocities.

Butterfly 44 left Laos in October 1966 with 413 combat missions in six months in his records.[3] Other Butterflies continued their operations wherever needed. Using standard USAF procedures familiar to the strike pilots, the performance of the Air Commando sergeants elicited neither curiosity nor complaints from the attacking air forces. Nor for that matter did the pilots or their commanders appear to even realize their attacks were being controlled by enlisted personnel. This lack of awareness was not a matter of any particular secrecy on the part of the Air Commandos but rather the simple fact that in this backwater "secret" war, nobody found reason to ask.

That is, nobody noticed until Lt Gen William Momyer, Seventh Air Force commander, introduced earlier to the reader, flew up in 1966 from Headquarters Seventh Air Force in Saigon to pay a visit to Air Commando leader Col Heinie Aderholt at Nakhon Phanom Royal Thai Air Force Base. Upon hearing that Butterfly controllers were neither officers nor pilots, the general responded with "one of the more impressive temper tantrums of the war," according to the recipient of the tantrum. Aderholt describes the memorable meeting:

> He [General Momyer] and I had not gotten along well, but I had lunch with him and mentioned the Butterflies. He had asked about the FACs in Laos and where they came from. I said, "The people FACing in airplanes are enlisted." He went about six feet up and hit the ceiling. "What do you mean? Who is flying the airplane?" I said "Air America [civilian] pilots." He said, "That will cease!"[4]

Tough lunch! And the general proved as good as his word. The Butterflies were phased out soon thereafter, to be replaced immediately by officer, jet-qualified pilots. To their credit, the new group carried on the Butterfly tradition of bravery and tenacity, in the process achieving well-deserved fame in their own right as "Raven" FACs.[5] Their respect for their Butterfly predecessors can be judged in part by their naming Charlie Jones "Raven One."

Notes

1. Charlie Jones, interview with author, 23 March 1994, Fort Walton Beach, Florida.
2. Ibid.
3. Author's review of USAF Form 5 (Flight Log) of Charlie Jones during the 23 March 1994 interview with the latter.
4. Brig Gen Harry C. Aderholt, USAF Oral History Interview (U) (K239.0512-1716), 12–15 August 1986, 130. (Secret) Information extracted is unclassified.
5. For an account of the colorful Ravens, read Christopher Robbins, *The Ravens: The Men Who Flew in America's Secret War in Laos* (New York: Crown Publishers, 1987).

Jungle Jim

At the Tip of the Spear

Most of the questions were perfunctory, until an unknown reporter asked General Curtis LeMay [Air Force Chief of Staff] about Operation "Jungle Jim." General LeMay was silent for a moment, just staring stonily at the man. "I've never heard of it," he said grimly.

Gen Curtis LeMay, 1962
news conference in Los Angeles

Generals don't lie. But at the very least, General LeMay's response stretched the truth like a bungee cord wrapped around the city of Los Angeles... twice. Only months earlier, the general had, at the urging of President John F. Kennedy, directed USAF's Tactical Air Command to establish a counterinsurgency (COIN)* unit so secret that even the name of the program was classified. It was called "Jungle Jim."

In sharp contrast to the secrecy that surrounded the establishment of Jungle Jim in April 1961, the political impetus that drove its establishment burst forth on the world stage only four months earlier with all the garish publicity and fanfare accompanying a public hanging. And the would-be executioner, red-faced and puffing with righteous indignation, was none other than Soviet premier Nikita ("We will bury you!") Khrushchev.**

In his televised speech to the Twentieth Communist Party Congress that January, a boastful Khrushchev had publicly told the West exactly how he would direct the spread of communism throughout the Third World: "Wars of national liberation are justifiable and inevitable. . . . Communists support wars of this kind wholeheartedly and without reservation."[1] Significantly, one of those who believed the Soviet premier was dead serious was the president of the United States.

Almost immediately, Kennedy responded with what subsequently became National Security Council Memorandum (NSCM) 56, the administrative vehicle by which all military services (save the Marines) were tasked to form their own COIN forces.[2] Existing Army Special Forces were expanded, while the Navy established its SEAL teams. For its part, the Air Force resurrected what would become known as the Air Commandos, a specialized, composite-type force not seen since World War II. So fast, in fact, did the military respond that these individual service initiatives were well underway before NSCM 56 was finalized in June 1961.

At General LeMay's instruction, Headquarters TAC directed its subordinate command, the Ninth Air Force, to activate the 4400th Combat Crew Training Squadron at Eglin AFB, Florida, on 14 April 1961.[3] Within weeks its original mission to train USAF personnel in COIN air operations, was expanded to include the training of foreign air force personnel in similar tactics. Four months later, Headquarters TAC withdrew the 4400th from Ninth Air Force supervision to assume direct operational control of the unit, a highly unusual step for a major command headquarters like TAC.[4] This move reflected both the growing sense of urgency attached to the Jungle Jim program, as well as the greatly expanded role and organization the concept was about to undergo.

The 4400th began with an authorized strength of 124 officers and 228 airmen.[5] It was an all-volunteer force in which every individual had completed stringent physiology testing at the Air Force's medical complex in San Antonio, Texas, as well as USAF's rugged survival training school at Stead AFB, Nevada. All-volunteer units such as the 4400th are relatively expensive to organize and always a drain of high-caliber talent from the ranks of existing forces. The activation of such units is one practice that every military tries to avoid if suitable alternatives can be found. And it is precisely for these reasons that when they *are* created, they are inevitably driven by urgent demands that they "absolutely, positively" must produce results *now.*

---

*So new was the counterinsurgency concept to the Department of Defense that a variety of names were used to describe this politico-military phenomenon. Many USAF records of the early 1960s, for example, refer to the concept as "sublimited warfare."

**Khrushchev's theatrical bombast, such as his earlier threat to "bury" the West, unquestionably fueled Western fears of Soviet expansionism. During one famous session of the United Nations, the Soviet premier actually pounded the table with his shoe to underscore his apparent anger at the proceedings.

But what results could the Air Force expect from a group developed from scratch for a mission never before tried by USAF and equipped with aircraft older than some of the pilots who flew them? Equally important, when would these results be produced? In April 1961, it was still too soon to tell.

The aircraft initially issued to the 4400th totaled 16 C-47 transports, eight B-26 medium attack bombers, and eight T-28 trainers. To fulfill the foreign advisory/training mission, an equal number of aircraft by type were placed in storage for eventual transfer to designated foreign air forces.[6] Unlike the stringent selection of the airmen, the aircraft were selected simply because the Air Force had no better alternative on hand for the kind of "bush warfare" described vaguely in military directives as "sublimited warfare and guerrilla operations."[7] Could these old aircraft produce the required results? As was the case with the still untried airmen, it was still too soon to tell.

The 16 C-47s were heavily modified at the Warner Robins Air Materiel Area, Georgia, after which USAF changed the designation of the transports to SC-47.[8] The modifications included installation of HF, VHF, and HF radio sets, a parapack system, an exhaust flame damper, JATO (jet assisted take-off) racks, loudspeakers for airborne broadcasting, anchor cables for personnel and equipment drops, and strap supports for litters.[9]

The eight World War II-era B-26s, a type which first entered active service in 1941, came from the Ogden AMA, Utah. These were updated with UHF, VHF, long-range aid to navigation (LORAN), radio compass, radio altimeters, a solid nose with .50-caliber guns, 2.75- and 5-inch high-velocity air-to-ground rockets, napalm and bomb racks, and a chemical capability; four were further modified for aerial reconnaisance cameras and a paraflare capability.[10]

The T-28Bs came from Navy depots, as this two-seat trainer was still in active use in Navy flight school. They came to Eglin modified for the ground attack role. Modifications included installation of six armament pylons capable of carrying a combination of .50-caliber heavy machine guns, 500-pound bombs, 2.75-inch air-to-ground rockets, ferry tanks, self-sealing fuel tanks, and armor plating for pilot protection.[11]

Clearly intended to fly in harm's way, this heavily armed COIN force was equipped to help take a bite out of Khrushchev's ambitions for Communist-supported insurgency in the Third World. But before biting, they first needed training in this odd assemblage of aircraft,* and it had to be done in complete secrecy. To help assure this secrecy, the group assembled at one of the many small airstrips on Eglin's vast reservation.** Officially known as Eglin Auxiliary Field No. 9, the airfield would soon become much better known by its name, Hurlburt Field.

Though the Jungle Jim men and equipment were only beginning to sort themselves out during the early summer months of 1961, plans were already in place to begin their Operational Readiness Inspection (ORI) early the following year; by USAF standards, a very short-time fuse indeed. Then Headquarters TAC cut the fuse shorter still, scheduling the ORI "graduation exercise" to begin 8 September, less than four months after assembling this experimental composite force! From the beginning, pressure from the highest levels to produce quick results never let up on the young group at Hurlburt.

Hurlburt Field became a pressure cooker with heat coming from every direction. President

---

*In 1962 the fleet was expanded still further with the addition of C-46 twin-engined transports of World War II vintage and L-28 single-engined liaison aircraft.

**In terms of size, Eglin AFB and its ranges comprise the largest USAF base in the world.

By the austere Air Commando standards of the early 1960s, this crude airfield "control tower" provides unexpected comfort to a pair of combat controllers. To guide blacked-out aircraft onto remote dirt airstrips at night, combat controllers on the scene frequently used only flashlights with cutout Styrofoam cups taped to the lens as guidance beacons. First learning these low-technology tactics and then teaching them to foreign air forces quickly became part of the Air Commando mission. The *Forward Air Guide* shown here provided the basis for such instruction to many Laotian and mountain tribesmen in Southeast Asia.

Charlie Jones

Charlie Jones

Kennedy's obvious interest, the growing clamor from the Army for its own air arm to support its Special Forces troops, and the deteriorating situation in South Vietnam all drove the training pace for the 4400th CCTS. Fortunately for the Air Force, the "stew" in this pressure cooker was the 350 "Type A" personalities it had so carefully handpicked for Jungle Jim.

Pitting this high-performance group against an impossible schedule in the sauna-like summer of the Florida panhandle created an astounding spectacle. Snarling piston engines reverberated around the clock, as did bursts of heavy machine-gun fire, rockets, and bomb explosions conducted all over the Eglin reservation. Parachutes blossomed over remote drop zones day and night from low-flying C-47s as new tactics were discussed, cussed, and finally agreed upon by the sweating aircrews and combat controllers on the drop zones. The scene in the maintenance hangars wasn't any prettier, of course. But a backbreaking, 24-hour-a-day effort succeeded in doing what it had to do. It kept this "junkyard air force" in the air and on schedule.

In July the C-47s exceeded their flying hours during the already demanding training schedule by 47 percent; the T-28s by 35 percent.[12] The following month, the C-47s and their crews were pushed to 65 percent over the flying schedule; the T-28s an incredible 72 percent.[13] Only the B-26s suffered, their tired airframes kept down for lack of spare parts as the bombers flew 21 and then 5.5 percent under schedule for July and August, respectively.[14]

Without notice and at random intervals, aircrews returning from exhausting missions were taken straight from the postflight debriefing room into the nearby swamps for three-day escape survival treks.[15] After the first such surprise, a sharp increase was noted in the number of airmen wearing their aircrew survival vests as required by regulation.

Training for the 4400th stopped on 8 September, allowing the unit a short, deep breath before the all-important ORI was launched three days later.* All the effort, all the team spirit, and all the work over Eglin's ranges would amount to nothing if the ORI team declared the airmen "not operationally ready." And nature, as an unofficial member of the ORI team, added a thoughtful touch to the realism by scheduling an especially heavy downpour just as the exercise kicked off.

In the ensuing six days, the 4400th demonstrated everything it had learned and how well it had been learned. Four times the old C-47 "Gooney Birds" were flung into the skies as if out of a slingshot to the roar and smoke of the multiple JATO bottles strapped to their fuselage sides. Meanwhile, the B-26s and T-28s thrashed nearly every blade of "enemy" grass on Eglin's gunnery ranges with a mixture of machine-gun, rocket, and bomb attacks. Problems—stemming primarily from malfunctioning of old equipment**—were noted, but the ORI credited the 4400th with "maximum training in a minimum amount of time."[16] More importantly, the new unit won the coveted "operationally ready" designator. From this date forward, life for the 4400th airmen divided into those remaining at Hurlburt to advance COIN concepts, and those deploying overseas to execute these concepts.

From the beginning, the 4400th had conducted much of its training with US Army Special Forces troops deployed to Eglin from their base at Fort Bragg, North Carolina. To support this joint COIN training, the Army had even provided a Special Forces liaison officer to the Jungle Jim program to assist with paradrop missions. In return, selected airmen from the 4400th were sent

---

*So sensitive was the Jungle Jim project in the summer of 1961 that even its ORI was classified secret.

**The wear and tear on the B-26s in particular was a problem that could come back to haunt the airmen in the worst of all possible ways.

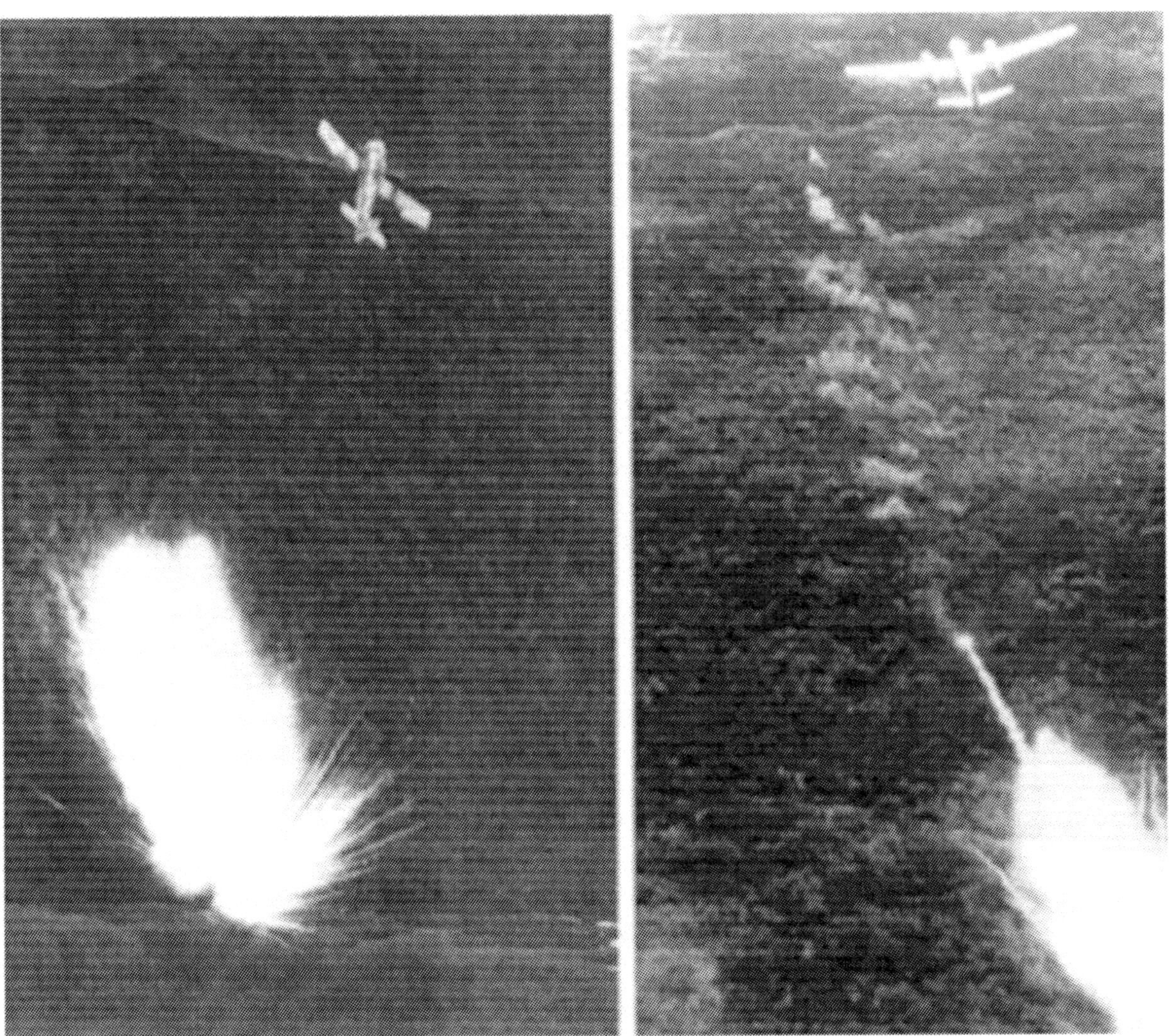

Air Commando Association

USAF's response to President John F. Kennedy's 1961 directive to form a counterinsurgency force took the Air Force a long way from the "wild blue yonder." The T-28B strike/trainer and twin-engined B-26 bomber shown here highlight the "propellers in the weeds" concept that developed. For different reasons, both the Kremlin and the US Army would soon find cause to complain about this unique band of airmen.

to Fort Bragg to attend Special Forces Indoctrination School while others participated in "survival training" missions with Army Rangers.[17]

On 26 March 1962, the Army took this joint-training effort a step closer by establishing the Remote Area Conflict Office near the 4400th headquarters.[18] It was an investment that would pay off handsomely in some of the most desperate battles soon to take place in faraway Southeast Asia. Still other investments would pay off even sooner.

In March 1962, the 4400th was expanded from squadron to group status. Within another 30 days, it expanded yet again—this time to become USAF's Special Air Warfare Center. And with the activation of the SAWC came the concurrent reactivation of a subordinate unit, this one boasting the colors, heraldry, and proud heritage of one of World War II's most famous combat units—the 1st Air Commando Group. Clearly this frenetic expansion rate was being driven by some very serious political clout. Despite the obvious signals, however, already there were rumbles of discontent coming from some equally serious players in the Pentagon, ones wearing US Army uniforms.

The Army had long recognized air support as the key to expanding the number of Special Forces units it could support in remote locations, especially those in South Vietnam. To provide this air support, it purchased several twin-engined C-7 Caribou STOL transports, aircraft approximating the performance of Air Force's C-123 Provider transports. During this same period, Army helicopter companies began expanding to a size that would reputedly give the US Army the world's fourth largest air force by the late 1960s. And finally, the Army began arming its twin-engined OV-1 Mohawk reconnaissance aircraft with air-to-ground rockets to conduct armed reconnaissance missions over hostile territory.

To the Army's proponents of an organic air force, the newly activated Air Commandos appeared a direct competitor for funds pouring into the Department of Defense for the hottest politico-military game in Washington in 1961—counterinsurgency. Flying from areas in which the Air Force did not routinely operate, the Air Commandos could be viewed fairly, if crudely, as a "propellers in the weeds" air force whose mission seemed to take them a long way from the "wild blue yonder."

On the other hand, the Army's ambitious air initiatives clearly jolted some Air Force nerve endings concerning the always sensitive interservice

Air Commando Association

Nearly half of the original 4400th Combat Crew Training Squadron, the all-volunteer nucleus of the future Air Commandos, deployed to the Republic of South Vietnam in November 1961 in the Farm Gate deployment. This photo shows the primitive conditions for both man and machine during the early days. Note the machine gun and rocket armament under the T-28's wings.

debate over control of air support. Helicopters were one thing, but multiengine fixed-wing aircraft were another. And strapping guns and rockets on the Mohawks proved the final straw. In the end, the Army eventually gave up its Caribous and took the weapons off the Mohawks, while the Air Force chose not to challenge Army supremacy in the employment of helicopter forces.

In retrospect, it is interesting to note the catalyst that brought the two services close to bureaucratic blows was the simultaneous expansion of their respective "elite counterinsurgency forces." Given other circumstances, neither the Army nor the Air Force would likely have selected these tiny COIN forces as sufficient justification for a major interservice missions-and-roles fight. But in 1962 the circumstances were such that the mere presence of the Air Commandos and the Green Berets made just such a fight virtually inevitable.

The stateside Air Commando organization proved as restless as the airmen who manned it. If the organizational changes (table 5) seem to have gone by in a blur, they were locked in chronological concrete compared to the operational pace set from the start by the airmen themselves. Like birds of prey unleashed from their mount, the Hurlburt airmen were already deploying straight

Table 5
Evolution of Hurlburt Field Air Commando/Special Operations Organization 1961–1979

Date	*Event*
April 1961	4400th Combat Crew Training Squadron (CCTS) activated at Hurlburt Field, Florida
March 1962	4400th Combat Crew Training Group (CCTG) activated at Hurlburt Field (as supervisory headquarters for 4400th CCTS)
April 1962	Special Air Warfare Center (SAWC) activated at Eglin, Florida; concurrent activities: Activation of 1st Air Commando Group (ACG) and 4400th CCTS redesignated 4410th Air Commando Squadron (ACS)
July 1963	1st ACG redesignated 1st Air Commando Wing (ACW)
January 1966	1st ACW transferred to England AFB, Louisiana; Hurlburt Field contingent designated Detachment 2, 1st ACW
July 1968	SAWC redesignated USAF Special Operations Force (USAFSOF); all subordinate Air Commando units redesignated Special Operations wings/squadrons
July 1969	1st SOW returned to Hurlburt; England AFB contingent designated 4410th Special Operations Training Group (SOTG)
July 1973	4410th SOTG deactivated; assets moved to Hurlburt Field
July 1974	USAFSOF deactivated; function and staff moved to Hurlburt Field; redesignated 834th Tactical Composite Wing (TCW) ; redesignated 1st SOW July 1975
July 1979	1st SOW falls below Headquarters USAF budget cutoff for active units; scheduled for assignment to Reserve component forces

USAF

A classic photo of the Vietnam era. Many Americans found it difficult to understand the Vietnamese lack of American-style aggressiveness. But while the Americans would rotate out of combat after relatively short tours, the Vietnamese knew their rotation out of combat would come only after death, crippling injury, or termination of a war seemingly without end.

into harm's way less than 60 days after their successful ORI.

Such was the pressure on the 4400th for quick results that not all its airmen were still present at Hurlburt Field to celebrate their ORI "graduation." Some of the birds had in fact already been deployed for COIN duty in faraway Africa. A month before the ORI, this deployment had taken place as a joint Army–Air Force Mobile Training Team (MTT) dubbed "Sandy Beach."

Sandy Beach deployed two C-47s and an Army Special Forces team to the Republic of Mali, on Africa's west coast.[19] The Air Force element of the MTT, Detachment 1, 4400th CCTS, provided the aircraft necessary for the paratrooper training requested by the Malis. Flying through a terrible rainstorm and landing without airfield tower assistance, the Air Commandos became a big hit among all the locals who came to watch the training "show."

The only exception to this enthusiasm came from Russian and Czechoslovakian aircrews already at the airfield, flying their aircraft from the same ramp as the C-47s while conducting their version of COIN with the Mali air force! Following their redeployment to the US, the Air Commando leader concluded, "We thought it was an interesting touch. . . . We didn't bother them and they didn't bother us."[20] Unfortunately, this example of an uneasy but still civilized coexistence was seldom repeated elsewhere. Indeed, the fur was about to fly between the two superpowers as they squared off in a bloody catfight a long way from Africa.

Leaving Hurlburt nearly two months to the day from their ORI, nearly half the 4400th CCTS deployed to the Republic of South Vietnam between 5–10 November 1961.[21] The airmen flew four of their C-47s across the Pacific, while eight T-28s and 140 personnel were airlifted by USAF's Military Airlift Transport Service. The four B-26s included in this deployment package were not 4400th CCTS aircraft, but were instead pulled from storage in Okinawa, refurbished in Taiwan, then sent to join the Air Commandos at Bien Hoa Air Base, a major Vietnamese airfield on the outskirts of Saigon.[22] The deployment itself was code-named "Farm Gate," while the deployed force was designated Detachment 2A, 4400th CCTS.

For the record, the Air Commandos became the first USAF airmen to conduct combat operations in Vietnam.[23] Off the record, they ran into so many problems it frequently seemed to them that their erstwhile Communist adversary, the Vietcong, were the least of their problems. For openers, the Detachment 2A airmen were not happy to discover that training the Vietnamese Air Force (VNAF) was their primary mission. As one TAC historian noted, "They [Air Commandos] had landed at Bien Hoa AB all heady with the cloak and dagger, super secret bit, and they bitched and yelled like the devil at having to do a standard job."[24]

Perhaps the Air Commandos could be forgiven if from the cockpit of a T-28 or B-26 on a strafing run, their job looked, at least to them, very "*non*-standard." Few air-to-ground gunnery training ranges in the US featured burning villages and enemy gunners trying to kill instructor and student pilots. The most aggravating problem encountered by the Air Commandos, however, was the lack of American-style aggressiveness demonstrated by most of their "students," many of whom were in fact already seasoned pilots in other types of aircraft. Many Americans, themselves on six-month rotational tours to Vietnam, found it difficult to understand the caution that developed within Vietnamese pilots. But unlike their American advisors, the Vietnamese understood they would never rotate out of combat until they were killed or the war ended.

Air Commando aggressiveness turned to frustration as they watched villages overrun, convoys ambushed, and airfields mortared without an

The primitive conditions in which the Air Commandos fought would not permit the introduction of highly advanced, complex systems requiring extensive maintenance support. On the other hand, the propeller-driven aircraft handed off to the Air Commandos in the early 1960s were already old even by that time. Efforts to achieve low-technology alternatives included this single-seat reconnaissance aircraft made from a much-modified fuel tank from a C-130 transport! The sleek-looking YT-28 (facing page) seen here with wing-tip missiles and upgraded engine, still shows its basic T-28 heritage. In the end, neither aircraft was selected for active service.

effective VNAF response. A particular event in South Vietnam's southern delta region highlighted the dilemma faced by the Farm Gate aircrews in the early days.

During the night of 10 September 1963, the Vietcong attacked the Soc Trang airfield with a mortar barrage, pinning down the VNAF T-28s stationed there, while the main attack took place against two small towns 70 miles to the southwest. Running through the mortar fire, four Air Commandos scrambled two armed T-28s to help town defenders drive off the Vietcong attack. The four airmen later received commendations for their initiative and courage—and reprimands for engaging in combat without a VNAF "student" in either T-28.[25] *C'est la guerre!*

When fighting the Vietcong, the Air Commandos at least had the satisfaction of viewing the devastating results achieved when their lethal skills were brought to bear on the enemy. Using those same skills against the US Army, however, was obviously out of the question, whatever the frustration. And in 1962, the frustrations coming from their khaki-clad Army brethren in Vietnam were plenty.

Driven mainly by the desire to meet increasing Army requests for air support, Headquarters PACAF requested in October 1962 a substantial augmentation of the Air Commando force in Vietnam.[26] The SAWC argued against the request, quoting the low monthly utilization rates for the T-28/B-26 strike force already in Vietnam as evidence the Army wasn't effectively using the Air Commandos already in country.[27]

On the one hand, the Army eagerly used all the C-47 airlift it could get. The Farm Gate C-47s flew 2,500 sorties in support of the 5th Special Forces Group in 1963, tripling its support to the Green Berets from that of 1962.[28] But when it came to close air support, it seemed to some that the Army was deliberately ignoring the strike aircraft as a bureaucratic tactic to validate its requests for more helicopter gunships.

The SAWC argument was bolstered by Maj Gen Rollen H. Anthis, commander of USAF's 2d Air Division based in Saigon. His reports detailed the Army's desire to "rely solely on its own aircraft . . . unless it ran into trouble."[29] In the end, however, the PACAF-requested augmentation was approved, with the rationale that "PACAF did not

Air Commando Association

Air Commando Association

want to be placed in a position of refusing [Army] requests regularly and thereby opening the opportunity for Army aviation to fill the gap."[30]

There was another, darker factor that favored the augmentation request. The Air Commandos flying these T-28/B-26 strike aircraft were being stalked by an unexpected enemy, one who would ultimately win regardless of the valor and skill of the airmen. Without warning, this unseen predator ripped entire wings off the aircraft in flight or caused catastrophic failure of major components during combat maneuvers against the Vietcong below. Age was finally catching up with the old airframes.

In February 1964, all USAF B-26s were grounded after a wing failed in flight during a night demonstration at Eglin AFB, Florida, before an audience that included 19 journalists.[31] The following month, a wing sheared off a Farm Gate T-28 during a bomb run. Less than a month later, it happened all over again.[32] Replacing General Anthis as 2d Air Division commander in Saigon, Maj Gen Joseph H. Moore observed, "The 2d Air Division is practically flat out of the [strike] business."[33] The proud US Air Force was reduced to borrowing nine T-28Bs back from the Vietnamese to keep a viable strike capability in Vietnam.[34] It did so, but Air Commando morale dropped to its lowest point yet.

Having received its marching orders to augment Farm Gate, the SAWC shelved other plans and concentrated on supporting the augmentation. On 1 July 1963, the 1st Air Commando Squadron (Composite) was activated at Bien Hoa AB, South Vietnam, with 275 officers and men, 18 B-26s, 10 SC-47s, and 13 T-28s.[35] The temporary duty tours that rotated individuals in and out of the Farm Gate deployments were terminated, as was SAWC "ownership" of the Vietnam-based Air Commandos. Newly arriving personnel came with orders for one-year tours,

Once-secretive Hurlburt Field grew to a size beyond which secret programs could hope to escape the notice of the public and the always inquisitive media. With the cat out of the bag, USAF decided to show off its elite force to the public (facing page). While the multiplicity of aircraft types was admittedly a maintenance officer's nightmare, it also provided the Air Commando/Special Operations force unparalleled flexibility (below).

Air Commando Association

USAF

Air Commandos from the Panama-based 605th ACS conducted civic action programs with a number of South and Central American air forces. Just getting to some of the more remote areas required many of the skills previously learned during training at Hurlburt Field.

and PACAF assumed operational command of the unit.

It was hard to believe all this had happened in just the first two years of the Air Commandos' existence. Without question, the continued high-visibility support coming from the Air Commandos' senior political mentor was a key factor in their growth. The previous May, President Kennedy had visited Eglin, ostensibly to view an Air Force firepower demonstration. Once on the base, however, he made clear his principal interest in the development of the Air Commando concept.[36] The COIN airmen responded with a full-blown "dog and pony" show that evidently left the commander in chief well satisfied that the Air Force had indeed responded to his encouragement.

Only a month before the president's visit to Hurlburt, the Air Commandos had launched Bold Venture, another major overseas deployment, this time to Panama. Like the earlier Farm Gate deployment, these airmen were given a

USAF

In response to a 1963 request from the Shah of Iran, the US sent a classified Air Commando/ Green Beret mission to Iran to help subdue a Kurdish rebellion in Iran's western provinces. The Air Commandos modified these two-seat World War II trainers with rockets and machine guns to provide the first effective air support to isolated government outposts. Less than a year after the Americans' arrival, the Kurdish threat to the government was virtually nil.

detachment designation: Detachment 3, 1st Air Commando Group. And with nearly half the old 4400th already in Vietnam, this deployment was limited to two each T-28, L-28, B-26, and C-46 aircraft.[37] Interestingly, Bold Venture was led by Lt Col Robert L. Gleason, the same officer who led the original Farm Gate airmen to Vietnam.[38]

Detachment 3 became the 605th Air Commando Squadron in November 1963. Flying from Panama, the unit honed its bush-flying skills in numerous civic action programs throughout rural South and Central America. Later transferred to the Air Force component of the US Southern Command (SOUTHCOM), it was redesignated the 24th Composite Wing in 1967 and remained so until its deactivation in April 1972.[39]

Even before the Panama detachment became a squadron, the Joint Chiefs of Staff had approved a similar deployment to Europe. Thus, Detachment 4, 1st Air Commando Wing, deployed to Sembach, West Germany, in January 1964 under the code name "Gold Fortune."[40] From the beginning, the European-based detachment (it became the 7th ACS that July), was different in two key aspects from all other Air Commando units.

One of the most easily spotted differences was the absence of propeller-driven strike (T-28, B-26, A-1) and UH-1 helicopter aircraft in the squadron. The 7th ACS was equipped only with C-47, C-123, and U-10 airlift. This odd configuration was largely influenced by the needs of the

7th's primary "customer," the 10th Special Forces Group, also based in West Germany at the time.

Like the 7th, the 10th was unlike the other COIN forces of its parent service. Its wartime mission had still not been "converted" from insurgency to counterinsurgency warfare, as had all other Special Forces groups by the early 1960s. What the 10th needed was airlift to carry its A Teams behind enemy lines into eastern Europe and the Soviet Union, to support anti-Communist partisans should general war between the US and the Soviets erupt.

In addition to major deployments such as Farm Gate, Gold Fortune, and Bold Venture, the Air Commandos supported dozens of smaller efforts throughout the world. A Special Air Warfare fact sheet of the period describes the scale of these deployments:

> Such deployments, lasting from six weeks to 90 days, were made to Honduras, the Dominican Republic, Guatemala, Peru, Venezuela, El Salvador, Nicaragua, Colombia, Argentina, Ecuador, Chile, Portugal, Iran,* Ethiopia, the Congo, and Saudi Arabia.[41]

Needless to say, the cost of this furious operational pace resulted in enormous (for the size of the force) requirements for men and materiel. Like a skinny teenager asking for a third cheeseburger, the Air Commandos demanded still more personnel and food (materiel) to feed their growth, putting continuing pressure on USAF's personnel system. In early 1961, all the initially small Jungle Jim cadre had been selected from an all-volunteer pool. Only 12 months later, the overly rapid expansion of the force led the Air Force to direct that only the 1st Air Commando Group within the SAWC would be manned on an all-volunteer basis.[42] It had not had much choice, since Headquarters USAF had just announced its intention to expand the force still further, from the current 795 to *five thousand!*[43]

But if the demand for more personnel continued unabated, so did the line of volunteers trying to get in the door. When Headquarters USAF established a COIN officer career specialty code and publicized its recruiting program, the personnel system was quickly awash in applications. Overwhelmed, the Air Staff was soon forced to ask the major field commands to defer accepting volunteer applications for a period.[44] Observing this administrative upheaval from their editorial desks, *Air Force Times* journalists noted in their 9 June 1962 issue that "special air warfare apparently appealed to many more airmen than did the scientific impersonality of the space age."[45]

By early 1965, the original 352-man Jungle Jim program had expanded to 11 active duty squadrons: six in South Vietnam, three at Hurlburt Field, and one each in Panama and West Germany.[46] In addition, National Guard Air Commando units were activated in California, West Virginia, Maryland, and Rhode Island.

Learning and continually adapting from field experience gained in its worldwide deployments, the Air Commandos recruited medics, combat controllers, combat weather teams, and forward air controllers, many of whom were put through US Army parachute training at Fort Benning, Georgia.[47] To consolidate and build on this hard-earned wealth of operational experience, a Special Air Warfare School was established at Hurlburt Field in 1966; it was subsequently redesignated the USAF Special Operations School in 1969.[48]

Impressive as the Air Commando expansion was, the force still represented far less than one percent of USAF strength. More impressive still was the individual talent that continued flowing

*In 1963 an Air Commando/Green Beret COIN operation supported the Shah of Iran's forces against the Kurds in northwestern Iran. For an insightful look at this rare COIN success, see Richard Secord with Jay Wurts, *Honored and Betrayed: Irangate, Covert Affairs, and the Secret War in Laos* (New York: John Wiley & Sons, Inc., 1992).

into Hurlburt Field. One measure of this talent can be gauged by the fact that between 1962 and 1965, airmen from this small fringe group were recognized by Headquarters USAF with the presentation of the Aviator's Valor Award (1962), the Mackay Trophy and Cheney Award (1963), and the Air Force Outstanding Unit Award (1964).[49]

The recognition continued in 1965, when the 1st Air Commando Squadron, flying the rugged A-1 Skyraiders, introduced to the Air Commandos just the previous year, won a Presidential Unit Citation for its combat in South Vietnam. It was the first USAF unit to win this level of recognition since the Korean War.[50] But the price for flying and fighting "at the tip of the spear" was proving expensive for those who dared. Forty Air Commandos died during this period, the majority as might be expected, in Southeast Asia.[51]

Still further expansion lay ahead for the Air Commandos, along with a 1965 shift in mission emphasis from training indigenous personnel to direct combat. Demonstrating an incredible diversity of capabilities, they fought with distinction throughout Southeast Asia from the beginning to the end: close air support, interdiction, civic affairs, psychological operations, defoliant operations, and much more.

In July 1968, all Air Commando units were redesignated "Special Operations." Throughout the incredible kaleidoscope of combat operations in America's longest war, the Air Commandos, whatever their name, could always be found . . . *anytime, anyplace.*

Richard Secord

Air Commando Richard Secord and his Iranian counterpart prepare for a counterinsurgency mission against rebellious Kurds in northwestern Iran in 1963. The Air Commando/Green Beret COIN mission proved a complete success, one of the very few times such an unqualified result would be achieved by the United States during the cold war.

Viet Nam Craft Down

SAIGON, South Viet Nam (AP) — A Vietnamese air force fighter-bomber piloted by two U.S. Air Force captains crashed and exploded in jungle-covered mountains today while on a strike mission.

There was no immediate indication whether either of the two American or the Vietnamese observer with them survived.

It was the second crash of an American-piloted B26 fighter bomber in four days. Sunday, a B26 crashed or was shot down on a strafing mission 110 miles southwest of here, killing both American pilots and the Vietnamese observer.

Today's crash, about 260 miles northeast of here, occurred while the B26 reportedly was strafing a suspected Viet Cong target. It was not known whether the plane had been hit by ground fire.

Flier Hunted In Viet Nam

SAIGON, South Viet Nam, Feb. 7 (UPI)—A rescued Vietnamese crewman reported today that a U.S. airman bailed out of their B26 bomber before it crashed yesterday. The report touched off a massive air-and-ground search of Communist-infested regions north of here.

A U.S. Air Force major was killed when the World War II vintage bomber, which had been strafing Viet Cong guerrilla positions, crashed and burned in the mountains about 250 miles north of Saigon.

His burned body was found in the wreckage by Vietnamese rangers who reached the crash site early today. Sixty-seven Americans have died in South Viet Nam since the United States launched its massive assistance program in 1961.

The bomber's Vietnamese radio operator was sighted from the air near the crash site by a U.S. helicopter.

He said the navigator, a U.S. Air Force lieutenant, bailed out ahead of him but the major who was piloting the bomber stayed with the plane as it hit a mountainside.

The B26 bomber was the second to crash in a week. Last Sunday, two U.S. officers and a Vietnamese crewman were killed while on a similar strafing mission against the Reds. Cause of that crash has not been determined.

USAF/Air Commando Association

The ease with which the phrase "flying into harm's way" is written on paper stands in stark contrast to the price in blood paid by many of those who chose to do so. While Air Commando/Special Operations forces never approached 1 percent of USAF's total personnel strength, its members received nearly half the Medals of Honor awarded the Air Force during the Second Indochina War.

Notes

1. 1st Lt John A. Koren, "History of USAF Special Operations Forces" (Background paper, USAF Special Operations School, 5 September 1982), 1.

2. Ibid.

3. History, Tactical Air Command, 1 January–30 June 1961, 20. (Secret) Information extracted is unclassified (declassified by AFSHRC, 19 October 1994).

4. History, Tactical Air Command, 1 July–31 December 1961, 59. (Secret) Information extracted is unclassified (declassified by AFSHRC, 19 October 1994).

5. Ibid., 21.

6. Maj John Hawkins Napier III, USAF, "The Air Commandos in Vietnam, November 5, 1961 to February 7, 1965" (master's thesis, Auburn University, 1967), 64.

7. History, Tactical Air Command, 1 January–30 June 1961, 433. (Secret) Information extracted is unclassified.

8. Ibid., 274.

9. Ibid., 275.

10. Ibid.

11. Ibid., 276.

12. "Tactical Air Command in Southeast Asia, 1961–1968," Office of TAC History, Headquarters Tactical Air Command, Langley AFB, Va., August 1972, 490. (Secret) Information extracted is unclassified (declassified 25 October 1994). Hereafter cited as "Tactical Air Command."

13. Ibid.

14. Ibid.

15. Ibid., 486.

16. Ibid., 490.

17. Ibid., 487.

18. Ibid.

19. Napier, 65.

20. Ibid.

21. "Tactical Air Command," 496.

22. Ibid.

23. James L. Cole Jr., "USAF Special Operations Forces: Past, Present, and Future," *Aerospace Historian* 27, no.4 (December 1980).

24. "Tactical Air Command," 18.

25. Carl Berger, ed., *The United States Air Force in Southeast Asia, 1961–1973: An Illustrated Account* (Washington, D.C.: Office of Air Force History, 1984), 26.

26. "Tactical Air Command," 10–11.

27. Ibid., 9.

28. Harve Saal, *MACV Studies and Observations Group*, vol. 4, *Appendixes* (Ann Arbor, Mich.: Edward Brothers, 1990), 13.

29. Ibid., 19

30. Ibid., 11.

31. Philip D. Chinnery, *Any Time, Any Place: A History of USAF Air Commando and Special Operations Forces, 1944–1994* (Annapolis, Md.: Naval Institute Press, 1994), 78.

32. Berger, 29.

33. Ibid.

34. Ibid.

35. Ibid., 12.

36. Napier, 103.

37. "Tactical Air Command," 50.

38. Napier, 102.

39. Chinnery, 76.

40. Ibid., 88.

41. *Special Air Warfare Fact Sheet*, 16; and US Air Force news service release, 7 May 1965, 313.

42. "Tactical Air Command," 56.

43. Napier, 105.

44. Ibid.

45. As quoted in ibid.

46. Ibid., 110.

47. Ibid., 111.

48. Koren, 2.

49. Napier, 197.

50. Ibid., 196.

51. Ibid., 197.

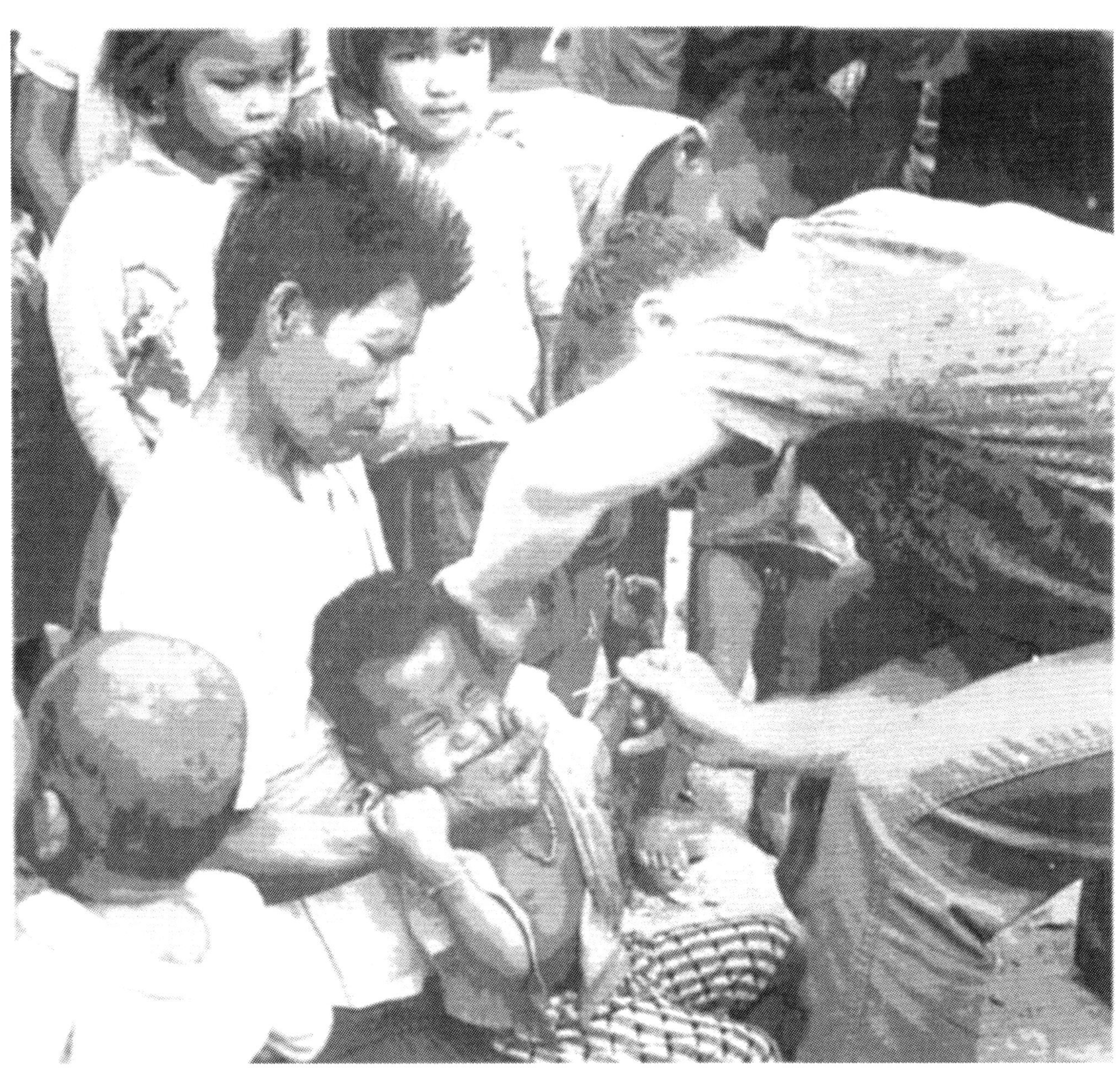

Air Commando
Civic Action

Fighting with the Heart

Poor little Ban Bu Phram. Only the Americans could build the bridge it so desperately needed during the annual monsoon floods. But American help went first to villages that lay within enemy rocket range of its big air bases, and no such base lay nearby. Without building its own 122mm rocket factory and painting a picture of Ho Chi Minh's face on its roof, Ban Bu Phram was going to stay in the cellar of the American Air Force's "threat to air bases" priority list.

Some days your civic action program meets its lofty "strategic" goals. Some days Mama just gets a sharp set of teeth in her thumb. The quiet courage and steadfastness of USAF's civic action teams provided one of the finest legacies of America's long and torturous experience in Southeast Asia.

Just the cry *Air Commando!* brings forth popular images of daring missions and courageous airmen fighting in the midst of mortal danger. These heroic images, however, tend to obscure more lasting Air Commando contributions made to the indigenous people the US sought to help in the first place, contributions appreciated long after the last Americans left Southeast Asia. The following story describing the Air Commando's military civic action teams, laboring in the heat, rain, and danger of rural Thailand was one such contribution.

Unlike similar US Army and Marine Corps efforts launched earlier in South Vietnam, the Air Force Military Civic Action Officer (MCAO) program conducted in Thailand received relatively little publicity. In retrospect, this probably facilitated their success. Using an intentionally low-profile approach, handpicked officers and airmen, assembled and trained in small teams, labored throughout the war in duty that often seemed more appropriate to the Peace Corps than the United States Air Force.

But unlike the Peace Corps, the humanitarian programs implemented by the MCAOs were motivated by a much more pragmatic rationale than simple altruism. With continual patience and ingenuity, they implemented a classic foreign internal defense program that effectively neutralized the once-dangerous Communist insurgent threat to the multiple Thai air bases hosting USAF combat forces for the war against North Vietnam. All the more remarkable, they accomplished this notable feat on a minuscule budget that by the standards of wartime expenditures came out of the USAF's petty cash drawer.

Following their individual arrival in Thailand, the MCAOs were quickly moved to their assigned base and put to work with the briefest of orientations. Extensive stateside training was helpful, but in the end it was the character and personality of the individual MCAO that would determine the effectiveness of his tour of duty. On site, the MCAO first prioritized the areas to receive the bulk of the limited MCAO resources available, with basic security considerations to the large air bases determining which particular areas came first. Those villages within a 16-kilometer (approximately 10 statute miles) radius of the air base got top priority for MCAO manpower and financial resources. Why 16 kilometers? Sixteen kilometers is the maximum effective range of the deadly, Soviet-made 122 mm rocket, used so effectively against US airfields and bases in neighboring South Vietnam. Although determination of this "security ring" was important, it was by far the easiest part of the MCAO program.

To the casual social observer, the ingredients for a successful civic action program appear deceptively easy. What could be more basic than building roads, hospitals, and schools? Add to that some mobile medical teams giving vaccinations, engineers digging wells, and perhaps a few civic action volunteers supporting the local orphanage, and success is in the bag. A piece of cake!

Well . . . not exactly. In reality, the complex geographic and cultural demands placed on any would-be MCAO were (and remain so today) so extreme that a worldwide catalogue of major civic action projects attempted by numerous countries would list far more failures than successes. Bitter experience has shown that the mere presence of more schools, dams, and wells does not necessarily translate into good will between two very different cultures.

The Soviets, for example, spent years building Egypt's giant Aswan Dam, the largest in the world, only to be later ejected by the Egyptians for their grossly offensive personal behavior. Fortunately for the Air Commandos, their flair for picking the right people for unusual jobs made for a totally different type of civic action story in Thailand. As noted earlier, their first civic action initiative in Thailand was launched by Project Water Pump medical personnel as an off-duty, unofficial addition to their primary duty of tend-

USAF

Military civic action officers were always looking for creative ways to boost their local budgets. This self-help crafts project initiated by one such MCAO draws Air Commandos (and their flight pay) from the 311th Air Commando Squadron.

ing to the Air Commandos. That all changed in 1966 with the arrival of the 606th Air Commando Squadron at Nakhon Phanom RTAFB.

With the arrival of the 606th ACS, Water Pump's unofficial efforts were formalized into a Civic Action Branch (CAB), which functioned as part of the US ambassador's overall "country team."[1] By the following year, the CAB had grown to a Civic Actions Center with 84 Air Force officers and airmen operating with the assistance of 12 Thai interpreters.[2] And it was in 1967 that this creative civic action team hit on one of those mad schemes that was brilliant not only for the low cost involved, but for the impact it had on their entire civic action program.

The genesis for the idea was found in the annual floods that sweeps over much of low-lying Thailand every monsoon season. Isolating villages, contaminating water, and causing a variety of potentially deadly diseases, the floods were more feared than the Communist insurgents. It was a challenge the Air Commando civic actions teams couldn't ignore, and they didn't.

At the suggestion of the Civic Actions Center, the Thai government leased a commercial river boat, which a joint US-Thai medical team converted to a floating medical clinic. Manned with joint US-Thai medical teams on a rotational basis, the "Floating Mekong Medical Clinic" was launched, literally, into the flooded lowlands. Immediately proving a great success, it was as one chronicler of the times described it, the "pride and joy" of both American and Thai civic action personnel.[3] As exciting as this high-visibility achievement was, however, the overall civic action struggle for the hearts and minds of the villagers was fought on a much more subtle battlefield—a field so deceptive in its outward calm that it took even the most alert MCAO months just to discover who and where the real enemy was.

In Thailand's remote villages, the MCAOs encountered a mixture of oppressive heat, unsafe drinking water, widespread disease, and poverty. Quite naturally, these circumstances took their toll on the village population's loyalty to a faraway government. More to the point, they also created a potential recruiting ground for anti-American insurgents. With the arrival of the first MCAOs in the mid-1960s, the insurgents and Americans soon squared off in a subtle but high-stakes contest for the elusive loyalties of these remote villages.

The most urgent and complex problem facing each MCAO in this battle was the need to determine the real agenda of the various key participants. Cultural and personality differences, profiteering, local politics, and generations-old animosities all combined to place a nearly impenetrable curtain of confusion between the MCAO attempting to assess the needs of villagers and the villagers themselves. Amidst this confusion, the MCAO often had little to rely on except his decidedly foreign American instincts and whatever resources he could cajole out of frequently harried American base commanders wrestling with a thousand other problems.

The MCAO would also learn that while insurgents might present the most deadly threat, aspiring entrepreneurs with an eye on the Yankee dollars in his civic action budget were far more numerous and equally ambitious. At least that was the experience of Capt Daniel Jacobowitz, who spent a 14-month MCAO tour in Thailand, part of which was in Nakhon Phanom with the 56th Special Operations Wing. In his 1975 end-of-tour "lessons learned" report, he observed that "50 percent of an alert MCAO's time is spent trying to outsmart his contractors, who are spending 100 percent of their time trying to outwit him. Frankly, paranoia can become an occupational hazard."[4]

Fortunately, there did exist a substantial pool of dedicated local and regional Thai officials and military commanders through which the MCAOs could establish new programs, or better yet, support existing programs identified by the Thais themselves. And this the MCAOs did, compiling some astonishing achievements that highlight not only their successes, but the scope of the problems they faced even around major towns like Korat.

In his monthly activity summary for November 1974,[5] MCAO team chief captain August G. "Greg" Jannarone notes a highly successful on-base fund raiser for both Korat's city/province orphanage and the Khon Kaen Leper Colony, ongoing construction at numerous new schools and health centers, and completion of similar projects at other schools, clinics, and water systems. In the same month, Jannarone also generated the first-ever rotation of Thai army hospital doctors and medics in weekly medical civic action patrols through the nearby villages—with a predictably positive response from the population.[6]

Not so predictable but very encouraging was the news that Korat's anti-American publisher of the *Korat Daily* praised these activities in his paper.[7] And these developments represented just one MCAO office, in one town, in one month.

The payoff to successful MCAO programs such as those around Korat and the collocated air base became increasingly evident to most echelons of USAF command. They proved incredibly cost-effective when compared to the massive American expenditures seen when once-small insurgencies escalated to the levels seen elsewhere in Southeast Asia. Noting a 1975 US government proposal to prop up neighboring, war-ravaged Cambodia for four months with a $220-million aid package, MCAO Jacobowitz observed, "This [amount of money] would run the present Thailand MCAO program for *four hundred years!*" (emphasis added).[8]

Occasionally, the MCAO would be urged by the American embassy in Bangkok to undertake a program of considerable long-range, bilateral political importance at the state level, but of little military value to the local Air Force base commander, who was also known as the MCAO's performance rating officer. The MCAO caught in such a bureaucratic power struggle had a major problem, especially if he believed in the embassy proposal.

And this is precisely where MCAO captain Jannarone found himself in July 1975 when both the US Embassy and the US Military Assistance Command, Thailand, wanted the Ban Bu Phram bridge built in the remote Prachinaburi Province. Ban Bu Phram presented two challenges in particular for the solution-seeking Jannarone.

First, the village was stranded from outside food, medical support, or other government services for long periods of the rainy season by encircling river waters that rose more than 10 feet above normal. Other than cutting off the village from access to school, market, and highway, the waters also brought to the village an unusually high malaria rate. The latter factor was of major interest to the Southeast Asia Organization (SEATO) medical laboratory in Bangkok. Finally, Ban Bu Phram was also considered politically sensitive, in part because of the history of success of Thai and Cambodian recruiting of insurgents in the area. Ban Bu Phram really needed that bridge!

The second challenge was tougher still. Unfortunately for Ban Bu Phram, it was located about 114 kilometers beyond the 16-kilometer-wide security ring protecting the nearest American air base. Without building its own 122 mm rocket factory complete with a picture of Ho Chi Minh's face on the roof, tiny Ban Bu Phram wasn't going anywhere on the Air Force's "threats to air bases" priority list.

In Ban Bu Phram's difficulties Jannarone found his solution. By communicating the village's nonmilitary priorities, as well as the potential for a serious military problem in the future, through a maze of US and Thai bureaucratic obstacles the savvy MCAO got Ban Bu Phram its bridge. From this experience and others, Captain Jannarone concluded at the end of his tour that an MCAO became optimally effective only after completing eight to nine months of the one-year tour of duty

August Jannarone

How do you warn curious children not to pick up something they haven't seen before? Civic action teams continually strove to get the word out by every means possible, including the widespread distribution of cartoon-type posters in every possible village and school.

that was standard US policy for American servicemen in Southeast Asia.

While this policy had an obvious impact on experience levels in every field, nowhere was this impact more of a handicap than in the civic action arena. In an Asian culture that traditionally measures "short-term" gains by the generation, traditional Yankee impatience and current military rotation policy continually hampered the execution of a coherent, long-term MCAO program.

As Captain Jacobowitz observed, it is extremely difficult for the MCAO to assess the enduring success of this program. The local population and officials, USAF and Thai military, and the US Embassy each have very different agendas by which they judge civic action activities. And unfortunately, the most valuable judges of the MCAO's effectiveness, the insurgents themselves, are not prone to participate in these "effectiveness survey" reports.

It is a matter of record that during the USAF's long stay in Thailand, not a single major attack was ever mounted by insurgents against the dozen or more Thai airfields and bases hosting US forces. This success is due at least in part to the valuable flow of local intelligence that continued to come from the grass-roots level in which American MCAOs and their Thai counterparts struggled year after year.

Beyond this easily observed military reality, the impact of the basic humanity the MCAOs demonstrated to those in need, the reduction in disease, illiteracy, infant mortality, and poverty are more difficult to satisfactorily measure. Amidst the death and destruction of war, the Air Commandos struggled and endured, emerging a decade later with something that, like these imponderables, can never be measured in a computer: the satisfaction of helping others help themselves.

USAF

How do you rate the effectiveness of a military civic action program? In Southeast Asia, one such measure was the steady stream of intelligence about Vietcong activity in the local area, which was provided to the civic action teams by grateful villagers, such as those pictured here.

Notes

1. Carl Berger, ed., *The United States Air Force in Southeast Asia, 1961–1973: An Illustrated Account* (Washington, D.C.: Office of Air Force History, 1984), 292.

2. Ibid.

3. Ibid.

4. Capt Daniel W. Jacobowitz, chief, Military Civic Action, Headquarters, 56th Combat Support Group (PACAF), Lessons Learned, a report in response to a request for same from Thirteenth Air Force ADVON/CA, message 22/0910Z, January 1975, 4. Hereafter cited as Jacobowitz.

5. Capt August G. Jannarone, Military Civic Action officer, Korat RTAFB, Thailand, Staff Agency Monthly Activity Summary for November 1974, dated 9 December 1974, 5.

6. Ibid., 3.

7. Ibid., 4.

8. Jacobowitz, 17.

RANCH HAND
紫
VIETNAM

A Dangerous Task, Thankless Missions

The Ranch Hand Project

When executed with surprise, speed, and ruthless violence, the ambush has proven over the centuries to be one of the deadliest tactics of warfare. Those caught in such a trap do not engage in battle so much as endure horrific slaughter until their surrender or death terminates the carnage. Of the three key factors noted, it is surprise that requires the essential element of concealment. But what if, in a campaign against an adversary whose foremost tactic is the ambush, *your* force could strip away the concealment that made his bloody victories possible?

The Ranch Hand shoulder patch is unusually descriptive of the mission. The red and yellow reflect the national flag of the Republic of South Vietnam, the green center the forests sprayed by defoliant aircraft, the brown swath the results of the spray missions, and the Chinese calligraphy the symbol for the color "purple," the slang expression for the herbicide used by Ranch Hand during the early years.

USAF

When Ranch Hand's defoliant planes stripped the natural concealment away from the Vietcong, they also crippled the VC's single-most successful tactic against allied troops during the war: the ambush. These herbicide-exposed Vietcong fighting positions and communications trenches (above and facing page) were in the VC-controlled "Iron Triangle" northwest of Saigon.

In the answer to that question lies the story of a unique Air Commando unit so controversial during its active service that years later, President Gerald R. Ford would publicly renounce first use ever again of such a unit by the United States in any future war. To understand why such a force was created in the first place and its mission and its impact on the war, a short imaginary diversion into the bloody history of Southeast Asia is helpful.

If it were possible for the reader to experience modern guerrilla warfare through a "virtual reality" video, he or she could find themselves riding in a French armored column, *Group Mobiles* as they were known in French Indochina in the early 1950s. Dozens of armored vehicles and trucks carrying hundreds of troops, artillery, medics, and supplies are probing deep into Communist-controlled rural areas. Your group is searching for the elusive Viet Minh, the predecessor to the Vietcong (VC) and North Vietnamese Army the Americans will search for in these same areas years later during the Second Indochina War.

Threading slowly through twisting, narrow backcountry roads in the heat and choking dust, your convoy travels through forest so thick and wild that it is only a few yards or even feet from your heavily armed vehicles. Both you and the grim-faced soldiers in your truck peer vainly into the woods for signs of enemy presence. You've traveled for long, boring days like this, seemingly wasting everyone's time in an obviously deserted sector. *But there!* The sun catches something metal in the bush, and in less than a heartbeat your gut turns cold with terror as you realize too late what is happening to you.

The thick foliage in your face explodes with fire, deafening noise, and gunsmoke. Hundreds of unseen weapons are firing at point-blank range from expertly camouflaged positions virtually atop your vehicles, mortar rounds explode with devastating accuracy into the killing zone you have entered, while heavy machine guns send streams of red-hot slugs slicing through trucks and the human flesh packed tightly in them. Within minutes, an incredibly short time, it's over. Return fire from the convoy has ceased; the shrieks of fear and death have fallen away to a few pitiful moans from the handful of wounded survivors. Only their futile pleas and the crackle of flames disrupt the graveyard silence that only moments earlier was a world gone mad with fury.

This "imaginary" scene really took place over and over again as thousands of French and colonial soldiers were driven, sometimes literally, to their deaths. Of all the factors that made this French nightmare possible, the most important was concealment of the ambush from French (and your) view. And very relevant to the story told here, the expert practitioners of this ambush tactic passed on their expertise to the next generation, which would, in turn, aim for a repeat performance in the 1960s.

This time it would be the young soldiers from California, Virginia, and places in between who would conduct "search and destroy" missions into these killing zones. In their armored personnel carriers and on foot, they would traverse into forests so dense that large numbers of heavily armed enemy could lie undetected in ambush only scant yards from the unsuspecting Americans. That is, of course, unless the Americans could find some way to see through the dense forest and jungle, to strip away the foliage that so effectively blinded the French army.

By 1961, the repeat performance was well underway as the Vietcong demonstrated how well they had learned ambush tactics from their Viet Minh predecessors. The bloody tab for the performance was picked up by the Army of the

USAF

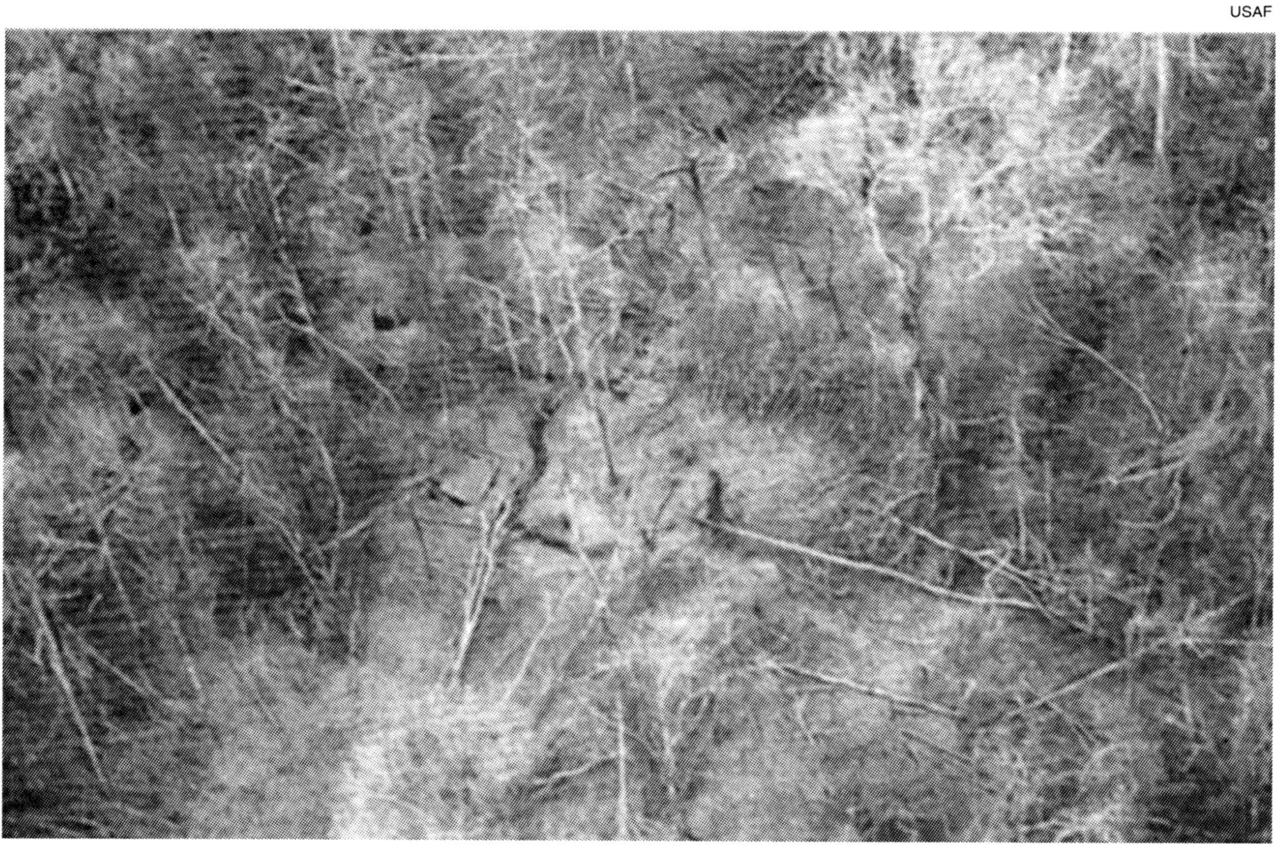

Republic of Vietnam (ARVN). But by this time, the Americans, who never quite left South Vietnam after the French departure in 1954,* thought maybe, just maybe, they had found the elusive "some way" to see what the French could not.

The Americans turned to action in November 1961, when six C-123 Provider transports, specially modified for aerial-spraying operations, left Pope AFB, North Carolina, en route to South Vietnam. Although earlier small-scale defoliation experiments had been conducted in Vietnam with both C-47 transports and H-34 helicopters, this decision to go to the more modern C-123 as the primary defoliant aircraft proved an excellent choice.

Originally designed as a glider, the C-123 had a rugged airframe, low-speed maneuverability, and good visibility that were near ideal for the spray mission. And the decision to add armor plating to the cockpit area would prove equally wise (and would be enjoyed on a repetitive basis by the aircrews). The most visible modification to the aircraft was the MC-1 Hourglass spray system, combining external spray booms on wings and fuselage and an internal 1,000-gallon herbicide tank and pumps in the cargo hold.

The all-volunteer aircrews flying these first Providers were solicited from the top of the list of nonselected volunteers for the original 4400th CCTS (Jungle Jim), which, as previously noted, had been activated the previous April.[1] And though not yet officially assigned to the Air Commando program, the airmen were scheduled to fly as part of the ongoing, trans-Pacific deployment flow of the 4400th's Detachment 2A (Farm Gate) to minimize public attention.

Only after their arrival in the Philippines were the aircraft separated from Farm Gate and given the code name that would later become synonymous with their mission: "Ranch Hand." At the same time, the group was designated Tactical Air Force Transport Squadron, Provisional One, and assigned to the 2d Air Division in South Vietnam.[2] The first three of the six defoliant airplanes flew into Saigon's Tan Son Nhut airport on 7 January 1962, on what was forecast as only a 120-day-long field test of the aerial spray concept. To avoid the media and ensure their security, they were immediately parked in a special area guarded 24 hours a day by Vietnamese Air Force (VNAF) police. But the precautions would prove only half successful, and the missing half was a killer.

If the American and South Vietnamese media remained temporarily unaware of the new special unit at Tan Son Nhut, two events quickly carried out at the airport in total silence shocked the American flyers into a new appreciation of "security" in Vietnam. The first was uncovered during a routine morning preflight of the aircraft when maintenance personnel discovered critical control cable turnbuckles on all the aircraft had been cut by saboteurs.[3] The second was an early morning, grisly discovery of one of their VNAF guards . . . with his throat slashed.[4] Thereafter, the Americans mounted their own guard of the aircraft every night.

Despite these problems, the program moved out smartly, one crew flying a successful test mission only three days after their arrival. During the early missions, a Farm Gate C-47 frequently preceded the spray aircraft with leaflet drop and loudspeaker messages to the villages below. The aerial communications explained to the population the purpose of the defoliant flights and, undoubtedly of much more interest to the listeners, the fact that the herbicides would not harm humans.

---

*The 1954 Geneva Protocols that mandated a phased French withdrawal from northern Vietnam said nothing about the 342-strong US Military Assistance/Advisory Group (MAAG) then based in Saigon to support French military operations. The MAAG remained, becoming the genesis of all future American involvement in Vietnam.

For their first three years, Ranch Hand flights primarily dispensed herbicide "Purple." Nicknamed from the purple band painted around each 55-gallon drum containing the liquid, it was a commercially proven weed-control agent then in wide use throughout the world.[5] Predictably, this fact was overlooked by the North Vietnamese government, which soon saw the propaganda potential for "gas warfare" in the admittedly ominous-looking flights.

In fact, because of the vulnerability of this high-visibility operation to Communist propaganda, a number of senior Defense and State Department officials had already voiced opposition to the program from its inception. But if the controversy in Hanoi and Washington surrounding Ranch Hand was growing, so were demands for more spray missions from Army commanders quick to pick up on the tactical implications for their units.

Less than a month after its first flight, a Ranch Hand Provider became the first Air Force aircraft lost in Vietnam.[6] On 2 February 1962, a Provider was apparently shot down while on a low-level training mission, killing Capt Fergus C. Groves II, Capt Robert D. Larson, and SSgt Milo B. Coghill. Although proof was never obtained that the C-123 was downed by hostile ground fire, Air Commando T-28s were soon tasked to fly armed escort for future spray missions.

By 1963 the "Cowboys," as the Ranch Hand aircrews called themselves, were busier than ever flying cargo, munitions, and personnel throughout Vietnam in addition to their primary mission. In August, the Thai government requested and received a Ranch Hand deployment that successfully destroyed a locust plague in that country.

By fall of that year, the increase in enemy ground fire against their spray flights were providing the Cowboys with a flattering, if deadly, confirmation that their program was having the intended effect on the Vietcong. In December, the Cowboys decided to forgo the flattery in exchange for better odds on their survival. This decision led in turn to the first spray missions at night in the hope that this would be one means of reducing the juicy target their Providers made when flying 150 miles per hour at an altitude of 150 feet above enemy gunners. If night missions proved practical, they would seem to provide a low-cost alternative to fighter-escorted missions, or the need for expensive new technology of some still-unspecified type.

The first night mission was accomplished with one aircraft dispersing flares from above while a lower-flying plane sprayed the foliage below. The mission was declared a success, though nervous Cowboys noted the same flares that helped them avoid impact with the ground also highlighted their aircraft to watchful eyes below. The second night mission confirmed their worst fears. Luck and surprise the first time had caught the Vietcong offguard. The second night an obviously alerted Vietcong greeted the spray plane with a heavy volume of fire, the tracer rounds from their rifles lighting up the sky as if to relieve the aircrews of simply guessing how many people below were trying to kill them. End of night spray flights as a tactic!

The VC may have hated the defoliant flights, but not as much as US and ARVN commanders loved them. The result was the continual expansion of the program, with the Special Aerial Spray Flight (as Ranch Hand had subsequently been designated) attached to the 309th Air Commando Squadron (also flying C-123s) in March 1965.[7] This move brought for the first time the formal inclusion of defoliant operations to the Air Commandos' already unusual repertoire of weapons. Included in this repertoire was a new herbicide Ranch Hand tested that same month, for the first time in the war.[8] Like Purple, this herbicide got its nickname from the painted band around the 55-gallon drums it arrived in. It was known as "Orange."

USAF

Precision formation flying below 200 feet is not a skill much in demand from most transport pilots. But Ranch Hand aircrews bet their survival on their ability to fly such disciplined formations, especially when taking enemy fire.

In addition to the organizational expansion, 11 more UC-123s were authorized in May 1966, scheduled to arrive in Vietnam before the year's end. During this period, the defoliant aircraft had been redesignated with the prefix "U" (UC-123) to differentiate them from standard cargo-hauling Providers. At no time during this organizational upheaval were the UC-123s pulled off combat operations, and the inevitable finally occurred in June 1966, when Ranch Hand took its first confirmed combat loss.

One of two UC-123s flying low, slow passes over a target area was hit by ground fire to an engine, crashing a short distance further down the flight path. Fortunately, a US Marine Corps helicopter flying in the vicinity rescued the three Cowboy crewmen grouped near the still-burning wreckage before the enemy could reach the site. In October, the same scene was played out again, and again a helicopter rescued the crew. Flying at spray altitudes that even pistol bullets could reach was, however, clearly pushing the Cowboys' luck. From this time forward, both expansion and attrition became inseparable for the Ranch Hand crews.

On 15 October 1966, the Special Aerial Spray Flight became the 12th Air Commando Squadron, assigned to the 315th Air Commando

Wing. Three months later, yet another Provider was downed, this one over Laos and this time with no survivors. In February 1967, Ranch Hand was sent into the dangerous demilitarized zone (DMZ) separating South and North Vietnam. These particular missions proved invaluable in exposing previously hidden North Vietnamese infiltration routes and supply dumps. By June of that year, the total number of UC-123s had risen to 20, but the following month still another Ranch Hand went down with the loss of all four aboard.

As the war's pace picked up, so did Ranch Hand operations. By 1967, the squadron was flying over 20 missions a day, with as many as three or four Providers flying spray runs in multiship formations for each mission. Each ship could defoliate a swath 80 yards wide on a track up to 10 miles long. Vietnamese observers were frequently carried aboard as "mission commanders," a development stemming from a rules-of-engagement requirement imposed on the squadron.

When the North Vietnamese Army and VC struck every major city and airfield in South Vietnam during the 1968 Tet offensive, the 12th ACS flew nearly 3,000 emergency airlift missions, carrying men and materiel to help stem the attack. Defoliant missions resumed two months later, and in May a fifth Ranch Hand went down under enemy guns. During the same month, some much-appreciated help came to the squadron with the arrival of the new K-model Providers, featuring two J-85 jet auxiliary engines mounted under the wings outboard of the two main piston engines.

By April 1969, all Ranch Hand UC-123s had received the K-model conversion.[9] The problem of enemy ground fire had continued to worsen, however, and that July new escort tactics were adopted to protect the spray planes. Reflecting the seriousness of the ground fire threat, the new escort tactics called for Air Commando-flown, propeller-driven A-1 Skyraiders to provide low-level, flank protection on the spray runs, while F-4 jets orbited overhead to strike enemy gun positions that had exposed their positions as the Providers flew overhead. The heavy escort tactic substantially reduced the number of hits taken by Ranch Hand crews.

By the fall of 1969, the Nixon administration's plan to withdraw US forces from Vietnam, "Vietnamization," was taking effect. In September, the US Military Assistance Command, Vietnam (MACV) directed Seventh Air Force to immediately begin reducing monthly herbicide sorties from their current average of 400 per month to a target figure of 280 sorties per month by July 1970.[10] In November, just after the 12th SOS reached its peak wartime strength of 25 defoliant aircraft, the squadron was reduced to 14 UC-123Ks to reflect the reduced operational schedule.[11]

But to the steadily shrinking number of American troops left in Vietnam, the Vietnamization process increased the danger of their situation and resulted in unabated demands for defoliant missions from Army field commanders. Despite this military reality, the 12th was further reduced from 14 to eight aircraft (two of which were configured for insecticide—not herbicide–spray operations only), by June 1970.[12] In February 1970, the Department of Defense approved just $3 million of the MACV-requested $27 million for herbicide operations for the period July 1970 to June 1971.[13]

Another event of note was the decision in 1970 to discontinue use of Orange amidst growing concern that contrary to earlier government claims one of its components, dioxin, could prove harmful to humans. From 1965 to 1970, Orange had become the primary herbicide in use, having affected an estimated "41 per cent of South Vietnam's mangrove forests, 19 per cent of the uplands forests and 8 per cent of all cultivated land."[14]

Missing, however, from all these operational statistics is the one number that motivated the

American government to start Ranch Hand in the first place and to continue using it despite growing apprehensions. This number will never be found for the simple reason that it—unlike missions flown, gallons of herbicide used, and acres of foliage affected—can never be computerized. In short, it is the unknown thousands of American and other allied troops who are alive today because herbicides stripped away the concealment needed by the Vietcong to execute the horrific ambush scene described in the beginning of this story. Oddly, this point of view remains conspicuous in its absence from most popular media treatment of the Agent Orange issue.

The 12th Special Operations Squadron (redesignated with all other Air Commando units in 1968) was deactivated on 31 July 1970, with the remaining UC-123Ks becoming A Flight, 310th Tactical Airlift Squadron. Ranch Hand flew its last mission on 7 January 1971, exactly 10 years to the day from its arrival at Tan Son Nhut airport. In nine years of defoliant operations, Ranch Hand aircraft and crews dispensed between 17.7 and 19.4 million gallons of herbicides in Southeast Asia. Approximately 11 million gallons of it were the controversial Orange herbicide.

On 8 April 1975, President Gerald R. Ford issued Executive Order 11850, renouncing first use of herbicides in war by the United States except for control of vegetation on and around the defensive perimeters of US bases.[15] With this order, President Ford ensured that an operation like Project Ranch Hand could never happen again.

*Epilogue:** In the years following the war in Vietnam, an increasing number of veterans came to Veterans Administration (VA) offices with complaints of numerous health problems, including birth defects in their children. The VA was slow to respond to these complaints, many of which were suspected by the veterans themselves to be associated with their past presence in herbicide-sprayed areas. Worse yet, the government's initial response denied that US troops were in areas undergoing spray operations at the time, a response subsequently shown to be false.[16] The media picked up on the story, and CBS television broadcast a particularly powerful show: "Agent Orange: Vietnam's Deadly Fog."[17]

Public indignation erupted in the late 1970s as the media rushed to publish without, in many cases, checking the credibility of the veterans' claims. One terminally ill Vietnam veteran described Agent Orange as so powerful that "within two days [it] could topple a hardwood tree 150 feet tall."[18] Also publicized were the comments of a widow: "Dioxins are what they sprayed in Vietnam. They make plants grow so fast they explode, so when it gets into humans, it must do much the same."[19] Still other veterans talked of being "drenched in an orange liquid," even though all herbicides used by the US were sprayed in a fine, colorless mist. The herbicide mist was dispensed at three gallons per acre, or the equivalent of 0.009 ounces per square foot, less if trees were overhead. All in all, such claims were hardly an environment for a calm, if admittedly belated, investigation into the facts.

As a result of the ensuing Agent Orange controversy, the US government began a number of studies on possible links between herbicides (Orange in particular) and Vietnam veterans' health problems. Chief among these is the ongoing Air Force Health Study (AFHS). This comprehensive epidemiology study of approximately 1,000 former Ranch Hand personnel is attempting to determine if the health profile of those individuals who worked with herbicides in Vietnam has been altered by such work.

The AFHS is now in its fourteenth year. Ranch Hand veterans and their scientifically

*This epilogue was written by Maj Jack Spey, USAF, Retired, president, Ranch Hand Vietnam Association, August 1996.

matched comparison group* have undergone four extensive physical examinations by the Kelsey-Seybold Clinic in Houston, Texas, and the Scripps Clinic and Research Foundation in La Jolla, California. The examinations include an emphasis on areas where animal studies suggest that dioxin might cause changes in health outcome.

To date, the mortality rate of the Ranch Hand group continues to be the same as the matched comparison group. In fact, the Ranch Hand mortality rate is significantly lower than the mortality rate for the male population of the Untied States. Health problems within the Ranch Hand group approximate those found in the comparison group.

As this book goes to print, the disparity between media reports and the results of scientific investigation remain as wide as ever. And as with the "Gulf War Syndrome" that emerged 20 years later, the real truth about Agent Orange, if there is only one truth, seems as elusive as ever.

Notes

1. William A. Buckingham, *Operation Ranch Hand: The Air Force and Herbicides in Southeast Asia, 1961–1971* (Washington, D.C.: Office of Air Force History, 1982), 11.
2. Paul Frederick Cecil, *Herbicidal Warfare: The Ranch Hand Project in Vietnam* (New York: Praeger Special Studies, 1986), 28.
3. Ibid., 31.
4. Ibid.
5. Philip D. Chinnery, *Any Time, Any Place: A History of USAF Air Commando and Special Operations Forces, 1944–1994* (Annapolis, Md.: Naval Institute Press, 1994), 73.
6. Carl Berger, ed., *The United States Air Force in Southeast Asia, 1961–1973: An Illustrated Account* (Washington, D.C.: Office of Air Force History, 1984), 15.
7. Cecil, 58.
8. Ibid.
9. Buckingham, 152.
10. Ibid., 161.
11. Ibid.
12. Ibid., 162.
13. Ibid., 162–63.
14. Chinnery, 74.
15. Buckingham, 185, 188.
16. Cecil, 167.
17. Ibid.
18. Ibid., 168.
19. Ibid.

*Other US Air Force aircrew and ground operations personnel in the same age group, but with no exposure to herbicide operations.

The Dragonship

I think we're going to find that the 4th Air Commando Squadron is the greatest thing since sex, so far as protecting a base is concerned.

Commander,
14th Air Commando Wing, 1966

By 1961, the popular sports metaphor "last ditch defense" had become a frightening reality to thousands in South Vietnam. With little hope of air support, even during daylight hours, isolated government outposts and the pro-government villagers they "protected" could only await their fate against a seemingly invincible Vietcong.

USAF

After the last hope for air support faded, the "last ditch" penetrated, and the radios gone silent, only smoking ruins and desolation marked the graveyard that only yesterday was a government outpost. Air Commando frustration grew to anger, then to something more useful. It was called a "Dragonship."

By the time the first Air Commandos arrived in South Vietnam in late 1961, Vietcong forces operating throughout the country had seized the initiative everywhere. In the process, they had demonstrated their contempt for South Vietnam's poorly trained and equipped air force by striking their targets even in broad daylight, contrary to traditional guerrilla tactics. Remote government outposts routinely fell to attacking Vietcong forces, as did outgunned progovernment villages whose elected officials frequently suffered follow-on atrocities at the hands of their "liberators."

The government's widespread introduction in 1962 of reliable, two-way radios to these isolated outposts and villages provided a much improved VNAF response, albeit one still limited to daylight-only operations as the fledgling VNAF had no night attack capability. The Vietcong responded to this government tactic with a switch to night attacks, and the dismal rate of government losses soon resumed. Looking to the recently arrived Air Commandos for help, the VNAF soon learned the Farm Gate contingent also had no night attack capability.

What the Air Commandos did have, however, was a small number of C-47 and (later) C-123 tactical transports and a license to use their imagination. If the Air Commandos couldn't yet effectively defend hamlets under siege at night, they could at least use one of their transports to circle above a beleaguered outpost and drop illumination flares, exposing the attacking Vietcong to the defending troops. This was done, at first with 50,000-candlepower and later with three-million-candlepower flares.[1]

The results obtained by these "flareship" tactics exceeded all expectations. To everyone's relief (everyone except the Vietcong, at least), the flares frequently had a spoiling effect on the attack, with the Vietcong sometimes withdrawing simply upon hearing a flareship approach.[2] In November 1963, when widespread Vietcong attacks attempted to exploit the confusion generated by the military overthow of Vietnam's president, the C-47s and C-123s dropped over 7,000 flares in night defensive operations.[3]

According to a *Newsweek* magazine article of the day, the flares terminated Vietcong attacks nearly 70 percent of the time.[4] But in response to the flareships, the adaptable Vietcong soon learned that they could simply outwait the flareship's fuel endurance before resuming the attack. In 1963, the limited number of transports/flareships available precluded all-night coverage over a single outpost, even one under attack.

It was only a matter of time until some imaginative soul thought of a way to improve the orbiting flareship's effectiveness. And when Capt Ronald W. Terry from the Aeronautical Systems Division at Wright-Patterson AFB, Ohio, proceeded to do just that, he also revolutionized the Air Force concept for close air support. Returning from field observations made during a 1963 trip to Vietnam, Captain Terry wondered why a C-47 flareship effectively illuminating an attacking force below couldn't also control available artillery and air strikes as well. Better yet, why couldn't an *armed* flareship do all these functions while helping these defenders still further with very accurate gunfire of its own?

Back at Wright-Patterson AFB, Terry's inquisitive mind led to the discovery of a dormant experimental effort to provide close air support from a single aircraft orbiting a specific spot on the ground, while its side-firing guns struck the spot. Appropriately, the effort was designated Project Tailchaser.[5] By August 1964, Terry and a small team had advanced Tailchaser to field testing the General Electric SUU-11A, a 7.62 mm minigun mounted on a C-131, over Eglin AFB's test ranges.[6] The equally inquisitive Air Commandos took one look at this test run right in their own backyard and took the "bait" like a world-record marlin hitting a lure.

Ninety days later, Captain Terry's team, including his ace weapons specialist, SSgt Estell P. Bunch, was back in Vietnam. This time the team modified two Farm Gate C-47s with the minigun and briefed crews from the 1st Air Commando Squadron on their employment.[7] Each gunship was to carry a USAF crew of seven and a Vietnamese observer. If the experimental program was off to a promising start in Vietnam, however, the same couldn't be said for its prospects in the United States.

In late 1964, the biggest threat to Tailchaser came from the corporate fighter pilot community (USAF's Tactical Air Command), headed by Gen Walter Sweeney Jr. An open skeptic of the gunship concept, General Sweeney predicted:

> This concept will place a highly vulnerable aircraft in a battlefield environment in which I believe the results will not compensate for the losses of Air Force personnel and aircraft . . . its employment might . . . be disastrous in a future conflict.[8]

Not surprisingly, this view soon formed the general opinion within TAC, which just happened to be the very command directed to employ the gunship![9]

Fortunately for Captain Terry and the Air Commandos, the Air Force chief of staff (CSAF) eventually overruled General Sweeney's objections, or at least most of them. When the fighter community learned the aircraft were to be desig-

USAF

When USAF's fighter pilot community heard that the new gunship was to be designated "FC-47" (for fighter cargo), the Pentagon didn't need telephones to hear the howls. Eventually, it was designated "AC-47," the first in a new line of attack aircraft that would perform incredible service throughout the Second Indochina War.

nated FC-47 ("F" for fighter), the Pentagon didn't need telephones to hear the howls from Headquarters TAC several hundred miles away.[10] The following year, the designation finally settled upon was AC-47 ("A" for attack).*

The CSAF's decision may have been influenced, at least in part, by a short but persuasive briefing by Terry to the CSAF himself. In a classic case of "bet-your-career" nerve, the young captain literally conned his way through the CSAF's outer office in a moment of administrative confusion to deliver his pitch for the gunship.[11]

With the CSAF's blessings, the "gunship show" was on, and, in the best Air Commando tradition, it started off with the simple expedient of poking three side-firing, multibarreled miniguns from the left side of the venerable C-47 "Gooney Bird's" fuselage, two through window slots, and the third

*The AC-47 was also known as "Puff the Magic Dragon," a reference to the seemingly unending sheet of flame and noise produced by the thousands of minigun tracer rounds pouring forth from the night sky directly onto the helpless Vietcong below. From this spectacular display, the aircraft predictably came to be known as "Dragonships."

through the main cargo door opening. Using the radio call sign "Spooky" in Vietnam, this "new, improved" Gooney had some impressive talons.

Each of Spooky's three 7.62 mm miniguns could selectively fire either 50 or 100 rounds *per second!* Cruising in an overhead orbit at 120 knots air speed at an altitude of 3,000 feet, the AC-47 could put a high explosive or glowing red incendiary bullet into every square yard of a football field-sized target in three seconds.[12] And, as long as its 45-flare and 24,000-round basic load of ammunition held out, it could do this intermittently while loitering over the target for hours.

So impressive were the Spooky aircraft in action that they were named after "Puff the Magic Dragon," a popular song at the time. Seen from a distance, these Dragonships seemed to roar as they spat a never-ending stream of bright red tracer rounds from the mouth of the miniguns to the ground below. If the show was spectacular, the results were deadly. On 8 February 1965, a Spooky flying over the Bong Son area of Vietnam's Central Highlands demonstrated both capabilities in the process of blunting a Vietcong offensive. For over four hours, it fired 20,500 rounds into a Vietcong hilltop position, killing an estimated 300 Vietcong troops.[13]

As in every army in every country, there's always somebody who doesn't get the word. A year later, a Vietcong company attacking a 32-man Vietnamese Popular Forces outpost shouted to the defenders through their loudspeaker, "We are not afraid of your firepower!"[14] Shortly thereafter, the first of four AC-47s that would be taking turns over the camp that night began dropping and shooting a combined total of 75 flares and 48,800 minigun rounds into the hapless Vietcong, then at first light called in two F-100 jet fighters for napalm strikes. Apparently reconsidering their boast, the surviving Vietcong broke

USAF

This time-delay photo of a Dragonship at work on the outskirts of Saigon provides a vivid display for another of the AC-47's names: Puff the Magic Dragon. The sheets of tracer fire raining down from the night sky represent only one of every five bullets fired from the gunship's miniguns.

off their attack.[15] Available reports do not mention whether they took their loudspeaker with them.

So successful were these early gunship "trials" that in July 1965, Headquarters USAF ordered TAC to establish an FC-47 squadron.[16] Training Detachment 8, 1st Air Commando Wing, was subsequently established at Forbes AFB, Kansas, to organize what would soon become the 4th Air Commando Squadron. In Operation Big Shoot, the 4th ACS grew to 20 AC-47s (16 plus four for command support and attrition[17]).

The 4th deployed the same year to Vietnam, all 20 FC-47 gunships landing at Tan Son Nhut airport on 14 November 1965.[18] In May 1966, the squadron, with its now-designated AC-47s moved north to the coastal enclave at Nha Trang to join the 14th Air Commando Wing, itself activated only two months earlier.* There it joined the 1st ACS (Attack), 20th Helicopter Squadron, and the 5th ACS (Psychological Warfare).[19] Just prior to this move, one of its gunships fought in one of the most harrowing battles of the war.

In March 1966, one of the 4th's gunships joined with the A-1 Skyraiders of the 1st Air Commando Squadron to support yet another endangered Special Forces outpost. One of the Skyraider pilots emerged from the battle with the Medal of Honor. The AC-47 aircrew met with a different fate. The site was the A Shau Special Forces camp, barely two miles from the Laotian border and under heavy siege from a regimental-sized North Vietnamese attacking force.

With a 400-foot-cloud ceiling keeping the United States Air Force off their back, the Communists were on the verge of overrunning A Shau's camp perimeter when a single AC-47 left the safety of altitude, broke through a hole in the cloud deck, and attacked at tree-top level with its three miniguns spitting 18,000 rounds a minute along the camp's perimeter. On the aircraft's second pass, both the tenacious AC-47 crew and the now thoroughly alerted North Vietnamese were firing thousands of rounds at each other at point-blank range. The Air Commandos' luck couldn't possibly hold out in such impossible conditions.

It didn't. Enemy rifle and machine-gun fire literally tore the right engine from the gunship's wing and stopped the left engine seconds later, hammering the plane to the ground. All six crewmen survived the crash, but so close was the crash site to the enemy that two crew members were killed almost immediately as the furious North Vietnamese assaulted the survivors.

A USAF helicopter attempting an emergency extraction of the four surviving crewmen came under heavy ground fire itself on its final approach path. Worse yet, the sound of the approaching helicopter provoked a final assault on the trapped Americans. Pinned down by enemy fire, exhausted, and with time running out, members of the crew awaited their fate. At this moment, the Spooky's copilot, Lt Delbert R. Peterson, broke cover to charge shooting into the oncoming enemy, sacrificing his life to ensure the successful extraction of the last three survivors. His body has never been recovered.[20]

The next day, Maj Bernard Fisher, 1st Air Commando Squadron pilot, pulled off one of the class acts of the entire war, landing his two-seat Skyraider on the littered A Shau airstrip in a hail of enemy fire to extract another Air Commando downed moments earlier in his Skyraider. (Fisher's story is told in the final Medal of Honor section of this book). A Shau fell later that day. Two years would pass before the Americans returned to the deadly A Shau valley.

By June 1966, four Dragonships had been lost in combat. In addition to the A Shau loss, three others had gone down due to ground fire over Laos as they attempted to interdict the flow of war supplies down the Ho Chi Minh Trail in the face of the most formidable antiaircraft defenses

*The 14th Air Commando Wing was activated 8 March 1966.

A rare photo of a Royal Laotian Air Force AC-47 taken in 1969. Despite initial misgivings about the capabilities of the RLAF to fight, the gunship's credible performance in defending a number of Lima Sites provided a major morale boost for Gen Vang Pao's outnumbered and outgunned irregulars.

USAF

they would ever encounter.[21] Following the losses in Laos, the gunships were called back to Vietnam, where they could remain until their return to Laos in 1969. The return trip proved considerably more successful as the gunships were selectively used in support of Gen Vang Pao's forces in northern Laos, away from the Ho Chi Minh Trail.

In January 1968, a second AC-47 unit, the 14th Air Commando Squadron (redesignated 3d Air Commando Squadron that May), was formed at Nha Trang as part of the 14th Air Commando Wing. The superb work of the two AC-47 squadrons, each with 16 AC-47s flown by aircrews younger than the aircraft they flew, was undoubtedly a key contributor to the award of the Presidential Unit Citation to the 14th Air Commando Wing in June 1968.[22] Recognition from the Republic of South Vietnam came the following year, when the 14th Special Operations Wing was awarded the Vietnamese Cross of Gallantry with Palm, the first time the Vietnamese government had so honored a USAF unit.[23]

From November 1965 to the last Spooky flight in December 1969, the 4th and 3d gunship squadrons compiled an incredible combat record. Perhaps the statistic most important to the AC-47 veterans, however, is that after four years of intense combat in Vietnam and Laos, no outpost was ever overrun while a Spooky flew protective orbit overhead. The time had long since come to replace the worn-out C-47 airframes, which had again served valiantly in yet another war. In all, 53 C-47s had been modified for gunship duty over the years, at an estimated cost of $6.7 million.[24] It was an incredible bargain by any standard.

As the US accelerated the transfer of its equipment to the South Vietnamese government in the fall of 1969 in a program referred to as "Vietnamization," the gunship squadrons began transferring their aircraft to the VNAF. A final twist was in store for the old gunships, however, as the VNAF transferred four of their newly acquired AC-47s to the Royal Laotian Air Force during this period.

Aftermath

Like the Phoenix rising from the ashes to fly again, 16 of the Dragonships from the 3d and 4th SOS were resurrected in 1969 as the VNAF's 817th Combat Squadron, popularly known as the "Fire Dragons."[25] The new squadron's performance awed USAF evaluators, one of whom was moved to report, "This squadron is better than any USAF AC-47 squadron that was ever over here."

Jack S. Ballard's *The United States Air Force in Southeast Asia: Development and Employment of Fixed-Wing Gunships, 1962–1972* is the definitive

Bill Keeler

These North Vietnamese Army sappers attempting to blast holes through a Lima Site's defenses the night before were caught in the open by the USAF- and RLAF-flown AC-47s orbiting overhead. Seventh and Thirteenth Air Forces described the gunships as "the deciding factor" in the successful defense of a number of such Lima Sites in northern Laos during 1969. Note the spades and taped explosives.

book on USAF gunship operations in Southeast Asia. In this book, which has already been cited, Ballard explains the superlatives given to the Fire Dragons by USAF observers. While the average American AC-47 pilot accrued 800 combat hours during his one-year tour in Vietnam, the Vietnamese gunship pilots began their AC-47 duty having already accumulated 6,000 to 12,000 hours in the C-47. And, as already pointed out elsewhere in this book, the Vietnamese pilots never rotated out of combat duty. If not killed or crippled in combat, they only got better and better at their deadly business. And, perhaps naturally, the Vietnamese pilots seemed to have a better knack for picking out terrain and enemy assault formations at night than did their USAF counterparts.

Within six months of the activation of the 817th, the squadron was flying AC-47s in all four military regions of South Vietnam. Acting as forward air controllers on occasion, the Fire Dragons also earned the trust of USAF fighter pilots who quickly discovered that the highly experienced Vietnamese gunship pilots knew their business. And in addition to the Fire Dragons, there were still other Asian pilots in Indochina capable of flying the AC-47 with deadly effect against the North Vietnamese.

While the AC-47s were no strangers to Laotian combat, they had in 1966 and again in 1969 been flown by the Air Commandos in support of Laotian and Hmong army forces. By late 1969, the concept of incorporating a gunship capability within the Royal Laotian Air Force had become an increasingly desirable option, given the growing momentum of the Nixon administration's Vietnamization process. The ability of the RLAF to fight with or even maintain the AC-47, however, remained an open question, at least until 7 October 1969, when the first RLAF–flown AC-47 went into action.[26]

In their first action, the RLAF crews simply held the triggers down until the minigun barrels melted. The reports don't indicate what, if anything, they hit, but the bundles of brass shell casing available for sale downtown was noted[27]—not an auspicious beginning! Nevertheless, the RLAF/AC-47 conversion continued with the result that by the following January the RLAF boasted 13 AC-47s. And to the surprise of many, the RLAF gunship crews learned the art of gunship fighting sooner than expected. And it was none too soon.

In December 1969, Gen Vang Pao's guerrilla army of Hmong tribesmen was finishing a bleak year in which its forces were being steadily ground down by a much larger and better armed North Vietnamese Army. Despite these setbacks, the general still responded with a firm "no" to the idea of RLAF–flown AC-47s supporting his mountain tribesmen. Long-standing animosities between the Hmong and the lowland Lao had built an instinctive distrust over the possibility of an accidental or even intentional use of the gunships against the Hmong themselves. Events proved that the general couldn't have been more wrong. When deteriorating weather and other USAF priorities left no alternative, Gen Vang Pao reluctantly took his first taste of RLAF gunship support. Much to his surprise and his troops' gratitude, the Laotian-flown Dragonships came to the rescue again and again over the following months of 1970. Numerous Lima Sites were successfully defended and hundreds of Hmong casualties were avoided as the RLAF fought hard in the final years on behalf of the Hmong army.

Already an aviation legend long before the gunship role, the C-47 earned yet another laurel for ushering in an entirely new concept in US Air Force combat operations. Tremendous advances in technology from that pioneer effort 30 years ago have made possible USAF's present-day, ultra-sophisticated gunship fleet. For all these unquestionable improvements, however, technical advances can never replace the qualitative link that binds today's gunship crews with the Dragonships that once roared as they spat streams of fire from the night skies over Indochina.

Notes

1. Maj John Hawkins Napier III, USAF, "The Air Commandos in Vietnam, November 5 1961 to February 7 1965" (master's thesis, Auburn University, 16 March 1967), 140.
2. Ibid., 139–40.
3. Ibid., 141.
4. Ibid.
5. Jack S. Ballard, *The United States Air Force in Southeast Asia: Development and Employment of Fixed-Wing Gunships, 1962–1972* (Washington D.C.: Office of Air Force History, 1982), 8.
6. Ibid., 9.
7. Ibid., 15–17.
8. Ibid., 13–14.
9. Ibid., 14.
10. Philip D. Chinnery, *Anytime, Anyplace: A History of USAF Air Commando and Special Operations Forces, 1944–1994* (Annapolis, Md.: Naval Institute Press, 1994), 99.
11. Capt Ronald W. Terry, Hurlburt Field, Fla., interviewed by author, 10 October 1994.
12 Napier, 151.
13. Ballard, 21.
14. Ibid., 37.
15. Ibid.
16. Ibid., 30.
17. Ibid., 34.
18. John Schlight, *The War in South Vietnam: The Years of the Offensive, 1965–1968* (Washington, D.C.: Office of Air Force History, 1988), 90.
19. Ibid., 129.
20. Ibid., 199.
21. Ballard, 47.
22. Schlight, 63.
23. Ballard, 71.
24. Ibid., 75.
25. Ibid., 252.
26. Victor B. Anthony and Richard R. Sexton, *The United States Air Force in Southeast Asia: The War in Northern Laos, 1954–1973* (U) (Washington, D.C.: Center for Air Force History, 1993). (Secret) Information extracted is unclassified.
27. Ibid.

AC-119s Crash the Party

The Shadow

When "uninvited guests" drop in,
call for "The Shadow!"

We provide: Lighting for all occasions
Beaucoup 7.62
Mortar suppression

We defend: Special Forces camps
Air bases
Outposts
Troops in contact

Who knows what evil lurks
in the jungle canopy?

The Shadow knows!

AC-119 "business card," circa 1968

A full two years before the final Spooky mission in December 1969, the Air Force had already narrowed the replacement for the old C-47s to either the 1950s-vintage, twin-engined C-119 Flying Boxcar, or the newer, four-engined C-130A Hercules. While the advantages of the latter over the former were clear to all involved, the cost of diverting scarce C-130 resources for gunship duty would severely penalize the already overtaxed airlift forces. The ready availability of C-119s in Air Force Reserve units finally decided the issue in favor of the Boxcars, at least as an interim measure until sufficient AC-130s could be brought on line. The next step proved far more controversial.

Because the G-model C-119's twin piston-engined performance was so marginal at combat gross weight, the Air Force intended from the beginning to upgrade selected Gs to a newly designated K-model configuration. The K bolstered the piston engines with two wing-mounted J-85 jet engines.[1] The difference was no small thing. While the rate of climb with one engine out was 500 feet per minute for the K, the G model's performance under the same conditions was listed "unsatisfactory at combat gross weight."[2] Perhaps to spare squeamish pilots, no performance numbers of any kind were included to describe just how "unsatisfactory" the situation was!

Overriding strong Air Force concerns in June 1967, Secretary of the Air Force Harold Brown, citing modification costs and deployment delays, chose to go with the G model as the AC-47 replacement. Later, in February 1968, he relented somewhat by approving a mixed C-119G/K fleet, with

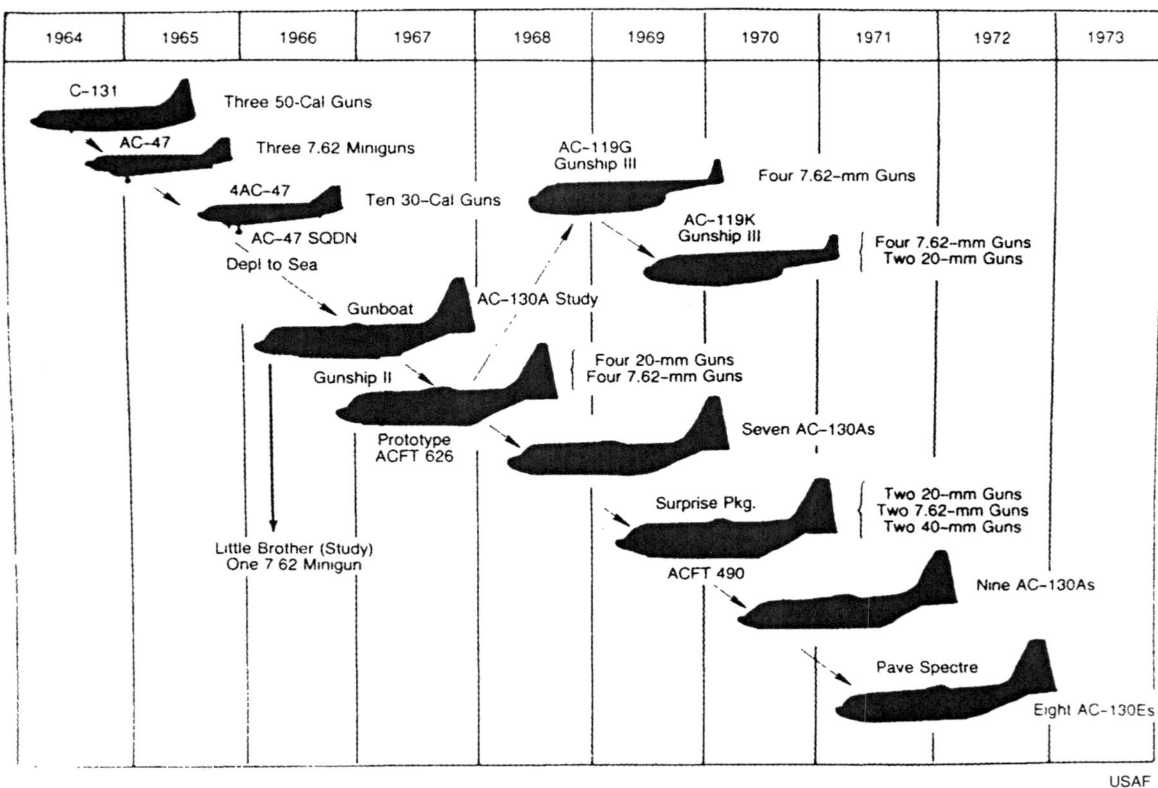

"Survival of the Fittest" was an apt description for the evolution of the gunship. A researcher of the subject would be hard-pressed to think of a manmade or natural obstacle that did not at one time or another attempt to knock the dangerous beasts out of the air, in Southeast Asia or the United States.

USAF

This picture-perfect gunship framed in a pretty blue sky seems oddly out of place for a war bird that did much of its deadly work under the cloak of darkness. The G-model AC-119 seen here was a significant improvement over its AC-47 predecessor . . . as long as both engines kept working. Single-engined performance at combat gross weights, however, was so poor that the flight manual simply substituted the word "unsatisfactory" for the usual performance figures.

16 of each type in two squadrons and an additional 10 of each type to absorb attrition losses.[3] The addition of a K squadron, however, did little to alleviate Air Force apprehension over the all-piston G model. In mid-1968, even the gunship-hungry Seventh Air Force in Saigon openly questioned whether the G should even be allowed into combat.[4]

If the G models *could* wangle an invitation to the party, they'd at least come "well dressed." In addition to carrying one more minigun than the three carried aboard the AC-47s, the Flying Boxcars carried much improved avionics to include target-acquisition radars, a fire control system, and a night observation device (NOD), which magnified starlight and moonlight several thousand times to provide a surprisingly clear, if still green, picture of the terrain below. The NOD's biggest drawback was that the tracer rounds fired by the gunship's miniguns provided so much more light that they effectively shut the NOD system down. As a result, flares became the primary means of identifying ground targets. Carrying 31,500 rounds of ammunition and 24 flares, it was more than capable of hurting anything it caught in its sights.

In what must have seemed to some like crashing the party uninvited, the first four C-119Gs of the 71st Special Operations Squadron finally arrived in Vietnam in December 1968 to begin a three-month combat evaluation.[5] An ill-considered attempt by Seventh Air Force to assign the radio call sign "Creep" to the 71st did at least give the squadron an early opportunity to demonstrate its fighting mettle to the headquarters staff. Following a "howl of indignation" from the squadron, Seventh Air Force agreed to change the call sign to the one that the 71st requested—"Shadow."[6]

The 71st displayed the same mettle in the early combat evaluations. During nightly armed reconnaissance missions, the Shadows flew down to 500 feet, using night observation systems to detect ground targets. *The flares became primary, even though their intensity effectively closed down the NOD after field experience in Vietnam revealed serious limitations in this early generation night viewing system.* Once a target was acquired by the flares, the Shadow established an orbit overhead and pummeled the target with one or more of its four 7.62 mm miniguns.[7] *As with the AC-47s, the range limitations of the 7.62 mm ammunition kept the orbit altitudes as low as feasible, but usually no higher than 2,000 feet.* Just two months after the arrival of its lead elements, all assigned aircraft were in country and the 71st SOS was declared "combat ready."[8]

To provide fire support to all four military regions in South Vietnam, the 71st began operating Alpha, Bravo, and Charlie flights, each with three gunships from three widely separated airfields throughout the country. In June 1969, the 71st SOS returned its flag to the United States, leaving some of its G models and two-thirds of its personnel* in Vietnam to fill out a new gunship squadron designated the 17th SOS.[9]

The first K-model gunships (call sign "Stinger") began arriving in Vietnam in October 1969, and by the following January, the second C-119 gunship squadron, the 18th SOS, was also combat ready. In addition to the two J-85 jet engines, the K model bolstered the four-minigun armament of the G with two 20 mm multibarrel cannon and 4,500 rounds of 20 mm ammunition.[10]

In addition to carrying the G-model NOD, the K models were also equipped with a state-of-the-art forward looking infrared (FLIR) system. This was a noticeable improvement over the seldom used NOD on the 17th SOS gunships because the FLIR did not require starlight or moonlight. In addition to the previously described flare equipment, both models were also equipped with a door-mounted, 20-watt "white light" illuminator. Its 1.5-million-candlepower variable beam could light up a football stadium with superb clarity on the darkest nights. Of course, it also told the bad guys below exactly where to point their weapons, a drawback that discouraged the gunship crews from using the illuminator whenever possible.

By the end of 1969, the 14th Special Operations Wing had 16 G-model and 12 K-model gunships operating from five different air bases throughout Vietnam.[11] And by this time, the Shadow and Stinger crews were already well into establishing their formidable reputation throughout Southeast Asia.

From the arrival of the K models, the two squadrons began dividing into separate missions, a reflection of their different sensors and armament. The crews of the G models had already learned the range limitations of their 7.62 mm minigun ammunition when firing against trucks from an altitude that kept the AC-119s beyond the reach of the enemy small-arms fire. Shadow navigator lst Lt Billy B. "Rusty" Napier recalls learning one such lesson, much to his crew's subsequent embarrassment:

> We found a solitary North Vietnamese truck one night, a rare catch for a Shadow crew. Popping up to 2,000 feet we opened up on the truck with all four miniguns. The truck disappeared in a cloud of dust as we showered it with thousands of rounds. After patting ourselves on the back and calling in our "kill" to home base, we were astonished to see the stationary

*The remaining one-third of the squadron's personnel strength was comprised of reservists called to six-months active duty to expedite activation of this first C-119 gunship squadron. Their departure and the squadron's move to another base during the same period caused considerable turmoil in the squadron throughout the rest of the summer.

USAF

The addition of a J-85 jet engine under each wing outboard the piston engine gave the K-model AC-119 a much better chance of survival in the event a single engine was lost. In fact, on one occasion, an AC-119K, abandoned by its crew after an engine malfunctioned, continued flying . . . straight toward mainland China!

> truck start back down the road! To pour salt in our wound, it even turned its headlights on.[12]

It was experiences like this that led the G models to specialize in defense of isolated outposts in South Vietnam, while the stronger Ks with their 20 mm cannon focused on the increasingly important truck-killing mission. This of course included Laos, where the gunship crews and US Army pilots flying their sophisticated OV-1 Mohawk surveillance plane formed into ad hoc hunter-killer teams during the late spring of 1970.

The hunter-killer-team concept brought together the best of the sensor capabilities mounted on both the OV-1s and the AC-119s, the former to find enemy trucks coming down the Ho Chi Minh Trail, the latter to acquire and destroy specific targets. As both aircraft were flying over the same territory looking for the same target, why not blend the two capabilities? With neither the Air Force nor the Army officially sanctioning the concept, both services allowed their aircrews to participate in a month-long test program from April to May 1970.[13]

Teaming up a total of 14 times during this period, the OV-1/AC-119 hunter-killer teams destroyed or damaged 60 of 70 trucks attacked.[14] While the field reports indicate not all truck kills stemmed from OV-1 sightings, the overall "trucks destroyed/damaged" totals surged an astonishing 60 percent over those achieved when the gunships operated alone.[15] More impressive still, this result was achieved with only the briefest and crudest coordination between the aircrews themselves. It seemed a promising start with an even more promising future.

Alas, the hunter-killer-team concept was not destined to last. What cooperation the aircrews could accomplish in the field was not repeated by their respective headquarters. The Seventh Air Force was loathe to put its aircraft in a subordinate command relationship with Army aircrews, while the Army was equally loathe to watch the Air Force getting all the credit for increased truck kills.[16] The ad hoc effort continued for a few months longer before dying quietly from lack of support.

Perhaps it was just as well things didn't pan out in "target rich" Laos, as the relative lull in enemy activity in South Vietnam terminated abruptly in May, with large-scale attacks against isolated government militia camps at Dak Pek and Dak Seang. Flying 147 sorties in seven weeks, the AC-119s expended over two million rounds of mini-

USAF

The four minguns and two 20 mm cannons of this 18th SOS gunship leave no doubt as to the gunship's grim mission. More than once, this firepower was all that stood between Special Forces camps only minutes from certain annihilation and the North Vietnamese assault troops already in the final barbed-wire defenses surrounding these camps.

gun ammunition and nearly 22,000 20 mm cannon shells defending the camps.[17] When the smoke cleared, the camps still held.

Dak Pek and Dak Seang also reminded everyone that gunships offered far more than gun support. After three Army C-7 Caribou transports were shot down attempting to resupply the camps, the pilots of the gunships and Caribous put their heads together and agreed to try something never before attempted.

This tactic called for the AC-119 orbiting the besieged camp to maintain suppressive fire until the Caribou reached the final approach to the parachute drop point. At precisely this time, the AC-119 lit up the drop zone like a nighttime Super Bowl game with its powerful 1.5-million-candlepower illuminator. Napier recalls the gunship crew's frightening sense of vulnerability to enemy fire once it identified its position by turning on the illuminator: "We left the illuminator on for a predetermined number of seconds, every one of which seemed an hour long once enemy tracer fire started coming toward the big white light in the sky."[18]

Immediately after dropping its cargo, the C-7 called for the AC-119 to kill the lights, while the Caribou escaped to safety in the darkness. It worked 68 times in three weeks without a single Caribou being hit.[19] More importantly from a command viewpoint, both camps held while the enemy took a considerable beating for their efforts.

Immediately following the Dak Pek/Dak Seang battles, the Shadows in particular supported the massive US and South Vietnamese attack later that same year on North Vietnamese base camps in Cambodia. But while the allied forces soon returned to South Vietnam, the gunships stayed deep in Cambodia in a desperate attempt to bolster government forces against the Khmer Rouge. This highly classified gunship operation required fake-flight and expended-ammunition logs showing operating locations within South Vietnamese borders. Fortunately for US public policy, no gunship was shot down in Cambodia during this period.

But gunship luck wouldn't hold forever. In April, a single engine failure on takeoff killed six crewmen; two months later, a runaway propeller caused the crew to abandon the aircraft over the South China Sea. While the crew was recovered safely, the aircraft continued to fly itself . . . straight towards China! It eventually disappeared from radar over international waters.

Against these losses, superb airmanship from a Stinger crew operating over Ban Ban, Laos, in May 1970 brought back a gunship despite extensive combat damage. On fire and with one-third of its right wing missing, the cumbersome Boxcar held together for a hair-raising return flight to Udorn, Thailand. The Air Force chief of staff later presented the crew with the 1970 Mackay Trophy "for the most meritorious flight of the year."

By 1972, the war was clearly winding down for the Shadow/Stinger squadrons. The AC-130s were coming on line in growing numbers, and the 17th SOS in particular was converting from a combat to a training squadron as its aircraft were turned over to the Vietnamese Air Force. The indisputable combat success of the AC-119 crews in Indochina is a story of persistence and faith in themselves as much as it is one of valor. Continual program delays, modification cost overruns, and bureaucratic opposition to the AC-119 program from Washington to Saigon threatened their deployment at every step.

With the advantage of hindsight, however, it can be argued that the truest testimony of the AC-119s' worth is not measured on engine performance charts, but rather in the hundreds of burned-out Soviet-built trucks littered across Indochina's landscape and the thousands of allied lives saved by the Shadow and Stinger crews who were always there when needed the most.

USAF

The 1.5-million-candlepower variable-beam illuminator shown here could light up a football field-sized area with brilliant white light. Of course, it also made the gunship a beautiful target for antiaircraft gunners determined to rid themselves of such unwanted visibility.

Notes

1. Jack S. Ballard, *The United States Air Force in Southeast Asia: Development and Employment of Fixed-Wing Gunships, 1962–1972* (Washington, D.C.: Office of Air Force History, 1982), 176.
2. Ibid., 262–63.
3. Ibid., 179.
4. Ibid., 188.
5. Ibid., 193.
6. Ibid.
7. Ibid., 194.
8. Ibid., 195.
9. Ibid., 203.
10. Eduard Mark, *Aerial Interdiction in Three Wars* (Washington, D.C.: Office of Air Force History, 1994), 336.
11. Ballard, 203.
12. Col Billy B. Napier, USAF, Retired, interview with author, 4 August 1996, Fort Walton Beach Fla.
13. Victor B. Anthony and Richard R. Sexton, *The United States Air Force in Southeast Asia: The War in Northern Laos, 1954–1973* (U) (Washington, D.C.: Office of Air Force History, 1993), 334. (Secret) Information extracted is unclassified.
14. Ibid.
15. Ibid.
16. Ibid.
17. Ballard, 208.
18. Napier interview.
19. Ibid., 209.

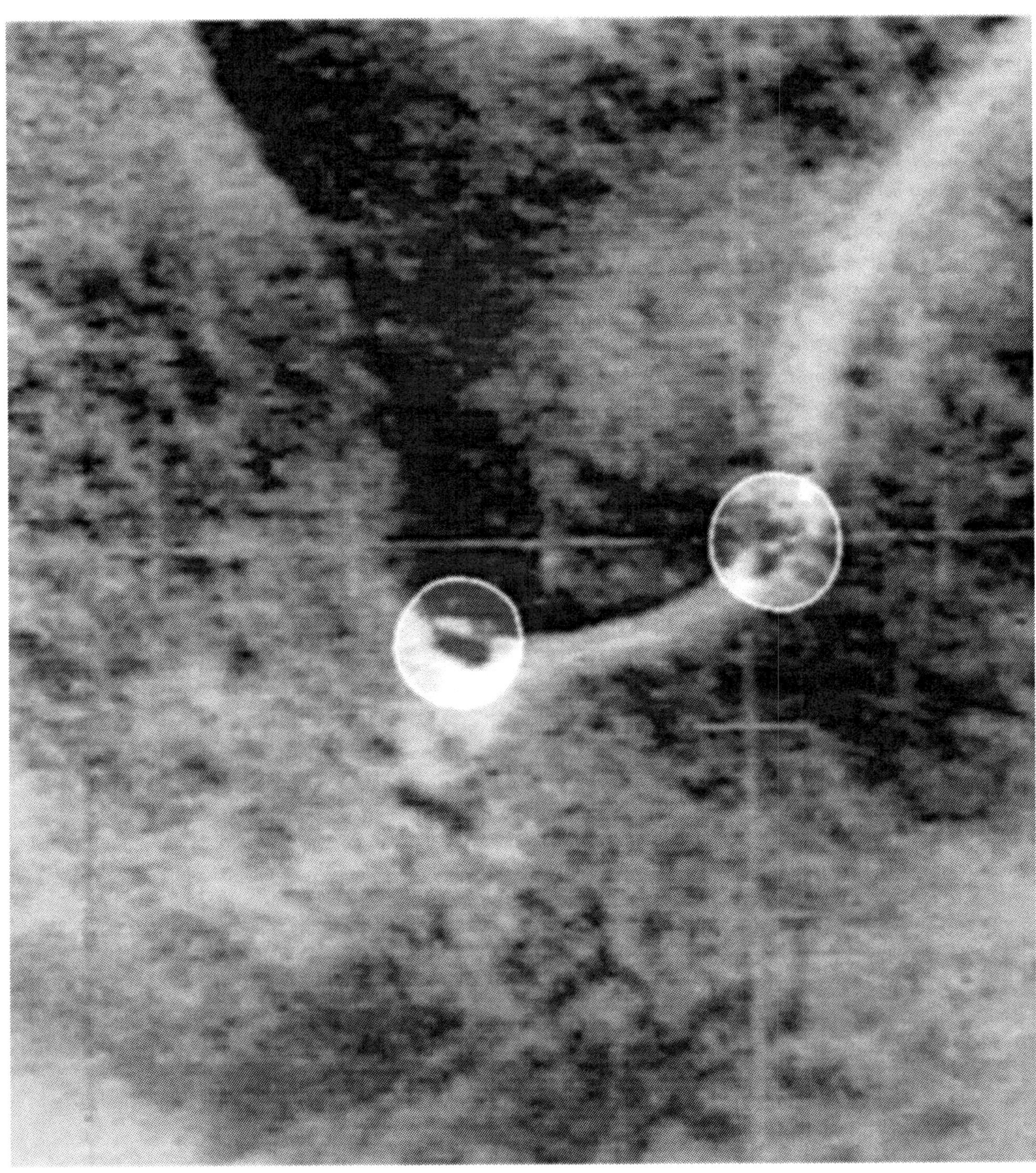

Spectre: (spek'ter), n. some object or source of terror or dread

The Predator

From its very first combat field evaluations in Southeast Asia in 1967, the C-130A Gunship II alerted both Air Force and Army commanders they were onto something special. And that "something" went far beyond mere replacement of the worn-out AC-47 and AC-119 gunships.

Despite their usefulness in armed reconnaissance missions, the AC-47 and its immediate successor, the AC-119, were seen by American commanders in Vietnam as most effective in defending isolated Vietnamese and US Army Special Forces camps. In this role, these two gunships were defending allied troops *from* trouble. The Gunship II was to conduct a far more predatory mission, one that sent the huge gunship actually looking *for* trouble.

So heavily armed that during early development stages it was initially designated "Gunboat," the C-130A could hardly be considered anything but a predator. Compared to the three miniguns on the AC-47, or the four miniguns and two 20 mm cannon on the AC-119s, the Gunboat boasted four miniguns and four 20 mm cannon. Later models added a modified US Army 105 mm field howitzer, the largest gun ever mounted in an aircraft. And that was just the armament.

The Gunship II's advanced electronic sensors stripped the night's protection away from the enemy as never before. Its night observation device (an improved version of that found on the AC-119K) intensified starlight and moonlight thousands of times to provide a greenish, but still very clear, view of the ground below on all but the darkest nights. The forward looking infrared radar system picked up heat emissions from both human bodies and vehicle motors regardless of star and moonlight conditions. And the "Black Crow" sensor detected spark-plug emissions from vehicles driving down a road, or even idling while hidden under camouflage nets or triple-layer canopy.

USAF

Boasting the latest sensor technology of its time, this early model AC-130A gives some idea of the complex systems integration that made the Spectre the premier truck killer in Southeast Asia. Soon after the details of the then-classified Black Crow system were published in a US defense industry magazine, gunship crews fighting over the Ho Chi Minh Trail noticed new North Vietnamese countermeasures intended to defeat this sensor.

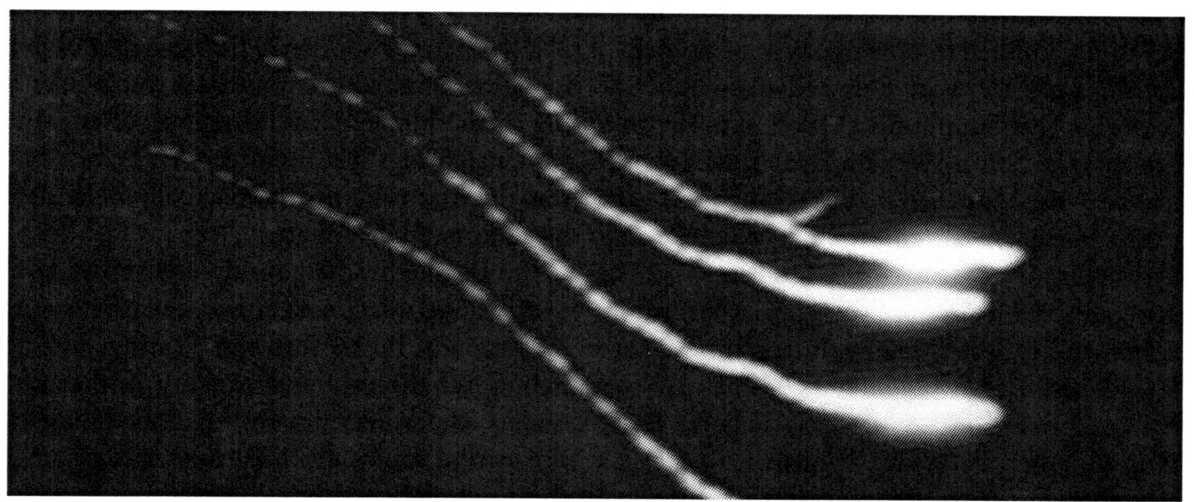

Spectre Association

Antiaircraft tracer rounds claw blindly into the night sky in an attempt to reach into the belly of a Spectre gunship, a source of torment for the North Vietnamese. The outcome of these vicious air-ground brawls taking place nightly over a blood-soaked stretch of real estate called the Ho Chi Minh Trail would decide the final outcome of the war.

The prototype Gunship II began its first combat evaluation in late 1967. Flying armed reconnaissance missions over both Laos and South Vietnam, the test-bed aircraft was an instant success, especially as a truck killer. Maj Gen William G. Moore, Air Force deputy chief of staff, research and development, concluded that the C-130A "far exceeded fighter-type kill ratios on enemy trucks and other equipment."[1] A still greater compliment came from the senior "customer" in South Vietnam, Gen William Westmoreland, commander of US Military Assistance Command, Vietnam, who was so impressed that he proved very resistant to letting the test-bed aircraft leave the country for a much-needed overhaul![2]

With an all-out effort expediting completion of the necessary modifications and overhaul, the Gunship II returned to South Vietnam in February 1968, much earlier than originally planned. And just as promptly, it proceeded to repeat its spectacular early successes. By November of that year, its crew reported 1,000 trucks sighted, of which 228 were destroyed and a further 133 damaged; nine of the 32 sampans sighted were destroyed and eight more damaged.[3] On one occasion during this period, the prototype was even sent north to the demilitarized zone separating the two Vietnams to search for North Vietnamese helicopters reported in the area.

A lengthy follow-on USAF analysis of this second combat trial divided the total financial costs of the prototype by the total number of "major events" (e.g., trucks and sampans destroyed, secondary explosions observed during attacks, gun sites destroyed). The findings concluded that "the Gunship II prototype to be one of the most cost-effective, close-support interdiction systems in the US Air Force inventory."[4]

What had started out as a relatively straightforward search for a follow-on aircraft to the AC-47 had now grown into an extremely complex, mixed-gunship fleet operating over Vietnam, Thailand, and Laos. By the end of 1968, the Air Force had four C-130s (now using the radio call sign "Spectre") operating from Thailand, as well as a mixed AC-47 and AC-119G/K fleet operating primarily in South Vietnam. It would not be until the early 1970s that the Air Force gunship force would be streamlined to only one type of aircraft.

Gunships of every type were active around-the-clock during the Communists' 1968 Tet offensive that swept over South Vietnam like a tidal wave of death and destruction.* This included the Gunship IIs that were deployed to Saigon's Tan Son Nhut airport. During this period, the C-130s were organized into the 16th Special Operations Squadron and for the first time officially designated "AC"-130s.[5] In November of the same year, the 16th moved to Ubon Royal Thai Air Force Base, arriving with 44 officers and 96 airmen.[6]

The closing days of 1968 saw a vicious cycle of combat become more so over attempts to dominate the Ho Chi Minh Trail. In December 1968, a Seventh Air Force study concluded that gunships escorted by fighters could probably kill more trucks than could gunships attacking alone.[7] Results from the first test of this tactic came quickly, as F-4 fighter escorts from the 497th "Night Owls" destroyed or silenced two 37 mm sites firing on the gunship.[8] It was a winning combination, even though some areas remained too hot even for fighter-escorted gunships.

With or without fighter escort, the gunships remained firmly in the center of this dangerous air-ground brawl over "ownership" of the Ho Chi Minh Trail. In January 1969, four Spectres with relatively inexperienced crews accounted for 28 percent of the reported kills along the supply line. Two months later, the 16th accounted for more than 44 percent of all truck kills in a 30-day period, despite flying only 3.5 percent of all allied interdiction sorties.[9]

The Thailand-based Spectres continued to rack up high kill ratios including, on 8 May 1969, a very unusual target for a gunship. Flying over Laos in the early morning darkness, a Spectre NOD operator spotted a slow-moving object flying a low-level course towards a rectangular clearing in the jungle. Ground reports of enemy helicopter sightings had been received before, but this was the first time one had actually been detected by an armed US aircraft.

On this night, the gunship crew moved quickly to secure permission to attack, then put several 20 mm cannon bursts into the clearing, hitting the helicopter directly and causing numerous secondary explosions nearby.[10] A Spectre veteran of this period recalls the 16th crew sparing no effort the next night as they described (ad nauseam!) their rare air-to-air kill to any and all of the collocated fighter pilots unfortunate enough to be in the bar with them.

But the fortunes of war inevitably swing both ways, and it was only two weeks after the helicopter shootdown that tragedy struck the Spectres. On 24 May, enemy antiaircraft gunners along the Ho Chi Minh Trail mortally wounded the first AC-130A, killing one crewman immediately and another as the aircraft burst into flames following a crash landing back at Ubon.[11] It could have been much worse but for some phenomenal flying by the pilots of the wounded Spectre.

As the gunship headed back to Ubon with two hydraulic systems shot away, the AC-130 began a nearly uncontrollable climb. Both pilots forced their control columns to the full-forward position as the aircraft commander, Lt Col William Schwehm, ordered all surviving crew members up to the flight deck to help force the aircraft's nose down. With the aircraft threatening to go out of control any minute, Schwehm ordered all nonessential crew to bail out as soon as the stricken ship reached the relative safety of Thailand. In

---

*Although a tremendous psychological victory for the Communists, particularly within the US television media, the Tet offensive saw the virtual annihilation of the South Vietnamese Communists (Vietcong) in the face of massed US firepower. As a military force the Vietcong never recovered from its Tet losses, and from this period forward, the North Vietnamese Army provided the overwhelming bulk of Communist forces in South Vietnam.

a single night, North Vietnamese gunners had reduced the four-aircraft-strong AC-130 force by 25 percent.

As the 16th SOS crewmen considered their loss, they received still another unpleasant reminder that in war the battlefield is only one of the many places where danger threatens their existence. Only two months after the shootdown, a Communist sapper attack against Ubon itself found the gunships in the unaccustomed role of defending their own air base in their first perimeter-defense battle.

The more the Air Force and Navy determined to cut the Ho Chi Minh Trail, the more antiaircraft defenses the North Vietnamese placed on that vital logistics lifeline. During the same period (1 November 1968–May 1970), North Vietnam increased its antiaircraft defenses along the Ho Chi Minh Trail by an estimated *400 percent!* The logistics lifeline was fast becoming a bloody example of the football cliché describing an "irresistible force meeting an immovable object." And it was about to become even more lethal for both "teams."

In February 1972, the first Spectre was equipped with a modified US Army 105 mm field

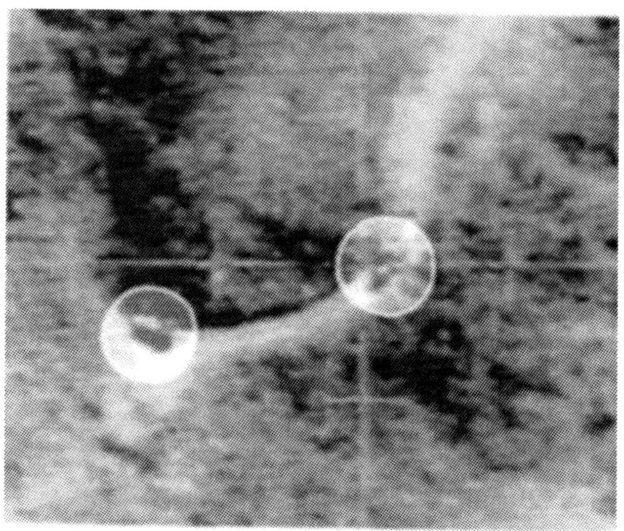

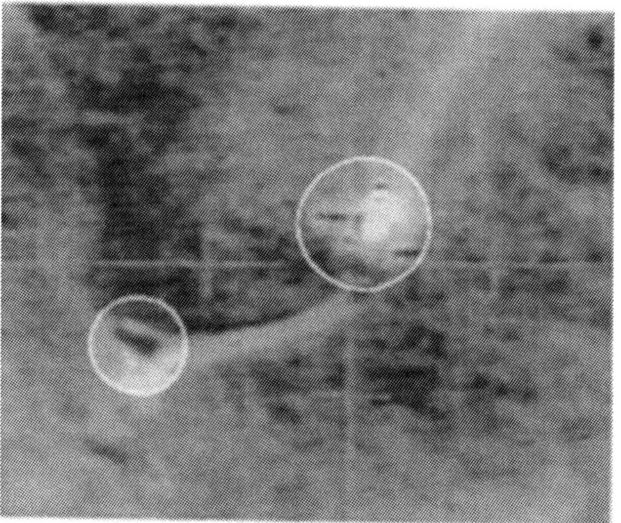

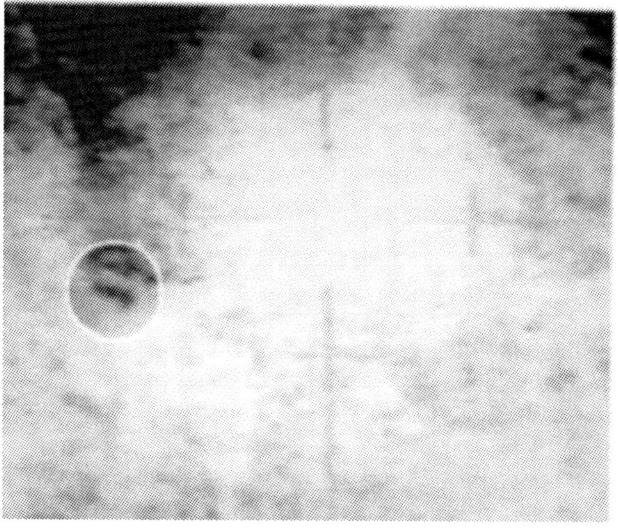

Top: Orbiting in the night sky 6,000 feet overhead, the Spectre is neither seen nor heard by these unsuspecting North Vietnamese truck drivers moving south down the Ho Chi Minh Trail. Fourteen airmen working in trained unison have already orchestrated millions of dollars worth of aircraft, electronic systems, and weapons to put the crosshairs on the lead truck.

Middle: Seen here at the precise moment of impact through the greenish glow of a weapon director's scope, a truck shatters from the impact of a direct hit from the Spectre's 40 mm cannon.

Bottom: A shattering blast from a secondary explosion and a crater in the road are all that's left to mark one truckload of ammunition that will not be fired at allied troops fighting in South Vietnam.

howitzer that could destroy anything on the Ho Chi Trail from a safer standoff distance than what the crews had enjoyed to date.[12] In response, the North Vietnamese upped the ante—big time. That same February, two Spectres were downed by enemy fire, one to a telephone-pole-sized SA-2 surface-to-air missile, a type never before seen on the Ho Chi Minh Trail.[13] On 5 May, the North Vietnamese played another surprise card, firing five SA-7 heat-seeking missiles at an AC-130 in another "first" for the Spectre aircrews.[14] Though the shoulder-fired SA-7s were much smaller than the SA-2s, a lucky hit from one of the man-portable missiles could still rip the wing off a gunship in flight.

During the five-month period from November 1971 through March 1972, allied aircraft destroyed or damaged an estimated 10,609 trucks traveling through the Laotian panhandle.[15] USAF statistics confirm that the top three truck killers, in descending order, were the AC-130, AC-119, and F-4 fighter.[16] As a matter of perspective, it is useful to remember all this activity reflects only those combat operations conducted over Laos.

In South Vietnam, the gunships were in demand more than ever. Spectres provided decisive defensive firepower against a North Vietnamese attack on the Ben Het Ranger camp on the 5th of May. On the same day, the big gunships beat back an attack on the government compound at Polei Kleng after the Communists had already driven troops and tanks into the camp's last-ditch, barbed-wire defenses.

Following another attack on the compound the next day, US Army advisors were removed in the face of seemingly inevitable defeat. Following their departure, the desperate ARVN commander found the only American support available in the form of a single Spectre orbiting over the compound. Staying in continuous contact with the commander, the Spectre emptied its entire load of

USAF

At the other end of the ammunition-caliber spectrum, this modified US Army 105 mm howitzer is the largest "gun" ever fired from an aircraft. Installed in the aftermost 40 mm station, the howitzer could destroy anything moving down the Ho Chi Minh Trail at a safer stand-off distance than previously possible.

USAF

Wounded but not killed, this AC-130 shows the scars from its encounter with a Soviet-made SA-7 Strela, a shoulder-fired, surface-to-air missile. Four more Strelas fired at the big gunship inexplicably missed. Even with its small warhead, the SA-7 missile was still capable of ripping the wing off a Spectre with a lucky hit.

ammunition, including 96 rounds of 105 mm howitzer shells, into the enemy below. The next month, the Spectre crew learned the Defense Intelligence Agency (DIA) had credited them with saving the surviving 1,000 ARVN soldiers in the compound from a full-scale regimental attack.[17]

By 1973, the remaining AC-119s had been turned over to the South Vietnamese Air Force, and USAF gunship efforts centered exclusively on the 16th SOS at Ubon. With a 14-man crew on each AC-130, the 16th had become the single largest USAF combat squadron in Southeast Asia.[18] The last Spectre combat mission in the region was flown over Cambodia on 15 August 1973.[19]

Over the war years, six of the big AC-130s had gone down before enemy gunners, taking with them 52 airmen.[20] As difficult as it is to conduct a cost-versus-benefit analysis where the loss of human life is concerned, the combat reality is that losses to the premier truck killer on the Ho Chi Minh Trail were far below those predicted by detractors of the gunship concept. Nor did the end of the American involvement in Southeast Asia spell the end of the gunship era.

USAF

These massive belts of armor-piercing 20 mm cannon shells represent the smallest caliber ammunition fired by the AC-130!

The 16th SOS redeployed to the United States in December 1975. Its H-model gunships were assigned to Hurlburt Field, Florida, by then home of the sole remaining USAF special operations force, the 1st Special Operations Wing. The original A-model AC-130s were sent directly to the Air Force Reserve's 711th SOS at nearby Duke Field, Eglin AFB.

As with the special operations force as a whole, the postwar years for the AC-130s at Hurlburt and Duke Fields were ones spent in relative anonymity as the force lapsed into the backwaters of Air Force priorities. This would end in 1980 when an American disaster in the desert wastelands of Iran would bring renewed Pentagon interest in the capabilities of these unique weapons.

Notes

1. *Jack S. Ballard, The United States Air Force in Southeast Asia: Development and Employment of Fixed-Wing Gunships, 1962–1972* (Washington D.C.: Office of Air Force History, 1982), 89.

2. Ibid.

3. Ibid., 90.

4. Ibid., 92.

5. "The Fabulous Four Engine Fighter" (paper presented at the 1975 Spectre Reunion in New Orleans, La.), 10.

6. Ibid.

7. Ballard, 116.

8. Ibid., 121–22.

9. Ibid., 119.

10. Ibid.

11. Ibid., 115.

12. "Fabulous Four Engine Fighter," 12.

13. Ballard, 231.

14. Ibid.

15. Ibid., 232.

16. Ibid.

17. Ibid., 239.

18. Lt Col Clay McCutchan, "USAF Gunship Overview: 1973–1993" (unpublished paper, March 1994), 2.

19. Ibid., 3.

20. Ibid.

The "Other" War

Americans traditionally have a hard time accepting "psychological warfare" as a legitimate weapon even in time of war. The "planned use of propaganda and other psychological actions to . . . influence hostile foreign groups"[1] demands in practice much more finesse and patience than the more quickly generated and visually impressive air strike. Nor can the results of an operation be seen by a satellite photo within days of its initiation.

An Air Commando O-2 Super Skymaster drops its leaflets over Communist-controlled territory, while its three 600-watt amplifiers broadcast surrender appeals to the enemy below. The Air Commando pilots pitched their broadcasts to a tough audience, which usually sent back its "audience appreciation" rating in 7.62 mm shells.

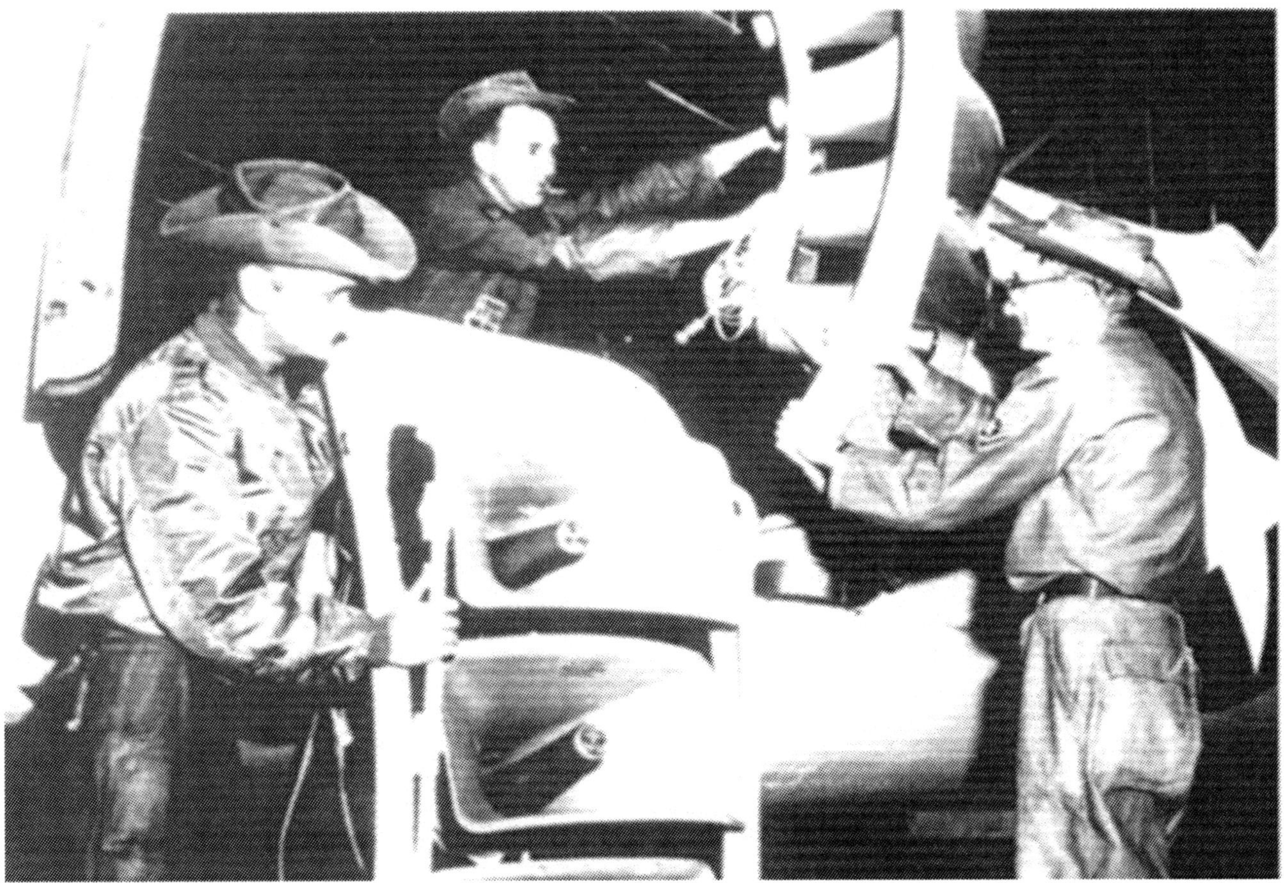

Air Commando Association

Three Hurlburt Field Air Commandos display an early loudspeaker setup for the C-47. Arguably the world's best political propagandists, the Communists proved extremely sensitive to its use against them!

But when done *right*, psywar can produce some astonishing results, and at a fraction of the cost of conventional war. Appropriately, it was the unconventional Air Commandos who were chosen from the beginning to lead the Air Force in Southeast Asia in what was frequently termed the "other" war.

With the arrival of the initial Farm Gate cadre in the Republic of Vietnam in November 1961, the Air Commandos brought four twin-engined C-47s equipped with belly-mounted loudspeakers for psywar missions.[2] On 4 December they flew their first mission, which soon revealed a critical flaw in their approach:

> [The belly-mounted speakers] cost about two years in redesign time. Like the train blowing its whistle as it comes down the track, the voice from the air kept changing pitch as the aircraft approached and departed, leaving no more than two or three intelligible words out of a complete sentence.[3]

As the C-47/loudspeaker combination had been used effectively in the Korean War, the problem raised once again the troublesome question that haunts the US military at the beginning of each war: do we have "lessons learned" from the previous conflict or simply "lessons recorded"? While design engineers were searching for a fix,*

*The solution was found in the development of lightweight, door-mounted speakers that could fit in either the C-47 or the much smaller U-10.

the C-47s switched to propaganda leaflet drops. And it was on one of these missions in February 1962 that the Air Commandos lost their first aircraft in Vietnam. Dropping leaflets during Tet, the Vietnamese Lunar New Year, the low-flying C-47 was downed by hostile ground fire.[4]

With the introduction of the improved, side-mounted speakers on the C-47s, voice clarity improved even when the aircraft flew at altitudes high enough to avoid most small arms fire. As one early observer recalls:

> Programs broadcast from 3,000 feet high are clearly audible on the ground. Broadcasts are often pleas to the guerrillas in the jungle to surrender. It is an eerie thing to hear a DC3 [C-47] droning high overhead, from which a monstrous celestial voice is enjoining the sinners to repent.[5]

Almost to the month, four years passed between the arrival of the initial Air Commando C-47s and the docking in Saigon of the USS *Breton*, a ship filled with 17 disassembled U-10 Super Courier light observation planes.[6] The source of the delivery had been initiated several months earlier at Forbes AFB, Kansas, where the 1st Air Commando Wing had established a training detachment to train its "psywarriors" under the auspices of Project Quick Speak. Assembled immediately and flown to the northern coastal enclave of Nha Trang, the single-engined U-10s joined the four C-47s in a newly organized unit dedicated solely to the psywar mission: the 5th Air Commando Squadron.

With only the 5th ACS and a handful of Vietnamese Air Force planes dedicated to psywar, their planes were soon spread thin throughout the country in small detachments. The missions were both difficult and dangerous for a number of reasons. Most notable was the fact that while the Communists were arguably the most effective exponents of political propaganda on Third World (and American) populations, they reacted immediately and violently upon

USAF

A rare photo of an Air Commando U-10 and a C-47 psywar aircraft flying formation. These two aircraft are from E Flight, 5th Air Commando Squadron, based in 1967 at Binh Thuy Air Base in South Vietnam.

finding themselves on the receiving end of their own style of psychological "poison."

A typical loudspeaker mission could last four hours, flying slowly at low altitudes over the same area. Of course, this prolonged aerial practice also gave the Vietcong down below the opportunity to organize their "audience appreciation" rating for this effort:

> Effectiveness can be judged by the fact that the VC shot at the psywar aircraft more than at any other, except those of Ranch Hand (the defoliant operations mission). They also banged pots and pans together in hamlet streets to drown out the speakers, and cut off the hands of villagers caught reading leaflets.[7]

Such ingratitude understandably made for a "long day at the office" for those in the cockpit of an unarmed and unarmored U-10 flying without escort a long way from friendly territory. As always, American humor found a way to fight the alternating boredom and fear that marked the psywar pilots' way of life. Aviation historian Philip D. Chinnery recalls an unusual interview with 5th Air Commando pilot Lt Col Ralph Evans:

> [I] remember the day Harvey Toffet fired up his U-10 during a psywar demonstration at Nha Trang. He started his takeoff roll, turned on his 3,000 watt speaker, and played a tape recording of an F-100 [jet fighter] after-burner kicking in. It tore the roof down, and some dumb Army general said, "That's an awful loud engine for such a small airplane![8]

On other occasions the psywarriors could find themselves smack in the middle of a major brawl still in full swing. In January 1966, Air Commando A-1, AC-47, and C-123 aircraft joined to support the first army division-sized "search and destroy" mission of the war. Dubbed Operation Masher,* it was a combined effort involving US, ARVN, and Korean army units.[9] Flying and fighting around-the-clock, the Air Commandos brought in the 5th ACS to round out a rare display of virtually all Air Commando capabilities at the same place and time:

> As the [friendly] soldiers moved forward, the [A-1Es] struck . . . sniper positions on their flanks. From overhead a U-10 from the 5th ACS dropped leaflets and beamed messages through its loudspeakers. After each period of heavy fighting, the PSYOPS plane broadcast funeral dirges and wailing sounds to play on the enemy's superstitions.[10]

Highly indoctrinated and isolated North Vietnamese and Vietcong troops were not easily susceptible to airborne psywar surrender leaflets and broadcasts. But as the Americans soon discovered, the leaflets were having the desired effect. In the same month that Operation Masher/White Wing took place, over 1,600 enemy soldiers using psywar leaflets as their safe-conduct pass became Chieu Hoi (ralliers) to the South Vietnamese government.[11] In 1967 alone, the annual total of Chieu Hoi reported from all allied psywar efforts was reported at 34,000, nearly double the previous year's total.[12]

By early 1967, the 5th Air Commando, still the lone US psywar squadron in South Vietnam, had become thoroughly saturated with tasks. To reinforce its early success and future potential, the squadron was split that March. The 5th retained coverage of South Vietnam's two southernmost regional corps, while the newly formed 9th ACS covered the two northernmost corps.[13] At the same time, the psywar C-47 and U-10 aircraft were supplemented by a third aircraft, the unusual looking Cessna 0-2, a twin-engined airplane with one tractor and one pusher propeller.

*Wide media attention present on the operation and the "potentially negative public reaction" to the name "Masher" led the Army to change the name of the lethal operation to the dovish-sounding and more politically correct White Wing.

USAF

All Air Commando psywar aircraft were equipped to conduct both loudspeaker and leaflet-drop missions. Note the leaflet-drop chute aft of the main cargo door. The leaflets falling from the other side of the aircraft are emerging from a "pipe" extended through an identical chute.

The overall effectiveness of any psywar program is invariably difficult to gauge. The cultural, subjective nature of the program, external factors beyond the control of the psywar planner, and difficulties encountered when attempting to measure success through the always-popular computer analysis all combine to complicate effective measurement of cultural behavior.

For all these problems, however, it still remains a fact that thousands of enemy soldiers became Chieu Hoi over the years, many the result of 5th and 9th ACS missions dedicated to achieving exactly this result. Also beyond quantification, but better still, every one of these Chieu Hoi was one less enemy soldier attempting to put an American in his (or her) gunsights.

Notes

1. Handbook, *Joint Special Operations Planning* (USAF Special Operations School, 1993), 225.
2. Army Pamphlet 525-7-2, *The Art and Science of Psychological Operations: Case Studies of Military Application*, vol. 2 (Washington, D.C.: Department of the Army, 1976), 731.
3. Ibid.
4. Maj John Hawkins Napier III, USAF, "The Air Commandos in Vietnam, November 5, 1961 to February 7, 1965" (master's thesis, Auburn University, 1967), 143.
5. Malcolm W. Browne, *The New Face of War* (Indianapolis: Bobbs-Merrill, 1965), 33, as quoted in Napier, 144.
6. John Schlight, *The War in South Vietnam: The Years of the Offensive, 1965–1968* (Washington, D.C.: Office of Air Force History 1988), 92.
7. Napier, 145.
8. Philip D. Chinnery, "PSYOPS: Vietnam to Desert Storm," in *Behind the Lines,* May/June 1994, 18.
9. Schlight, 195.
10. Ibid.
11. Keven M. Generous, *Vietnam: The Secret War* (New York: Gallery Books, 1985), 173.
12. Chinnery, 18.
13. Schlight, 243.

32 Air | 33 PsyWar | 34 Agent | 35 Recon | 80 JPRC

75th Air Studies Group

90th SOS	AIRLIFT	C-123K, C-130E
20th SOS 21st SOS	HELO	UH-1F/P, UH-1N, CH-3, CH-53
19th, 20th TASS 21st, 23rd TASS	FAC	0-1, 0-2, 0V-10
219th Avn Co 281st AHC	U.S. ARMY	0-1, UH-1H, AH-1
219th Sqdn 530th Sqdn	VNAF	CH-34, A-1H

The 75th Air Studies Group

We're funded and targeted by a nameless agency in Washington that's known by its initials most of the time . . . all our missions have the approval of the very highest authority. It can't get any higher. And I mean every target.

A SOG briefing officer

USASA/SF SOU

Taken from a reel of film found in the camera of a Vietcong killed in South Vietnam's southernmost delta region, this photo shocked US Military Assistance Command, Vietnam headquarters. The shock came not so much from the presence of North Vietnamese soldiers (khaki uniforms and helmets) with local VC (black uniforms and flop hats), but because of the year in which the photo was recovered. It was 1963, a year before SOG began providing MACV with the first real evidence indicating the true extent of North Vietnamese support to the South Vietnamese VC.

It was called simply the "Studies and Observations Group" (SOG).* But there was nothing simple about the top secret organization that included all of Indochina in its area of operations. The innocuous-sounding name conveyed an image of some obscure research function buried in the headquarters of MACV. But appearances are truly deceiving, and in this case the deception proved fatal for thousands of enemy soldiers. For SOG, as it was referred to by the few who had reason to hear its name, was arguably the most deadly combat force fielded by the United States in the Second Indochina War.

Activated on 24 January 1964, SOG was a unique Joint Unconventional Warfare Task Force comprised of Air Commandos, Green Berets, SEALs, and Marine Corps aircrew and reconnaissance personnel.[1] Drawn from the most elite units the US would field for this war, these Americans were the minority in SOG. Their mission was to

*Although initially identified as the "Special Operations Group" upon activation, security concerns for the top secret organization soon mandated a change in name to "Studies and Observations Group."

lead the real combat power in SOG, an indigenous force thousands strong comprised of Vietnamese, Cambodian, and Chinese civilians hired, trained, and led by the Americans for a vicious war so secret that neither North Vietnam nor the US mentioned their existence. How could they? Blood trails left by both SOG and North Vietnamese soldiers stained jungle floors where neither Washington nor Hanoi admitted to having forces in the first place!

So secret were SOG's missions, so politically sensitive their purpose, that SOG's targets were directed by the Joint Chiefs of Staff in the Pentagon.[2] Even in South Vietnam itself, only a select few offices were ever briefed on SOG operations: successive MACV commanders (generals Paul D. Harkins, William C. Westmoreland, and Creighton W. Abrams Jr.), MACV's flag-rank chief of staff and intelligence officers, the general commanding the Seventh Air Force, and the admiral commanding the US Naval forces, Vietnam.[3] Each MACV-proposed mission was reviewed and approved or disapproved by the White House.

The incredible secrecy and priority accorded SOG's primary unconventional warfare missions (strategic reconnaissance, direct action, and psychological warfare) were due in part to the nature of the operations themselves, but largely because of where these operations took place. While official US policy forbade its military personnel from operating beyond South Vietnam's borders, SOG operations worked almost exclusively in Laos, Cambodia, and North Vietnam.

To SOG's all-volunteer* Air Commando and ground teams infiltrating these deadly Communist sanctuaries, the impact of official Washington policy was twofold—and very personal. First, the Americans were operating beyond artillery and US fighter aircraft support for all but the most dire emergencies, and sometimes even then. As such, teams or downed aircrews could generally rely only on the limited SOG air support (helicopter gunships) in the event of such an emergency. Second, the US would (and consistently did) disavow all knowledge of captured SOG personnel operating in "unauthorized" areas. The families of those killed on operations in Laos, Cambodia, and North Vietnam were told their sons and husbands died in South Vietnam while performing anything else but SOG operations. "For the record," top secret SOG didn't even exist beyond its intentionally bland cover name!

To execute its unconventional warfare mission into North Vietnamese-controlled territory, SOG developed a "private air force" of carefully selected airmen from US Air Force, Army, and Marine units as well as the Vietnamese Air Force itself. Using primarily USAF assets, SOG provided staff oversight for its air operations with Operation 32, Air Studies Branch. The 75th Air Studies Group was made up of a multitude of USAF and other units that actually executed the Operation 32-tasked missions in the field.

In general, there were three categories of USAF special operations. For long-range infiltration of Operation 34 agents, the primary aircraft were the C-123K Provider and C-130E transports, both types commonly referred to as the "Blackbirds." USAF UH-1, CH-3, and CH-53 helicopters were used for the short-range infiltration of Operation 35 ground reconnaissance teams or the recovery of downed US aircrews. And finally, the 0-1, 0-2, and OV-10 observation aircraft were used for forward air control duty in "over the fence" flights into Cambodia and Laos.[4] Also warranting recognition for their outstanding performance, the VNAF provided A-1 Skyraiders and CH-34 heli-

*Since the beginning of recorded military history, "volunteers" have arrived in several different categories. These can range from super patriots to those "firing squad disadvantaged" souls who see the light . . . before the muzzle blast. For the most part, SOG got a rare combination of talent and courage from both sources.

copters piloted by some of the bravest and most combat-experienced pilots to fight in the war. The US Army, too, provided UH-1 helicopters and 0-1 Bird Dogs for some of the most dangerous low-level reconnaissance and FAC missions. Their stories follow.

Duck Hook, Combat Spear, and OPLAN 34A

Less than a week after SOG's activation, the US government made a formal decision to implement a highly classified plan identified as Operations Plan (OPLAN) 34A, which was an intensified program of harassment, diversion, political pressure, capture of prisoners, physical destruction, acquisition of intelligence, generation of propaganda, and diversion of resources *against the Democratic Republic of Vietnam.*[5]

The timing of OPLAN 34A and SOG's activation was no coincidence, as SOG was the chosen weapon to execute OPLAN 34A by air, land, and sea. Of the three infiltration methods, aerial delivery was of obvious importance to the US Air Force, the primary agency tasked to conduct the secret flights into North Vietnam. As always in covert operations, the concept of "plausible denial" became a critical factor in the conduct and organization of the first USAF unit to undertake OPLAN 34A missions. Fittingly enough, it began in the Air Commando nest at Hurlburt Field, Florida, just four months after SOG's activation.

The program was code-named "Duck Hook." Official Air Force history notes that on 25 May 1964, 38 Chinese and 18 Vietnamese aircrews began specialized low-level flight and bad-weather paradrop training in three specially equipped C-123Bs operating from the Air Commando field in the Florida panhandle.[6] Graduating on 15 July 1964 from their USAF training, the Asian aircrews, along with the American contingent assigned to Duck Hook, returned to South Vietnam to form Detachment 1, 775th Troop Carrier Wing.[7]

Detachment 1 was later redesignated "First Flight," and by 1968 its personnel and equipment would be carried for "cover" purposes on the records of the 15th Special Operations Squadron (C-130E Blackbirds) collocated with it at the coastal airfield at Nha Trang, 190 miles north of Saigon.[8] Equipped with six C-123s extensively modified with navigation and terrain avoidance radar, First Flight aircraft were painted in a distinctive black and green scheme in contrast to the standard USAF camouflage pattern.

For missions outside South Vietnam, First Flight utilized its all-Asian crews,* with the aircraft's US insignia decals on its fuselage removed.[9] It seemed a winning concept at Hurlburt Field, but in Southeast Asia, First Flight found the weather, terrain, and antiaircraft defenses over North Vietnam even tougher than expected. An official USAF history of the operation notes:

> Early activity was confined to high-altitude leaflet operations and routine airlift work. The first reinforcement-resupply mission to North Vietnam took place on December 25th, 1966. Seven more resupply missions to the north were completed in the first three months of 1967, followed by only ten more through the end of 1968. Completion rate was one sortie in three.[10]

Commanded by a USAF lieutenant colonel, First Flight's Chinese and American crews lived in downtown Nha Trang to minimize their contact with other American personnel. Among the American contingent in 1968 was Capt Peter M.

---

*On rare occasions, an American pilot or agent handler/jumpmaster accompanied a flight, but his presence alone compromised the politically important "plausible denial" cover should the aircraft be downed.

Bob Pinard

This C-123K painted in nonstandard US camouflage is parked at Nha Trang in the late 1960s. Assigned to USAF's top secret First Flight, it was one of six such aircraft flown by American, Chinese, and Vietnamese aircrews deep into North Vietnam for psychological warfare and agent infiltration missions. Neither before nor since has there been any comparable unit in the history of the US Air Force.

Hurd, an electronics warfare officer with a unique insight into the mission of this highly unusual unit. Like most of the other American aircrew, he served as an instructor for the Asian crews and took his turn flying SOG's routine "in country" missions throughout South Vietnam. But it was in his primary duty as First Flight's air penetration officer that he planned the dangerous flight routes into Laos, Cambodia, and North Vietnam for the Chinese flight crews. By this stage of the war, as many as two or three flights a month were delivering South Vietnamese agents (Operation 34) and propaganda material (Operation 33) prepared by SOG's "psywar" staff.[11]

While the highly experienced Chinese pilots earned the respect of their American counterparts, the range and payload limitations of the C-123K hampered the effectiveness of the Duck Hook program. This realization led to the decision to boost SOG's Operation 34 capability with another highly specialized aircraft, the C-130E Combat Talon. The addition of this capability also came with a special code name: "Combat Spear."

Like Duck Hook, the Combat Spear program began in the United States with carefully screened airmen being asked to volunteer for dangerous but unspecified duty in Southeast Asia. In 1966, C-130 flight engineer Bert Cartwright Jr. recalls that simply to be selected for an interview, flight engineers were required to have a minimum of 4,000 hours experience in the C-130.[12] In an intriguing twist (as well as a clue as to whom the volunteers would be working for), the airmen were also sent to Washington, D.C., for lie detector testing conducted by US intelligence officials.[13]

Those individual airmen successfully completing the lengthy screening process were assembled at Pope AFB, North Carolina, for three months of intensive training in the electronically sophisticated Talon. Air-to-ground pickups with the Blackbird's unique Fulton Skyhook Recovery System,* night low-level flying, and mastery of the aircraft's complex computer systems were all emphasized to bring the crews to a peak of team effectiveness. With the initial crews trained, four Combat Talons departed the US in December 1966 in a deployment dubbed "Project Stray Goose." They arrived at Nha Trang airfield the same month to augment SOG's First Flight.

Within the first several months of 1967, the Blackbirds** were logging as many as four night flights into North Vietnam each month.[14] Nha Trang was getting to be a busy place for "secret" operations and an inquisitive observer would notice some strange goings-on, "The SOG C-130s (at Nha Trang) typically taxied to some out-of-the-way airfield corner to pick up troops packing strange submachine guns or to unload men in North Vietnamese uniforms who scurried into unmarked civilian vans and sped away."[15]

The Blackbird missions were usually agent or propaganda leaflet drops, sometimes both on the same flight. Unlike the all-Asian crews flying the First Flight missions, the Combat Spear program was an all-American show from the start. So secret were the "out of country" flights that even the flight orders for each mission, listing the names of the crew but not its route, were classified top secret. During 1967, which appears from oral histories to have been the period of maximum Blackbird activity over North Vietnam, South Vietnamese agents were not the only personnel apparently dropped into the north.

During his 1967–68 tour with the Blackbirds, flight engineer Cartwright recalls that his crew, "Stray Goose 04," completed 17 missions into North Vietnam.[16] A "typical" flight might carry up to a dozen South Vietnamese agents with their American SOG jumpmaster, as well as a load of leaflets to be released after the agent drops. Such multitask flights over North Vietnam were both long and dangerous. Inevitably, one would prove deadly to its crew.

The inevitable happened during the early morning hours of 30 December 1967. With top secret flight orders listing only the crew members' names, duration of flight (seven hours, 15 minutes), and call sign "RA," a Blackbird departed Nha Trang at 0030 for a combination agent/leaflet drop mission into North Vietnam.[17] It was never heard from again. To this date the North Vietnamese deny all knowledge of the mission or the Blackbird's 11-man crew. There were other flights, too, recorded in the oral histories of the Combat Spear crews, which raise questions still officially unconfirmed to this day.

On one such mission, Cartwright recalls his Combat Talon landing in Laos to pick up a group of 20 to 25 Cambodian mercenaries, all wearing parachutes and North Vietnamese uniforms. The crew dropped the mercenaries in three different locations, less than 10 miles south of the Chinese/North Vietnamese border. Their mission? None of the Blackbird crew's business. Their method of exfiltration from North Vietnam? None of the crew's business either. Though missions of this sort were not common, the existence of Cambodian and Chinese mercenaries in SOG

*Despite the apparent advantages offered by the visually impressive Fulton Skyhook Recovery System, its potential was never once exploited in a combat situation in the decades the equipment remained on the Blackbirds. In late 1996, the Air Force Special Operations Command removed the Fulton systems from its MC-130E Combat Talon fleet, placing the Talon's once-famous "whiskers" in mothballs should Fulton's remarkable device ever be required.

**The term *Blackbirds* was frequently applied to both the First Flight C-123Ks and the four C-130Es assigned to a different squadron. The C-130E squadron went through several different designations during its tour in South Vietnam. Initially assigned as Detachment 1, 314th Tactical Airlift Wing, it subsequently became the 15th Air Commando Squadron, later the 15th Special Operations Squadron, then the 90th SOS before its departure to Kadena Air Base, Okinawa, in 1972. There it was redesignated yet again, this time to its current organization, the 1st SOS. The author uses the term *Blackbirds* as it was the one name that remained consistent throughout this period.

was a well-known feature of the organization from its earliest inception.

Only now, decades later, are the First Flight and Blackbird crews discovering what few of them could have suspected during their dangerous hours over North Vietnam. For decades after the war, it has been a secret to which only a few senior US intelligence and Army officers . . . and the North Vietnamese government were privy. OPLAN 34A's infiltration of South Vietnamese agents into North Vietnam had been virtually a 100 percent failure even before the military had assumed the program from US intelligence officials.

In his groundbreaking book, *Secret Army, Secret War*, historian Sedgwick Tourison details the fate of 456 agents captured or killed almost immediately after their delivery into Communist territory in 1960–68 alone; others are still listed as missing.[18] While most of the casualties occurred after 1964, one authoritative source notes that during the three years that preceded transfer of the program from US intelligence to military control during that year, no less than "18 of 23 teams were lost, mostly upon landing."[19] Those not killed immediately were invariably "doubled" by the North Vietnamese and used for disinformation purposes against the Americans. Tourison concludes:

> Thus, by the end of 1963 a program that [William E.] Colby [US intelligence official] knew to have been a failure in 1962 and had so informed Secretary [of Defense Robert S.] McNamara in November, 1963, was miraculously transformed on paper from a . . . low-level espionage operation into a magic bullet ostensibly to send a message its designers had never intended. . . . *New military commanders, however, were now assigned to carry out an impossible mission, soon to be dubbed Operations Plan (OPLAN) 34A.* [Emphasis added] [20]

The year 1968 is significant as an official "end-point" of known Vietnamese agent casualties because on 31 October of that year President Lyndon B. Johnson announced a halt to Operation Rolling Thunder, the US bombing campaign against North Vietnam above the 19th parallel.[21] For the following two years, only reconnaissance aircraft would fly north of the parallel. And what of the South Vietnamese teams previously infiltrated at such risk by the Blackbirds?

To those involved in Agent 34 operations at the time, the teams were seemingly abandoned. This cessation of US support followed a remarkable conclusion reached by a special team of intelligence and military officials flown into Saigon from Washington during one of the temporary bombing halts declared prior to the long-term bombing halt declared on 31 October. Reviewing the case histories of each team, the American special team "concluded that *all* teams were under hostile control and had probably been so since shortly after insertion" (emphasis added).[22] A former SOG commander, Maj Gen Jack S. Singlaub, US Army, Retired, recalls learning years after the war that a Vietnamese officer with access to SOG operational data was passing this information to a senior Vietnamese source later revealed as a North Vietnamese spy.[23]

Some of those teams confirmed as "under hostile control" might receive one last visit from a Blackbird, parachuting a final "resupply" drop into the darkened landscape below. These were "special" packages, booby trapped with high explosives set to explode when the container was opened by the double agents.[24] Without a "need to know," the Blackbird crews took the same risks to fly these elimination missions as they did for any other mission "out of country."

As in the Korean War a decade earlier, the US grossly overestimated the ability of infiltrated agents to establish a successful resistance movement within a totalitarian Communist regime. As noted earlier, the agent program inherited by the military (SOG) in 1964 from US intelligence operatives in South

Vietnam had in fact already been deemed a failure by its civilian American managers.[25]

Following the 1 November 1968 cessation of agent and leaflet flights into North Vietnam, the Blackbirds at Nha Trang flew only occasional unconventional warfare missions into Cambodia and Laos, while picking up a larger role in routine cargo flights within South Vietnam. But while the overall pace slacked off during this period, the 90th SOS Blackbirds still found themselves playing a leading role in a very specialized infiltration technique, one never before attempted by US special operations forces in combat.

The new infiltration technique was named high-altitude—low opening (HALO). Civilians would recognize it as the sport of skydiving. But it was anything but a sport to SOG, which was determined to find some infiltration alternative to the increasingly dangerous Operation 35 helicopter insertions. For by 1970, such insertions were provoking enemy responses more often than not before the team could even clear the landing zone. Was HALO a realistic alternative?

In the early morning darkness of 29 November 1970, SOG Recon Team Florida—comprised of three Americans, one Vietnamese, and two mountain tribesmen (Montagnards)—stepped silently off the darkened ramp of a 90th SOS Blackbird cruising over Laos at 18,000 feet, disappearing into the rain-swept, dark clouds below.[26] From the ground two miles below, the C-130E could neither be seen nor heard. The Blackbird's navigation radar rather than a jumpmaster call was used to send the jumpers off as the weather blocked the entire landscape below from view. The US had just initiated the first combat HALO jump in the history of its military forces.[27]

Given the storm conditions in the area, the six-man team was lucky to land without injuries, though separated into four groups. The four elements searched independently over the next four days—and without success—for their target area before being extracted by Thailand-based helicopters. Though a technical failure, SOG noted with satisfaction that HALO had been "proven as a means of entering [Laos] undetected since an active enemy search was not made to locate the team."[28]

The Blackbirds would go on to complete four more HALO missions for SOG over the following year, with drop zones in Cambodia and South Vietnam added to the mission list.[29] Results from the HALO insertions proved an operational disappointment. For while the silent insertions generally avoided provoking an enemy response, weather, terrain, and equipment problems invariably scattered the team members far from each other. It was a problem never satisfactorily resolved before SOG was deactivated in the spring of 1972.

On 31 March 1972 (coinciding with SOG's closure), both the First Flight and 90th SOS were withdrawn from clandestine operations.[30] While First Flight's aircraft were split up and distributed elsewhere, the C-130E Blackbirds were sent to Kadena Air Base, Okinawa, the following month and assigned to the 18th Tactical Fighter Wing. Redesignated yet again to the 15th SOS, the squadron continued to be tasked by SOG for missions over Cambodia and occasionally North Vietnam.[31] Col Bob Pinard, the Blackbird commander at the time, recalls leaving one C-130E in Thailand, first at Nakhon Phanom then Takhli, during this period for exclusive support to SOG.[32]

These SOG missions called for the Blackbirds to drop both propaganda leaflets and counterfeit currency, as well as resupply drops to indigenous personnel on the ground. On one such resupply mission during this period, former Blackbird Lee Hess recalls the distinctly American voice over the radio guiding the airdrops from below. But the voice wasn't really there at all, not officially, and, come to think of it, neither was Hess

Bob Pinard

Lifting off into the evening dusk from Nha Trang AB in 1968, a C-130E Blackbird begins a classified flight, carrying an unknown cargo to a destination unspecified on its top secret flight plan.

and his crew. In the special operations world, it's called "Ops Normal."

The "Bringers of Death"

In the unlikely event SOG had ever been ordered to forgo volunteers and place a brutally honest "Employment Offered" advertisement for forward air control pilots, it probably would have looked something like this:

> Wanted: Pilots looking for an exciting time, not a long time. Must be willing to fly small, unprotected observation aircraft within range of enemy weapons ranging in caliber from handheld pistols on up. Must not worry unduly that in the event of your untimely death, no one including your family will know where you were or what you were doing. Courage and reflexes valued much more highly than long-term, goal-planning skills. Good death benefits, all you can eat mess hall, pay could be better.

Fortunately, SOG was never put in the position of having to place such an ad. Unfortunately for the North Vietnamese Army and Vietcong, the Air Force somehow managed to find the odd character that actually thought this type of "flying and fighting" was just his ticket. Other airmen might face even more personal danger; others still have more firepower at their fingertips. But no one in the war ever combined firsthand danger with the authority to call in a massive, violent response than did the FACs. The North Vietnamese called them the "Bringers of Death," and they had every reason to know whereof they spoke.

Dale Bennett

The wreckage of a plane that shouldn't be there. This O-1 Bird Dog from the US Army's 219th Aviation Company lies in Cambodia, officially declared off-limits years earlier to US military personnel.

The SOG/FACs were the key element to the effectiveness and survival of what SOG called with disarming ease its "Ground Studies Group," or Operation 35. The "studying" done here was of the hands-on kind, and the grading was fairly straightforward. Green Beret-led reconnaissance (recon) teams comprised mostly of indigenous (Vietnamese, Cambodian, Chinese, or Montagnard) personnel were inserted into areas thought to be the most dangerous concentrations of North Vietnamese activity in Indochina. Invariably, this turned out to be exactly the case, and the teams either performed with skill, endurance, and valor, or they suffered tragically for their shortcomings.

The price for such shortcomings varied only between death, capture, and torture, or simply vanishing from friendly sight to be listed as "Missing in Action" for all time to come. Author and former SOG recon team veteran John L. Plaster describes the cruel reality on the ground succinctly, "Among SOG's [reconnaissance] units, Purple Hearts were earned at a pace unparalleled in American wars of this century, with casualties at times exceeding 100 percent [i.e., multiple wounds to the same individual, sometimes on the same mission]."[33]

A major reason for this extreme environment is that Operation 35 didn't officially exist. Recon teams detected and attacked in Laos or Cambodia couldn't be publicly acknowledged, much less supported, by the US command in South Vietnam. In the first case, the US had pledged to respect the "neutrality" of Laotian territory following the relevant 1962 Geneva Accords. As for Cambodia, it severed diplomatic relations with the US on 3 May 1965, in the process specifically and publicly forbidding any US military personnel on Cambodian soil.[34] Immediately evident to SOG from the start was that FAC support, especially the firepower it could call on from

Vietnamese and occasionally US tactical fighter aircraft, was the only way to keep the recon team operations from becoming suicide missions.

To provide this all-important FAC support to SOG, the USAF activated four tactical air support squadrons (TASS) over a period of time. Though not formally part of USAF's special operations force, their pilots were trained under the auspices of the Special Air Warfare Center at Hurlburt Field.[35] Inevitably, the Air Commando esprit and aggressiveness carried into their tactical training. None of the TASS units were committed solely to SOG, but each provided elements from within the squadron that specialized in classified SOG combat. The first to come on-line was the 20th TASS, activated at Da Nang AB on 26 April 1965 with "visual reconnaissance" over South Vietnam as its official cover story.[36]

Flying the little two-seat 0-1 Bird Dog and using "Covey" as its radio call sign, the 20th took part in SOG's first US-led, cross-border recon mission into Laos on 18 October 1965,[37] less than a month after President Johnson's personal authorization for such missions on 21 September. At this early stage of SOG's war, missions into Laos were code-named "Shining Brass," each tightly controlled on a case-by-case basis by the Joint Chiefs of Staff.[38] This first mission became a bloody omen for future cross-border missions, in the process also marking the date that began the death toll for the FACs, the Operation 35 teams, and the VNAF helicopter pilots that were a vital part of SOG's secret air force.

During the operation, a VNAF "King Bee" H-34 helicopter with a crew of three, two observers in a 20th TASS Bird Dog, and the recon team's point man were killed, for a total of six deaths (all attributed to locations in South Vietnam). Determined to achieve some success from the mission despite these losses, the recon team leader called on the 20th Covey FAC, who, in turn, promptly directed a total of 88 bombing runs on the enemy truck park that the team was originally inserted to pinpoint.[39] Multiple secondary explosions and strong antiaircraft fire erupted from the thick jungle, confirming the presence of high-value targets now worth considerably less on the military surplus market.[40]

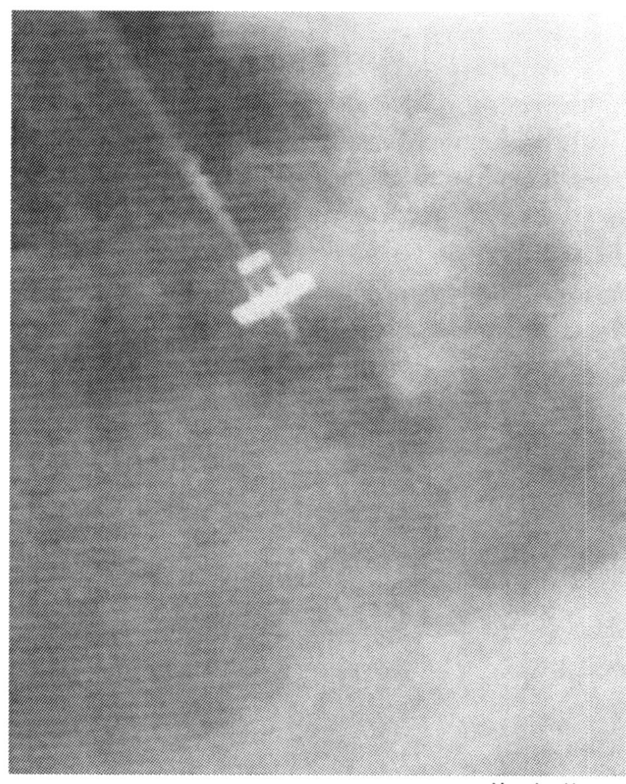

Mary Ann Harrison

A steep low-level dive provides the best chance for this SOG OV-10 Bronco to put a marker rocket exactly on target. Of course, such a maneuver also provides the same opportunity for North Vietnamese antiaircraft gunners to put their rounds exactly on target. The enemy called these dangerous forward air controllers the "Bringers of Death."

Of the many lessons SOG learned from its first missions, one of the most important was the benefits gained from the addition of a SOG recon veteran in the backseat of the FAC plane. Called "Covey riders," these former recon team leaders provided immediate, invaluable assistance to both the recon team down below, usually hidden from the FAC's view and the FAC pilot with whom they were riding.

Unforeseeable to SOG at the time, this first mission set a pattern of Operation 32/Operation 35 teamwork that would continue until SOG was finally withdrawn from combat just over six years later. The losses to the FACs and recon team members were particularly personal and painful as the numbers of volunteers involved were so few. Personal relationships abounded as the air-ground teams became a mutual admiration society. And from these relationships flowed a fanatical camaraderie that fully matched the enemy's equally fanatical determination to wipe out the recon teams operating in its rear area sanctuaries.

To eliminate the intrusive SOG recon teams, the North Vietnamese frequently came together in large numbers . . . and within view of the SOG/FAC overhead. Inevitably, that proved a big mistake, as from the beginning SOG/FACs were known to become obsessed with the safety of "their team" once it was inserted. Again and again, the fury from a merciless FAC, circling over an endangered recon team, brought wrathful, massive carnage upon the enemy. In his fascinating book *SOG: The Secret Wars of America's Commandos in Vietnam*, Plaster puts numbers to such words:

> SOG . . . consistently killed more than one hundred NVA for each lost Green Beret, a ratio that climbed as high as 150:1, which MACV documented in 1969. This was the highest documented kill ratio of any American unit in the war, exceeding the average by a factor of ten, and quite likely is the highest such ratio in U.S. history.[41]

USAF

The OV-10 Bronco was particularly valued by SOG, as the lightly armed aircraft was the closest thing to tactical fighter support usually allowed to support the recon teams. The two 7.62 mm machine guns mounted in pods on either side of the fuselage are visible here, although the centerline rocket pod is not present. On one SOG night mission, two OV-10s parachuted a six-man patrol recon team deep into Cambodia.

Dale Bennett

Officially, Air Force and Army observation aircraft flying over Laos and Cambodia worked different missions. But since "officially" they weren't there in the first place, the pilots invariably worked closely together with the SOG teams down below. It was, as one SOG pilot noted, "a lonely kind of war."

This phenomenal record underscores the thousands of air strikes called in by SOG/FACs from all TASS units, including in addition to the 20th, the 19th at Bien Hoa AB near Saigon, the 21st at Pleiku in South Vietnam's Central Highlands, and the 23d that supported SOG from Nakhon Phanom RTAFB in Thailand. From each of these squadrons, a small group of pilots had been asked to volunteer for "special missions." Flying the 0-1 Bird Dog, the 0-2 Skymaster, and finally the OV-10 Bronco at different stages of the war, the FAC pilots supporting SOG became the nemesis of NVA units from southern Cambodia to northern Laos. This dubious "compliment" from the enemy came with a steep price tag.

To the NVA in the jungle below, the FACs were quickly recognized as the source of all the cannon fire, napalm, and bombs that followed their arrival overhead. They were, of course, also recognized as the easiest target. In contrast to the jets that came in at hundreds of miles per hour or the heavily armored A-1 Skyraiders that were exceptionally tough to bring down, the flimsy, slow-moving FACs were a relatively easy target. By both priority and vulnerability, they thus became by default the "target of choice," second only to the even more vulnerable helicopters that inserted and extracted the recon teams.

If there were obvious (and rational) reasons why the flow of volunteers for FAC duty was something less than a stampede, the flow to SOG duty was even slower. In addition to the inherent dangers of FAC flying, the SOG volunteer could count on little more than the insertion team he was supporting to rescue him if he went down. Summing up the situation succinctly, OV-10 FAC Marshall Harrison called it "a lonely kind of war," in his excellent book of the same title.[42]

As previously mentioned, what Harrison and others like him got during their initial SOG in-brief was a clear reading of official US policy to emphasize just how "lonely" they were going to find themselves. And that policy was as clear as it was simple: no tactical air support for SOG in Cambodia, not even for a team in trouble or a downed pilot.[43] Once in the field at a forward launch site, however, the terms of their "contract" were driven home to them by less articulate speakers: the Special Forces who ran the operation.

In his book, newly arrived SOG/FAC Harrison recalls asking a SOG officer what help he could count on should he be shot down. The response was hardly comforting:

> As long as there's a chance in hell of pulling the pilot or crew out of there, then we'll be doing it. I'm going to be straight with you on this though. . . . If I decide that there's no way we can effect your rescue [in Cambodia], I'll order the gunships to fire at you to prevent the enemy from getting their hands on you. I

Dale Bennett

Unable to resist looking up, a North Vietnamese soldier breaks discipline (a rarity), exposing his pale face against the surrounding vegetation to a low-flying 219th Bird Dog. The firing slit of a bunker is circled in the center foreground, and what appears to be equipment lies in the small clearing in the center of the photograph.

can't risk having any of the [recon] teams compromised if they take you alive.[44]

As fate would have it, Harrison was shot down "over the fence," coming within a whisker of being captured before being snatched from the jungle floor at the end of a rope tied to a SOG helicopter. Upon his return, he learned that SOG's urgent radio request to Headquarters MACV in Saigon for fighter support to achieve his rescue had been disapproved as promised, as per stated policy.[45] Even the heroic efforts of his SOG rescue team—efforts that would have earned valor citations anywhere in South Vietnam—went unrecognized. How could such citations be written for people who didn't exist, doing a mission that never happened?

The SOG rescue team just mentioned came from Operation 80, another SOG operational staff section with the title Joint Personnel Recovery Center. Organized initially by a name now well familiar to the reader, Air Commando colonel Heinie Aderholt, Operation 80 was organized to recover US personnel already in captivity. Almost from the start, however, the retrieval of SOG personnel such as Harrison or split-up recon team members on the run became a priority for the Aderholt creation. The Bright Light rescue missions were extremely dangerous as the enemy was obviously in the immediate area of the personnel in distress. While more than a few SOG fighters owe their lives to the Bright Light operations, no American POWs were ever recovered from the camps in which they were held.

Another small band of Bird Dog pilots supported SOG in the dangerous skies over Cambodia. Though their mission was officially described as "visual reconnaissance" rather than FACing for the SOG recon teams, the pilots of the US Army's 219th Aviation Company took all the same risks and played by all the same skewed political rules that made Americans nameless and homeless in the most dangerous situations. Years after the war, 219th pilot Dale R. Bennett recalls personally learning, for example, that the death of another 219th pilot in Cambodia had been "relocated" back to South Vietnam . . . for the record.

Only the pilots assigned to the 219th's Second and Fourth Flight Platoons were actually dedicated to SOG. Always flying in pairs for safety and mutual support, the Second Flight was committed to Prairie Fire operations in Laos while the Fourth supported SOG's Daniel Boone missions in Cambodia. Generally, much younger than their Air Force counterparts, the 219th pilots flew with that certain assurance of immortality that comes with youth. They needed it, as their mission (and their exuberance) led them to take alarming risks at treetop level. They weren't immortal, of course, and they paid, sometimes dearly, for the priceless information they brought back to SOG's intelligence section.

It was all part of SOG's private air force. If there was one aerial target the NVA accorded a higher priority to than the low-flying FACs, it was the even lower-flying SOG helicopters that carried the despised recon teams into the bowels of the NVA's "protected sanctuaries" in Cambodia and Laos.

Green Hornets and Knives

"The Green Hornets . . . were the prime reason a lot of SOG men came out of Cambodia alive." So states John L. Plaster in *SOG: The Secret Wars of America's Commandos in Vietnam*.[46] To SOG's recon teams, the helicopter crews flew the "war wagons" that took them into harm's way, the gunships that attacked those who would harm them, and the lifeline that snatched them from harm's way when all hope seemed lost. To SOG's helicopter crews flying the recon teams, the prospect of close-quarters combat on virtually every mission tested their character, skill, and valor in ways few airmen would ever be tested. To abandon a team, regardless of the hopeless odds, was

USAF

A "Pony Express" mission into "denied territory" in June 1968 plucks a Special Forces patrol and indigenous troops from the jungle. The unusual presence of cameras suggests the equally unusual absence of North Vietnamese troops in the immediate vicinity.

unthinkable, and, as the records show, many died in desperate acts of courage rather than face this unacceptable failure.

The Green Hornets of the 20th Special Operations Squadron were the first American helo crews to join SOG's secret war with their UH-1s and CH-3s, followed later by the Dust Devils of the 21st SOS with their more powerful CH-53 machines. The VNAF provided the legendary King Bees of the 219th Helicopter Squadron with their piston-powered H-34s. It was a world-class lineup that was still bloodied over and over again in the all-out brawl that takes place in every war "at the tip of the spear."

Activated at Tan Son Nhut AB on 8 October 1965, the 20th Helicopter Squadron's 14 CH-3Cs

Dale Bennett

The first helicopters to support SOG came from the VNAF's 219th Helicopter Squadron. Identified by their radio call sign "King Bee," the fearless Vietnamese pilots who flew these CH-34s became a legend to the Americans who routinely trusted their lives to the skill and valor of these airmen. (Note that all insignia markings have been removed from this King Bee.)

performed a wide variety of useful "ash and trash" missions before the squadron was assigned to the 14th Air Commando Wing in March 1966.[47] An official US Air Force history written in 1982 notes: "The unit was soon occupied in tasks *beyond* its [original] mission statement "(emphasis added).[48] Indeed they were. A less formal but more contemporary and candid history might observe that the "rotorheads" were now up to their knickers with Green Beret "snake eaters" in places no official history is about to discuss in detail.

Less than three months after joining the 14th ACW, 11 of the 14 CH-3s were flown to Udorn RTAFB to support SOG's incursions into Laos "in support of the unconventional role."[49] Thus evolved the "Pony Express" flights that inserted both South Vietnamese agents and Operation 35 teams into the Laotian panhandle in the Shining Brass and Prairie Fire operations. That June, the 20th flew its first infiltration mission further north, into North Vietnam. The pace of infiltrations over the next several months hardly slowed, and by year's end, Pony Express had infiltrated North Vietnam and Laos no less than 315 times.[50]

Seven months later, in January 1967, the 14th ACW unexpectedly found itself the recipient of 15 UH-1F Hueys formerly based with the 606th Air Commando Squadron at Nakhon Phanom RTAFB, Thailand.[51] All were equipped with self-sealing fuel tanks and side-mounted miniguns; some with air-to-ground 2.75-inch rocket pods. The Hueys came with something else—a symbol stenciled on their tailbooms reflecting their name: "Green Hornets." Following a brief period of confusion, the 14th ACW introduced the "new guys in town" to SOG. Long on enthusiasm but short on combat experience, the Hornets got a rude

flage paint added to their Hueys upon arrival in Thailand covered the still partially noticeable blue and white SAC colors. The crews were primarily trained "to carry toilet paper and people to the missile silos in the Midwest."[52] It wasn't much of a training background for SOG, and within weeks of their arrival, the Hornets had suffered their first casualties.

To their credit and SOG's relief, the Hornets quickly adapted to their new environment, becoming "the preferred [helicopter] unit for SF [Special Forces] operations across the borders."[53] A major plus in their favor was the makeup of the crews—many of them older, experienced pilots with extensive fixed-wing flying experience.

The Green Hornets typically used four P-model gunships to escort the F-model UH-1 carrying the recon team "over the fence." The miniguns on the P models, a vast improvement over the infantry-type M-60 machine guns used on Army helicopters, were especially important. The US policy forbidding tactical air support for the recon teams meant that SOG's helicopters provided its primary aerial gunship support in officially designated "denied areas." For insertions, speed was critical to give the recon team maximum opportunity to elude the North Vietnamese troops drawn inevitably to the insertion site. Recovery was a daylight affair, given the obvious drawbacks to air-ground coordination at night, but it called for

Don Nieto

This excellent side shot of a UH-1P gunship gives a good indication of the sting carried by the 20th "Green Hornets" Special Operations Squadron. With tactical air support forbidden for SOG recon teams working beyond South Vietnam's borders, the presence of helicopter gunships frequently spelled the difference between life and death for teams cornered by vastly superior forces.

awakening as they worked their way into the starting lineup in the "big leagues."

Maj "Smokey" Hubbard, one of the original Green Hornets in the Nakhon Phanom/NhaTrang transfer, recalls that both the UH-1Fs and their pilots came from Strategic Air Command assignments in America's Midwest. The green camou-

Exiting with a very appropriate-sounding snarl, 6,000 rounds a minute pour out of the six barrels of the GAU-2 minigun. Of less value, but still comforting, is the way the minigun blocks out the sound of all the weapons firing back at you!

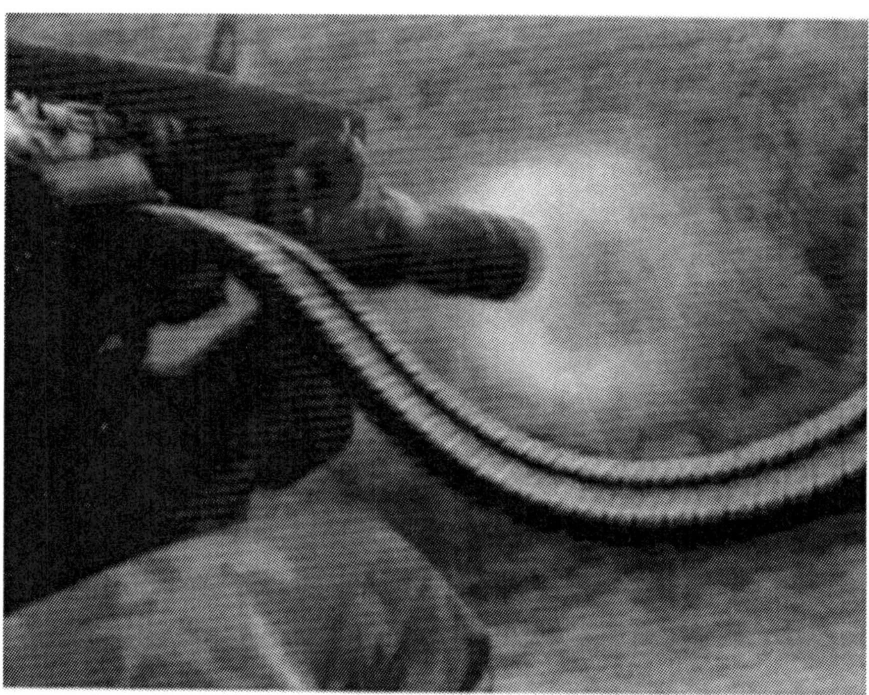
Don Nieto

brute firepower (rather than speed) to keep the enemy from overrunning a cornered team.

The saga of Air Force Medal of Honor recipient 1st Lt James P. Fleming (told in the Medal of Honor story), underscores the heart-stopping drama that frequently unfolded when a helicopter crew forced its way into a knockdown, drag-out fight between a recon team and the NVA waged, literally, within rock-throwing range. As always in war, some return miraculously unscathed, as did Fleming's team when it escaped from death or capture into the welcoming clear blue sky. For another SOG team, however, the end came when a Soviet-made RPG-7 (rocket-propelled grenade) found their helicopter leaving the pickup zone, bringing all aboard back into the green landscape in a ball of fire and molten aluminum. During their tour of duty in Southeast Asia, the Green Hornets lost 19 helicopter, 13 in direct combat.[54]

Rope-ladder extraction of a recon team leaves both helicopter and team members totally vulnerable to enemy machine-gun fire and even rocket-propelled grenade attacks. On 15 March 1970, SOG Recon Team Pennsylvania and a helicopter crew of four were eliminated by just such a grenade attack deep inside Cambodia. The bodies were never recovered.

Don Nieto

John Plaster

Facing down the camera with the cold stare of death, future Medal of Honor recipient SSgt Franklin Miller and his SOG recon team, pinned down at this time by enemy fire, await extraction by the Green Hornets. In supporting SOG, the Hornets suffered 13 of their 19 helicopter losses in direct combat.

In December 1967, the Air Force beefed up its helicopter force in both numbers and capability, with the establishment of the CH-3-equipped 21st Helicopter Squadron at Nakhon Phanom.[55] Initially involved in placing seismic sensors and "road watch" teams along the Ho Chi Minh Trail, the 21st began its first Prairie Fire missions in late 1968.[56]

Further organizational changes took place so that by 1970 the Green Hornets were equipped exclusively with UH-1s, while the Dust Devils began transitioning from the CH-3 Jolly Green Giant to the much more powerful CH-53C Super Jolly Green Giant. The massive CH-53 proved a real workhorse, with three times the payload and twice the power of the CH-3.[57]

The Dust Devils normally used two CH-53s for each SOG infiltration and exfiltration mission. For these operations, the "low bird" inserted or extracted the team while the "high bird" orbited nearby to complete the mission should the first aircraft encounter trouble. By this stage of the

James Fleming and John Plaster

The submachine gun with supresser, grenages, handgun, and other equipment carried by legendary recon team leader, SFC Jerry "Mad Dog" Shriver.

Jerry Gilbert

A CH-53 "Knife" from the 21st SOS lands in North Vietnam in 1971 to extract a small group of fully armed defectors guarded only by one "friendly," the other having been killed by the same defectors the night before this pickup. The unusually circular LZ appears to have been blown open from the surrounding jungle by a 15,000-pound BLU-82 "Daisy Cutter" bomb dropped from a C-130.

Jerry Gilbert

May Day! Moments before, this single-engined Air America plane lost all engine power obviously in broad daylight—but not so obviously right over the Ho Chi Minh Trail! This photo was taken from a 21st Knife as it followed the Pilatus Porter down for immediate extraction of pilot and passenger from one of the most dangerous pieces of real estate in the world in 1971.

war, both experience and high aircrew skill levels had nearly perfected the insertion/extraction tactics at the landing zone. Steep, high-speed approaches and departures were made to/from the LZ by CH-53s carrying armor plating and miniguns. Fighter escort aircraft, preferably the tough and highly accurate A-1, were also a standard feature. The practices paid off, as the 21st lost only one CH-53 (February 1971) to combat in the Prairie Fire target areas of Laos.[58]

By the early 1970s, the Dust Devils found themselves fighting in a role for which they had never been intended. It took place in Laos, in support of the irregular forces of Hmong general Vang Pao, America's primary ally in the country. Combining their airlift capabilities with that of other USAF assets and Air America's H-34s, the 21st flew a variety of airmobile assault and cargo missions in support of the irregulars. In June 1969, for example, 10 helos from the 20th SOS and 21st SOS, three HH-53s from the Air Rescue Service, and 11 Air America H-34s formed an ad hoc aerial task force to evacuate a 350-man Thai unit in two hours.[59] Other such missions became routine in Laos, as well as large-scale helicopter evacuations of civilian refugees.

Remaining at Nakhon Phanom after the American withdrawal from Laos, the 21st was called upon to play a key role in the chaotic evacuation of American citizens from Saigon (Operation Frequent Wind) and a similar operation (Eagle Pull) from the American Embassy staff in Phnom Penh, Cambodia. As dramatic as these

Jerry Gilbert

Knife crewmen race to the plane to pull two Americans from the wreckage before the North Vietnamese react to this "golden opportunity" in their own backyard. The "Dust Devils" CH-53 had been in the immediate area on an unrelated SOG recon team extraction when this plane went down.

operations seemed at the time, however, the Dust Devils could not possibly foresee that their bloodiest challenge still lay ahead.

A Bitter Postscript to the War

In May 1975, the US became involved in what has since become popularly known simply as the "*Mayaguez* Incident." The historical events are fairly straightforward. On 12 May, Cambodian gunboats seized a US vessel, the *Mayaguez,* in international waters, forcing its crew to leave the ship for an unknown destination. In the immediate confusion that followed, the US suspected that the crew might be held on the small Cambodian island of Koh Tang, 30 miles off the Cambodian mainland. Initial reports suggested the crew was being held by "only 20 Cambodian irregulars."[60] As the Dust Devils and others were about to discover to their tragic cost, the figures on enemy strength were woefully understated.

The day after the seizure, the 21st launched eight CH-53s (all its flyable aircraft) from its base at Nakhon Phanom to U-Tapao RTAFB in southern Thailand. Tragedy struck almost at once, as one of the giant craft went down in flight because of mechanical failure, killing the five-man crew and all 18 USAF security police aboard. Early on the morning of 15 May, five Dust Devils flying with their long-standing radio call sign "Knife" and three Air Rescue HH-53s carrying a combined total of 175 marines approached two separate LZs on Koh Tang Island.[61] The three Air Rescue helos managed to land their troops only after repeated attempts over a matter of hours. The situation for the 21st, however, was resolved much more quickly and bloodily.

Flying the first helo onto Koh Tang was Knife 21, flown by the squadron commander. It had no sooner touched down than it was hit by machine-gun, rocket, and mortar fire. Pulling away on its only remaining operational engine as the last of the marines cleared the tail ramp, the badly riddled helo stayed aloft for less than a mile before ditching into the sea. Knife 22, flying the number two position in the formation, was raked by enemy fire so intense it turned back to Thailand with its troops still aboard. Knife 23 was disabled on the beach, its crew trapped with its marine landing party. Knife 31 never made it to the beach, exploding in flight over the shallow waters leading up to the beach landing zone. Thirteen aircrew and marines were killed in the explosion. Knife 32 unloaded its marines and made it back to Thailand, so badly shot up it was grounded.

Three hours after the assault had begun, a Thai fishing vessel with a white flag prominently displayed from its mast was intercepted after it sailed from the Cambodian mainland.[62] Aboard was the entire crew of the *Mayaguez.* The next day, the 21st launched its last two flyable CH-53s, in conjunction with the Air Rescue helos, and managed to withdraw the remaining 131 airmen and marines from Koh Tang.[63]

One measure of the vicious fighting that broke out at Koh Tang is found in the subsequent awarding of two Air Force Crosses to Knife crewmen and the multitude of Purple Hearts and Silver Stars awarded to many others for their actions that day.

In retrospect, SOG's private air force can justifiably claim it never succumbed to the popular but misplaced myth that the aircraft's pilots are simply the "bus drivers up front." The Air Force has a long and proud tradition that claims its mission is "to fly and *fight.*" Contemporary modifications to that claim made by a recent USAF chief of staff notwithstanding, the Air Force will not likely find a better example of its proud heritage than that provided by SOG's special operations aircrews who had to be pulled from the fight after the last bell kept ringing.

Notes

1. Harve Saal, *SOG: MACV Studies and Observations Group,* vol. 1, *Historical Evolution* (Ann Arbor, Mich.: Edwards Brothers, 1990), 79.

2. Sedgwick Tourison, *Secret Army, Secret War: Washington's Tragic Spy Operation in North Vietnam* (Annapolis, Md.: Naval Institute Press, 1995), 112.

3. John L. Plaster, *SOG: The Secret Wars of America's Commandos in Vietnam* (New York: Simon & Schuster, 1997), 23. See also Maj Gen John K. Singlaub, USA, Retired, with Malcolm McConnell, *Hazardous Duty: An American Soldier in the Twentieth Century* (New York: Summit Books, 1991), 294.

4. Tourison, 111.

5. Ibid., 112.

6. Ray L. Bowers, *The United States Air Force in Southeast Asia: Tactical Airlift* (Washington, D.C.: Office of Air Force History, 1982), 429. See also History, Special Warfare Center (U), 1 January–30 June 1965, page number obliterated. (Secret) Information extracted is unclassified (declassified by the Air Force Historical Research Agency, 19 October 1994).

7. Philip D. Chinnery, *Any Time Any Place: A History of USAF Air Commandos and Special Operations* (Annapolis, Md.: Naval Institute Press, 1994), 106.

8. Col Bob Pinard, USAF, Retired, former commander of the 90th SOS, interview with the author, 19 October 1996. See also Bowers, 429.

9. Plaster, 24.

10. Bowers, 429

11. Peter M. Hurd, former First Flight officer, interview with the author, 24 October 1996.

12. MSgt Bert Cartwright Jr., USAF, Retired, former C-130E Blackbird flight engineer, interview with author, 20 October 1996.

13. Ibid.

14. Plaster, 71.

15. Ibid.

16. Cartwright interview.

17. USAF Flight Order, Detachment 1, 314th Tactical Airlift Wing, 29 December 1967. Received from Col Bob Pinard, USAF, Retired, and in author's possession.

18. Tourison, 331–40.

19. Plaster, 69.

20. Tourison, 109.

21. Charles T. Kamps Jr., *The History of the Vietnam War* (New York: The Military Press, 1988), 104.

22. Tourison, 217.

23. Singlaub, 303.

24. Ibid., 304.

25. Ibid., 100–9.

26. Plaster, 299.

27. Ibid., 301.

28. Ibid.

29. Ibid., 290–312.

30. Bowers, 431.

31. Col Bob Pinard, USAF, Retired, former commander 90th SOS, telephone interview with the author, 11 February 1997.

32. Ibid.

33. Plaster, 339.

34. Saal, 106.

35. Chinnery, 120.

36. Ibid., 109.

37. Ibid.

38. Ibid.

39. Saal, vol. 3, 54.

40. Ibid.

41. Plaster, 340

42. Marshall Harrison, *A Lonely Kind of War: Forward Air Controller, Vietnam* (Novato, Calif.: Presidio Press, 1989), title page.

43. Ibid., 104.

44. Ibid., 214.

45. Ibid., 259.

46. Plaster, 109.

47. Bowers, 235–36.

48. Ibid., 236.

49. Chinnery, 110.

50. Bowers, 455.

51. Ibid., 425.

52. Lt Col Warren "Smokey" Hubbard, USAF, Retired, telephone interview with author, 29 January 1997.

53. Wayne Murtza, "Covertly into Cambodia," *Air Enthusiast* 32 (December 1986–April 1987): 26.

54. Ibid., 28.

55. Ibid.

56. Bowers, 455.

57. Chinnery, 163.

58. Bowers, 428.

59. Ibid., 458.

60. Ibid., 645.

61. Ibid.

62. Chinnery, 220.

63. Ibid.

Son Tay

Barbara's Secret

It looks like Son Tay is empty...the prisoners have been moved.

Lt Gen Donald V. Bennett
Director, Defense Intelligence Agency,
24 hours prior to launch of Operation Kingpin

We are going to rescue 70 American prisoners of war...from Son Tay. This is something American prisoners of war have a right to expect from their fellow soldiers. The target is 23 miles west of Hanoi.

Col Arthur D. "Bull" Simons
Deputy Commander,
Joint Contingency Task Group Ivory Coast,
four hours prior to launch of Operation Kingpin

Don't let anyone tell you that this mission was a failure. We will learn, as the results develop, that many benefits will accrue as a result of having done this.

Adm John S. McCain
Commander in Chief, Pacific Command,
24 hours after Operation Kingpin was terminated

Following his shootdown over North Vietnam, Lt Col J. L. Hughes, USAF, is paraded through Hanoi for propaganda photographers. Once the cameras were gone, the fate of the already-injured airman would take a decided turn for the worse at the hands of his captors.

Vice President Richard M. Nixon made a brief visit to the obscure village outside Hanoi during a tour of northern Vietnam in late 1953.[1] Today, Son Tay is the home of scenic Kings Island Golf & Country Club, a beautiful, world-class golf course with a glossy brochure that invites prospective English-speaking visitors, "If you are planning a trip to Hanoi, please call us."[2] Kings Island's highly exclusive membership roster includes at least two retired US Air Force generals. Both dreaded and hated by the North Vietnamese during the war, the now-welcomed presence of these two former Air Commandos speaks volumes about the human capacity for both war and forgiveness.

But for all the civility and grace these two images summon forth in the mind's eye, there are darker images of Son Tay from which the mind retreats in horror. These images of despair come from the Americans who fought for their lives and their sanity in the POW camp activated at Son Tay in May 1968. Mostly Air Force and Navy aircrew downed over North Vietnam, the Americans were held in isolation and tortured beyond comprehension for years.

For most POWs, their pain ceased only when they were beaten into unconsciousness; for others, only when they died of neglect and injuries inflicted at the hands of their captors. The nightmarish world of the Americans was one in which deliberately and continuously delivered pain killed 11 of every 100 prisoners in captivity before the war was over.[3]

At first with disbelief, then with helpless anguish, Americans learned of the stories written by foreign journalists detailing the agony of the American POWs. The worst fears of Americans were seemingly confirmed on major TV networks as they watched badly injured airmen forced to march through mobs of frenzied North Vietnamese civilians screaming for American blood. As the American public's fury over the maltreatment of its POWs mounted, so inevitably did pressure on the Nixon administration to "do something."

The personal anguish over the POWs was brought home directly and forcefully into the White House in late 1969, when President Richard M. Nixon held his first private audience with 26 wives of POWs. Visibly shaken from their quiet despair during the meeting, Nixon turned to Secretary of Defense Melvin Laird to query the Pentagon for "some unconventional rescue ideas."[4]

The Players

The Pentagon's response evolved into one of the most spectacular, complex, and controversial military operations ever conducted in the 300-year history of American arms. And after military prowess and heroism failed to produce the desired results, Washington's time-honored hunt for scapegoats resumed with a vengeance. Beyond Washington, political shock waves from the mission reverberated through the international power centers of Moscow, Peking, and, of course, Hanoi as well.

The top secret mission, code-named "Kingpin," had its genesis in a startling discovery that occurred in May 1970, six months before the raid. President Nixon would later take a personal briefing on the mission in the White House, but that May the real action was taking place at Fort Belvoir, Virginia, just 15 miles south of the president's Oval Office. Located in an isolated section of Belvoir, the shabby wooden building hardly seemed worth the rolls of barbed-wire providing its security from unwanted visitors. Only the small sign outside indicating its occupants as the 1127th USAF Special Activities Squadron gave a clue as to its special importance.

Inside, a small group of intelligence analysts, all specialists in POW activities, stared in disbelief at the photos before them. After nearly two years of searching, it appeared they had discovered at last the location of a long-rumored POW camp in North Vietnam. It was located in the small village of Son Tay, some 23 miles northwest of Hanoi. Staring through their magnification scopes at the aerial photography, the analysts were stunned to see discreet physical signals from the POW compound—signals asking for an urgent rescue mission!* It was the first time in the war the analysts had seen anything like it.

After additional aerial photography seemed to confirm the analysts' initial assessment, the team immediately sent a high-priority intelligence summary through secret channels to the Pentagon. Two weeks later, the summary landed on the desk of US Army brigadier general Donald D. Blackburn, who was special assistant for counterinsurgency and special activities (SACSA) to the chairman, Joint Chiefs of Staff (CJCS).

Keenly aware of both the president's request for "some unconventional rescue ideas" and the likely political reaction to a combat operation so close to Hanoi, the JCS consumed two full months reviewing rescue feasibility studies. Finally, on 8 August the CJCS authorized activation of Joint Contingency Task Group (JCTG) Ivory Coast, the ad hoc team that would, only if authorized personally by the president, launch Operation Kingpin right into the outskirts of Hanoi's suburbs.

Designating General Blackburn's SACSA as the office of primary responsibility, the JCS proceeded to make two critical decisions affecting Kingpin. First, it picked superb combat-proven Air Force and Army talent to lead the mission. Second, it gave this talent the freedom it needed to plan, organize, and train for the mission as it saw fit.

Selected to command the JCTG was Brig Gen Leroy J. Manor of the Air Force. Then commanding USAF's special operations forces at Eglin AFB, Florida, the general was not only the highest ranking unconventional warfare officer in the Air Force but a highly experienced fighter pilot whose combat record went back to World War II. Quiet, precise in manner, and effective, Manor enjoyed the complete confidence of his superiors. Underneath his suave exterior, however, General Manor had other qualities that surfaced when necessary. He was, as a senior JCTG officer put it, "the steel hand in a velvet glove."[5]

US Army colonel Arthur D. "Bull" Simons, then on the staff of XVIII Airborne Corps at Fort Bragg, North Carolina, became the JCTG's deputy commander. The colonel had earned the nickname "Bull" with his own combat record going back to World War II, not to mention the massive face, barrel chest, and huge hands that intimidated so many in his presence. No one ever accused Simons of the smooth efficiency for which Manor was known, but the man was a natural combat leader whose fierce appearance belied an excellent mind. General Blackburn described Simons succinctly: "When Bull Simons undertook an operation . . . the research and planning behind it were meticulous."[6]

A measure of the remarkable freedom and confidence granted these two officers by the CJCS was later acknowledged by General Manor, "We had practically a blank check when we left there [Office of the CJCS]. It is the only time in my 36 years of active duty that somebody gave me a job, simply stated, and the resources with which to do it, and let me go do it!"[7]

If the JCS believed it had picked good leaders in Manor and Simons, so evidently did the airmen and Green Berets who responded to the call for volunteers in numbers far beyond mission requirements. As obviously no details of the mis-

*The POWs hung their laundry out to dry in a pattern that suggested "SAR," the military acronym for "search & rescue." And the alphabetical "rescue" letter *K*, apparently dug into the dirt by the prisoners further reinforced the analysts' perception the POWs were attempting to communicate. Other signals, still classified a quarter-century later, were reportedly used as well.

sion could be revealed, the men were asked to volunteer blindly, even after being told the mission would entail "considerable risk." As one JCTG officer observed: "It was sort of by invitation only. . . . The invitation didn't indicate when the dance would be over, but it did mention it would be dangerous."[8]

From Duke to Takhli

Moving swiftly, the JCTG began training on 20 August, less than two weeks after its activation. The vast training ranges and the presence of both special operations and Aerospace Rescue and Recovery Service forces at Eglin AFB made the Florida panhandle the chosen area to prepare for the mission. At Eglin's Auxiliary Field 3 (Duke Field), the Ivory Coast group threw itself into an exhausting two-and-a-half month training regime. Working through the Defense Intelligence Agency, the JCTG received additional photography of the Son Tay compound through both high-altitude SR-71 Blackbirds and low-altitude Buffalo Hunter photoreconnaissance drones.[9]

Early plans to build a full-scale 140 x 185-foot replica of Son Tay for training purposes had to be scuttled after the group learned Soviet Cosmos 355 photoreconnaissance satellites passed over Eglin twice a day.[10] An easily disassembled lumber and target cloth substitute was used to simulate Son Tay's walls and buildings, and daylight training was limited to the few "satellite free" hours available.[11] In addition, US intelligence built an elaborate small-scale model of the camp for "wargaming" the actual assault. The top secret model was code-named "Barbara."*

In fairly short order, the Ivory Coast team determined the weather, terrain, and North Vietnamese enemy order-of-battle factors that would drive the training program at Eglin. Son Tay would be a night assault, emphasizing surprise and shock action at close quarters. Good weather for aerial refueling was essential, as well as enough (but not too much) moonlight to identify the target without highlighting the aerial force for enemy gunners. Precision in the air and on the ground was mandatory, as the tolerance for error in such a small force was virtually nil.

By this time, Lt Col Warner A. Britton, an Air Force member of both the original feasibility study group and the mission planning staff,** had culled some two dozen highly experienced helicopter crewmen from the Aerospace Rescue and Recovery Training Center,*** located at Eglin.[12] Headquarters, Aerospace Rescue and Recovery Service would also provide the crewmen for the two HC-130P aerial tankers that would refuel the helicopters over Laos prior to their low-level dash into North Vietnam. From the special operations force at Eglin would come the A-1 strike pilots and the crews for the two C-130E Combat Talon aircraft, the latter serving as pathfinders for the force right up to its target.

Many years after the war, with the aid of much improved technology, the Air Force's special operations aircrews would perfect the dangerous tactics used by the Son Tay airmen. But in 1970, a prudent flyer observing the training would have been justified in wondering whether even this mission warranted such risks. One of the mission planners described Ivory Coast's nightly activity over Eglin's dark swamps:

---

*The model is now on display in the Air Force Museum at Wright-Patterson AFB, Ohio.

**Britton was the only member of Ivory Coast to have participated in the mission all the way from the original 12-man study group to the actual assault on the compound. At Son Tay he flew Colonel Simons's Support Element in HH-53 call-sign "Apple 1."

***The Aerospace Rescue and Recovery Training Center had the only heavy-lift, air-to-air refuelable HH-53 and H-3 helicopters (the type selected for the raid) then stationed in the US.

Air Commando Association

Code-named "Barbara," this scale model of the Son Tay POW compound was built by US intelligence as a training aid for Operation Ivory Coast raiders. As the postmission hunt for political scapegoats picked up steam in Washington, the organization that built Barbara leaked the news that it had not been involved in the premission planning!

> Aircrew training began with night formation [flying] involving dissimilar aircraft [two types of C-130s; three types of helicopters and fighters] . . . low level was introduced as well as objective area tactics which included helicopter landings and extractions; airdrops by the C-130s of flares, fire-fight simulators and napalm; and close air support by the A-1s.[13]

In 77 days of training, the aircrews flew 1,054 hours, mostly under the conditions described above, without a single scratch to any of the aircraft.[14] (A few bad frights maybe, but no damage to the outside of man or plane!) It was a good omen, and the performance fully warranted the enthusiastic approval of JCS observers who declared Ivory Coast ready after watching two five-and-one-half-hour-long full-profile mission rehearsals.[15]

On 10 November, just 10 days before the mission, two C-130Es departed Eglin to begin Ivory Coast's long deployment across the Pacific Ocean to Takhli Royal Thai Air Force Base. Four days later, the bulk of the men and material were lifted out via four C-141 jet transports for the two-day deployment to Takhli.[16] As this movement was going on, Manor was busy adding some vital "insurance" to the upcoming mission.

By 1970, the Hanoi-Haiphong urban area possessed the densest (and most proficient) concentration of antiaircraft defenses in the world. To fly down the throat of such defenses even in a night surprise raid required some obvious precautions. These precautions came in the shape of F-105G Wild Weasel fighters—specialists in attacking surface-to-air (SAM) missile sites with antiradiation

Air Commando Association

With the entire compound measuring only 140 x 185 feet, the "landing zone" targeted for the HH-3's crash-landing point was little more than the size of a volley-ball court. The intentional destruction of the helicopter was the price paid to ensure the Assault Element could reach the POW cells before the guards had the chance to kill their prisoners.

missiles that homed in on the SAM site's own search radars.

In the long chance North Vietnamese MiG fighters would make a rare night appearance, F-4 fighters were also added as a protective umbrella, or combat air patrol (MIGCAP) over the raiders. Finally, the United States Navy would put on a massive deception operation with fighters from Carrier Task Force-77, dropping illumination flares* over North Vietnam's most sensitive coastal areas.

Taking off from seven airfields and three aircraft carriers, the aerial armada for this mission would ultimately total over 116 aircraft before the raid was finished.[17] Just to keep this massive force in the air required 12 Strategic Air Command KC-135 tankers, eight for the MIGCAP and another four for the Navy jets over the Gulf of Tonkin.[18]

*Under then-current US policy, no ordnance (bombs) could be dropped on North Vietnam north of the 19th parallel. This unilateral US policy, declared nearly two years earlier, spared North Vietnam's capitol, major harbor, and other critical targets from US attack.

Back at Takhli, bitter news awaited nearly half the Army raiders present, as the final assault force was pared down from the 100 men present to the 56 considered the minimum essential force to accomplish the mission. The US Army UH-1 helicopter crew that had trained since the beginning with Ivory Coast at Eglin also got its "lay-off" message. The decision had been made to use the Air Force's larger twin-engined HH-3 helicopter to carry the 14-man assault team that would stun the prison guards by crash-landing directly into the prison compound, a volley-ball-court-sized area surrounded by trees.

With the final lineup established, Ivory Coast needed two more decisions to launch Operation Kingpin. The first would come from the White House, as President Nixon reserved for himself the final approval for mission launch.* The second would come from Manor, who upon receiving the president's approval would pick the exact launch date based on weather over the target.

As simple as the latter decision might seem at this late stage, Mother Nature stepped in to put the general through another (but not his last) agony. Bad weather developing over North Vietnam threatened to scrub the mission that was from the start totally dependent on a very narrow set of weather criteria. Receiving the president's approval on the 18th, Manor took a calculated gamble on a particular 24-hour weather window and set the launch date for 20 November, 24 hours ahead of the original schedule.

So tight was mission security that not until 1600 hours on the 20th were all raiders finally informed of the target and the mission. Pent-up energy from months of training exploded in applause as the national-level significance of their task spread over the assembled group.

Execute!

At 2200 hours on the 20th, the raiders were flown eastward from their staging base at Takhli to Udorn RTAFB, their launching point from Thailand. At Udorn, the force split up to board three helicopters: the Assault Element on the HH-3 and the larger Support and Command Elements on two separate HH-53s. These three were joined by three other HH-53s—one dedicated as a "gunship" to knock out Son Tay's two guard towers, the final two serving as backup flareships and transport home for the 50-plus POWs expected at Son Tay.

Within an hour of the raiders' arrival at Udorn, the heliborne force was airborne, following two Ivory Coast HC-130P tankers leading them over Laos for the aerial refueling leg. Refueling silently, the helos watched their tankers peel away, to be replaced by a Combat Talon that would lead them into North Vietnam and to the very doorsteps of Son Tay, 337 miles from their departure point at Udorn. Both lead and backup Talons were specially equipped with forward looking infrared navigation equipment and no less than three navigators in each plane to ensure absolute pinpoint accuracy.[19]

As the Talon-helo flight departed Laos heading eastward, a second Talon was then leading a flight of five A-1s to a rendezvous with the helos. With the linkup completed, the Talon-led force continued eastward, flying low to slip underneath enemy radars. Above them, the MIGCAP F-4s and Wild Weasel F-105s were already slipping into their predetermined positions.

Like a pack of wolves moving silently through the forest with total concentration on its doomed quarry, this force of heavily armed and dangerous men moved steadily through the night sky

*Without much hope, President Nixon had made one last public appeal to North Vietnam to negotiate the release of American POWs. As in previous years, North Vietnam's response alternated between stony silence or bitter propaganda tirades.

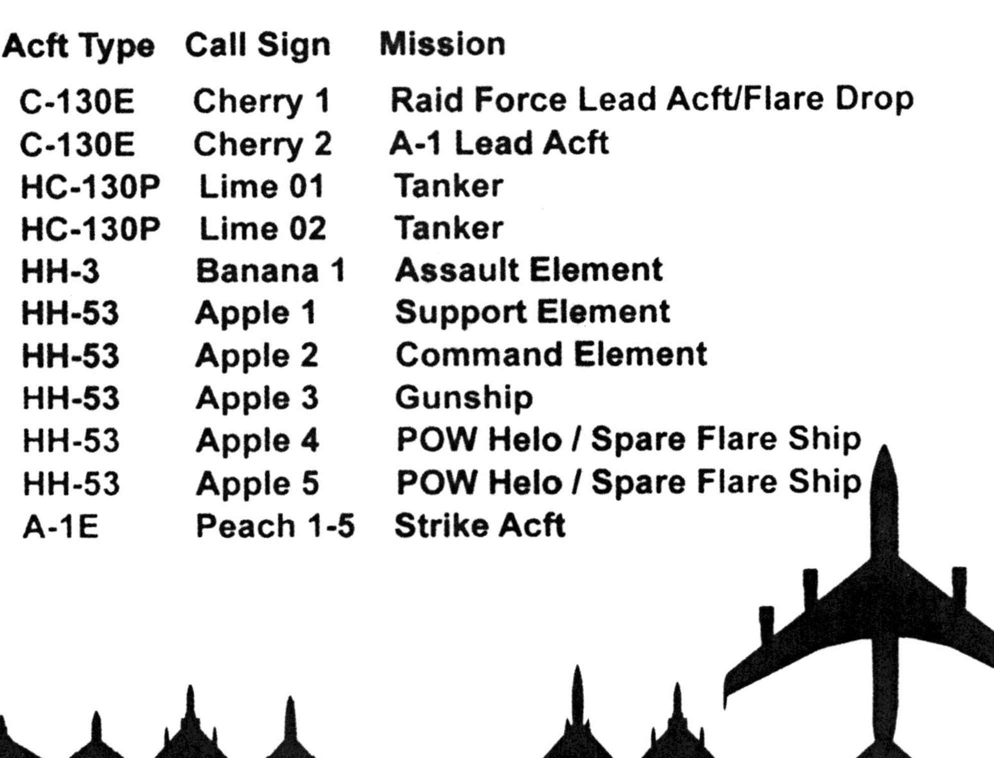

Acft Type	Call Sign	Mission
C-130E	Cherry 1	Raid Force Lead Acft/Flare Drop
C-130E	Cherry 2	A-1 Lead Acft
HC-130P	Lime 01	Tanker
HC-130P	Lime 02	Tanker
HH-3	Banana 1	Assault Element
HH-53	Apple 1	Support Element
HH-53	Apple 2	Command Element
HH-53	Apple 3	Gunship
HH-53	Apple 4	POW Helo / Spare Flare Ship
HH-53	Apple 5	POW Helo / Spare Flare Ship
A-1E	Peach 1-5	Strike Acft

A-6 A-7 F-4 F-8

Primary U.S.Navy Support (CTF-77)

F-105 F-4 KC-135

Primary U.S.Air Force Support

Graphics by Wayne Thompson

Source: Comdr William H. McRaven, USN, "The Theory of Special Operations" (graduate thesis, Naval Postgraduate School, 1993)

towards Son Tay. The 56 raiders were armed with no less than 111 machine guns, grenade launchers, rifles, and pistols, not to mention the demolitions. Every Green Beret had also been issued a combat knife, as well as some stone-cold command guidance from the Bull:

> You are to let nothing, nothing, interfere with the operation. . . . Our mission is to rescue prisoners, not to take prisoners. . . . If we walk into a trap, don't dream of walking out of North Vietnam. . . . We will back up to the Song Con River . . . let them come across the open ground and we'll make them pay for every foot across.[20]

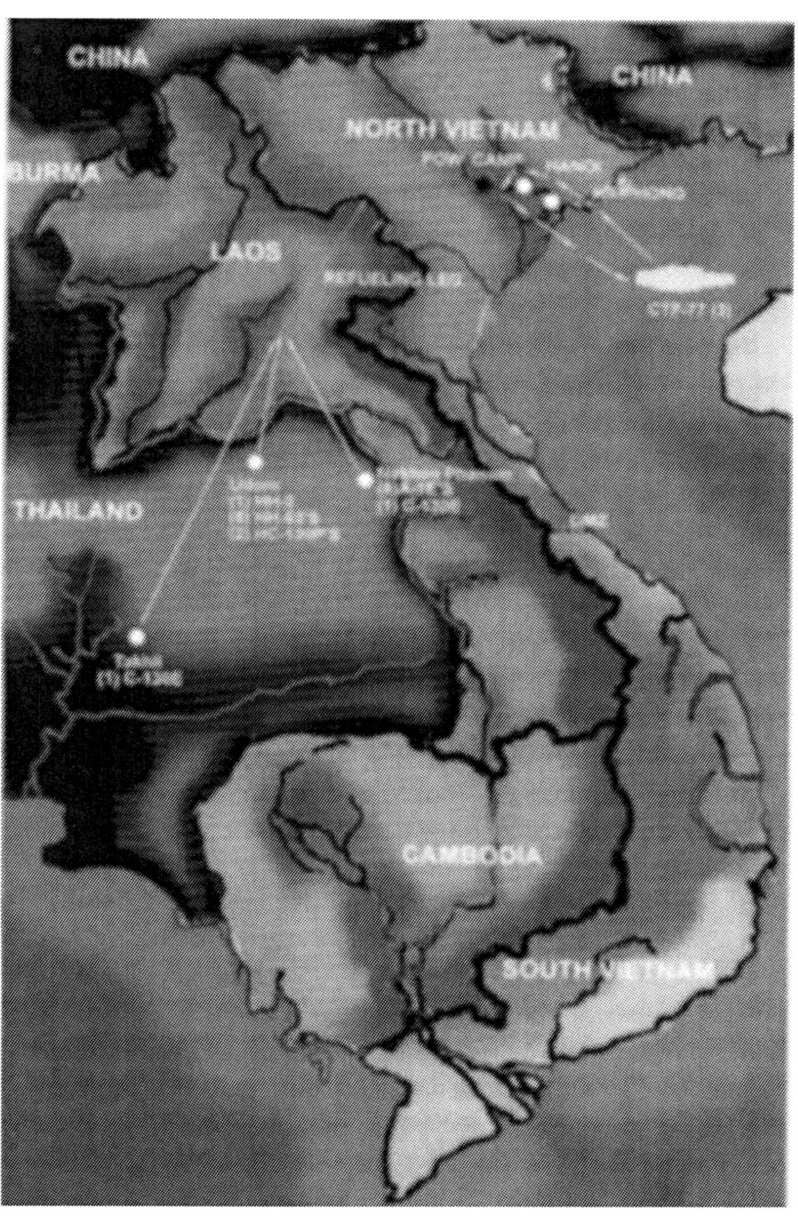

Graphics by Wayne Thompson

"Like a pack of wolves moving silently through the forest with total concentration on its doomed quarry, this force of heavily armed and dangerous men moved steadily through the night sky towards Son Tay." The 56 Army raiders were armed with no less than 111 personal weapons plus explosive charges for the foray that brought them and their aircrews within 23 miles of Hanoi.

Three and a half miles west of the camp, the lead Talon radioed a final course correction to the helos, then pulled ahead up to 1,500 feet to drop illumination flares over the POW camp. Seeing the effective deployment of the flares, the two HH-53 backup flareships (Apple 4 and 5) diverted to their holding area on an island in a lake* to await a call-in for POW pickup. Apple 3, the HH-53 "gunship," began descending toward the camp, followed in turn by Banana 1 with the Assault Element, then Apple 1 and 2 in trail with the Support Element and Command Element, respectively. At this moment, the plan started to unravel. As the copilot on Apple 2 later recalled:

*The island where the two HH-53s waited is now the site of the Lakeside Course at the Kings Island Golf & Country Club described in the opening paragraph of this story.

> As we neared our objective, I sensed we were not going the right way to the Son Tay camp. . . . The amazing thing to me at the time, and remains so, is that no one had the forethought to break radio silence and say so! Indeed, Apple 3 had almost taken the [wrong] camp under fire, discovered his error in time, and turned north to the correct place.[21]

Recovering from his mistake, Apple 3 flew another 400 meters northward to obliterate the two guard towers at Son Tay with its miniguns as planned. Following Apple 3, Banana 1 slammed into the camp's tiny courtyard, chopping down some unexpectedly large trees "like a big lawn mower" before delivering the Assault Element less than 50 feet from the POW cells.[22] What neither Apple 3 nor the Assault Element knew was that something dreadfully wrong was happening behind them. Only one of the two helicopters following them had reached Son Tay.

In taking their eyes off Apple 3 and Banana 1 to pick out their own touch-down point outside the darkened compound, the pilots of Apple 1 (the third helicopter in line carrying Simons's Support Element) missed the first two helos veering off toward the Son Tay compound. As Apple 1 touched down at the wrong place, the pilots of Apple 2 (the fourth helicopter in line carrying the Command Element) overflew it and continued on to Son Tay in radio silence. In the last few seconds before arriving at Son Tay, the Command Element leader was notified Simons's helicopter was missing.

Even before the Assault and Command Elements landed 400 yards away at Son Tay, Simons and the 21 other raiders in the Support Element poured out of Apple 1 into a compound labeled simply on their target area photos as a "secondary school." As Apple 1 flew off to its nearby holding area, a nasty shock awaited the Support Element.

Apple 1's landing had an effect on the compound much like someone kicking over a hornet's nest. From seemingly everywhere, darkened forms spilled out of the buildings, firing on the run into the American intruders. It was an infantryman's worst nightmare and happening way too fast to call for the A-1s overhead. Something else was wrong, too.

These soldiers were much more heavily armed than those predicted at Son Tay, and much taller than any North Vietnamese these American combat veterans had ever before encountered—"5-foot-10 to 6-feet tall, Oriental, not wearing the normal NVA dress, but instead . . . T-shirts and fitted dark undershorts."[23] While the nationality of the troops was never identified, or at least publicly released, it was at the moment obviously a moot point for those dodging all the hot lead coming their way.

Realizing the error, Simons immediately called for the return of Apple 1 and extraction even as his men counterattacked the compound. In a masterpiece of understatement, the laconic Simons would later remark that his Support Element attacked "with great violence."[24] Apparently so. Nine minutes after its insertion at the "secondary school," Simons's team was back aboard Apple 1 enroute to Son Tay. Behind them, the 22 raiders left the compound burning "like a Roman candle," the flames casting eerie shadows and a yellowish glow over the estimated 100 to 200 enemy dead and wounded littering its grounds.[25]

"Let nothing, nothing, interfere with the operation. . . . Our mission is to rescue prisoners, not take prisoners."

Most of the estimated 55 North Vietnamese guards at Son Tay had already been killed or wounded by the Assault and Command Elements before Simons's team arrived.[26] The raiders then received the worst shock of all. The POW cells were found empty, the POWs gone. Apparently Son Tay had been a dry hole for some time, as the raiders had landed in waist-high grass. Simons immediately called for the HH-53s to extract the force.

Graphics by Wayne Thompson

Racing from the glare of a North Vietnamese surface-to-air missile exploding overhead, the last Kingpin HH-53 escapes the deserted POW camp moments before a demolitions charge inside HH-3 "Banana 1" explodes. Though no POWs were rescued, the political aftershock from this classic high-risk, high-gain mission generated a controversy that rocked both Hanoi and Washington.

But if there was a heartbreaking shortage of American POWs at Barbara, there was no shortage of heavily armed—and now thoroughly upset—North Vietnamese. As the A-1s began working over the area adjacent Son Tay, Soviet-made SA-2 missiles flashed skyward over Son Tay, seeking anything in the air. Approximately 16 of the telephone-pole-sized missiles were launched in a matter of minutes. The Wild Weasels fought back, firing eight Shrike antiradiation missiles into the launch sites.[27] Both sides drew blood before the American force left the area.*

Twenty-seven minutes after the HH-3 had crash-landed into Son Tay, the last group of raiders were back in the air with only two slightly wounded personnel. It was a long, long ride back to Thailand, with everyone agonizing over the effort and risk expended only to come home empty-handed. They were met at Udorn by Manor, who, after a quick debrief of the key personnel, communicated the mission results back to the JCS.

*Two of the eight Wild Weasels were damaged, with the crew of one having to bail out over Laos. Its two crew members were later rescued by Apples 4 and 5 performing in their secondary role of rescue aircraft.

The Scapegoats

Both Manor and Simons were directed to proceed back to Washington via the quickest means possible. Once there, they were to help the JCS and the Nixon administration answer a barrage of questions from the media and Congress, as well as counter North Vietnamese allegations the US had actually bombed Son Tay!

In the melee of public finger pointing over the ensuing few days, it became difficult at times to tell who was more hostile to the failed gamble. But if the North Vietnamese response was a given, the Nixon administration was shaken by the congressional hostility exhibited by some powerful Democrats to the attempted rescue.

Senator J. William Fulbright (D-Ark.), chairman of the Senate Foreign Relations Committee, virtually parroted North Vietnamese cries of outrage when he called the mission "a major escalation of the war . . . a very provocative act to mount a physical invasion [of North Vietnam]."[28] Senator Edward M. Kennedy (D-Mass.) "deplored the [Nixon] policy" that sent the raiders forth, while Senator Birch Bayh (D-Ind.) referred to the "John Wayne approach" in which the mission was undertaken.[29]

The government's military and civilian intelligence agencies were publicly vilified for their "intelligence failure" in not knowing the Son Tay camp was devoid of POWs. The public accusations were safe enough, as the finger pointers knew that by the very nature of its business the intelligence community is virtually forbidden to defend itself against such public attack. But if the allegations could be made without fear of public repudiation, the senior military and political officials responsible for the Son Tay raid knew even then that the allegations were fundamentally false.

The day before the raid, no less an authority than the director of the Defense Intelligence Agency, Lt Gen Donald V. Bennett, told both Blackburn and the chairman of the Joint Chiefs of Staff that late-breaking intelligence strongly suggested the Son Tay POWs had been moved to another camp earlier that year.[30] Bennett's information came from a "usually reliable" foreign source with credible access to POW-relevant information.

The source reported many POWs, including those at Son Tay, had been moved to a new camp until then unknown to the Americans. A photoreconnaissance of the alleged camp confirmed a significant enlargement of the facility to include guard towers that were currently manned.[31] Bennett's stunning news was delivered less than 24 hours after President Nixon had sent the mission launch-approval message to Manor.

With every passing hour, a giant, incredibly complex machine was moving inexorably toward launching Operation Kingpin. What neither Bennett, his DIA analysts, nor any other intelligence organization in the US could do was *prove* the absence of POWs at Son Tay. In fact, infrared imagery of the camp showed the presence of "someone" at the compound.

In Benjamin F. Schemmer's authoritative book *The Raid*, Blackburn described his reaction to this uncertain intelligence in exceptionally candid terms:

> Had I known [Son Tay held no POWs] I'd have had to call it off. But I didn't want to know the truth, I just wanted any shred of evidence to let us hang in there. It was bigger than getting the POWs out. There were too many people who didn't have the perception to understand what this was really about, or could accomplish.[32]

As if to reaffirm just how ugly decision making can really get "at the top," Bennett's news to the JCS chairman arrived with another bit of POW-related intelligence. Only a week before, antiwar protester Cora Weiss had publicly released the names fed to her by the North Vietnamese of six POWs who had died in captivity. Bennett had

Table 6
Operation Kingpin Chronology of Events

Date	*Event*
May 1968	Son Tay POW camp is activated.
May–Nov 1968	Fifty-five American POWs are transferred to Son Tay.
May 1970	1127th USAF Special Activity Squadron first confirms POW camp at Son Tay, as well as unique POW signals requesting urgent rescue.
2 June	Defense Intelligence Agency provides Special Assistant for Counterinsurgency and Special Activities, Joint Chiefs of Staff, with SR-71 photos confirming 1127th report.
10 June	With JCS authority, SACSA convenes 12-man rescue feasibility study group from all three military services, as well as from DIA.
10 July	JCS informed that a rescue effort at Son Tay is feasible.
?? July	Removal of POWs from Son Tay due to flooding of area. Removal is undetected by US intelligence.
8 August	JCS authorizes Joint Contingency Task Group Ivory Coast to "organize and train" for rescue mission designated Operation Kingpin. JCTG commander is Brig Gen Leroy J. Manor, USAF, commander of Special Operations Force, Eglin AFB, Florida, and deputy commander is Col Arthur D. Simons, USA, J-4, XVIII Airborne Corps, Fort Bragg, North Carolina.
20 August	JCTG mission training begins at Field 3 (Duke Field), Eglin AFB, Florida.
8 September	JCTG commander confirms mission feasibility to JCS.
1 November	Chief, JCS, authorizes JCTG commander to coordinate mission with senior (US) Army and Navy commanders in South Vietnam.
8 November	JCTG mission training at Duke Field terminates.
14 November	JCTG and logistical support arrive at Takhli Royal Thai Air Force Base, Thailand.
18 November	President Nixon approves JCTG's Operation Kingpin.
20 November	The mission is launched from Udorn RTAFB; recovered early A.M. hours of 21 November.

Source: Comdr William H. McRaven, USN, "The Theory of Special Operations" (graduate thesis, Naval Postgraduate School, 1993), 441–50.

just learned Weiss was about to release the names of 11 more such deaths.

Twenty-four hours before the launch of Kingpin, America's top military and civilian leadership were in an agonizing human quandary. The enormous risks in such high-stakes decisions are most assuredly glamorized most by those who have never had to make one. In the end, Bennett bowed to the enormous pressure not to be the one who said "no" to grasping at the "thin shred of evidence" waiting at Son Tay.

In the few short hours remaining, the situation was kicked up to the White House. President Nixon listened intently, then reaffirmed the go signal issued 24 hours earlier. No one in Ivory Coast was informed of these events taking place in Washington during the 24 hours prior to launch.

Son Tay with 20-20 Hindsight

In hindsight, it seems fair to say that Son Tay was neither the splendid example of operational excellence some have since proclaimed, nor the failure that seemed so obvious to most at the time. So what exactly was Son Tay? And what was it not?

Son Tay was a demonstration of what can be accomplished when excellent leadership is selected for a task, given the necessary resources, and the operational freedom necessary to execute that task. Adm Thomas H. Moorer and General Blackburn deserve every credit for their role here, as do Manor and Simons, who assured the same philosophy was given their subordinates.

Son Tay was a reaffirmation that the really good talent makes its own luck. The critical error in putting the Support Element down at the "secondary school" could easily have changed Son Tay from a disappointment to a disaster had Simons's group been pinned down or even overrun by the much superior forces they encountered. Instead, the raiders turned this error into a mission-saving plus by eliminating the major, and totally unexpected, threat to their mission.

The nationality of the heavily armed, oddly dressed troops encountered at the so-called secondary school has remained one of the most intriguing mysteries of the Son Tay legend for over a quarter of a century. After the raid, it was the question no one in the US government wanted to ask, for fear they couldn't stand the answer. Chinese? Russians? The options brought implications no one wanted to face; and the North Vietnamese weren't talking either. Not until 1997 has a just-published book submitted a plausible explanation as to the identity of these "mystery soldiers."

In his authoritative book *SOG: The Secret Wars of America's Commandos in Vietnam*, author and special operations veteran John L. Plaster describes the existence of a special NVA "counter-reconnaissance" unit dedicated to tracking down US Special Forces reconnaissance teams operating in Laos, North Vietnam, and Cambodia. This deadly special operations unit was manned from personnel handpicked from North Vietnam's only paratroop outfit, the Soviet-trained and superbly equipped 305th Airborne Brigade.[33] Both the 305th's base and the training school for the counterreconnaissance unit were the same: Son Tay.

Son Tay was a modern-day example of a concept in the profession of arms that goes back to biblical times. Its motivation and execution speak in terms more eloquent than words can express of the valor, loyalty, and commitment to those ideals that represent America and its military at their best.

Son Tay was not an "intelligence failure." To his credit, Secretary Laird said as much to various congressional committees and took the heat for their derisive response. The reality is that the mission could never have been planned or prepared

Air Commando Association

American POWs forced to appear as stage props for Jane Fonda's propaganda films in Hanoi were in a far stronger position to deflect her verbal assaults as a result of the earlier "failed" raid on Son Tay. Improvements in morale and the establishment of a surreptitious but effective chain of command in the POW camps followed North Vietnam's decision to bring Americans together in larger groups to discourage "another Son Tay."

for without excellent support from the intelligence community. To his discredit, the secretary could not or would not bring himself to tell the whole truth: the National Command Authorities had been briefed prior to the mission launch that no POWs would likely be found at Son Tay.

Son Tay underscored yet again why senior military and political leaders understandably cringe at the prospect of these high-risk, high-gain special operations. The historical success rate of these gambles is hardly reassuring to those who inevitably take the heat for authorizing their execution. The fact remains that the only thing these leaders can truly count on from missions such as Son Tay is that the political fallout will be enormous, taking directions not foreseen even by their advocates.

Son Tay generated tangible improvements in the conditions of the POWs' captivity. To discourage a repeat of Son Tay, the North Vietnamese concentrated their American captives in two large camps in downtown Hanoi.[34] As many POWs came together for the first time, the resultant improvements in communications and cohesion created a substantial and much-needed improvement in their morale.

Son Tay also allowed the senior US officers in the two remaining POW camps to establish surreptitious but effective command of the 591 POWs finally released three years later. The timing of these improvements was more critical than many knew at the time, as the POWs would later face an ordeal the likes of which no American prisoner in the history of this country had ever before suffered.

Jane Fonda's singular decision to personally harangue the vulnerable American POWs in their camps took the antiwar sentiment in America to an extreme to which no POW could possibly have been prepared. Those POWs forced to undergo her abuse as stage props for the filmed sessions endured a torture coming from a direction they did not expect. Those who refused to appear in such sessions were savagely beaten for their refusal.[35] Had it not been for Son Tay and the improvements it alone made possible in the POW camps, the impact of Fonda's personal actions on the debilitated prisoners could have been catastrophic.

Notes

1. James R. Arnold, *The First Domino: Eisenhower, the Military, and America's Intervention into Vietnam* (New York: William Morrison & Co., 1991), 127.
2. *Kings Island Golf & Country Club News*, June 1993, 3.
3. Benjamin F. Schemmer, *The Raid* (New York: Harper & Row, 1976), 13.
4. "Acting to Aid the Forgotten Men," *Time* 96, no. 23 (7 December 1970): 15–21.
5. Comdr William H. McRaven, USN, "The Theory of Special Operations" (graduate thesis, Naval Postgraduate School, 1993), 444.
6. Schemmer, 80.
7. McRaven, 462.
8. "Acting to Aid the Forgotten Men," 15–21.
9. McRaven, 449.
10. Schemmer, 76.
11. Ibid.
12. History, Aerospace Rescue and Recovery Service, 1 July 1970–30 June 1971, Annex, "The Son Tay Raid," 10.
13. Lt Gen Leroy J. Manor, USAF, Retired, "The Son Tay Raid: November 21, 1970," *Daedalus Flyer* 35, no. 4 (Winter 1995): 9.
14. Ibid.
15. Ibid.
16. Manor, 10.
17. McRaven, 479.
18. Earl H. Tilford Jr., *Search and Rescue in Southeast Asia* (Washington D.C.: Center for Air Force History, 1980), 108–9.
19. Ray L. Bowers, *The United States Air Force in Southeast Asia: Tactical Airlift* (Washington D.C.: Office of Air Force History, 1982), 431.
20. Schemmer, 159.
21. Manor, 14.
22. Schemmer, 167.
23. Ibid.
24. Ibid., 171.
25. Ibid. See also Manor, 13.
26. Schemmer, 172.
27. McRaven, 491.
28. Ibid., 190.
29. Ibid.
30. Schemmer, 140.
31. Ibid., 142–43.
32. Ibid., 220.
33. John L. Plaster, *SOG: The Secret Wars of America's Commandos in Vietnam* (New York: Simon & Schuster, 1997), 84–85.
34. Manor, 16.
35. Maj Gen John K. Singlaub, USA, Retired, with Malcolm McConnell, *Hazardous Duty: An American Soldier in the Twentieth Century* (New York: Summit Books, 1991), 350.

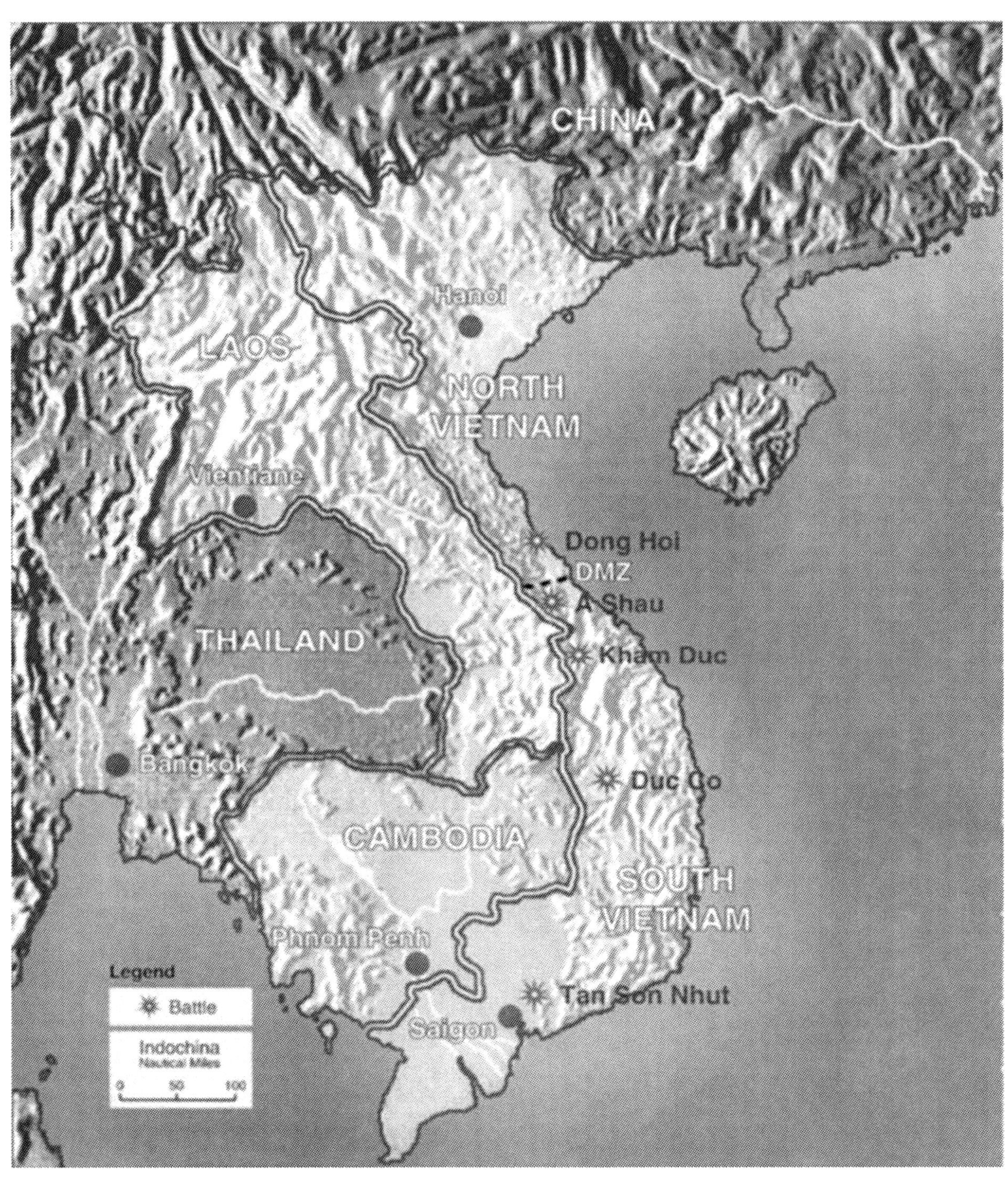

CHINA
Hanoi
LAOS
NORTH
VIETNAM
Vientiane
Dong Hoi
DMZ
A Shau
THAILAND
Kham Duc
Bangkok
Duc Co
CAMBODIA
SOUTH
VIETNAM
Phnom Penh
Legend
Battle
Tan Son Nhut
Saigon
Indochina
Nautical Miles
0
50
100

Medal of Honor

Air Commandos above and beyond the Call

Five of the 12 Air Force Medals of Honor awarded during the Vietnam War went to Air Commando/Special Operations personnel. Considering that even at the peak of their strength in Southeast Asia, the Air Commandos never accounted for more than 5 percent of the total Air Force effort, this remarkable record of valor underscores as nothing else can the dangerous world in which the Air Commandos fought and sometimes died at "the tip of the spear."

Maj Bernard F. Fisher

1st Air Commando Squadron

In the humid early-morning darkness of 9 March 1966, an entire North Vietnamese Army assault regiment slammed down on a remote Special Forces camp near South Vietnam's mountainous border with Laos. Mortar shells rained down on the small camp, quickly reducing critical defensive bunkers to rubble and temporarily disrupting the camp's vital communications lifeline to the outside world.

The camp, located in the Communist-dominated A Shau Valley, usually had only two kinds of weather: either rain or rain with fog. Having learned to their bitter cost what American airpower could do against them under clear skies, the NVA forces wisely scheduled their attacks during the worst possible weather.

Despite their precaution, however, the attack was momentarily stymied when a particularly determined Air Commando AC-47 managed to get in under the low-hanging clouds to fire its miniguns into the front ranks of the assault troops. But flying under the 400-foot cloud base also made the gunship an easy target. Concentrated NVA ground fire quickly disabled one engine, then blew the other entirely off its mount before driving the gunship into a hillside near the camp.*

Responding to the AC-47's last-minute distress call, fighters scrambled from Pleiku, Qui Nhon, and Nha Trang to join the fray. Maj Bernie Fisher, 1st Air Commando Squadron, was piloting one of the first propeller-driven A-1 Skyraiders to reach the camp. He and his wingman flew with priority orders to keep the downed AC-47 out of enemy hands by completely destroying the still partially intact gunship.

Quickly finishing off the AC-47, the two Skyraiders moved to cover two C-123 Providers parachuting medical supplies and ammunition into A Shau's increasingly desperate defenders. Hit hard by ground fire as they made their low-level drops, the Providers were lucky to escape from the valley. Major Fisher's flight, low on fuel, was also forced to abandon the camp and return to base for refueling.

*The story of this valiant but doomed AC-47 attack is told earlier ("The Dragonship") in this book.

With the next morning's weather only marginally better, Fisher's three-ship flight was ordered back into the deadly A Shau Valley. Arriving just as the camp was being overrun, Fisher's and two other A-1s immediately began strafing passes right up to the camp's last-ditch perimeter. So desperate was the plight of the remaining defenders that Fisher's flight attacked with their 20 mm cannon without first dropping their bombs, the standard procedure in ground attack missions. Picking up the Skyraiders' attack pattern, the NVA hit the number three A-1 piloted by Maj "Jump" Myers of the 602d Air Commando Squadron. With the Skyraider's engine dead and spewing fire at very low altitude, Myers had little choice but to ride his plane in.

USAF

A Special Forces proverb states, "You have not lived 'til you've almost died. For those who dare, life has special flavor the protected will never know." Air Commandos Bernie Fisher and "Jump" Myers minutes after returning from one of the most spectacular feats of airmanship in the annals of American history.

If the plane went into the surrounding jungle, Myers had little chance of surviving the crash. His only chance was the pierced-steel-planking (PSP) runway that served the camp . . . a runway now controlled by the North Vietnamese. Out of choices and altitude simultaneously, Myers jettisoned his bomb load into the jungle and made for the runway. Smashing down hard in a wheels-up landing, he skidded sideways nearly 600 feet before hitting an embankment and bursting into a fireball.[1] Overhead, Myers's wingman, also hit by ground fire, had been blinded and forced to leave the area. In moments Fisher had become the sole survivor in his flight.

Taking in this carnage, Fisher thought surely Myers had died in the crash and in fact reported this back to his airfield. But just then, the smoke cleared momentarily to reveal Myers running out of the inferno and into a nearby ditch. Fisher promptly asked a nearby Marine helicopter for a rescue pickup, then returned to the fight.

When 10 minutes passed with no chopper in sight, Fisher again called, only to learn the chopper was at least 20 minutes away—not good enough because NVA troops were only yards away from Myers. Twenty minutes might as well have been 20 days. With little time and perhaps less inclination to consider his odds, Fisher made the snap decision to rescue Myers himself.

Flying through the smoke and fire surrounding the camp, he broke into the clear just over the edge of the runway. In spite of the litter cluttering the strip and damage from mortar fire to the PSP runway itself, Fisher somehow avoided a crash of his own. Skidding as he braked hard, he finally brought the huge fighter to a stop near a fuel dump at the far end of the runway. Ignoring the damage to the rugged A-1's wings and tail from the runway debris, Fisher turned the aircraft around and headed back up the runway toward the burning wreckage of Myers's aircraft. Seeing Myers jump up as he passed by, Fisher braked his plane for the pickup.

As Fisher later recalled, sitting there waiting for Myers was the worst moment of all. Every second became an hour as he steeled himself to remain still amidst the chaos of blazing structures, smoke, machine-gun fire, and desperation that made up his entire world in that moment. "The enemy was so close I was afraid a couple of them might actually jump aboard my Skyraider before Myers could make it."[2] Of little comfort was his sudden realization that his wingmates, their ammunition already expended, were now making fake strafing runs around him with the dubious hope that this alone would keep the heads of the enemy down.

Myers made it to the A-1 only to find the propeller wash generated by the Skyraider's massive 18-cylinder, 2,700-horsepower engine was keeping him from mounting the wing. Seeing Myers's plight, Fisher momentarily throttled back, allowing Myers to clamber up the wing before spilling headfirst into the side-by-side, two-place cockpit. Without waiting for Myers to strap in, Fisher turned the plane around again and jammed the throttle against its forward stops. With Fisher holding the plane down until the last possible moment, the A-1 raced down the runway before leaping for the sky and safety. Following his return to home base, ground crews counted no fewer than 19 bullet holes in Fisher's sturdy Skyraider.

Maj Bernard F. Fisher's bravery under fire as he risked his life to save a comrade from capture or death earned a much deserved Medal of Honor. In the process, Fisher also became the first recipient of the Air Force Medal of Honor in Vietnam.

Lt Col Joe M. Jackson
311th Air Commando Squadron

On 12 May 1968, Lt Col Joe Jackson, aircraft commander of a 311th Air Commando C-123K Provider, diverted his unarmed transport to the besieged Special Forces camp at Kham Duc in response to an urgent radio call for help. Having held out for two days in the face of nonstop infantry, sapper, and mortar assaults by the North Vietnamese Army's Second Division, the camp was now dying in agony only moments after its last defenders were evacuated. Or so everyone thought.

Then a frantic radio call sent a shock through the aircrews circling overhead. Down below, three remaining members of an Air Force combat control team, inserted during the final evacuation over the protests of the C-130 crew delivering them,* had been left behind in the confused scramble to board the last escaping aircraft. Now trapped in a small pocket near the runway, they faced certain death or capture.

Another Provider ahead of Jackson's had already braved intense enemy antiaircraft fire as well as debris and the wreckage of a helicopter cluttering the runway in an attempted last-ditch rescue of the CCT. Helpless to prevent heavy enemy fire from pinning down members of the CCT where they crouched, the transport crew had no choice but to abandon the attempt and flee for their own lives. For his courageous attempt, the pilot received the Air Force Cross, the second highest award for valor America can bestow on its airmen. So desperate now was the situation for the CCT that, incredibly, the nation's ultimate award for valor was only moments away from being earned by another airman.

As Jackson and his copilot, Maj Jesse W. Campbell, watched the chaos below from 8,000 feet above Kham Duc, they knew their aircraft was the CCT's last hope for escape. Dumping the aircraft's nose sharply, Jackson spiraled the C-123 wildly down in a combat

*The airlift control center responsible for the camp's evacuation ordered the CCT inserted, despite reports from the C-130 crew delivering the team that the camp was nearly deserted. When an airborne control ship over Kham Duc reported the evacuation complete only minutes later, the angry C-130 crew "immediately and vehemently" set the record straight.

approach that strained the design limits of the bulky transport. Jackson's unorthodox maneuver was not the act of desperation it might seem to many. Not generally known in previous accounts, Jackson was then in his 25th year on flight status, with a great many of those years flying fighters. Prior to this tour in Vietnam, Jackson had flown aircraft as diverse and famous as the legendary F-51 Mustang to the high-altitude U-2 reconnaissance "spy plane."

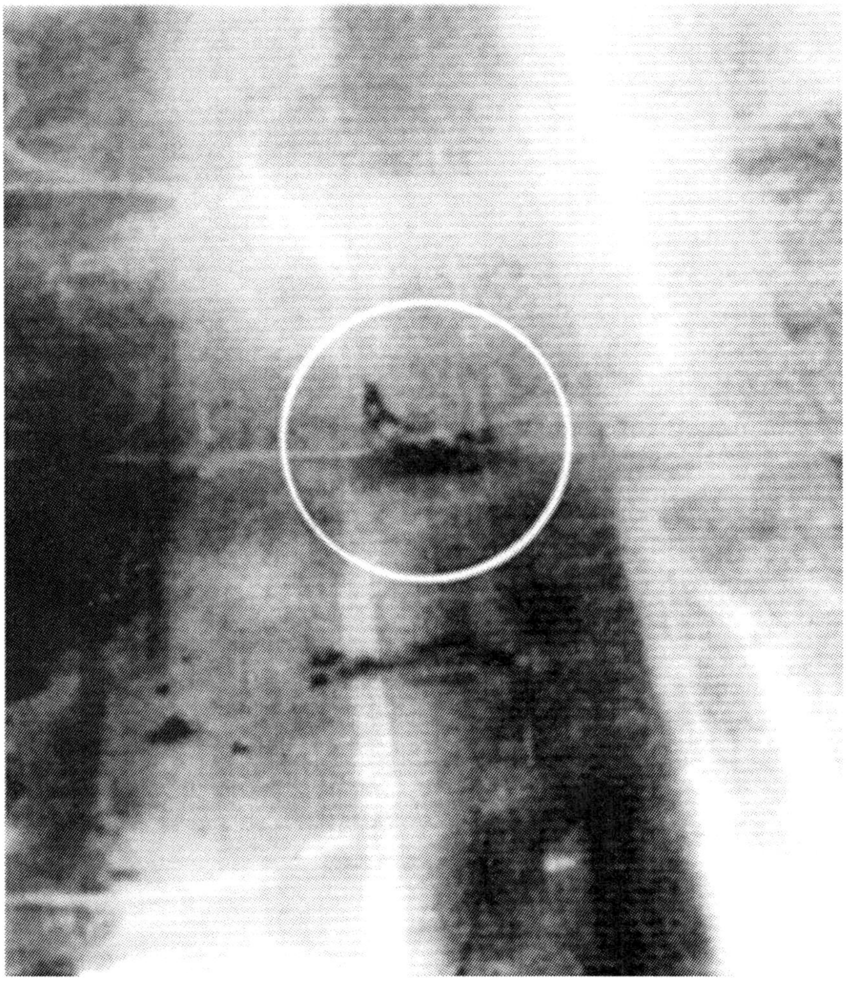

Pulling the nose of the straining aircraft toward the strip and flaring at the last possible second, he thumped the C-123 down hard onto Kham Duc's airstrip. Standing on the brakes, the two pilots brought the aircraft to a shuddering halt just as an enemy rocket landed on the runway ahead of the aircraft... and failed to explode.

Running literally for their lives, the three controllers leapt aboard the Provider.[3] With maximum power on its two piston and two jet engines, the transport raced down the runway as mortar rounds fell all around the aircraft. Intense but fortunately inaccurate automatic-weapons fire swept through the confusion all around the Provider, miraculously missing the transport. As Jackson later recalled with a laugh, "Before take-off that day, I was notified that I would receive my operational proficiency check on this flight. I never did hear whether I passed or not."[4]

USAF

This is the only known photo of a Medal of Honor being won even as it happened. Lt Col Joe Jackson's C-123 is on the airstrip at Kham Duc, now in enemy hands, as he picks up the three combat controllers who were stranded there after the last aircraft had left Kham Duc earlier.

As the Air Commandos say, you can get away with anything . . . *once!* Jackson's cool nerve and superb flying skills saved the lives of the besieged combat controllers, establishing in the process another Air Commando legend. For his performance, he was awarded the Medal of Honor, Major Campbell the Air Force Cross, and the rest of the crew Silver Stars.

Lt Col William A. Jones III
602d Special Operations Squadron

Lt Col Bill Jones, flight leader for four 602d Special Operations Squadron Skyraiders just scrambled off Nakhon Phanom Royal Thai Air Base, was a busy man on 1 September 1968. Coordinating with airborne rescue controllers, his flight, and two air rescue helicopters he was escorting deep into enemy territory was much like choreographing a complex play. But this "play" would take place in North Vietnam before a very hostile audience waiting and hoping Jones would make a fatal mistake . . . just one would do. Because if he did, the price for that mistake could well be the lives of the two crew members of a downed F-4 Phantom jet fighter that the rescue force was en route to save—or perhaps even his own life.

As the lead Skyraiders arrived over the estimated location, they discovered from the downed pilot that they were too late to rescue the Phantom's backseater, who was already a North Vietnamese prisoner of war destined for years of brutal imprisonment. Using his handheld survival radio, the injured and shaken but still free pilot attempted to bring Jones's flight over his position. But dense foliage and low-hanging clouds prevented a clear line-of-sight vision of both the downed pilot and his would-be rescuers.

Flying with the radio call sign "Sandy One," Jones led his flight down below the overcast towards the homing beacon transmitting from the downed pilot's survival radio. He found the terrain below to be as treacherous as the North Vietnamese gunners waiting for him. With the tops of some mountains hidden by clouds, Jones continued to be frustrated in his attempts to get a visual reference to the downed pilot's location. A further critical hour was lost when the downed pilot's wingman directed the search eight miles in the wrong direction. When Jones finally made visual contact with the downed pilot, he also became quickly and painfully aware that enemy gunners had also made visual contact with him as well.

Jones's A-1 was hit by a 37 mm AAA shell almost immediately as he approached the downed pilot's location, the high-explosive shell momentarily filling the cockpit with smoke. Jones continued on, frantically zigzagging to avoid more of the heavy antiaircraft shells exploding all around him. He was now so low enemy gunners in the hills were firing downwards on him. Jones's attempts to draw fire to mark enemy positions for a flight of F-4s overhead was a valiant and selfless act . . . and one that couldn't go on much longer.

Low on fuel and with his aircraft clattering loudly from the effect of numerous antiaircraft hits, Jones was still the only pilot so far to have pinpointed the downed pilot's exact position. Then he spotted something much worse, a heavy antiaircraft gun emplacement on a slope just above the downed pilot. Ordering the other aircraft in the area to standby, Jones wheeled his Skyraider over to bring his guns to bear on the target. Peppering the enemy position with 20 mm cannon fire and CBU-38 cluster bombs, he could feel his heavily armored A-1 shuddering as enemy bullets found their mark again and again.

Charlie Norton

What else besides a downed and injured pilot desperately calling for help lies beneath these clouds? How low are the valleys, how high the jagged karst cliffs? Where are the North Vietnamese gunners patiently using the pilot as bait for the inevitable rescue attempt?

Smoke and fire filled the cockpit as the inevitable fatal hit struck, this one igniting the rocket motor in Jones's ejection seat. Jones jettisoned the canopy and triggered the ejection seat for bailout. Nothing! He tried the secondary release. Again, nothing! The flames were burning him as his wingman began shouting, "Get Out! You're on fire! Bail out now!"[5]

Trapped in the fire of a dying plane, unable to escape, Jones continued attempting to point out the survivor's exact position to his wingman. By now the Skyraider was enveloped in flames, leaving a trail of smoke across the sky. Jones was in extreme pain, but still trying to orient the rest of the rescue force to the downed pilot. Only when fire destroyed his radio did he finally break off, to be escorted by his wingman back to NKP and a straight-in approach to the runway.

Rolling his aircraft to a stop, Jones was pulled from the cockpit in extreme pain from burns but still refusing medical treatment until he had passed on his information while lying on the ambulance stretcher. With this information, the remaining force fought through the enemy fire to complete a successful rescue of the F-4 pilot later that day. His badly riddled Skyraider was later declared a 100 percent write-off.

For his bravery under fire, Colonel Jones was nominated for the Medal of Honor. Returning to the United States to a well-deserved welcome, Jones's good luck finally ran out. An aircraft accident took this valiant Air Commando's life before the medal could be presented by President Richard M. Nixon. Nixon presented the Medal of Honor to Jones's widow on 6 August 1970.

1st Lt James P. Fleming

20th Special Operations Squadron

First Lt Jim Fleming, a UH-1F helicopter pilot with the 20th Special Operations Squadron's "Green Hornets," was awarded the Medal of Honor for bravery and what the Air Force later described as "a feat of unbelievable flying skill" during the rescue of a trapped, six-man Special Forces reconnaissance team on 26 November 1968.[6]

Just inserted into a heavily forested area near Duc Co in South Vietnam's central highlands, the sudden presence of the Green Berets had provoked a sharp firefight with a much larger enemy force in the immediate area. The team leader's urgent request for an emergency extraction had been overheard by a Green Hornet flight of five helicopters returning to their base from a separate mission. The two gunships and three "Slicks" (troop carrying UH-1s), already low on fuel, turned immediately and raced to the relief of the trapped patrol.

They arrived overhead to find the team surrounded on three sides and trapped with its back against an impassable river. The gunships quickly attacked with rockets and 7.62 mm miniguns. Just as quickly, one of the gunships was hit by enemy machine-gun fire and forced to make an emergency landing in a small clearing near the ongoing battle. Following the crippled gunship down, the Slick rescued the crew only scant minutes before enemy troops arrived in the clearing. That left one gunship and two Slicks over the team.

One of the two remaining Slicks was soon forced to withdraw for lack of fuel, leaving only Fleming's Slick and the sole-surviving gunship to rescue the desperate Special Forces troopers. After ordering the patrol to move the 20 yards separating it from the river bank and another small clearing, the gunship fired into the dangerously thin strip separating the enemy from the patrol as Fleming flared his helicopter into the clearing.

Enemy gunners already firing to keep the team pinned down now added Fleming's helicopter to their targets. With the helicopter's nose in the clearing and the tail of the 48-foot-long helicopter extending back out over the river, the stationary helicopter crew could do little but wait for the team to make its break.

As special operations historian John L. Plaster recounts in his excellent book *SOG: The Secret Wars of America's Commandos in Vietnam*, the wait was bad. Then another NVA assault almost rolled right across the tiny team, and Lieutenant Fleming heard their radio operator scream, "They've got us! They've got us! Get out, Get out!"[7]

Seeing the team's escape route cut off, the 25-year-old Fleming, now experiencing only his second mission as an aircraft commander, finally backed the chopper out over the river as his door gunners kept the enemy at bay. Once in the clear, he climbed rapidly above the small-arms fire to plan his next move.

The Green Hornet emblem on this UH-1F's tail boom identifies the 20th Special Operations Squadron in which Lieutenant Fleming flew what the Air Force would later call "a feat of unbelievable flying skill." The feat took place on the second day of the 25-year-old lieutenant's upgrade to aircraft commander.

Despite facing the heaviest enemy fire he'd ever seen, and keenly aware of his dangerously low-fuel state, Fleming knew his helicopter was the team's only hope for escape. Bringing his aircraft around and diving back again into the deadly clearing on the river bank, he knew the North Vietnamese would be waiting and ready . . . and they were.

As Fleming nudged his helicopter into the clearing yet again, the reconnaissance team was also ready. To help cover their withdrawal, the team had set up a series of Claymore mines* around their position to cover their escape. As they raced from a hail of gunfire towards the chopper in the clearing with the enemy hot on their heels, the closest North Vietnamese hit the Claymore trip wires, bring a swath of death back into their ranks.

Though heavily burdened with rucksacks and weapons, the seven-man team leaped for the helicopter and was "helped" aboard by adrenaline-filled door gunners even as Fleming was backing out over the river once more. The last of the recon team was literally dragged through the water by helping arms before finally being hauled aboard the helicopter. As Fleming climbed away from the river, gunfire shattered the windshield, miraculously missing the six-foot, four-inch Fleming, his crew, and the team. Returning to Duc Co with near empty fuel tanks, Fleming landed his shot-up helicopter and a very grateful team of Green Berets.

---

*A Claymore mine, in size fitting neatly into a shoebox, detonates with the effect of a huge shotgun shell, spewing a lethal pattern of hundreds of antipersonnel pellets in the direction in which the Claymore is pointed.

Airman 1st Class John L. Levitow

3d Air Commando Squadron

The night of 24 February 1969 found Airman Levitow, a loadmaster aboard one of the 3d Air Commando's AC-47 gunships, in combat air patrol over Tan Son Nhut, Saigon's major airport. When the nearby US Army base at Long Binh called for assistance in fending off a mortar attack, the AC-47 diverted immediately . . . without the smallest of clues as to the frightening events about to befall them.

Defending camps was a gunship specialty, and the AC-47's multibarreled miniguns soon knocked out two of the mortar positions attacking Long Binh. As the gunship pummeled the mortars, Levitow set the ejection and ignition timers on the gunship's MK-24, two-million-candlepower magnesium flares used to highlight the targets. Spotting other mortar flashes in the distance, the gunship then turned in their direction. Suddenly a brilliant violent explosion over the right wing rocked the aircraft, shredding the paper-thin fuselage with thousands of fragments and lethal shards of hot metal. Against odds of at least one in a million, an enemy mortar round had struck the gunship.[8]

Levitow, standing near the open cargo door to drop illumination flares, was knocked to the cabin floor with more than 40 wounds in his back and legs. An already-activated magnesium flare he and a fellow crewman were handling was flung from their arms into a pile of spilled high-explosive and tracer ammunition. Timed to ignite in seconds and burn at 4,000 degrees Fahrenheit, the flare would easily generate an explosion that would in turn instantly destroy the aircraft and all aboard.

Ignoring his pain and loss of blood, Levitow threw himself on the flare, which was already spewing highly toxic smoke throughout the cabin. Dragging it painfully back to the open cargo door, he shoved it out only an instant before it ignited into a ball of flame. As the gunship's aircraft commander later reported, "It is my belief that this story could not have been told by any other member of my crew had Levitow failed to perform his heroic actions."[9] By Levitow's own account, he was so stunned from the explosion and pain that he reacted entirely from his training and instinct, not fully realizing until told later by others what he had accomplished.[10] His honest account remains a considerable testimony to both USAF training and Levitow's personal character.

Levitow's heroic actions earned for him the Medal of Honor, making him the only Air Force enlisted man to be so awarded during the decade-long conflict in Vietnam.

USAF

These magnesium-burning illumination flares being loaded aboard an AC-47 Dragonship ignite with such intensity that they will continue to burn even underwater . . . or completely through the fuselage of the gunship if ignited before they exit the aircraft.

Notes

1. Robert F. Dorr, *The Illustrated History of the Vietnam War: Douglas A-1 Skyraider* (New York: Bantam Books, 1989), 153, 156.
2. Col Bernard F. Fisher, USAF, Retired, speaking at the USAF Special Operations School Symposium for Medal of Honor recipients, 28 February 1997, Hurlburt Field, Fla.
3. Ray L. Bowers, *The United States Air Force in Southeast Asia: Tactical Airlift* (Washington, D.C.: Office of Air Force History, 1983), 317–18, 346.
4. Col Joe M. Jackson, USAF, Retired, speaking at the USAF Special Operations School Symposium for Medal of Honor recipients, 28 February 1997, Hurlburt Field, Fla.
5. Dorr, 162–63.
6. John L. Plaster, *SOG: The Secret Wars of America's Commandos in Vietnam* (New York: Simon & Schuster, 1997), 110–15. See also Bowers, 426.
7. Ibid., 113.
8. Jack S. Ballard, *The United States Air Force in Southeast Asia: Development and Employment of Fixed-Wing Gunships, 1962–1972* (Washington, D.C.: Office of Air Force History, 1982), 71.
9. Ibid., 72.
10. John L. Levitow, speaking at the USAF Special Operations School Symposium for Medal of Honor recipients, 28 February 1997, Hurlburt Field, Fla.

Valor

For a moment
Everything a person is
Becomes a fiery spirit.
Everything a person dreams
Lies at the foot of God
Hidden from men's eyes.
All a person's strength,
Physical, intellectual, spiritual,
Fuses into a single act
Of extraordinary grace
And achieves supreme humanity,
Denies defeat, and vanquishes evil.
It is bold, brash, . . . almost irrational.
Its logic eludes the poets.
A logic which weaves
Our mantle of sacrifice
And separates mankind
From all other beings
At the foot of God.
Everything a person dreams
Becomes a fiery spirit.
Everything a person is
For a moment
Valor.

Dick Schaller

Reflections

Air Commando Association

Any attempt to place the astonishing operations of the Air Commandos in perspective must begin with an understanding of the extraordinarily hostile environment in which they were placed during much of the cold war. Only with this initial understanding can both their missions and their unorthodox tactics be understood. But the most important element in formulating such a perspective is found in the nature of the individual airmen themselves—those who volunteered, fought, and led the remarkable Air Commando/special operations force.

In evaluating the hostile environment in which the Air Commandos were placed, there is a natural tendency on the reader's part to become distracted by the extreme diversity of the operations recounted in this short history. For all this operational and geographic diversity, however, common threads run through these stories that combine to form a composite picture of a surprisingly uniform and very dangerous environment. These include a lethal and unforgiving battlefield, physically harsh terrain and climate, limited resources, aging weapons, and almost always the knowledge that capture behind enemy lines meant probable torture and death. Even the psychological assurance of fighting in large numbers was usually denied individuals and small aircrews flying, often at night, into areas in which the US denied even its presence. All these realities had to be faced . . . and in one way or another they all took their toll on the individual's mental and physical health.

Many such missions undertaken in these conditions are by definition considered high-risk, high-gain gambles. The price tag for failure has historically been worldwide embarrassment to the US government at the highest levels and worse for those airmen attempting to carry out the mission (e.g., at Son Tay and the Bay of Pigs). Both the dangerous nature of such missions and the mandatory requirement for the element of surprise in their execution combine to place exceptional demands on those who would dare them. And this historical fact leads in turn to the inescapable observation that truly few among us possess the exceptional courage, skill, and imagination to fight and survive at this extreme level of performance.

One of the most enduring arguments against the formation of elite units is that "the best and brightest" inevitably flow to them, to the expense of the remaining majority. Ironically, the distinguished performance of the Air Commandos simply lends credence to this argument. This fact alone plays a large part in the historical ebb and flow in which such elite forces are found in the ranks of America's military forces.

In 1979, the hollow remnants of the once proud special operations force learned from Headquarters USAF that Air Force priorities and funding limitations precluded the continued existence of this force in active service. Transfer of the remaining aircraft to the reserve components the following year was likely; transfer to USAF's aircraft "boneyard" in Arizona was a possibility. Once again, the end seemed clearly in sight. And once again, fate would intervene in a time and manner few could possibly have anticipated.

Fate arrived in 1980, before the active duty special operations force could be transferred or scrapped. The manner in which it stepped in took form in a fiery aircraft explosion that leapt into the night skies over a frozen piece of Iranian desert soon to be known around the world as "Desert One." Again the national embarrassment of a failed high-risk, high-gain mission; again death as the price paid for those who dared. The special operations cycle was about to repeat itself yet again. But that's another story.

Bibliography

Books and Articles

Anthony, Victor B., and Richard R. Sexton. *The United States Air Force in Southeast Asia: The War in Northern Laos, 1954–1973.* Washington, D.C.: Office of Air Force History, 1993.

Arnold, James R. *The First Domino: Eisenhower, the Military, and America's Intervention into Vietnam.* New York: William Morrison & Co., 1991.

Ballard, Jack S. *The United States Air Force in Southeast Asia: Development of Fixed-Wing Gunships, 1962–1972.* Washington, D.C.: Office of Air Force History, 1982.

Berger, Carl. *The United States Air Force in Southeast Asia, 1961–1973: An Illustrated Account.* Washington, D.C.: Office of Air Force History, 1984.

Blair, Clay. *The Forgotten War: America in Korea, 1950–1953.* New York: *Times* Books, 1987.

Bowers, Ray L. *The United States Air Force in Southeast Asia: Tactical Airlift.* Washington, D.C.: Office of Air Force History, 1982.

Browne, Malcolm W. *The New Face of War.* Indianapolis, Ind.: Bobbs-Merrill, 1965.

Buckingham, William A. *Operation Ranch Hand: The Air Force and Herbicides in Southeast Asia, 1961–1971.* Washington, D.C.: Office of Air Force History, 1982.

Castle, Timothy N. *At War in the Shadow of Vietnam: U.S. Military Aid to the Royal Lao Government, 1955–1975.* New York: Columbia University Press, 1992.

Cecil, Paul Frederick. *Herbicidal Warfare: The Ranch Hand Project in Vietnam.* New York: Praeger Special Studies, 1986.

Chinnery, Philip D. *Any Time, Any Place: Fifty Years of the USAF Air Commando and Special Operations Forces, 1944–1994.* Annapolis, Md.: Naval Institute Press, 1994.

———. *Any Time, Any Place: A History of USAF Air Commandos and Special Operations.* Annapolis, Md.: Naval Institute Press, 1994.

Conboy, Kenneth. *Shadow War: The CIA's Secret War in Laos.* Boulder, Colo.: Paladin Press, 1995.

Davis, Larry. *MIG ALLEY: Air to Air Combat over Korea.* Carrollton, Tex.: Squadron/Signal Publications, 1978.

Dorr, Robert F. *The Illustrated History of the Vietnam War: Douglas A-1 Skyraider.* New York: Bantam Books, 1989.

Ferrer, Edward B. *Operation PUMA, The Air Battle of the Bay of Pigs.* Miami, Fla.: Open Road Press, 1975.

Generous, Keven M. *Vietnam: The Secret War.* New York: Gallery Books, 1985.

Hagedorn, Dan, and Leif Hellstrom. *Foreign Invaders: The Douglas Invader in Foreign Military and US Clandestine Service.* Leicester, UK: Midland Publishing Limited, 1994.

Hamilton-Merritt, Jane. *Tragic Mountains: The Hmong, the Americans, and the Secret Wars in Laos, 1942–1992.* Bloomington: Indiana University Press, 1993.

Harrison, Marshall. *A Lonely Kind of War: Forward Air Controller, Vietnam.* Novato, Calif.: Presidio Press, 1989.

Kamps, Charles T., Jr. *The History of the Vietnam War.* New York: The Military Press, 1988.

Mark, Eduard. *Aerial Interdiction in Three Wars: Air Power and the Land Battle.* Washington, D.C.: Office of Air Force History, 1994.

Nichols, Donald. *How Many Times Can I Die?* Brooksville, Fla.: Brooksville Printing, 1981.

Paddock, Alfred H., Jr. *US Army Special Warfare: Its Origins.* Washington, D.C.: National Defense University, 1982.

Peissel, Michel. *The Secret War in Tibet.* Boston: Little, Brown and Company, 1973.

Persons, Albert C. *Bay of Pigs: A Firsthand Account of the Mission by a U.S. Pilot in Support of the Cuban Invasion Force in 1961.* Jefferson, N.C.: McFarland & Company, Inc., 1990.

Phillips, David Atlee. *The Night Watch: 25 Years of Peculiar Service.* New York: Atheneum, 1977.

Plaster, John L. *SOG: The Secret Wars of America's Commandos in Vietnam.* New York: Simon & Schuster, 1997.

Prados, John. *Presidents' Secret Wars: CIA and Pentagon Covert Operations since World War II.* New York: William Morrow and Company, 1986.

Prouty, Col L. Fletcher, USAF, Retired. *JFK: The CIA, Vietnam and the Plot to Assassinate John F. Kennedy.* New York: Carol Publishing Group, 1992.

———. *The Secret Team: The CIA and Its Allies in Control of the United States and the World.* Englewood Cliffs, N.J.: Prentice-Hall, Inc., 1973.

Robbins, Christopher. *Air America: The Story of the CIA's Secret Airlines.* New York: G.P. Putnam's Sons, 1979.

———. *The Ravens: The Men Who Flew in America's Secret War in Laos.* New York: Crown Publishers, 1987.

Saal, Harve. *SOG: MACV Studies and Observations Group*, vol. 1, *Historical Evolution.* Ann Arbor, Mich.: Edward Brothers, 1990.

——— *SOG: MACV Studies and Observations Group*, vol. 4, *Appendixes.* Ann Arbor, Mich.: Edward Brothers, 1990.

Schemmer, Benjamin F. *The Raid.* New York: Harper & Row, 1976.

Schlight, John. *The War in South Vietnam: The Years of the Offensive: 1965–1968.* Washington, D.C.: Office of Air Force History, 1988.

Schuetta, Lt Col Lawrence V. *Guerrilla Warfare and Airpower in Korea, 1950–1953.* Maxwell AFB, Ala.: Aerospace Studies Institute, January 1964.

Singlaub, Maj Gen John K., USA, Retired, with Malcolm McConnell. *Hazardous Duty: An American Soldier in the Twentieth Century.* New York: Summit Books, 1991.

Tilford, Earl H., Jr. *Search and Rescue in Southeast Asia.* Washington, D.C.: Center for Air Force History, 1980.

Tourison, Sedgwick. *Secret Army, Secret War: Washington's Tragic Spy Operation in North Vietnam.* Annapolis, Md.: Naval Institute Press, 1995.

Van Staaveren, Jacob. *Interdiction in Southern Laos, 1960–1968: The United States Air Force in Southeast Asia.* Washington, D.C.: Center for Air Force History, 1993.

Warner, Roger. *Backfire: The CIA's Secret War in Laos and Its Link to the War in Vietnam.* New York: Simon & Schuster, 1995.

Wyden, Peter. *Bay of Pigs: The Untold Story.* New York: Simon & Schuster, 1979.

Periodicals

"Acting to Aid the Forgotten Men." *Time* 96, no. 23 (7 December 1970): 15–21.

Aderholt, Brig Gen Harry C., USAF, Retired. "Setting the Record Straight." *Arc Light* 11, no. 4 (October 1995).

Cole, James L., Jr. "USAF Special Operations Forces: Past, Present, and Future." *Aerospace Historian* 27, no. 4 (December 1980): 218–26.

Chinnery, Philip D. "PSYOPS: Vietnam to Desert Storm." *Behind the Lines*, May/June 1994, 18.

Evanhoe, Ed. "Reported Alive: Three U.S. Spec Ops Men Still Missing in the Korean War." *Behind the Lines*, November/December 1993.

Manor, Lt Gen Leroy J., USAF, Retired. "The Son Tay Raid: November 21, 1970." *Daedalus Flyer* 35, no. 4 (Winter 1995): 8–16.

Mullen, Chris. "Tibetan Conspiracy." *Far Eastern Economic Review* 89, no. 36 (5 September 1975): 30–34.

———. "Tibet: A God Escapes." *Newsweek*, no. 15 (13 April 1959): 46, 48.

Murtza, Wayne. "Covertly into Cambodia." *Air Enthusiast* 32 (December 1986–April 1987): 26.

Paschall, Col Rod. "Special Operations in Korea." *Conflict* 7, no. 2 (1987): 155–78.

"POWs Hold Reunion." *Arc Light* 1, no. 4 (October 1985).

Wickstrom, Lt Col Tom, USAF, Retired. "Nimrods, Truck Killers on the Trail," *Air Commando Association Newsletter*, July 1968.

Historical Studies

Headquarters, Fifth Air Force, Office of Deputy for Intelligence. Letter. Subject: Special Activities Unit Number One (Operating Instructions), dated 5 March 1951, found in "UN Partisan Forces in the Korean Conflict." Prepared by 8086th Army Unit (AFFE) Military History Detachment, January 1953.

Jannarone, Capt August G. Military Civic Action Officer, Korat RTAFB, Thailand. Staff Agency Monthly Activity Summary for November 1974, dated 9 December 1974.

Koren, 1st Lt John A. "History of USAF Special Operations Forces." Background paper, USAF Special Operations School, 5 September 1982.

"Lucky Tiger Combat Operations" (U), Project CHECO (Contemporary Historical Evaluation of Counterinsurgency Operations) report. Headquarters PACAF, Directorate of Tactical Evaluation, CHECO Division, 15 June 1967. (Secret) Information extracted is unclassified.

"The Origin and Development of the United States Air Force Psychological Warfare Program, 1946–1952," chapter 1. Historical Research Agency Archives, Maxwell AFB, Ala., 1 June 1953.

"Tactical Air Command in Southeast Asia, 1961–1968," Office of Tactical Air Command History. Headquarters Tactical Air Command, Langley AFB, Va., August 1972.

News Releases and Messages

Jacobowitz, Capt Daniel W., Chief, Military Civic Action. Headquarters, 56th Combat Support Group (PACAF). Lessons Learned. Message 22/0910Z January 1975.

Message from US Embassy (Vientiane), 18 May 1964, DDRS 1990, as cited in Conboy, Kenneth. *Shadow War: The CIA's Secret War in Laos.* Boulder, Colo.: Paladin Press, 1995.

Secretary of the Air Force Office of Information. "US Air Force News Service Release," 7 May 1965.

Air Force Special Operations Command, History Office, *Special Air Warfare Fact Sheet,* 16.

Unit Histories

History. Aerospace Rescue and Recovery Service, 1 July 1970–30 June 1971, Annex, "The Son Tay Raid."

———. Air Resupply and Communications Service, 1 July–31 December 1951.

———. Air Resupply and Communications Service, 1 July–31 December 1953, pt. 1, "The ARCS Mission and Program."

———. Air Resupply and Communications Service, 1 July–31 December 1953, "Balloon Launching Squadron."

———. Far East Air Forces, 1 June–31 December 1951.

———. Special Warfare Center, 1 January–30 June 1965.

———. Tactical Air Command, 1 January–30 June 1961.

———. 21st Troop Carrier Squadron, October 1950.

———. 21st Troop Carrier Squadron, March 1951.

———. 21st Troop Carrier Squadron, April 1951.

———. 580th Air Resupply and Communication Wing and 580th ARC Group, 1 November–31 December 1951.

———. 580th Holding and Briefing Squadron, 1 January–29 February 1952.

———. 581st Air Resupply and Communications Wing, Operations Plan 3-52, 14 July 1952.

———. 582d Air Resupply and Communications Wing, 1 January 1953–30 June 1953.

———. 581st Air Resupply Group, vol. 2, 1 July–31 December 1955.

———. 582d Air Resupply Group, 1 July–25 October 1956.

———. 6004th Airborne Information Systems Squadron, May–June 1952.

———. 6004th Airborne Information Systems Squadron, 1 July–31 December 1952.

———. 6004th Airborne Information Systems Squadron, Monthly Report, August 1952.

———. 6160th Air Base Group, no. 5, 25 June–31 October 1950.

———. 6160th Air Base Group, Detachment 1, April 1952.

———. 6167th Air Base Group, 1 July–1 December 1952.

———. 6167th Air Base Group, 1 January–30 June 1953.

———. 6167th Air Base Group, 1 July–31 December 1953.

Published Government Reports

Anthony, Victor B., and Richard R. Sexton. *The United States Air Force in Southeast Asia: The War in Northern Laos, 1954–1973* (U). Washington, D.C.: Center for Air Force History, 1993. (Secret) Information extracted is unclassified.

Army Pamphlet 525-7-2. *The Art and Science of Psychological Operations: Case Studies of Military Application*, vol. 2. Washington, D.C.: Department of the Army, 1976.

Handbook. *Joint Special Operations Planning*. USAF Special Operations School, 1993.

McRaven, Comdr William H., USN. "The Theory of Special Operations." Graduate/Thesis, Naval Postgraduate School, 1993.

The 1952 Historical Research Origin and Development of the United States Air Force Psychological Warfare Program, 1946–1952. Maxwell AFB, Ala: USAF Historical Division, 1 June 1953.

Unpublished Government and Military Sources

Aderholt, Brig Gen Harry C., USAF, Retired. USAF Oral History Interview (U) (K239.0512-1716),

12–15 August 1986. (Secret) Published passages declassified. USAF Historical Research Agency, Maxwell AFB, Ala., 6 January 1994.
Brewer, 1Lt Robert B. "Study Regarding Parachute Agent Problems" (U). Joint Special Operations Center, FEC/LG, 3 September 1950, attached as appendix 2 to vol. 2, "Intelligence Information to Partisans for Armor" (U). (Confidential) Information extracted is unclassified.
Chapman, Capt William C., USN, Retired. "The Bay of Pigs: The View from PRIFLY." Paper presented at the Ninth Naval History Symposium, US Naval Academy, 20 October 1989. Janet Ray Weininger Collection, Miami, Fla.
"The Fabulous Four Engine Fighter." Paper presented at the 1975 Spectre Reunion in New Orleans, La.
Fondacaro, Maj Steve A. "A Strategic Analysis of U.S. Special Operations during the Korean Conflict, 1950–1953." Thesis, US Army Command and General Staff College, 1988.
Garth, Lt Col Steven et al. "Intelligence Information by Partisans for Armor" (U), vol. 1. Research report, Armored Officer Advanced Course, Fort Knox, Ky., 1952. (Confidential) Information extracted is unclassified.
McCutchan, Lt Col Clay. "USAF Gunship Overview: 1973–1993." Unpublished paper, March 1994.
Napier III, John Hawkins. "The Air Commandos in Vietnam, November 5, 1961 to February 7, 1965." Master's thesis, Auburn University, 1967.
Pfeiffer, Jack B. "The Taylor Committee Investigation of the Bay of Pigs," 9 November 1984. Janet Ray Weininger Collection, Miami, Fla.
Putney, Diane T. "Origins of USAF HUMINT in Korea." Booklet, 40th Anniversary of AFSAC, USAF History Office, date unk.
Schuetta, Lt Col Lawrence V. "Guerrilla Warfare and Airpower in Korea, 1950–1953." Paper, Aerospace Studies Institute, Maxwell AFB, Ala., January 1964.
Sullivan, Maj Robert F., USAF, Retired. Former pilot, Helicopter Flight, 581st Air Resupply and Communications Wing. Memoirs. Author's Collection.
Tyrrell, Col Robert L. F. USAF Oral History Interview (U) (K239.0512-895) (U), 12 May 1975. (Secret) Information extracted is unclassified.

Memorandums

Memorandum. Combat Doctrine, B Flight, 6167th Operations Squadron (U). Korean War-era date obliterated by declassified stamp. Declassified April 1977. (Secret) Information extracted is unclassified.
Technical Memorandum ORO-T-4 (EUSAK). Kilchoon Kim and E. A. Johnson. *Evaluation of Effects of Leaflets on Early North Korean Prisoners of War* (U). Johns Hopkins University, February 1951. (Secret) Information extracted is unclassified.
Technical Memorandum ORO-T-64 (AFFE). Frederick W. Cleaver et al. *UN Partisan Warfare in Korea, 1951–1954* (U). Johns Hopkins University, June 1956. (Secret) Information extracted is unclassified.

Military Orders

Detachment 1, 314th TAW. US Air Force Flight Order, 29 December 1967.
Fifth Air Force General Orders no. 637. Award of the Distinguished Flying Cross, First Oak Leaf Cluster, to Major Paul G. Moore, 27 September 1953.

Headquarters Far East Air Forces General Orders no. 336. Activation, Special Activities Unit No. One 20 July 1951.

Letters

Adams, Lt Col Lester M., Jr., former commander 22d CRBS, to author. Letter, subject: History of USAF Crash Rescue Boats, 5 May 1995.

Budway, Col George, USAF, Retired, former CCRAK officer, to Mr. Ray Dawson, former CCRAK NCO. Letter, subject: CCRAK Operations, June 1987.

Brewer, Robert B., former FEC/LG officer, to Joseph C. Goulden, author, *Korea: The Untold Story.* Letter, 12 December 1984.

Fifth Air Force, Director of Intelligence. Letter, subject: Reorganization of the 6004th Air Intelligence Service Squadron, 12 September 1953.

Headquarters FECOM Liaison Detachment (Korea) to Commanders: Leopard, Wolfpack, Kirkland, Baker Section. Letter, 11 April 1952.

Nichols, Donald, Commander, Detachment 2, 6004th AISS, to Commanding Officer, Headquarters Squadron, 6160th Air Base Group. Letter, subject: Letter of Appreciation, 11 January 1952. Filed in History, Detachment 1, 6160th ABG, January 1952.

Pittman, Col George, USAF, Retired, former commander, 581st Air Resupply and Communications Wing, to author. Letter, 13 December 1994.

US Intelligence Employee to Jack B. Pfeiffer. Letter, subject: Bay of Pigs, 20 May 1976. Janet Ray Weininger Collection, Miami, Fla.

Index

LaVergne, TN USA
09 September 2010

196508LV00001B/11/A

9 781410 200099